Algrove Publishing Limited
1090 Morrison Drive
Ottawa, Ontario
Canada K2H 1C2

Canadian Cataloguing in Publication Data

Lever, Darcy, 1760?-1837
    The young sea officer's sheet anchor, or, A key to the leading of rigging, and to practical seamanship

(Classic reprint series)
3rd ed.
Includes index.
Reprint of the ed. published London : Longman, Hurst, Rees and Orme, 1808, together with the additions made
    by George W. Blunt in the ed. published New York : E. & G.W. Blunt, 1858, as compiled by Robert S. Lee.
ISBN 0-921335-71-7

    1. Masts and rigging. 2. Seamanship. I. Blunt, George W. (George William), 1802-1878. II. Lee, R. S.
(Robert Stanley), 1932- III. Title. IV. Title: Key to the leading of rigging, and to practical seamanship. V. Series:
Classic reprint series (Ottawa, Ont.)

VK541.L65 2000   623.8'62   C99-901576-1

Printed in Canada
#21000

Editor's Preface to
The Young Sea Officer's Sheet Anchor

*Combining the Original 1808 British Version by Darcy Lever
and the 1858 American Version by George W. Blunt.*

When we decided to reprint Darcy Lever's magnificent *The Young Sea Officer's Sheet Anchor* of 1808, it was with the intention of providing authoritative details to ship modellers, specifically for the Royal Navy ships of Napoleonic times. A secondary intent was to enrich the enjoyment of the many readers of Patrick O'Brian and C.S. Forester, authors who so vividly portray the lives of the men of iron who sailed those ships of oak.

We then realized that this would be an ideal opportunity not only to reprint Lever's original work but to add to it the changes made by George W. Blunt in his American edition of 1858. Since the Blunt version is essentially a modified version of Lever's, it seemed sensible to note Blunt's changes and additions in an appendix rather than print both texts complete since there is much duplication in the two works and readers would be put to much extra work sorting them out. We did the work for you. Lever's original clearly portrays the authentic rigging and methods of seamanship with the flavor of the time. Blunt's edition showed many changes in rigging and some of the changes in the English language caused by the separation of fifty years and the Atlantic Ocean.

Rigging changes arise from three sources: British vs. American practice, early 19th century vs. late, Royal Navy vs. commercial shipping. Minor points of rigging had been somewhat simplified in the U.S. military vessels and in commercial shipping, with the trend being to reduce both weight and manual labor. An example of the latter is the change of cringles from plain hemp to those worked around thimbles. The Royal Navy had more spare manpower than the merchant vessels, so it could bend new cringles more often. Other differences show the concern for availability of materials. Where the British edition speaks of "large pieces of elm", the American advises "stout pieces of oak or locust".

The American version includes in its latter part much interesting detail on total canvas for different classes of vessels, weights of chain and cordage, details on the clipper ships (just coming into service at time of publication), weights, characteristics and testing methods for armament (ball and shot), and notes and illustration describing the Porter anchor and Forbes rig.

Many differences in the text are of interest to students of the development of English, since Blunt and Lever were of the same social class and education, their language differences are clearly based in nationality and time.
- The use of the subjunctive, now almost obsolete, was beginning to fade in 1858. Where the British version said, "If the wind increase and it be . . .", the American version replaces the first verb form with the present indicative, saying, "If the wind increases and it be . . .".
- The American version uses both "reeved" and "rove", while the British version standardizes on "reeved". Other minor differences in both text and punctuation exist, raising the question of whether the editor or the typesetter instigated them, as typesetters sometimes took on proofreading responsibilities, whether assigned to them or not.
- Capitalization: The time difference of fifty years as well as the different language development affected capitalization. The British (older) version still tended to capitalize important nouns in a sentence, a practice that was less in evidence by the mid-19th century.
- Spelling, still somewhat inconsistent in the British version ("sails are maid of canvas", "gear" and "geer") had become more standardized by 1858, though "geer" and "gear" still remained.

We provide footnotes wherever Blunt's text differed from Lever's, and provide appendices containing all of the material that Blunt added. We believe the result is the most complete and authoritative source available for this arcane knowledge. We hope that you enjoy it.

Robert S. Lee, Editor
January, 2000

THE

Young Sea Officer's Sheet Anchor;

OR,

A KEY TO THE LEADING OF RIGGING,

AND TO

PRACTICAL SEAMANSHIP.

BY

DARCY LEVER.

Leeds:

PRINTED BY THOMAS GILL.

LONDON: SOLD BY LONGMAN, HURST, REES, AND ORME, PATERNOSTER - ROW; AND ALL THE BOOKSELLERS.——1808.

TO THE

RIGHT HONORABLE HENRY LORD MULGRAVE, (FIRST LORD)

AND THE

LORDS COMMISSIONERS OF THE ADMIRALTY.

MY LORDS!

YOUR Permission to dedicate this Work to the Heads of the first Maritime Power in the World, is so very flattering, that were I not conscious how inadequately its Merits are proportioned to the Patronage, my Vanity would be excessive.

YOUR Lordships, interested for the Welfare of the junior Branches of the Service, have been pleased to encourage a Book of little Invention or Novelty, of meer explanatory Description, intended to facilitate their Improvement, and as a Vehicle to the Study of more important Treatises on the same Subject.

BY your Lordships' Notice of this Trifle, the rising Generation will know, that any Attempt to lessen their Toil in the Pursuit of a glorious Profession, will meet the same liberal Sanction which has been given to,

MY LORDS,

Your Lordships'

Most humble,

Most obedient,

And most grateful Servant,

DARCY LEVER.

Leeds, July 30, 1808.

The Author's Design.

IN elucidating the Theory of Seamanship where very few technical Terms are necessary, explanatory Figures have always been deemed indispensible.---The Author imagined they might at least be equally useful in a Description of the Practice, which *must* be given in Terms of Art: particularly, as it might induce many to study the Profession who have no previous Knowledge of Geometry.

A meer verbal Explanation often perplexes the Mind, as no one but a Seaman can clearly comprehend it, and he is not the Object for whom such Aid is intended.

There has been scarcely any Improvement in the working of Ships, since the Production of a Treatise on practical Seamanship, by the late *Mr. William Hutchinson*, of *Liverpool*, which was given to the Public about thirty Years ago, a Work of great Merit, written by a real Seaman; the first of any Consequence on this Subject ever published, and perhaps the only one, in which a few Figures of Ships have been given to explain the working of them. In the leading of Rigging there have been some useful Varieties since that Period, of which as many are given in this Volume as the Author is acquainted with.

To make the Study less irksome, he has provided a Plate for every Page of Letter Press, that the Ideas may not be disturbed, nor taken from the immediate Subject by a Reference to Figures in another Part of the Work. This he has avoided, except where a Repetition takes Place; and when that occurs, the Figure will be found with the Explanation. He has comprized the Whole in One Hundred and Eleven Pages.

In this Book there is no Attempt at any Thing new, what may not have been treated on before, or with which every good Seaman is not perfectly acquainted. It is intended *solely* as a *Key* to the leading of Rigging and to practical Seamanship, as an Assistant to render the Knowledge of them easy and familiar to the young Gentlemen of the Royal Navy, the Honorable East India Company's Service, and others, who may not have been long enough at Sea, or have had an Opportunity of acquiring it by practice. If it possess this Utility, it has all the Merit it can claim.

Young Officers sometimes feel a Diffidence in soliciting Information, either from a Fear of exposing their Ignorance, or an Idea that such a Request may be treated with Ridicule.—A Reference like a Work of this Nature, which can be applied to with Privacy, will obviate the Difficulty: it was not a secondary Consideration in the Prosecution of it.—In the Pursuit of this Object, the Author has done his best.

THE Plan of this Work was laid many Years ago, and subsequently, the Manuscript was finished nearly as it now appears, for the Advantage of a young Gentleman whose Inclinations at that Time led him to the Choice of a Sea-faring Life.

Being seen by many Gentlemen of known professional Abilities, on both the Eastern and Western Coasts, who thought an Explanation of this Nature might be of Service to young Seamen in general, they presented the Author with Testimonials of their good Opinion, and wished him to give it Publicity. It was afterwards, through the friendly Zeal of *Captain Joshua Sydney Horton*, of the Royal Navy, introduced to the Notice of several Officers of Rank and Experience, who with a Liberality worthy of their high Stations, gave their Signatures of Approval.

To the highly respectable Individuals who have thus kindly sanctioned his Attempt, he takes this Opportunity of returning his most grateful Acknowledgments. He feels himself inadequate to express his Obligations to those public Bodies, who have honored him with their Countenance on this Occasion---the *Lords Commissioners of the Admiralty*, the *Honorable the Court of Directors of the East India Company*, and the *Corporation of the Trinity House at Hull*, having confered their Patronage in a Manner equally flattering to the Author's Feelings, and favorable to the Interests of his Publication.

N. B. It is to be observed, that the Figures are not drawn to any Scale, but are placed to answer the Description independently; and that no more Rigging, in general, is shewn, than is necessary to explain the Part described.——The Plates are engraved by *Messrs. Butterworths*, of *Leeds*, to whose Perseverance and Abilities the Author feels himself greatly indebted.

b

The under-mentioned OFFICERS *of* His MAJESTY's ROYAL NAVY

Have been pleased to give their Signatures of Approval to this Work, as worthy the Attention of young Officers and Others.——The Names are placed in the Order and Manner they were signed in the Two First Pages of the Manuscript :

J. Holloway, Vice-Admiral
Keith, Admiral
Robert Jackson, Captain H.M.S. Edgar
E. W. C. R. Owen, Captain H.M.S. Clyde
John Laugharne, Captain H.M.S. Isis
Joshua Sydney Horton, Captain H.M.S. Princess of Orange
Henry Bazely, Captain H.M.S. Antelope
A. C. Dickson, Captain H.M.S. Orion
Charles Ekins, Captain H.M.S. Defence
George Montague, Admiral
Isaac Coffin, Rear-Admiral
William Young, Admiral
E. Gower, Vice-Admiral

B. S. Rowley, Vice-Admiral
H. E. Stanhope, Vice-Admiral
J. Vashon, Rear-Admiral
Phillip Patton, Admiral
George Grey, Captain R.N.
Thomas Dundas, Captain R.N.
Loftus Otway Bland, Captain R.N.
C. P. Hamilton, Vice-Admiral
Walter Lock, Captain R.N.
P. Somerville, Captain H.M.S. Nemesis
Joseph Larcom, Captain R.N.
Don. H. Mackay. Captain R.N.
Charles Adam, Captain H.M.S. Resistance
R. Moorsom, Captain R.N.

THE FOLLOWING TESTIMONIALS

Were also given by Gentlemen of known Experience in the Merchant Service:

WE, the under-signed, have examined Mr. LEVER's *Demonstration of Rigging and Seamanship.*—The Explanation throughout is so judiciously managed by the Introduction of numerous Figures, that it may be justly stiled a KEY to the ART.—We are therefore of Opinion, that it is a Work which promises to be of National Utility, and every Way suited to forward the Author's Design, who has in this Treatise opened an easy Channel for the Improvement of young Sea Officers in every Service.

Caleb Fletcher,
James Finchett,
Roger Leatham,
Joseph Fletcher,

Jacob Fletcher,
William Ward,
Robert Bibby,
Hamlet Mullion,

George Brown,
Richard Hall,

LIVERPOOL.

WE, the under-signed, have perused this Work, and find it executed on a Plan clear and Seaman-like, particularly the plain and progressive Explanation of SWINGING A SHIP AT SINGLE ANCHOR :---We therefore recommend it to all those who wish easily to obtain a Knowledge of this important Part of a Seaman's Duty :

Thomas Pyman, Whitby.
William Brown, Newcastle-upon-Tyne.
John Curby, Ditto.
Thomas Smith, Ditto.
Nathan Wood, Hull.
Michael Teasdale, Sen. Ditto.
Michael Teasdale, Jun. Ditto.
Thomas Chilton, Whitby.
Richard Hutchinson, Whitby.

Andrew Scott, Master of the American Ship Washington.
John Wood, Master of the American Ship John Adams.
Joseph Smith, Master of the American Ship Felicity.
Joseph Trott, Master of the American Ship Packet.

CONTENTS.

CONTENTS.

RIGGING AND SAILS.

SEAMANSHIP.

Appendices follow the section "A Dictionary of Sea Terms".

SEAMANSHIP.

ERRATA

Page 6, in the 8th line from the top, for ' Jib Horses,' read ' Jib Guys.'
Page 12, for ' Fig. 97,' read ' Fig. 98.'
Page 18, in the last line, for ' Fig. 372,' read ' Fig. 366.'
Page 53, in line 4 from the top, for ' are reeved through these Blocks, then through the Blocks (f) on the Yard,' read ' are reeved through the Blocks (f), then through the Blocks on the Yard.'
Page 55, in line 26, for ' the principal Objection is,' read ' the principal Objection are.'
Page 75, line 3 from the top, for ' perfect understanding,' read ' perfect undertaking.'
Page 67, line 18 from the bottom, for ' Sheet Cable,' read ' Sheet's Cable.'
Page 71, line 23 from the top, for ' in a direct Line,' read ' a direct Line.'
Page 60, line 6 from the top, for ' leading in,' read ' leading it.'
Page 69, line 7 from the bottom, for ' outer End,' read ' inner End.'
Page 83, line 15 from the top, for ' Burton Tackles, read ' Burton Pendents.'
Page 95, line 16 from the top, for ' Fig. 507,' read ' Fig. 512.'

ERRATA IN THE PLATES.

Page 15, Fig. 134 should be 131.——Pages 29 and 30---in Figs. 202 and 208, the upper Seizings should be throat ones.
Page 23, in the top, Fig. 172, the Battens should be laid fore and aft.
Page 34, Fig. 222, the Block of the lower Lift is hooked to the fore End of the Cap, instead of the fore Part of the Side of it.

Publisher's Note: to maintain the historical accuracy of the text, we have included the original Errata, despite the fact that, compared to modern usage, they state the reverse of their intent. Changed Errata have been added to the relevant pages.

THE

Young Sea Officer's Sheet Anchor;

OR,

A Key to Rigging and Seamanship.

RIGGING.

THE Rigging of a Ship consists of a quantity of Ropes, or Cordage, of various Dimensions, for the support of the Masts and Yards. Those which are fixed and stationary, such as Shrouds, Stays, and Back-stays, are termed *Standing Rigging;* but those which reeve through Blocks, or Sheave-Holes, are denominated *Running Rigging;* such as Halliards, Braces, Clew-lines, Bunt-lines, &c. &c. These are occasionally hauled upon, or let go, for the purpose of working the Ship.

Ropes are a combination of several Threads of Hemp, twisted together by means of a Wheel in the Rope-Walk. These Threads are called Rope-Yarns, and the Size of the Rope in Diameter, will be according to the Number of Yarns contained in it.

A Proportion of Yarns (covered with Tar) are first twisted together. This is called a Strand; three, or more of which being twisted together, form the Rope: and according to the number of these Strands, it is said to be either *Hawser-laid, Shroud-laid,* or *Cable-laid.*

ROPES

ROPES—SPUN-YARN WINCHES.

A HAWSER-LAID ROPE, Fig. 1.

Is composed of three single Strands, each containing an equal Quantity of Yarns, and is laid right-handed, or what is termed *with the Sun.*

A SHROUD-LAID ROPE, Fig. 2.

Consists of four Strands of an equal Number of Yarns, and is also laid *with the Sun.*

A CABLE-LAID ROPE, Fig. 3.

Is divided into nine Strands of an equal Number of Yarns: these *nine* Strands being again laid into *three*, by twisting *three* of the small Strands into *one.* It is laid left-handed or *against the Sun.*

SPUN-YARN,

Is made as follows: A Piece of Junk or old Cable is untwisted, the Yarns drawn out, knotted together, and rolled up in Balls round the Hand. Three or four of these Balls are laid upon Deck, and an End out of each being taken, they are coiled in Fakes upon a Grating, or other thing, (to keep the Tar from the Deck) and upon every three or four fakes Tar is rubbed by a Brush. These are fastened by their Ends to a kind of Reel called a Spun-yarn Winch, Fig. 4. and a half-hitch is taken over one of the Spokes, E. The Man who spins the Yarn, retires to a convenient Distance: and then with a brisk Motion, (holding the Yarns in his hands) he whirls the Winch round against the Sun. When it is spun sufficiently, he rubs it backwards and forwards, with a piece of old Canvas, which he keeps in his hand, reels it on the Winch, takes another half-hitch round the Spoke E, and proceeds as before. When the Reel is full, it is taken off and balled.

There is a Winch, Fig. 5. on a much better construction, used in the Merchant Service, with which two boys may spin a considerable quantity of Spun-yarn in twelve hours. A Crutch (1.) is stepped into a mortise of the Windlass (2.) A Wooden Spindle goes through the Holes in the upper part of the Crutch, having a small Wheel or Truck fixed to one end. That part of the Spindle which lies between the two Arms of the Crutch is four Square (3.) The Part without, is rounded, and in the End is fixed a Peg (4.) A piece of Line, such as small Rat-line (5.) well chalked, is taken with a Turn round the *squared* Part (3.) The Rope-Yarns are fixed to the Peg (4) on the rounded Part: one Boy walks aft with them, rubbing them with a piece of old Canvas, whilst the other (having a part of the Ratline in each Hand (5) pulls briskly on the under Part (a), then slackens it, restoring it again to its former Position, by hauling on the upper one.

Thus the Wheel and Spindle are kept in a continual Whirl, which renders this Method very expeditious; for the Boy may walk the length of a large Ship with the Yarns, before there is occasion to reel them up. When it is sufficiently spun, the Bight is laid over a Hook fastened by a Laniard to one of the Fore Shrouds, opposite the *rounded* Part of the Spindle, on which it is reeled by the ratline Stuff. The Bight is then taken over the Peg again, and they proceed as before.

WORMING

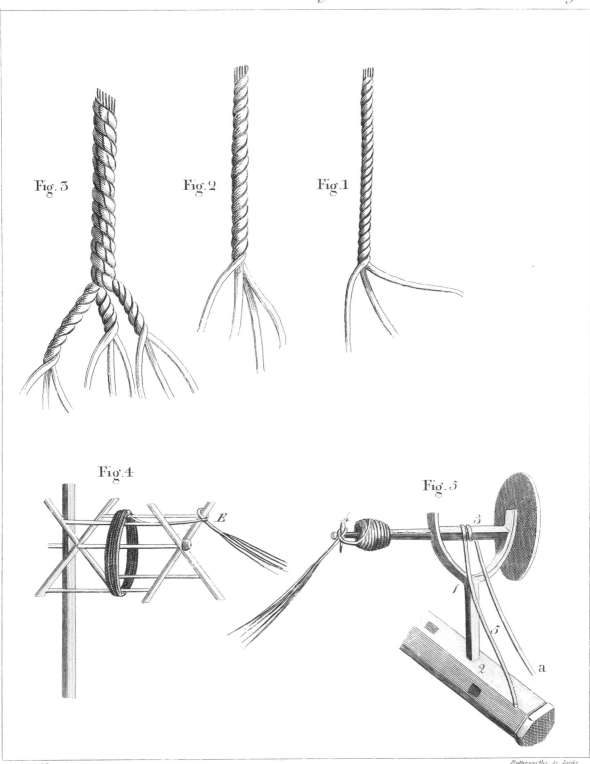

Fig. 3

Fig. 2

Fig. 1

Fig. 4

E

Fig. 5

Oliver del.

Butterworths, sc Leeds.

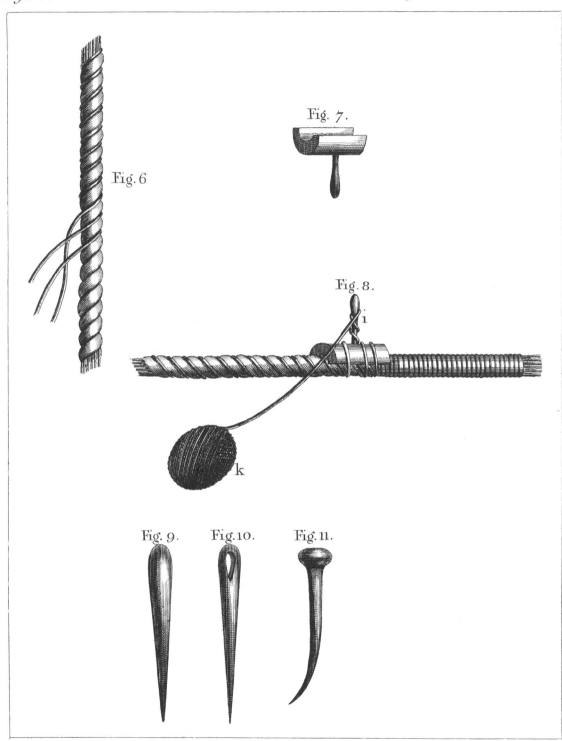

Fig. 6.

Fig. 7.

Fig. 8.

i

k

Fig. 9.   Fig. 10.   Fig. 11.

WORMING—SERVING—SPLICING.

Spun-yarn is used for *worming, serving, seizing, &c.*

WORMING A ROPE,

Is filling up the divisions between the Strands by passing Spun-yarn, &c. along them, Fig. 6. This is done, in order to strengthen it, for various purposes: and to render its surface smooth for parcelling.

PARCELLING A ROPE,

Is wrapping old Canvas round it, well tarred, which prepares it for serving, and secures it from being injured by rain Water lodging between the parts of the Service when worn.

THE SERVICE,

Is clapped on by a wooden Mallet, Fig. 7. made for the purpose. It is round at the Top; but has a Groove cut in the head of it to receive the Rope, that the turns of the Spun-yarn may be passed with Ease and Dispatch. It is done thus: The Rope is first bowsed hand-taught by a Tackle, then wormed. The End of the Spun-yarn for the Service is laid upon the Rope, and two or three turns passed round the rope and over *it*, hauling them very taught. The Mallet is laid with its Groove upon the Rope Fig. 8. a turn of the Spun-yarn is taken round the Rope and the Head of the Mallet, close to the last turn which was laid by hand: Another is passed in the same manner, and a *third* also on the *fore* part of the Mallet, leading up round the Handle (i) which the rigger holds in his hand. The Service is always passed *against* the lay of the Rope, so that as the latter stretches, the tension of the former is not much decreased. A Boy holds the Ball of Spun-yarn (k) at some distance from the Man who is serving, and passes it round, as he turns the Mallet, by which he is not retarded in his Operation. The end is put through the three or four last turns of the Service, and hauled taught.

SPLICING.

Ropes are joined together for different purposes, by uniting their Strands in particular forms, which is termed *Splicing.* A Splice is made by opening, and separating the Strands of a Rope, and thrusting them through the others which are not unlaid. The Instruments used on this Occasion, are Fids and Marling Spikes.

A FID,

Is made according to the Size of the Rope it is meant to open, and is tapered gradually from one end to the other, Fig. 9. It is commonly made of hard Wood, such as Brazil, Lignum Vitæ, &c. and sometimes of Iron: when of the latter, it has an Eye in the upper End like Fig. 10.

A MARLING SPIKE,

Is an iron Pin of a similar Mould, on the upper End of which is raised a Knob, called the Head, Fig. 11.

SPLICING.

SPLICING.

A SHORT SPLICE.

To splice the two Ends of a Rope together, proceed thus : Unlay the Strands for a convenient Length ; then take an End in each hand, place them one within the other, (Fig. 12) and draw them close. Hold the strands (a. b. c.) and the end of the Rope (d) fast in the left hand, or if the Rope be large, stop them down to it with a Rope-yarn : then take the middle end (1) pass it over the strand (a) and, having opened it with the Thumb, or a Marling-spike, (Fig. A.) push it through under the strand (c) and haul it taught. Perform the same operation with the other Ends, by leading them *over* the first next to them, and *th ough* under the second, on both sides : the Splice will then appear like Fig. 13 ; but in order to render it more secure, the work must be repeated : leading the Ends *over* the third and through the fourth ; or the ends may be untwisted, scraped down with a Knife, tapered, marled, and served over with spun-yarn.

AN EYE SPLICE, Fig. 14. (a)

Is made by opening the End of a Rope, and laying the Strands (e. f. g.) at any distance upon the standing part, forming the Collar or Eye (a). The End (h) Fig. B. is pushed through the Strand next to it (having previously opened it with a Marling Spike) ; the End (i) is taken *over* the same strand, and through the second ; and the End (k) through the third, on the other side.

THE LONG SPLICE, Fig. 15.

To make this splice, unlay the Ends of two Ropes to a convenient distance, and place them one within the other as for the short splice : unlay one strand for a considerable length, and fill up the intervals which *it* leaves with the opposite strand next to it. For Example, the Strand (1) being unlaid for a particular length, is followed by the space which it leaves by the Strand (2). The Strand (3) being untwisted to the left hand, is followed by the Strand (4) in the same manner. The two middle Strands, (5 and 6) Fig. C. are split : an overhand Knot is cast on the two opposite halves, and the Ends lead over the next Strand and through the second, as the whole Strands were in the short splice : the other two halves are cut off : Sometimes the *whole* Strands are hitched, then split, and the *half* Strands put through in the same manner ; but the surface is not so smooth, and the former method seems sufficient. When the Strand (2) is laid up to the Strand (1) they are divided, knotted, and the Ends cut off in the same manner ; and so with (3) and (4). This Splice is used for lengthening a Rope which reeves through a Block, or Sheave-hole, the Shape of it being scarcely altered.

A FLEMISH EYE, Fig. 17.

Take the end of a Rope and unlay one Strand (7) Fig. 16. to a certain Distance and form the Eye Fig. 17. by placing the two Strands (8) along the standing part of the Rope, filling up the intervals (marked by the Shade) with the Strand (7) till it returns and lies under the Eye with the Strands (8). The Ends are scraped down, tapered, marled, and served over with spun-yarn.

AN ARTIFICIAL, OR SPINDLE EYE, Fig. 18.

Unlay the End of a Rope, then open the Strands, separating every Yarn : Take a piece of Wood or Rope the size of the intended Eye, and hitch the Yarns round it, as described by the figure : scrape them down, marl, parcel, and serve them. This makes a neat Eye for the End of a Stay. The Yarns are here drawn greatly out of Proportion, in order to render the figure distinct.

KNOTTING.

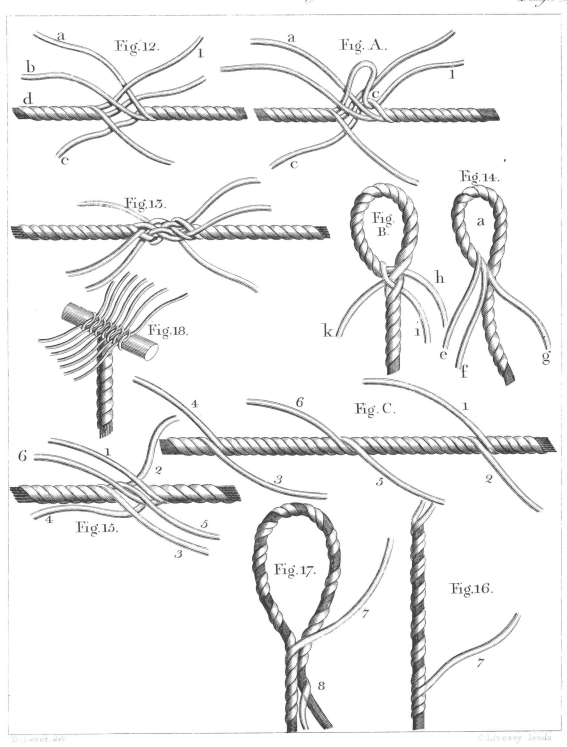

Fig. 12.

a
b
d
1
c

Fig. A.

a
1
c
c

Fig. 13.

Fig. B.

Fig. 14.

a
h
k
i
e
f
g

Fig. 18.

6
1
4
2
3
5
Fig. 15.

4
6
3
Fig. C.
1
5
2

Fig. 17.

7
8

Fig. 16.

7

D. Lever. del.   C. Livesey Leeds.

Splicing_Knotting.

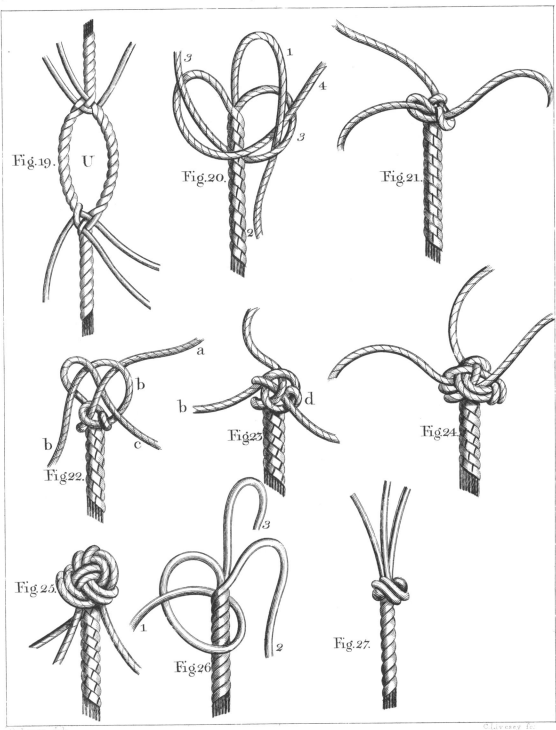

Fig.19. U

Fig.20.

Fig.21.

Fig.22.

Fig.23.

Fig.24.

Fig.25.

Fig.26.

Fig.27.

KNOTTING.

To make the CUT or BIGHT SPLICE, Fig. 19.

Cut a Rope in two, and according to the size of the Collar or Eye you mean to form, lay the end of one Rope upon the standing part of the other, and push the ends through, between the Strands, in the same manner as for the Eye Splice, shewn in the former page. This forms a Collar or Eye, (u) in the bight of the Rope. It is used for Pendents, Jib-Guys, &c.

To make a WALL-KNOT, Fig. 21.

Unlay the end of a Rope, Fig. 20, and with the Strand (1) form a Bight, holding it down on the side of the Rope at (2) : pass the end of the next (3), round the Strand (1) : the end of the Strand (4), round the Strand (3), and through the Bight which was made at first by the Strand (1) : haul them rather taught, and the Knot will then appear like Fig. 21.

To CROWN this Knot, Fig. 23.

Lay one of the ends over the top of the Knot, Fig. 22, which call the first (a), lay the second (b), over it, and the third (c), over (b), and through the Bight of (a) : haul them taught, and the Knot with the Crown will appear like Fig. 23, which is drawn open, in order to render it more clear. This is called a *Single Wall*, and *Single Crown*.

To DOUBLE WALL this Knot, Fig. 24.

Take one of the ends of the single Crown, Fig. 23, suppose the end (b), bring it underneath the part, of the first walling next to it, and push it up through the same Bight (d) : perform this operation with the other Strands, pushing them up through two Bights, and the Knot will appear like Fig. 24, having a *double Wall*, and *single Crown*.

To DOUBLE CROWN the same Knot, Fig. 25.

Lay the Strands by the sides of those in the single Crown, pushing them through the same Bights in the *single* Crown, and down through the *double* Walling : it will then be like Fig. 25, viz. *single* walled, *single* crowned, *double* walled, and *double* crowned. This is sometimes called a Tack Knot, and is also used for Topsail Sheets. The first walling must always be made *against* the lay of the Rope : the parts will then lay fair for the double crown ; so that if Figure 20 had been a hawser-laid Rope, or *with the Sun*, the Strands (1. 3. 4.) would have been passed the contrary way. The ends are scraped down, tapered, marled, and served with spun-yarn.

MATHEW WALKER's KNOT, Fig. 27,

Is made by separating the Strands of a Rope, Fig. 26, taking the end (1) round the rope, and through its own Bight: the end (2) underneath, through the Bight of the first, and through its own Bight, and the end (3) underneath, through the Bights of the Strands (1 and 2), and through its own Bight. Haul them taught, and they form the Knot Fig. 27. The ends are cut off. This is a handsome Knot for the end of a Laniard.

N.B. The Knots are in general drawn very slack and open, that the parts may be more plainly demonstrated : on which account they have not so neat an appearance in the plates, as when they are hauled taught. More bights and turns are also shewn in the drawings, than can be seen at one view in the Knots, without turning them backwards and forwards.

B   KNOTTING.

KNOTTING.

To make a SINGLE DIAMOND KNOT, Fig. 29.

Unlay the End of a Hawser-laid Rope for a considerable Length, Fig. 28, and with the Strands form three bights down its Side, holding them fast. Put the End of Strand (1) over Strand (2), and through the Bight of Strand (3), as in the Figure: then put the Strand (2), over Strand (3), and through the Bight formed by the Strand (1): and the End of (3), over (1), and through the Bight of (2). Haul these taught, lay the Rope up again, and the Knot will appear like Fig. 29. This Knot is used for the Side Ropes, Jib Guys, Bell Ropes, &c.

To make a DOUBLE DIAMOND KNOT, for the same Purpose, Fig. 30.

With the Strands opened out again, follow the lead of the single Knot through *two single* Bights, the Ends coming out at the Top of the Knot, and lead the last Strand through *two double* Bights. Lay the Rope up again as before, to where the next Knot is to be made, and it will appear like Fig. 30.

To make a SPRIT-SAIL SHEET KNOT, Fig. 33.

Unlay two Ends of a Rope, and place the two Parts which were unlaid, together, Fig. 31. Make a Bight with the Strand (1). Wall the *six* Strands together, *against* the lay of the Rope (which being *Hawser-laid* must be done from the right Hand to the left) exactly in the same manner that the single Walling was made with three: putting the second over the first, the *third* over the second, the fourth over the third, the fifth over the fourth, the sixth over the fifth, and through the Bight which was made by the first: haul them rather taught, and the single walling will appear like Fig. 32; then haul taught. It must be then crowned, Fig. 33, by taking the two Strands which lie most conveniently, (5 and 2) across the Top of the Walling: passing the other Strands (1. 3. 4. 6.) alternately over, and under those two, hauling them taught: the Crown will be exactly similar to the Figure. It may be then double walled, by passing the Strands (2. 1. 6 &c.) under the Wallings on the left of them, and through the same Bights, when the Ends will come up for the second crowning, which is done by following the lead of the single Crown, and pushing the Ends down through the Walling, as before, with three Strands. This Knot, when double walled, and crowned, is often used as a Stopper Knot, in the Merchant Service.

A STOPPER KNOT, Fig 34,

Is made by single walling, and *double* walling (as described page 5) *without crowning*, a three stranded Rope, against the lay, and stopping the Ends together as in the Figure. The Ends if very short are whipped, without being stopped.

To make a SHROUD KNOT, Fig. 35.

Unlay the Ends of two Ropes Fig. 36, placing them one within the other, drawing them close as for splicing: then single-wall the Ends of one Rope against the lay (i.e. from left to right, if the Rope be cable laid, as in the Figure) round the standing Part of the other, Fig. 35. The Ends are opened out, tapered, marled down, and served with Spun-yarn. This Knot is used, when a Shroud is either shot, or carried away.

To make a FRENCH SHROUD KNOT, Fig. 37.

Place the Ends of two Ropes as before Fig. 36, drawing them close. Lay the Ends (1. 2. 3.) back upon their own Part (b), single-wall the Ends (4. 5. 6.) round the Bights of the other three, and the standing Part (b), and it will appear like Fig. 37. The Ends are tapered, &c. as before. This Knot is much snugger, and equally secure as the other.

HITCHING

---

*Although original Erratum reads *"in the 8th line from the top, for 'Jib Horses,' read 'Jib Guys.'"*, it should be *"in the 8th line from the top, for 'Jib Guys,' read 'Jib Horses.'"*

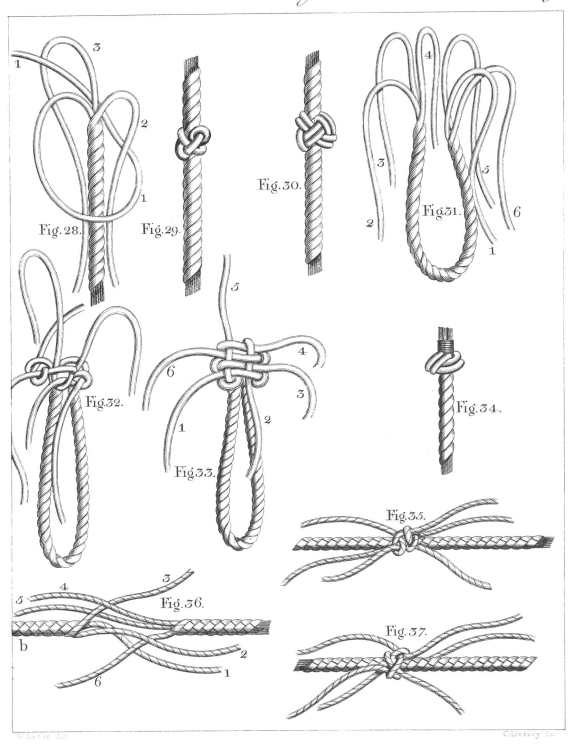

Fig. 28.

Fig. 29.

Fig. 30.

Fig. 31.

Fig. 32.

Fig. 33.

Fig. 34.

Fig. 35.

Fig. 36.

Fig. 37.

Knotting.

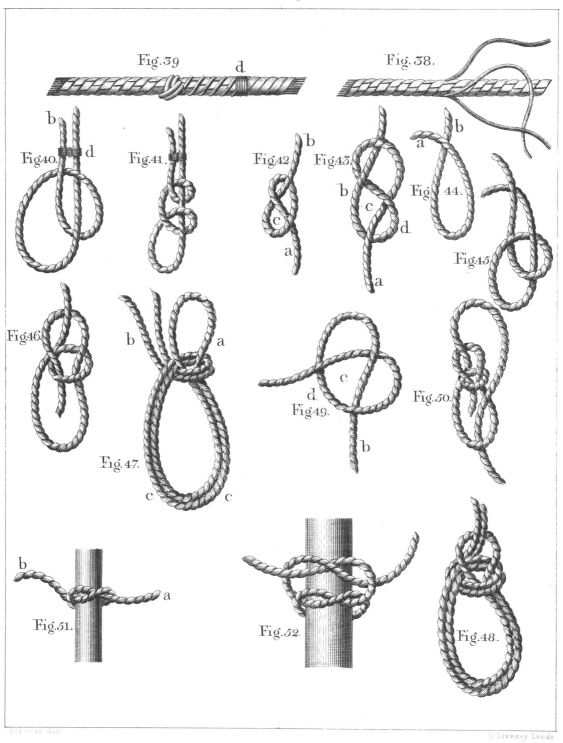

Fig. 39.   d   Fig. 38.

b   d   Fig40.   Fig.41.   Fig42.   b   Fig43.   a   b

b   c   a   Fig. 44.

c   d   Fig45.

a

Fig46.   b   a   c   Fig.49.   d   b   Fig.50.

Fig. 47.   c   c

b   Fig.51.   a   Fig.52.   Fig.48.

HITCHING----KNOTTING.

To make a BUOY ROPE KNOT, Fig. 39.

Unlay the Strands of a Cable-laid Rope, and also one of the *small* Strands out of each large one; laying the large ones again as before, and leaving the small ones out, like Fig. 38---then *single* and *double* wall the small Strands (as directed for the Stopper Knot, page 6), round the Rope, Fig. 39, worm them along the Divisions, and stop their Ends with Spun-yarn, (d).

HITCHING a ROPE, Fig. 40,

Is performed thus---pass the end of a Rope (b) round the standing part: bring it up through the Bight, and seize it to the standing part at (d). This is called a *Half-Hitch*. Two of these, one above the other, Fig. 41, is called a *Clove-Hitch*.

To make an OVER-HAND KNOT, Fig. 42.

Pass the end of a Rope (b), over the standing part (a), and through the Bight above (c).

To make an OVER-HAND, or FIGURE-OF-EIGHT KNOT, Fig. 43.

Take the end of a Rope (a), round the standing part (b), under its own part (d), and through the Bight (c).

To make a BOWLINE KNOT, Fig. 46.

Take the end of a Rope (a), Fig. 44, in the right hand, and the standing part (b), in the left, laying the end over the standing part: with the left hand, turn a Bight of the *standing* part over it, Fig. 45: lead the end round the standing part, through the Bight again, and it will appear like Fig. 46.

To make a BOWLINE KNOT upon the BIGHT of a ROPE, Fig. 48.

Take the Bight (a) in one hand, Fig. 47, and the standing parts (b) in the other. Throw a Kink or Bight over the Bight (a) with the standing parts, the same as for the single Knot. Take the Bight (a) round the parts (b), and over the large Bights (c c), bringing it up again; it will then be complete, Fig. 48.

To make a RUNNING BOWLINE KNOT, Fig. 50.

Take the end of a Rope, Fig. 49, round the standing part (b), and through the Bight (c): make the single Bowline Knot upon the part (d), and it is done, Fig. 50.

To make a REEF KNOT, Fig. 52.

Make an over-hand Knot as before directed, Fig. 51, round a Yard or Spar: bring the end (a) (being the next towards you) over to the *left*, and (b) to the right: take (a) round (b), draw them taught, and it is done, Fig. 52.

HITCHING

HITCHING----BENDING.

To make a TIMBER HITCH, Fig. 53.

Take the end part of a Rope (a) round a Spar or Timber Head: lead it *under* and *over* the standing part (b): pass several turns round its own part (c), and it is done.

To make a ROLLING HITCH, Fig. 54.

With the end of a Rope (a) take two round turns over a Spar, &c. at (c): pass two Half-Hitches (see page 7th) round the standing part (b), and it is finished : the end may be stopped to the standing part.

To make a MAGNUS HITCH, Fig. 56.

Pass two round turns with the end of a Rope (a) over a Spar, Fig. 55; then bringing it before the standing part, pass it again under the Spar, and up through the Bight which it made, Fig. 56, the end part being jambed by the Bight (d).

To make a BLACKWALL HITCH, Fig. 58.

Form a Bight, (c) Fig. 57, by putting the end (a) across under the standing part (b). Put this Bight over the Hook of a Tackle, Fig. 58, letting the part (d) rest upon it, and the part (a) be jambed by the standing part at the Cross. This is used with a Laniard, when setting up the Shrouds.

To make a CAT's-PAW, for the same Purpose, Fig. 60.

Lay the end of a Rope (a), Fig. 59, over the standing part (b), forming the Bight (e), take the side of the Bight (c) in the right hand, and the side (d) in the left---turn them over from you, three times, and there will be a Bight in each hand, (c d) Fig. 60. Through these put the Hook of a Tackle.

To make a SHEET BEND, Fig. 61.

Pass the end of a Rope (a), through the Bight of another Rope (b), then round both parts of the Rope (c d), and down through its own Bight.

To make a FISHERMAN's BEND, Fig. 62.

With the end part of a Rope, take two turns (c), round a Spar: a Half-hitch (see page 7), round the standing part (b), and under the turns (c); then another Half-hitch round the standing part (b). This is used for bending the Studding-sail Halliards to the Yard.

To make a CARRICK BEND, Fig. 64.

Form a Bight (c), Fig. 63, by laying the end of a Rope (a), across the upper surface of its standing part (b). Lay the end (e) of another Rope (d) under (a and b); then following the lead of the dotted Line, pass it *over* (a), *through* the Bight, *under* (d), and up through the Bight again, Fig. 64: (c) there representing the end (e) in the other figure.

HAWSERS are sometimes bent together thus: Fig. 65. The Hawser has a Half-hitch cast on it, a Throat Seizing (see the next page), clapped on the standing part (b), and a *round* one at (a). Another Hawser is reeved through the Bight of this, hitched in the same manner, and seized to the standing part at (d e).

And frequently the ends of two Ropes (a c), Fig. 66, are laid together: a *Throat* Seizing (see the next page) is clapped on at (e), the end (a) is turned back upon the standing part (b), and the standing part (d) brought back to (c): another throat Seizing is put on each, as at (f), Fig. 67, and a round Seizing near the end at (g): the same Security is placed on the other side.

HITCHING

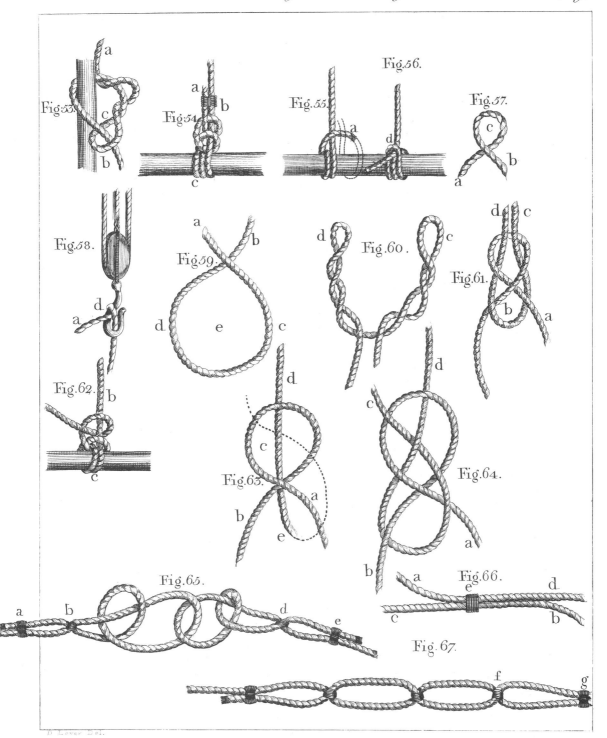

Fig.53.
Fig.54.
Fig.55.
Fig.56.
Fig.57.
Fig.58.
Fig.59.
Fig.60.
Fig.61.
Fig.62.
Fig.63.
Fig.64.
Fig.65.
Fig.66.
Fig. 67.

D. Lover Del.

Hitching_Seizing.

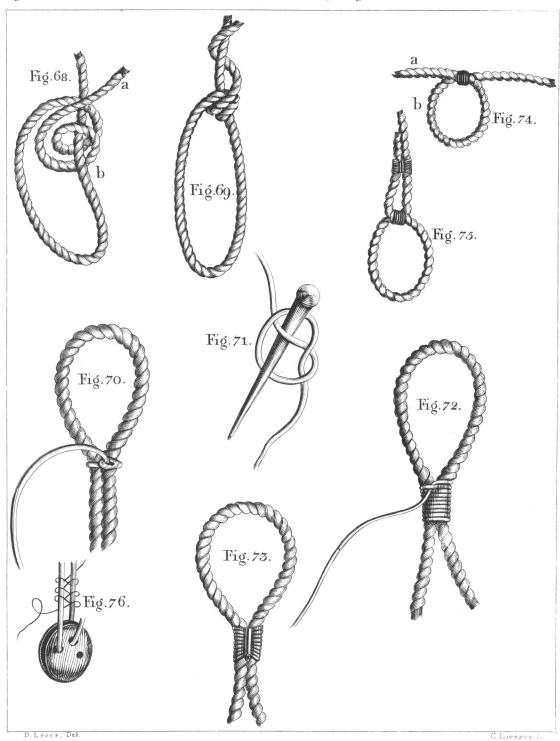

Fig. 68.

a

b

Fig. 69.

a

b

Fig. 74.

Fig. 75.

Fig. 70.

Fig. 71.

Fig. 72.

Fig. 73.

Fig. 76.

D. Lever, Del.

C. Livesey, Sc.

HITCHING—SEIZING.

To make a MIDSHIPMAN's HITCH, Fig. 69.

With the end of a Rope, (a) Fig. 68, take a half-hitch round the standing part (b); take another turn through the same Bight, jambing it between the parts of the Hitch---when hauled taught, it will appear like Fig. 69. The end may be taken round the standing part, or stopped to it. It is thus a Tail-tackle is clapped on a Rope, or fall, to augment the purchase.

SEIZING a Rope is binding the two parts together with Spun-yarn, House-line, Marline or small Cordage.

To make a ROUND SEIZING, Fig. 73.

Splice an Eye in the end of a Seizing, Fig. 70, and taking the other end round both parts of the Rope, reeve it through the Eye---pass a couple of turns---haul them taught by hand; then make a kind of Cat's-paw on the Seizing, Fig. 71, by taking a turn with the Seizing by the Marling-spike, laying the end part over the standing part, pushing the Marling-spike *down* through the Bight, *under* the standing part, and up through the Bight again. Heave these two turns well taught, by the Heaver or Marling-spike: pass the rest, and bind them in the same manner, making six, eight, or ten turns, according to the size of the Rope; then push the end through the last turn, Fig. 72. Over these pass five, seven, or nine more, (which are termed *Riders)* always laying one less above, than below. These are not to be hove too taught, that those underneath may not be separated. The end is now pushed *up through* the Seizing, and two cross turns, Fig. 73, are taken betwixt the two parts of the Rope and round the Seizing, (leading the end through the last turn) and hove well taught. If the Seizing be small Cordage, a WALL KNOT (see Page 5) is cast on the end; but if Spun-yarn, an over-hand Knot. When this Seizing is clapped on the two ends of a Rope, it is called an END SEIZING. If upon the Bight, as in the Figure, an EYE SEIZING---and if between the two others, a MIDDLE SEIZING.

A THROAT SEIZING, Fig. 75,

Is passed with riding turns, but *not* crossed. A Bight is formed Fig. 74, by laying the end (a) over the standing part (b). The Seizing is then clapped on; the end put through the last turn of the Riders, and knotted. The end part of the Rope, Fig. 75, is turned up and fastened to the standing part, as in the Figure, with a *round Seizing.* This is used for turning in dead Eyes, Hearts, Blocks, or Thimbles.

STOPPING, is fastening two parts of a Rope together, like a round Seizing, but not crossed.

NIPPERING, is making fast the two parts of a Laniard or Tackle-fall, whilst the purchase is fleeted. The turns are taken cross-ways, Fig. 76, between the parts, to jamb them; and frequently a round turn is taken over the Laniard, before every cross: These are called *Racking* Turns. Riders are passed over these, and the ends fastened with a REEF KNOT, (see Page 7) if they be to remain.

The neatest method of securing the ends of Ropes from untwisting, is by POINTING.

C

POINTING---

POINTING——GRAFTING——MOUSE.

To POINT a ROPE, Figs. 79 and C.

Unlay the end of a Rope, as for splicing, and stop it. Take out as many Yarns as are necessary, and make Knittles : (this is done by taking separate parts of the Yarns when split, and twisting them) Comb the rest down with a Knife, Fig. 77. Make two Knittles out of every Yarn which is left : lay half the Knittles down upon the scraped part, and the other, back upon the Rope, Fig. 78. Take a length of twine, which call the *Warp*, and pass three turns very taught, jambing them with a Hitch at (a). Proceed, laying the Knittles backwards and forwards, as before, and passing the Warp. The ends may be whipped and snaked with twine, or the Knittles hitched over the Warp, and hauled taught. The upper Seizing must also be snaked, Fig. 79. The Pointing will appear like Fig. C : a small Becket is often worked at the end, when the Rope is large (g). If the tapered part be too weak for pointing, a piece of stick may be put in, proceeding as before.

SNAKING is for the better securing of a Seizing, which is passed round the single part of a Rope, and therefore cannot be crossed. It is done by taking the end parts under and over the lower and upper turns of the Seizing, Fig. 80.

GRAFTING a ROPE, Fig. 82,

Is done by unlaying the two ends of a Rope, placing the Strands one within the other, as for splicing, Fig. D, and stopping them at the joining. The Yarns are then opened out, split, and made into Knittles, as before, for pointing. The Knittles of the lower part (a), Fig. 81, are divided, the Warp passed as before, and pointed over the Rope. Proceed with the Knittles of the upper part in the same manner, snaking the Seizing at each end, Fig. 82. Straps of blocks are often grafted instead of the short Splice, particularly on the quarter-deck : this is by no means so secure as the Splice, for if the pointing be worn by wet and friction, the Strap may give way---it is therefore better, that the Straps of blocks which are to be pointed for neatness, and without a Splice, should be made *Selvagee* fashion, (see *Selvagee*, Page 12, Fig. 96) all the parts of which bear an equal strain, and if the pointing give way, the Strap will hold.---N. B. The Knittles in the plates are much too large, and only a few represented, to avoid confusion.

A MOUSE for a STAY, Fig. 83,

Is generally raised with Spun-yarn, taking a number of turns, heaving them well taught, jambing them with Rope-yarns laid under, and over, alternately, and then parcelled and pointed. It is, however, found by practice in the Merchant service, that the parcelling alone is sufficient, which is tapered and marled down, according to the shape required.---Fig. 83 represents the Mouse made with parcelling. Knittles for pointing, made of Hambro' line, &c. according to the size of the Stay, are middled, laid with their Bights just above the head of the Mouse at (b), and the Warp passed round, proceeding as before-mentioned in pointing. As they rise on the Mouse, more Knittles are added ; and when got past the thickest part, they are decreased. They are frequently worked a little distance below the Mouse, on the Stay, according to fancy : the service of the Stay is taken over their ends, to secure them---the Warp is House-line, Marline, &c.

PUDDINGS for the YARDS or MASTS, Fig. 84,

Are made by splicing an eye (see Page 4) in each end of a piece of Rope, according to the size intended, then serving it over with Spun-yarn, increasing the turns from each end towards the middle ; which tapering gives it the shape of the figure. If it be for a mast, it is pointed over, for neatness---a Laniard or Lashing is spliced into one of the eyes.

GASKETS---

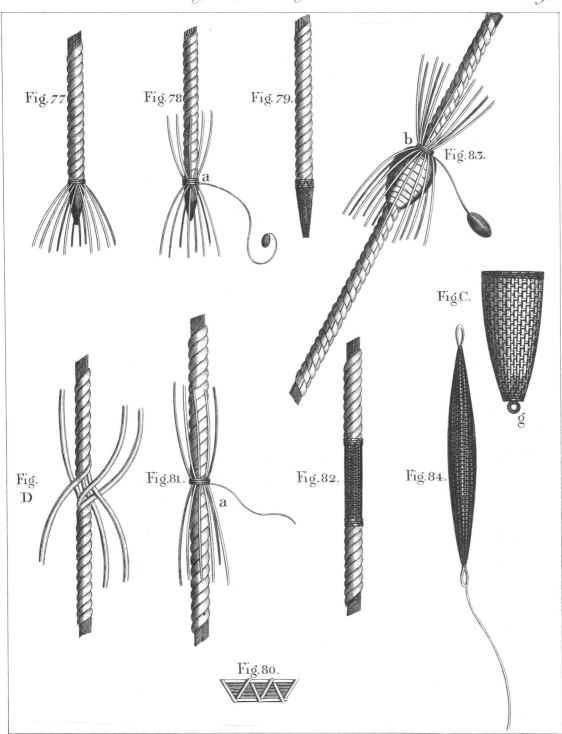

Fig. 77.

Fig. 78.

a

Fig. 79.

b

Fig. 83.

Fig. C.

g

Fig.
D

Fig. 81.

a

Fig. 82.

Fig. 84.

Fig. 80.

Gaskets_ Matts &c.

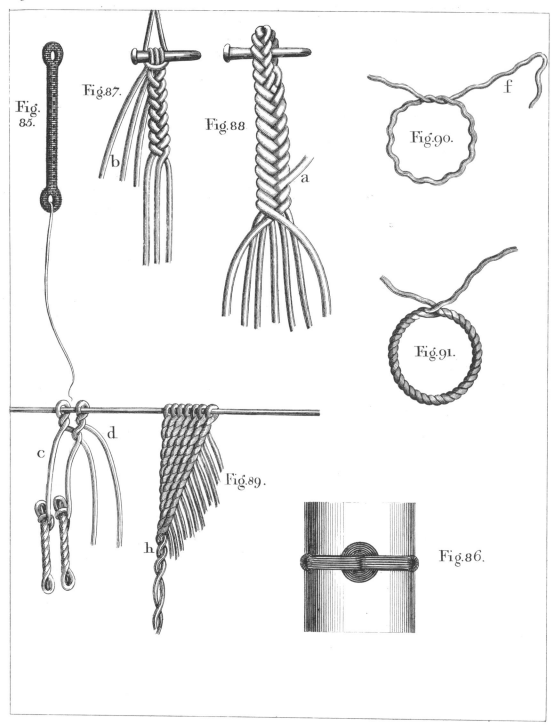

Fig. 85.

Fig. 87.

b

Fig. 88.

a

Fig. 90.

f

Fig. 91.

c

d

Fig. 89.

h

Fig. 86.

GASKETS——MATS, &c.

A DOLPHIN, Fig. 85,

Is made in the same manner that the Pudding was begun, having an Eye in each end ; but no Service raised. It is wormed, and parcelled, to make the surface even, and then pointed over Fig. 85. In one End is spliced a Lashing, or Laniard, and when the two Ends are lashed round the Mast, &c. the Lashing is passed cross-ways, over and under one Eye, then over and under the other, and the End part afterwards taken in a circular form round the crossing : Fig. 86. This is called a *Rose-lashing*.

Foxes for Gaskets, &c. are made by taking a number of Rope-yarns from three upwards, according to the size intended, and twisting them on the Knee, rubbing them well backwards and forwards with a piece of Canvas.----*Spanish* Foxes are made by twisting single Rope-yarns in the same manner. They are then made into a kind of Coil over the Thumbs, and twisted (that they may hang clear, and not impede the operation) like those represented in the Figure for the Mat.

GASKETS, Fig. 88,

Are made by taking three or four Foxes according to the size, middling them over a Pump-bolt, &c. and plaiting the three or four Parts together for the length of the Eye, Fig. 87. The Plaiting is formed by bringing the outside Fox on each side alternately over to the middle. The outside one is laid with the right hand, and the remainder held and steadied with the left. When this is done, take the other Parts (b), (having shifted the Eye part so that it lies over the Bolt, Fig. 88.) and work the whole together in the same manner ; add another Fox at (a), and work it for a convenient length, then diminish it towards the End, taking out a Fox at proper Intervals. When finished, one End must be laid up, the others plaited, and then the one hauled through.

POINTS for reefing Sails are plaited with Foxes. They are sometimes of one Piece, or *single*, and when this is the case, the Plaiting is begun in the Middle with seven or more Foxes, worked in the same manner, and tapered, by reducing the Foxes towards each End. Over-hand Knots are cast on, when reeved through the Gromets in the Sails, and jambed taught by reeving one End through the Hole of a Sheave, taking hold of the End, and pushing the Sheave with the feet. They are more commonly made what is called Rope-band fashion, in two Parts, having an Eye in one End of each Leg like the Gasket, Fig. 88 ; but this Eye is worked long and small, that a Turn may be taken in it before the End of the other Leg is put through, which makes it double, (as will be mentioned page 53.) One Fox is turned up as before ; but as they are continually beating against the Sail, the Ends are whipped with Twine, and stuck through the whole with a sail Needle.

SENNIT is made by plaiting Rope-yarns in the same Manner that the Foxes were worked for the Gasket.

To make a WROUGHT MAT, Fig. 89.

A Piece of Hambro' Line, &c. is stretched in an horizontal Direction, as in the Figure : and Foxes, according to the Breadth intended, are hung over it. The Fox nearest the left Hand (c), has a Turn twisted in its two Parts, and one Part given to the Man opposite, (two People being employed). The next Fox (d), has also a Turn twisted in its two Parts, and one Part given back : the remaining End is twisted round the *first* which was given back, (as in the Figure), and that again round *its own* Part. Proceeding in this manner with the other Foxes, the Mat will appear in the working as described in the Plate, until the whole of the Foxes are put in. The two to the left (h), are always twisted together, till those to the *right* Hand are worked to them, in order to keep in the Turns each time. At the Bottom, another Piece of Hambro' Line is put in : the Ends of the Foxes split, and hitched round it, then put through the other Twists with a Marline-spike. To render the Surface of these Mats softer, Strands of old Rope are cut in Pieces of about three Inches in length, pushed through the Divisions of the Twists, and then opened out. These Yarns are called *THRUMBS*.

A GROMET, Fig. 91,

Is made by unlaying a Strand of a Rope, Fig. 90, placing one Part over the other, and with the long End, (f), following the Lay till it forms the Ring, Fig. 91, casting an over-hand Knot, (Fig. 51, page 7), on the two Ends, and if necessary, splitting and pushing them between the Strands, as in the long Splice.   MAT-

MAT—TURKS-HEAD—LEAD—LENGTHENING a ROPE.

To make a WOVE MAT.

A flat Piece of Wood called a Sword (d), Fig. 92, is used. This is put alternately between the Parts of the Spun-yarn, or Sennit, stretched over two Pieces of Hambro' Line, as in the figure. The Warp of Spun-yarn (e), is placed through the Parts which the Sword has opened, and jambed by it, close to the Head: a Piece of Spun-yarn (i), is put slack through the same Divisions at the opposite End, and left there. The Sword is taken out, passed under, and over the other Parts, as before, and each End of the Warp passed, and jambed taught. The Piece of Spun-yarn (i), which was left at the opposite End, is now lifted up, and brings the Parts as they were first divided by the Sword: the Warp is passed as before, and the Work continued until the Whole is completed.

A TURKS-HEAD, Fig. 95,

Is worked with Log-line, &c. as an ornament to Bell or Man-ropes, and is made thus---Take a *clove-hitch* (see page 7) with the Line round the Rope, Fig. 93: bring the Bight (d) under the Bight (g), and take the end up through it: it will then appear like Fig. 94---make another cross with the Bights, and take the end down, after which follow the lead, and it will form a kind of Crown or Turban, Fig. 95.

A SELVAGEE, Fig 96,

Is made by laying *Rope-yarns* in a Bight, round two Timber-heads, &c. and marling them down with Spun-yarn. Large ones of Spun-yarn are sometimes made for getting in the lower masts, as will be mentioned hereafter. Straps for Blocks are very neat made in this manner, particularly leading Blocks on the Shrouds for the running Rigging, which are sometimes worked with *Spanish Foxes*.

A SHEEP SHANK, Fig. 98,

Is made for shortening a Back-stay, &c---a half-hitch is taken with the standing parts (a), round the Bights (b), when it will appear like the Figure.

The HAND-LEAD, Fig. 98,

Is a Plummet of 7, 8, or 9 pounds weight. It is shaped like the Figure; having a hole in the upper extremity, through which is reeved a Gromet (c), being well served over, to keep it from chafing. In the end of the lead-line there is a long Eye spliced, which is also served over. The eye is reeved *through* the Gromet, and taken *over* the Lead, being thus secured. This Line is about twenty fathoms in length, and particularly marked as follows :---At the distance of *two* and *three* fathoms, a piece of *black leather* is thrust through the Strands---at *five* fathoms, a *white rag*---at *seven* fathoms, a *red* one---at *ten*, and *thirteen*, black leather; and at *seventeen*, a red rag.

The DEEP-SEA LEAD,

Is shaped like the hand lead; but is more ponderous, weighing from twenty to thirty pounds.

To LENGTHEN a ROPE by an ADDITIONAL STRAND.

Cut the Strand at the bottom of the plate, Fig. 100, and unlay it as far as (b), and there cut the Strand (b)---Unlay those two Strands the same length, Fig. 99: and cut the Strand (c) at (d). Draw the two parts of the Rope asunder to the proper distance, laying the end part of the longest Strand (d), on one side over the shortest on the other (e). Introduce the additional Strand (e), lay it on at (d) to (e), and then follow up the lay with the two longest Strands to (a). The ends are knotted, and pushed through, as in the long Splice. This Splice is used for lengthening the head and foot Ropes of sails, when intending to put in another Cloth. If it be lengthened *two* feet, the Strands must be cut *three* feet apart: and the additional Strand must be upwards of nine feet in length.

BLOCKS,

*Although original Erratum reads *"for 'Fig. 97,' read 'Fig. 98.'"*, it should be *"for 'Fig. 98,' read 'Fig. 97.'"*

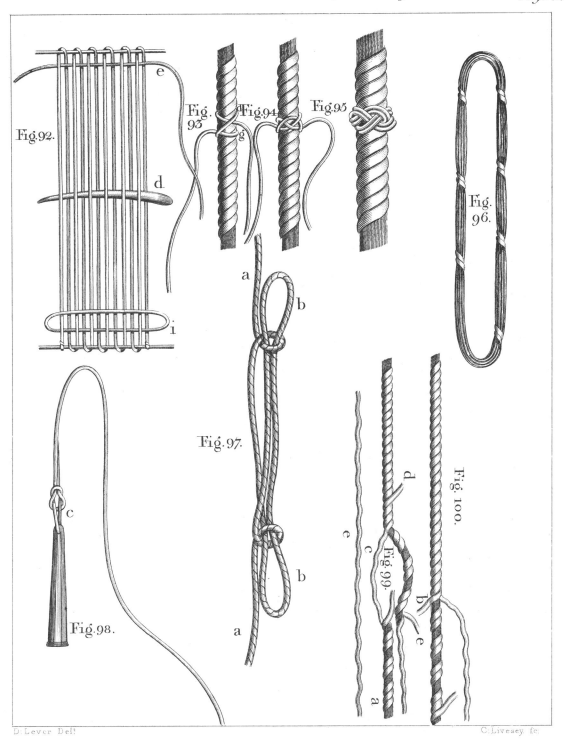

Fig. 92.

Fig. 93

Fig. 94

Fig. 95

Fig. 96.

Fig. 97.

Fig. 98.

Fig. 99.

Fig. 100.

D: Lever Del.

C: Livesey. fc:

Fig. 101

Fig. 102

Fig. 103

Fig. 104

Fig. 105

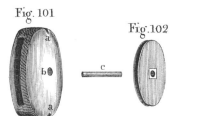

Fig. 106

Fig. 107

Fig. 108

Fig. 109

Fig. 110

Fig 111

BLOCKS.

BLOCKS are variously shaped, according to their Use and Situation in the Ship. A Block consists of a Shell, Sheave, and Pin : and from the Number of these Sheaves it derives its Name, viz. a Block with one Sheave is called *single* : with two, *double* : with three, *treble* : and with four, *four-fold*.

The *SHELL* of a Block is made of Ash, or Elm, Fig. 101, and has one or two Scores or Notches cut at each End (a), according to its size : these Scores are for the Purpose of admitting a Strap which goes round the Block; and in its Center is a Hole for a Pin (b). The Shell is hollow, and in the Inside is placed a solid Wheel called a *SHEAVE*, Fig. 102, made of Lignum Vitæ, Brass, or Iron. In the Center of this Sheave is a Hole for a Pin or Axis, on which it turns. This is frequently strengthened by letting in a Piece of Brass, called a Coak or Bush. Round the Circumference of the Sheave is a Groove, that the Rope which goes over it may play with ease. The Sheave is placed in the Shell, and the Pin (c), is put through both the Shell and Sheave.

The *SINGLE BLOCK* appears like Fig. 103,---the *DOUBLE BLOCK* like Fig. 104, and the *TREBLE BLOCK* like Fig. 105.

TOPSAIL SHEET BLOCKS, Fig. 106,

Have a Shoulder or Projection at the lower End, to prevent the Sheets or Ropes which reeve through them from jambing.

LONG TACKLE BLOCKS, Fig. 107,

Are made like two single Blocks, the one large, the other small : the large one being above the small one.

SHOE, or LEG-AND-FALL BLOCKS, Fig. 108,

Are also made like two single Blocks ; but the Sheave of the upper one lies in a contrary direction to that of the lower one.

SNATCH BLOCKS, Fig. 109,

Have one side of the Shell open above the Sheave, by which the *Bight* of a rope may be placed in, and taken out at pleasure, without the necessity of reeving the end through. A hole is bored through the upper end, to admit a lashing. Small ones are used for hauling in the deep-Sea Lead, and large ones, iron bound, for receiving the Bight of Hawser, when warping the Ship. (see Iron-bound Blocks, page 16.)

SISTER BLOCKS, Fig. 110,

Have two Sheave-holes, one above the other ; but frequently in the Merchant Service, only a round hole in the lower Block, instead of the Sheave, like the Figure. A Score (g) is cut between the Blocks, and one at each end of them, for Seizings. They are hollowed out on each side of the Shell, for a Shroud to lie in.

CLEW-LINE BLOCKS, Fig. 111,

Are strap-bound---that is, they have a shoulder on each side of the Cheek, next to the end where the rope reeves. In these Shoulders are holes, bored vertically, (h), to receive a strap.

D   BLOCKS,

BLOCKS, &c.

A MONKEY BLOCK, Fig. 112,

Is made with a Saddle, to nail upon the Topsail Yards in Merchant Ships, for the Bunt-lines to reeve through. Sometimes it has a Swivel above the Saddle, to permit the Block to turn, when used for a Leech-line.

A DEAD EYE, Fig. 113,

Is a large circular piece of wood, having a Groove in its circumference, for a Shroud to lie in. The three holes or eyes are for a Laniard to reeve through.

A HEART, Fig. 114,

Is a block of wood with a large hole in the center, at the bottom of which are four or five scores round the outside, a Groove is cut, to admit a rope, called a *Stay*, &c.

A HEART for a COLLAR, Fig. 115,

Is sometimes open at the lower end, opposite to which the Laniard is passed. It has a Groove on each side (k), for the Seizing to lie in. A Heart, Fig. 116, is often used in the Merchant Service, with a round hole (l), for the heel of the Jib Boom to rest in, which is bevelled for that purpose. The bottom of the Heart (m), is also bevelled according to the Steeve of the Bowsprit.

A NINE-PIN BLOCK, Fig. 117,

Is shaped something like the Pin from which it derives its name; and is placed in the Breast-work, for the running rigging which leads down by the Mast, to reeve through.

A TRUCK, Fig. 118,

Is rounded, having a hole bored vertically for a Rope to reeve through. In the middle is a score (n), for a Seizing, and down the back a Groove, for a Shroud to lie in.

A BULL's EYE, Fig. 119,

Is a kind of wooden Thimble, with a hole in the center, and a Groove in the circumference.

A RACK, Fig. 120,

Is a piece of wood, through the holes of which belaying Pins are stuck---at the back part are several Scores for the Shrouds to lie in, to which it is seized.

An EUPHROE, Fig. 121,

Is a long piece of wood, having a number of holes, through which the Crow-foot for the Awning, &c. is reeved.

CLEATS

Are pieces of wood for various purposes, as represented by the different Figures. Fig. 122 is called a SLING CLEAT. One of these is nailed on each side of the slings on the Yards. Fig. 123, a STOP CLEAT. Such are nailed on the Bowsprit for the Gammoning, Collars, &c. and sometimes on the Yard Arms. Fig. 124, a BELAYING CLEAT. This is nailed or bolted to the side, for the purpose of belaying the Running-rigging to. Fig. 125, a MAST CLEAT. This is made with a Score, to admit a Seizing, a long hole in the center for an *under* Seizing, and two round holes by which the Seizing may be crossed. A COMB CLEAT, Fig. 126, is merely used for leading a rope through, or for keeping it in its place.---For a Shroud Cleat, see page 16.

STRAPPING.

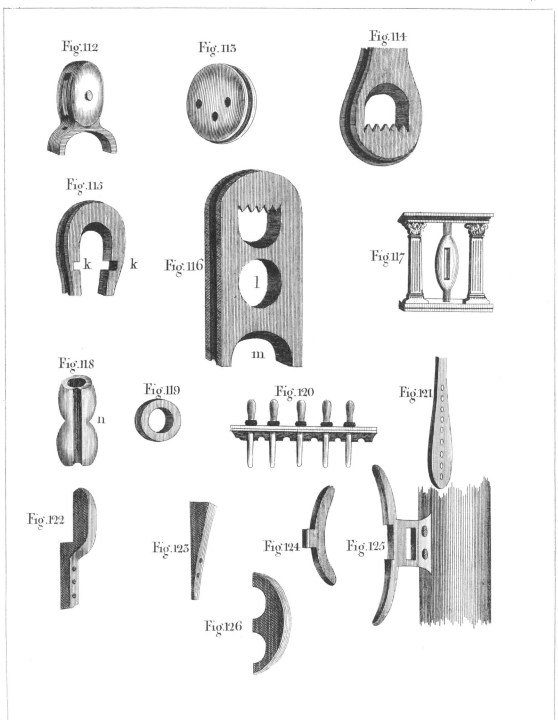

Fig. 112   Fig. 113   Fig. 114   Fig. 115   Fig. 116   Fig. 117   Fig. 118   Fig. 119   Fig. 120   Fig. 121   Fig. 122   Fig. 123   Fig. 124   Fig. 125   Fig. 126

Strapping.

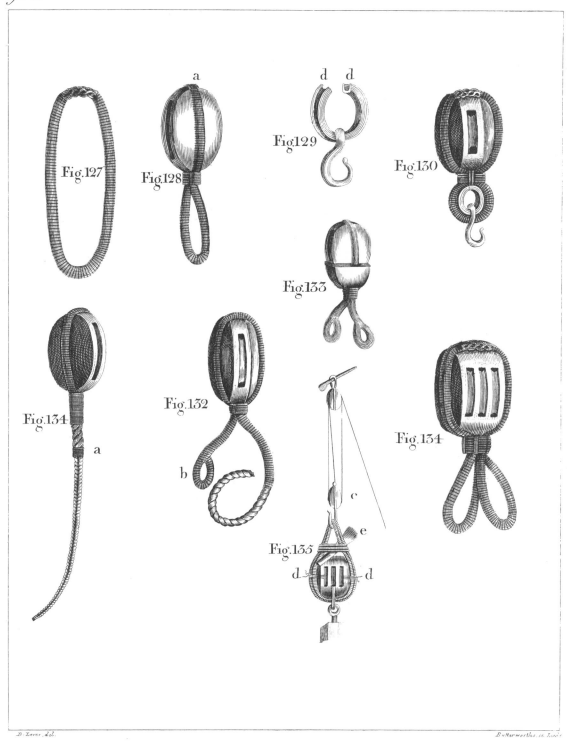

Original Erratum: *"Fig. 134 should be 131."*

STRAPPING.

A STRAP for a BLOCK, Fig. 127,

Is served over with Spun-yarn, and the two ends are spliced together with a *short* splice, (see page 4) the Scores being well tarred. This Splice, Fig. 128, (a) is placed over the end of the Block, opposite to where the Rope reeves. Close under the Block, a round Seizing (see page 9), is clapped on with Riding-turns, and crossed.

An IRON THIMBLE, with a hook, Fig. 129, is frequently strapped to Blocks. When this is done, the Strap is reeved through the eye of the hook, and over the Groove of the Thimble (d).--- The Splice is then made, placed as above, and the Thimble Seizing is clapped on between the Thimble and the Block, Fig. 130.

A TAIL BLOCK, Fig. 131,

Is strapped with an Eye-splice (see page 4). This Splice, which lies *under* the Block, having the ends combed and marled down, is served over with Spun-yarn, and the end of the rope whipped; but more frequently a stop (a), is put on at some distance from the Splice: The Tail is then unlaid, and the Strands plaited, as mentioned for Gaskets (page 11): and often, instead of this, the Yarns, when opened out, are marled down like a Selvagee (see page 12).

A BLOCK, strapped with a LONG and SHORT LEG, Fig. 132,

Is seized in the Eye or Bight with a round Seizing (see page 9): the Short Leg (b) has an Eye spliced in the end of it: the other Leg is left long, to pass round a Yard, &c. reeve through the Eye (b), and be hitched or seized to its own part. Blocks are also strapped in the same manner, with *two short* Legs, having an Eye in each, for a Seizing to pass through.

A CLUE-LINE BLOCK, Fig. 133,

Is strapped in the last-mentioned manner: the Bight of the Strap is put over the head of the Block, and the ends are reeved through the shoulder on each side: the Seizing is clapped on as before.

A THREE, or FOUR-FOLD BLOCK, Fig. 134,

Is double strapped, having two Scores in the Shell for that purpose: the Strap is wormed, parcelled, and served, (sometimes only wormed and served) and spliced together: then being doubled, the Splice and the other Bight are put over the Block. The Seizing is clapped on both parts as before, with this only difference, that it is crossed *both* ways, through the double parts of the Strap.

These Blocks being so unweildy, require a purchase to heave the Strap out, and a wedge or large Fid to fix it in. When this Block is strapped on board Merchant Ships, it is generally done in a vertical direction, reeving a rope through one of the Sheave-holes, and making it fast to a ring-bolt, &c. then hooking a Stay Tackle, (c), Fig. 135, to the two Bights of the Strap, and setting it taught. A Frapping or temporary Seizing is next put on above the Block, and hove well taught by a heaver. A large Fid (e) is driven in betwixt the head and the frapping, and a Stop of Spun-yarn (d), (which is too low down in the plate) is clapped on, being reeved through the *upper* part of the Sheave-hole on each side, and nippered round the strap with a Heaver, which keeps it in its place. The Fid is then knocked out, the frapping taken off, and the Seizing clapped on as before. In Men of War and East Indiamen, when these Blocks are strapped, they use a Chock instead of a Fid, and a Wedge is driven in between the Chock and the Block. The Nipper (d), is taken round both the Strap and Block, and hove taught with a Heaver.

BLOCKS---

BLOCKS——TACKLES, &c.

Blocks strapped with iron, are either single, double, or treble.

A TOP BLOCK, Fig. 136,

Is a single Iron-bound Block, and is used for reeving the top rope pendent through, when swaying up the Topmasts.

The UPPER TOP-TACKLE BLOCK is double or treble, and strapped similarly to the Top Block.

The LOWER TOP-TACKLE BLOCK, Fig. P,

Is either double or treble, and is also iron-bound, having a Swivel in the iron Strap (g), that the Turns may be taken out of the Top-tackle Fall, if twisted, by slueing the Block round.

A SHROUD CLEAT, Fig. F,

Omitted in page 14, is shaped like the Figure, having Scores for the Seizings (i), which are snaked, (see page 10) and a Groove in the part where the Shroud lies.

A TACKLE

Is a purchase formed by reeving a rope through two, or more Blocks, to render easy the hoisting of any weight. The smallest purchase of this kind is made by reeving a rope through a single Block, Fig. 138. This is called a *Whip*.

A GUN TACKLE PURCHASE, Fig. 139,

Is made by reeving a rope through a single Block (a), then through another single Block (d), and making the end (c), fast to the Strap of the single Block (a). (c) is called the *standing* Part, because it is fixed: (e) the running part: and (f) the Fall, or part hauled upon.

If a rope be reeved through a single Block, Fig. 140, it is called *a Whip*, as before mentioned: and if the Block of another Whip (i), be strapped to the Fall of that, it is called *Whip upon Whip*.

A LUFF TACKLE, Fig. 141,

Consists of a double and single Block, each strapped with a Hook and Thimble. The Fall (b), is reeved through one of the Sheave-holes of the double Block (a); then through the single one; through the double one again, and the end makes fast with a Sheet-bend (see page 8) to a Becket (c), spliced round the Strap of the single Block (d).

If these Blocks be strapped with Tails, instead of Hooks and Thimbles, the purchase is then called a *Tail*, or *Jigger Tackle*.

A RUNNER TACKLE, Fig. 142,

Is the same Purchase as a Luff Tackle, applied to a Runner; which is a large Rope (c), reeved through a single Block (a), hooked to a Thimble in the end of the Pendent (b).

A SNATCH BLOCK, Fig. G,

Is frequently iron-bound, with a swivel Hook (a). This is used for placing the Bight of a Hawser or large rope in, when warping the Ship, &c. and to prevent the Bight from slipping out, if the rope be suddenly slackened, an iron clasp is fitted in the Strap which goes over the Snatch, and is fastened by a Toggle Bolt (b).

BLOCKS——

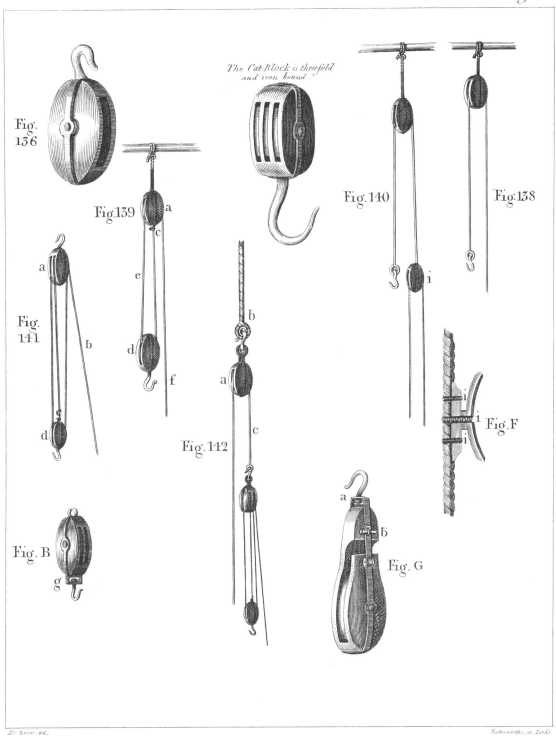

The Cat-Block is threefold
and iron bound.

Fig.
136

Fig.139

Fig.140

Fig.138

Fig.
141

Fig. F

Fig. 142

Fig. B

Fig. G

D. Lever, del.

Butterworths, sc. Leeds

Getting in the lower Masts.

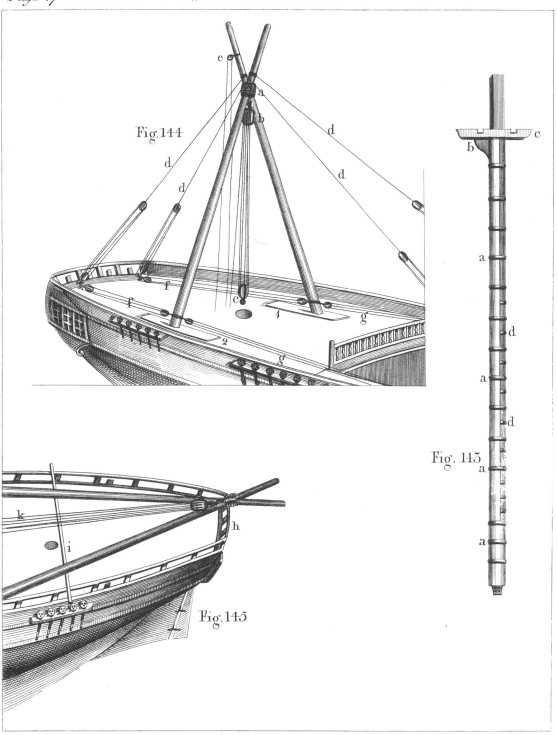

Fig.144

Fig. 143

Fig.145

D. Lever del.

Butterworths sc. Lond.

GETTING IN THE LOWER MASTS.

Ships have three lower Masts, and the Bowsprit, which may be also termed a Mast. These are of various lengths and diameters, according to the size of the vessel.

The first of these is called the *Fore-Mast*, from its situation, being placed in the fore part of the Ship. The second and largest, the *Main-Mast*, being near the center; and the third, the *Mizen-Mast*, which is nearest to the Stern. The Bowsprit projects over the Stem, and rises upwards in a sloping direction, which is termed *stiving*.

Ships of War and East-Indiamen have their Masts formed of different pieces. They are called *Made Masts*.

Fig. 143 represents one of these Masts---(a) the Iron Hoops---(d) the Hoops of the Fish---(c) the Tressle-Trees, with Scores to admit the Cross-Trees. The Tressle-Trees are strong pieces of Oak bolted together, and to the Mast-head: They rest on the Cheeks or Hounds of the Mast, which project out, and are farther supported by two large Brackets on each side, called *Bibbs* (b).

SHEERS, Fig. 144,

For getting in the lower Masts and Bowsprit, are made of two large Spars: a strong lashing secures them by their heads (a): Over the head of the Sheers, at the lashing, a large three or four-fold Block (b), according to the size of the largest Mast to be got in, is secured, connecting itself by a fall to another Block (c). At the head of the Sheers are four ropes, called *Guys*, two leading forwards, and two aft (d). Also at the upper end of one Spar, a Girt-line Block (e), is made fast, and its line reeved through it. This is to hoist up a man in case of emergency. At each heel of the Sheers there is a Tail-tackle (f), leading aft: and two others (g), are overhauled forwards.

Previously to the Sheers being raised, two planks (1.2.) long enough to lie over three beams, which are shored below, are placed upon deck on each side, for their heels to rest on.

The lashing of the Sheers is passed like a Throat-seizing, not too taught; and then the heels of the Sheers are drawn asunder:---They are laid over the Taffarel (h), Fig. 145; and (if the Ship do not carry a Poop,) to make them rise easier, a Spar is laid athwart over the Fife-rails (i). The lower Purchase Block is then taken forwards, (the fall (k), being overhauled) to the Breast-hook, or the Ring-bolt in the Stem, for the Main-Stay. The fall being taken through a leading Block, is brought to the Capstern, and hove upon. The cross Spar (i), cants the Sheers, and their heels are prevented from flying forwards, by the Tail-tackles.

When the Sheers are up, they are moved forwards or aft, by the Guys and Heel-ropes.

The Guys are hauled taught, and the Block cast off from the Breast-hook.

E   GETTING

GETTING IN THE MASTS—BOWSPRIT.

The Mizen-mast is first got in; for which purpose the Sheers are placed before the partners or hole (d), which the Mast is to enter; and the lower Purchase Block is lashed on a little above the center of gravity of the Mast, that it may have a Cant upwards. But in preference to this lashing, a stout Selvagee, made of Spun-yarn, should be taken round the Mast (a), Fig. 146, the Bight put through the Strap of the lower Purchase Block, and a Toggle clapped in. This, from its pliability, will be sure to hold, and is quickly done.

Two Girt-line Blocks, one on each side of the Mast-head (b), are lashed, to be ready to get the rigging over-head, and to hoist men on the Tressle-trees, in order to place it properly. The end of the Girt-line, which was made fast to one of the Sheer Heads (c), is taken round the Mast under the Bibbs. This is called a *Back Rope.*

When the Mast is high enough, this *Back Rope* is hauled upon, which places it in a vertical direction, over the Partners, or Hole (d). Some Hands on deck also assist at the Heel of the Mast, to make it enter. The purchase fall is then eased, and when fairly entered, they lower away: the people in the Hold placing the Tenon (e), in the Heel, into a Mortise of a large piece of Oak Timber, called a *Step,* which is bolted on the upper part of the Kelson.

When the Mizen-Mast is fixed, the Sheers are moved forwards by the Guys and Heel Ropes, as seen in Fig. 144, and placed before the Partners of the MAIN-MAST. This, and the *Fore-Mast,* are got in, and stepped, in the same manner.

The *BOWSPRIT,* Fig. 147,

Has its part within board, to the Heel, eight square; and from thence, rounded all the way to the Cap.---The Cap (A), is a large Block of Elm, with two holes, one round, the other square: it is driven on the outer end of the Bowsprit, the square hole going over the Tenon. In this Cap are several iron bolts, the use of which will be mentioned hereafter.

* Within the Cap, large pieces of Elm are bolted on each side to the Bowsprit; and underneath these, two Blocks with Sheeves. The former (e), are called the *Bees,* and the latter, the *Bee Blocks.* Without the squared part are Cleats, which are called the *Gammoning Cleats* (d), and above them is a piece of wood called a *Saddle* (f), having holes in it for the running-rigging to reeve through. About two-thirds out, is a Saddle for the Jib-boom (g), (except the heel rests in the Fore Stay Heart, shaped like Fig. 116, page 14), and another (h), for the Parral of the Spritsail Yard.

When the Bowsprit steps on Deck, it is slung like the lower Masts; but if it step between decks, then the after Guys of the Sheers are eased, so that their heads may project forwards.

** To get the Bowsprit in by the Fore-yard, see page 70, Fig. 366.

GETTING

---

*Blunt's second paragraph under the heading "The BOWSPRIT" contains a number of examples of change in word use and in availability of materials (see Appendix 2).
**Although original Erratum reads "In the last line, for 'Fig. 372,' read 'Fig. 366.'", it should be "In the last line, for 'Fig. 366,' read 'Fig. 372.'"

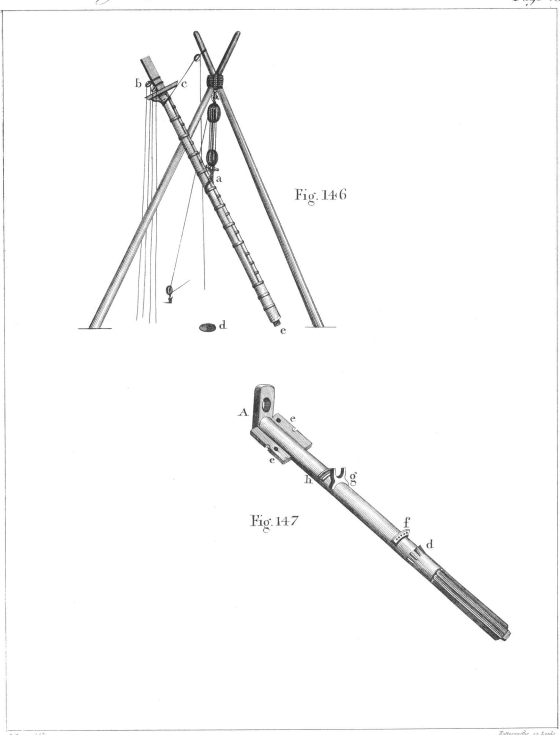

Fig. 146

Fig. 147

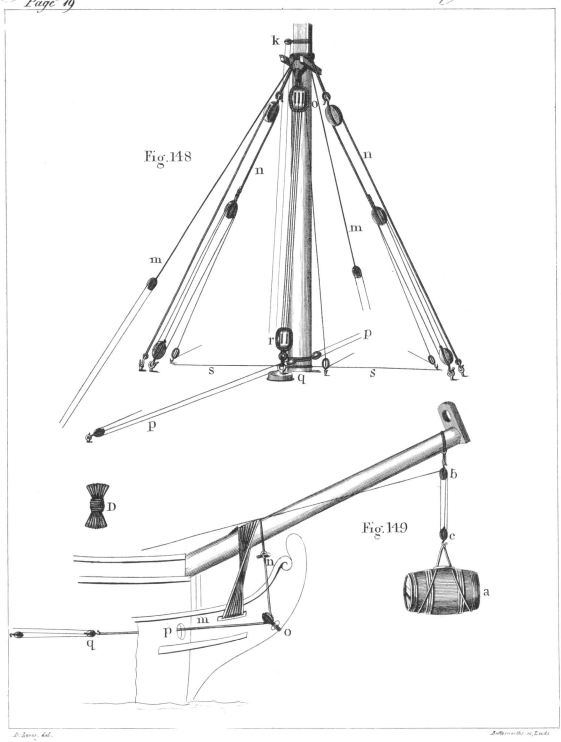

Fig. 148

Fig. 149

GETTING IN THE MASTS.

TO GET IN A NEW MAST BY THE OLD ONE, WITHOUT SHEERS, Fig. 148.

If a vessel have a damaged Mast, and be so circumstanced that she cannot procure Spars of sufficient dimensions to hoist in a new one by : Strip all the rigging, except the Runner Pendents (n), off the damaged Mast : take the Runners and Tackles to the Chains, setting them taught, two fore and aft Guys (m), to the Mast-head, and also a Girt-line Block (k). Secure the Mast above the Partners with fore and aft Tackles (p), and Heel-ropes from side to side (s). Lash the Purchase-block (o), to the Mast-head. Whilst this is doing, let the deck be well shored below. When all is secured, saw the old Mast off close to the Deck, wedging it as it is sawn : and being cut through, move it aft by the Guys and Heel-ropes, as before. Drive a large bolt into the head of the stump (q), remaining in the hold ; and (the lower Purchase-block (r), being lashed to it) hoist it out. The new Mast is then got in by the purchase, as before : and when stepped, the upper Purchase-block (o), may be shifted to the new Mast-head, the lower one toggled to the Selvagee, (see page 18) on the old Mast, and the Runners, Guys, &c. being cast off, the old Mast may be hoisted out by the new one.

The lower Masts and Bowsprit being stepped, the Ship is ready for rigging ; and as the Masts forwards depend greatly on the *latter,* it may be first secured.

In order to keep the Bowsprit down firm, and to resist the great force of the Stays, which support the Masts forwards, it is confined to its situation by the Gammoning, Bobstays, and Shrouds. Previously to these being fixed, it is swigged down by a cask of water (a), Fig. 149 ; or by a boat, suspended to its outer extremity. A pair of slings, or a strap, is passed round the Bowsprit end : the double Block (b), of a Luff Tackle is hooked to it, and the lower one (c), to a pair of slings round the cask, which is hoisted up, and remains till the Gammoning is secured.

The Gammoning is a rope passed with eight, ten, or twelve turns, (according to the size of the ship) over the Bowsprit, and through a hole in the Cutwater (m). The end is passed through the hole, over the Bowsprit, and either clinched, or spliced with an eye round the standing part : another turn is taken over the Bowsprit, through the hole, and over the Bowsprit again. The turns on the Bowsprit lie one *before* the other : those in the hole, one *abaft* the other ; because the Cleats on the Bowsprit lie before the hole in the Cutwater. The Bight of the Gammoning is put through the eye in the end of a Runner (n), and either toggled, or Cat's-pawed to a hook at the end of it. This Runner reeves through a Tail-block, made fast (or a block lashed) to the hole for the Bobstay (o), in the Cutwater ; and leads through the Hawse-hole (p). The double Block of a Luff-tackle (q), is hooked to the Runner within board, and the single Block being hooked to one of the Ring-bolts, the fall is taken to the Capstern.

The Gammoning is then hove well taught, and when sufficiently so, nippered with Spun-yarn to the standing part, by passing some turns round both parts, and a few alternately round one and the other : These are called *Racking Turns.* (see page 9, Fig. 76). The Luff-tackle (q), is then eased off, the Toggle taken out, and one or two more turns passed, and hove taught in the same manner : and so on with the rest.

When the regular number of turns is taken, the end part is passed round the whole of them, and hove taught, as before, till the whole is expended. These last are called *frapping* Turns (D) ; by which great power is gained in taughtening the other---the end is stopped to the standing part.

GAMMONINGS---

Blunt's version of Figure 149 (see Appendix 3) shows different methods of counterweighting when installing the bowsprit, and different methods of gammoning (lashing of bowsprit to cutwater), as the Americans began using iron for the purpose (Figure 147 in Appendix 2).

GAMMONINGS——STAY-COLLARS, &c.

The GAMMONING, Fig. 150,

Is frequently used. A large Strap has its two ends spliced together, wormed, parcelled, served, and then doubled. One Bight of the Strap reeves through a large bolt, (well leathered) in the top of the Cutwater (q), and in each Bight is seized a small heart (r. s.). The Bight (r), goes over the Bowsprit, and is secured to the Bight (s), by a Laniard (w). This Laniard is set up by a Spanish Windlass, thus :---A Spar (t), is laid over the Bowsprit and the Cathead, or Bows, and the Laniard being taken round it, is Cat's-pawed to the Heaver (v), (like the Seizing to the Marling-spike, Fig. 71, page 9), and hove round, till sufficiently taught : the parts are nippered, as in the former page, fresh turns are taken ; and when as many as requisite are passed, the Laniard (w), and the Bights (x), are frapped together as before.

When the Ship has no Cutwater, Fig. 151, the Gammoning is taken through a Ring-bolt (a), driven into the fore part of the Stem. It is set up with a Spanish Windlass, as before, and as many frapping turns taken as will conveniently lie.

When there is no Ring-bolt, Fig. 152, the Gammoning is taken through a hole in the Stem ; but in this case, no frapping turns can be taken ; therefore, as it is set up, each turn is nailed down to the Bowsprit, having a piece of leather under the head of every nail. It is commonly set up with a Spanish Windlass on each side. The Gammoning being middled, is nailed down ; one turn taken before, and another abaft, set up on both sides, and nailed, till the whole is expended.

Many Ships have a projecting Knee, with a Griffin's Head, &c. carved on (c). The Bowsprit is then secured by two Gammonings, as in the Figure : one through the hole in the Stem (b), and the other round the Knee (c). If a space were left between the Knee and the Bowsprit, and the hole in the Stem made lower down, these Gammonings might be frapped. Many masters object to the Bowsprit being confined down on the Knee, thinking it better that it should have a little play.

The Collars for the Fore Stays, Bobstays, and Bowsprit Shrouds, are next got on ; for which purpose two Spars are lashed together, in the form of a pair of Sheers, and the ends of these Spars rest one on each side over the Bows, Fig. 153. The other ends which are lashed together, are slung under the Bowsprit, just below the Cleats (e), which are nailed on to stop the Collars from coming in ; and upon these Spars is placed a grating (f), for the men to stand on.

When the Ship carries a FORE SPRING STAY, its Collar is put on next to the Cleats ; but when there is no Spring Stay, the Fore Stay Collar is placed there, and fitted to the Heart thus : the Collar is wormed, parcelled, and served, the two ends spliced together, and doubled, Fig. 154 ; after which the Splice and the Bight next to it, (h), are laid over the Heart (i), Fig. 155, and the parts then lie down the sides in the Groove. It is secured to the Heart, by a Seizing passed round the Heart and Collar, two scores being made for that purpose (k). As this round Seizing cannot be crossed, it is snaked, as mentioned page 10, Fig. 80. A Lashing is spliced round one of the Bights (l), the Heart is laid on the upper side of the Bowsprit, and the Bights hanging down on each side, the Lashing is passed through them alternately, underneath the Bowsprit, by the men on the grating, and hove taught by a Heaver.

BOBSTAYS.

Blunt adds a note to say, "All this applies to the old cumbersome mode of rigging ships, called the old school, which is nearly extinct."

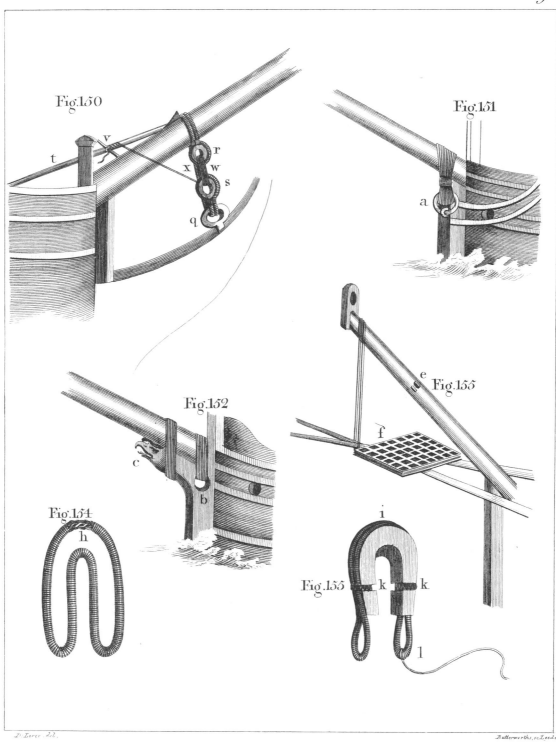

Fig.150

Fig.151

Fig.152

Fig.153

Fig.154

Fig.155

D. Lever del.

Butterworths, sc Leeds

Bobstays.

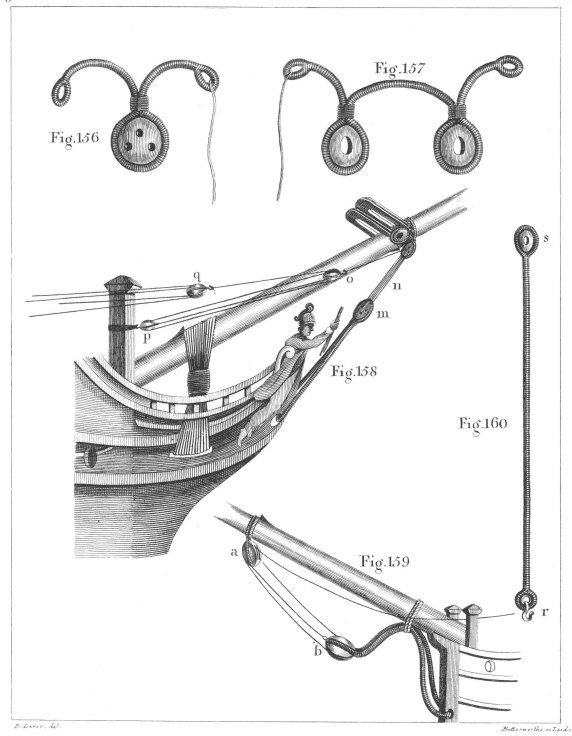

Fig.156

Fig.157

Fig.158

Fig.159

Fig.160

D. Lever, del.

Butterworths, sc Leeds.

BOBSTAYS.

The BOBSTAY COLLAR, Fig. 156,

Is wormed, parcelled, and served, having an Eye spliced in each end : A Dead Eye is placed in the   *
Bight, and a round seizing (see page 9), is clapped on. This lies underneath the Bowsprit, and the
lashing is passed through the Eyes over the upper part of it. In the Royal Navy there are two of
these, one placed before the other.

BOWSPRIT SHROUD COLLARS,

Of which there are two, are lashed over the Bowsprit in the same manner, with a Heart, or Dead
Eye, one lying on each side; but more frequently in Merchant Ships, the Hearts are both seized
into one Collar, Fig. 157, and the lashing is passed through the Eyes over the Bowsprit. The ends
of all the lashings are whipped, and seized down to the standing part.

The BOBSTAYS, Fig. 158,

In large vessels, are Cable-laid ; but in smaller ones Hawser-laid : They are wormed, parcelled, and
served, led through a hole in the Cutwater, and have the two ends spliced together. A Dead Eye
(m), is seized in with a round Seizing (see page 9), the splice laying on the upper side of it. They
are set up thus : A rope called a *Laniard* (n), is spliced to the Heart or Dead Eye, under the Bowsprit,
passing alternately through the Heart or Dead Eye (m), in the Bobstay, and the one it is spliced
to : the double Block of a Luff-tackle (o), is hooked to a Cat's-paw or Black-wall Hitch (see Figs.
57 and 59, page 8), on the Laniard : the single Block (p), hooks to a Selvagee, round the Knight-head.
This is bowsed taught, and another Luff-tackle (q), being hooked in the same manner to the fall of
this, it is set up. The Laniard is then nippered with Rope-yarn (see page 9), and the Tackles taken
off. This purchase of the Tackles is called *Luff-upon-Luff.* The end is taken through between the
Seizing and Dead Eye (m), one turn taken round the single part of the Bobstay, the remaining turns
round both parts, and the end stopped ; or if it be long, it may be frapped round the parts of the
Laniard (n). Ships in the Merchant Service, which carry two pair of Bobstays, frequently have the
Laniard of the outer pair to lead through a Heart or Dead Eye, the Collar of which is lashed to the
Bowsprit end, just within the Cap, a Cleat being nailed there for that purpose.

   Ships which carry no Figure Head, such as Coasters, whose Cat-heads are in general very forward,
have their Bobstays led through a hole in the Stem, like Fig. 159. They have a double Block turned
into the Collar (a), and a single one (b), seized in the Bobstay. The reason why they have not Dead
Eyes, is, because when the Anchor is hove up, the Bobstay laying so near the Bows, the Stock is apt
to get foul of them : They are therefore let go occasionally, and the Bights of the Bobstay triced up
to the Bowsprit, as in the Figure.

The BOWSPRIT SHROUD, Fig. 160,

Has a hook and thimble (r), spliced into one end, and a Heart or Dead Eye (s), into the other. It
is served over. The lower end (r), is hooked to an Eye-bolt in the Bends forward, and the upper one
(s), is set up with a Laniard to the Heart or Dead Eye in the Collar, with Luff upon Luff, like the
Bobstay.

F   RUNNER

---

*Blunt's versions of text and Figures 156 and 158 (see Appendix 4) define changes to bobstay collars (use of iron) and sig-
nificant changes in bobstay rigging.*

RUNNER PENDENTS.—SHROUDS.

The Fore-mast may be now fitted with its standing Rigging, which consists of Runner Pendents, Shrouds, Stays, Backstays, Cat-harpins, and Futtock Shrouds.

The Rigging is got over the Mast-Head by the Girtlines, which are reeved through Blocks (t), Fig. 163, lashed on each side of it, as mentioned before when getting in the Masts.

The RUNNER PENDENTS, Fig. 161 and 162,

Are first got over-head.---They are originally of one piece, and have an eye with a Thimble spliced in each end, (v) Fig.161. They are cut in the middle, and then joined by the Cut-splice (see page 5, Fig. 19), forming a Collar (w), to fit the Mast-head. In the Merchant Service, the Runner Blocks are often spliced into each end of the Runner, Fig. 162. They are wormed, parcelled, and served.

The end of the Girtline is made fast round the Pendents: they are hoisted up, and the men on the Tressle-trees place the Collar over the Head of the Mast: thus they hang on each side (y), Fig. 163. They rest on a Bolster, which is a piece of wood rounded and nailed on the Tressle-tree on each side, close to the Mast: and strong canvas, tarred, having Oakham underneath, is nailed on them; which prevents the Rigging from chafing. Sometimes in the Merchant Service the Bolsters are not nailed on, but merely stopped with Spun-yarn.

SHROUDS in the Royal Navy are Cable-laid; but small Ships in the Merchant Service have theirs Shroud, or Hawser-laid (see page 2). They are taken round two Fids or short posts (a.c.), Fig. 164, distant from each other according to the length of the Shrouds from the Tressle-tree on the opposite side, to the Partners, and stretched hand-taught. The Bights (c), are then cut asunder, so that every Bight on the Fid (b), is the middle of a pair of Shrouds; the foremost pair laying within the Coil.

Each pair is then taken its whole length, Fig. 165. A Bight is made at one end (d), and it is toggled through the strap of the double Block of a Tackle, the other end (e), is made fast to a strap round a Fid, with a Sheet-bend (see Fig. 61, page 8). The fall of the Tackle (f), being taken to a Windlass (g), it is bowsed a little taught, and wormed: then hove well on the stretch. The foremost pair are served from the middle (h), to the end (e), and on the other side, one-fourth towards the end (d): the rest are served one-fourth from the middle (h), on each side. Many Seamen object to worming the Shrouds; as the worming when stretched, is apt to lodge rain water, which may rot them.

They are now cast off: and an Eye is made in each pair, to fit the Mast-head, by clapping on a round Seizing (see page 9), which will lie just below the Bolster on the Tressle-trees: the middle (h), Fig. 166, making the upper part of the Eye. The Seizing for the Eye of the second pair of Shrouds is clapped on about its own breadth below the first, the third below the second, &c. By this they will hang clear of each other, and not chafe.

Near the end of each pair of Shrouds a Dead Eye is turned in, with a Throat-seizing, (see page 9): left-handed, if *Cable-laid*: right-handed, if *Hawser-laid*. In the former case, the ends of the Shrouds will lie *aft*, on the *Larboard side*: and *forwards*, on the *Starboard side*: Fig. 167 represents a Dead Eye on the Larboard side, and the inner side of the Dead Eye. The end part of the Shroud (i), is stopped to the standing part (k), by two round Seizings (see page 9): the end is whipped: and a piece of Canvas, tarred, is put over it, called a Cap (l).

TOPS

Blunt's version of text and Figure 164 (see Appendix 5) define slightly different procedures in making shrouds.

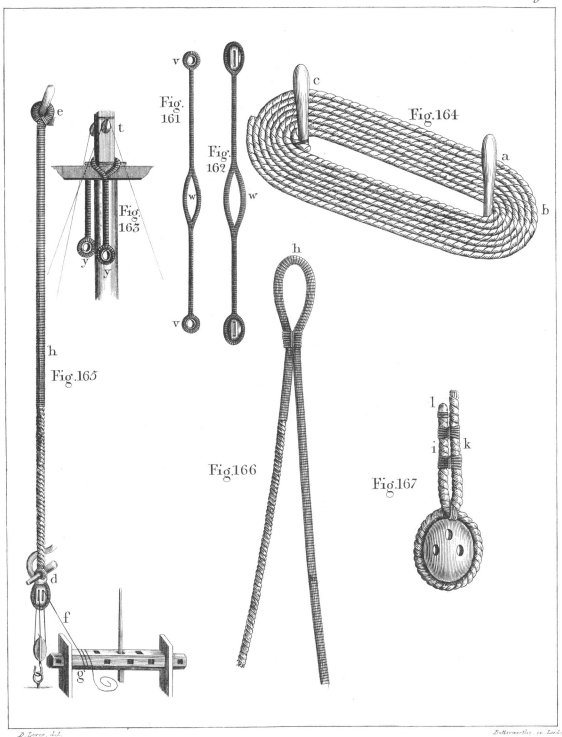

Fig.
161

Fig.
162

Fig.164

Fig.163

Fig.165

Fig.166

Fig.167

D. Lever, del.

Butterworth, sc. Leeds.

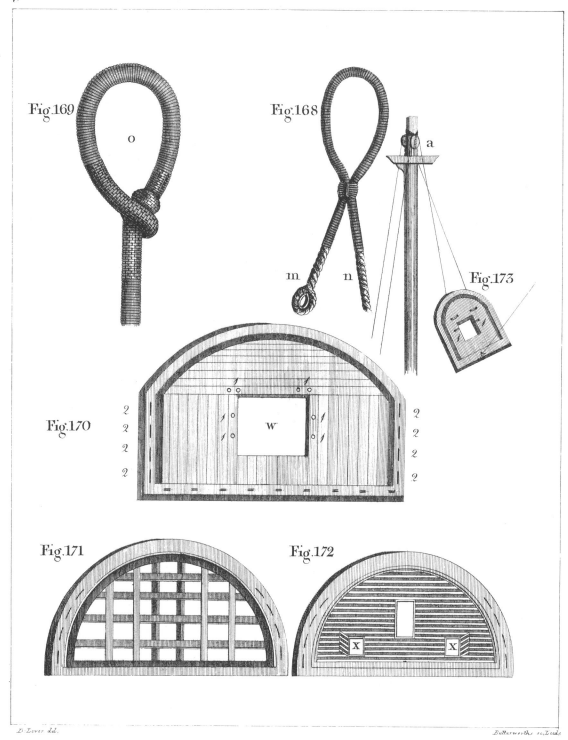

Fig.169

o

Fig.168

a

m   n

Fig.173

Fig.170

2
2
2
2

w

2
2
2
2

Fig.171

Fig.172

x   x

D. Lever del.

Butterworths sc. Leeds.

Original Erratum: *"in the top, Fig. 172, the Battens should be laid fore and aft."*

TOPS.

The Girtlines are over-hauled from the Mast-head, as before, for the Shrouds, which are got over in pairs. First, a pair on the starboard, then a pair on the larboard side, alternately, until the whole are completed.

If there be an odd Shroud on each side, it is hitched round the Mast-head, and seized; but in the Merchant Service, the odd Shrouds (which are called *Swifters*) are generally the foremost; and have the Runner Pendents in the same piece: an Eye being seized for the Mast-head, as before, Fig. 168, (m) the Pendent, and (n) the foremost Shroud.

The SPRING STAY and FORE STAY are next got overhead.---The Spring Stay, when carried, is sometimes put over the Mast-head, before the Fore Stay; but more frequently the Fore Stay is put over, and the Collar of the Spring Stay is taken up through the Collar of the other, and then put over the Mast-head, so that the Collar lies *over*, and the Stay *under* the fore Stay. The Spring Stay lies under, for the convenience of bending a Fore-stay Sail to it.

The Fore-stay is a large four-stranded rope, Cable-laid, and has an Eye worked in one end when made; but if not, a Flemish or Spindle Eye (see page 4), is made, combed out, marled, parcelled, and served (the Eye is commonly pointed over). The service is continued for one-third the length of the Stay, and it is stretched for that purpose as the Shrouds were. At that distance the Mouse is commonly raised (see page 10). The end of the Stay is reeved through the Eye to the Mouse, Fig. 169, and the Collar (o), formed by this, is put over the Mast-head, like the Shrouds, only that the Stay hangs before the Mast and the Shrouds on each side. The pointing of the Mouse is sometimes continued for a little distance down the Stay, for neatness; but in this case, a piece of parcelling should be placed just below the Mouse, that the Knittles may not be chafed by the Eye.

The TOPS are next got over.---They are in the shape of D's, framed on Cross-trees, which fit into a score left in the upper part of the Tressle-trees, and are for the purpose of spreading the Topmast Shrouds.

The Tops in Men of War and East-Indiamen are decked over, Fig. 170, and have a square hole (w), in the middle, called *Lubber's Hole*: on each side of this, and in its front, are holes bored (1), for the Girtlines to reeve through, and be stopped. In the rim of the Top are Mortises for the Futtock Plates (q): and sometimes within them holes for the Swivels. In the after rim of the Top there are holes for the Netting Stantions.

In the Merchant Service the Tops are seldom decked. Sometimes they are made what is called *Grating fashioned*, like Fig. 171, having three or four Cross-trees let into the Tressle-trees, when made. Sometimes they are made with light Battens, like Fig. 172: these have no Lubber's Hole; but a Scuttle on each side (x), with a kind of Trap-door, which a boy can, without difficulty, push up with his head. The battened Tops are framed on the Tressle-trees, and bolted to them: and the Mast is got in with the Top on, by the Sheers, as before-mentioned.

When the decked Top is to be got over the Mast-head, the Girtlines (a), Fig. 173, are overhauled down abaft the Mast, taken underneath the Top, and reeved through the small hole (1), down through Lubber's Hole, and the end hitched round the standing part. They are then stopped with Spun-yarn to the holes in the fore part of the Top. One of the Girtlines from the Main-mast head is hitched through a hole in the after part of the Top.

The Fore Top is then swayed up by the fore Girtlines (a), and guyed clear of the Tressle-trees, by the main one. When high enough, the stops at the fore part of the Top are cut: and then by hoisting on the fore Girtlines (a), it will fall over the Mast head: the Girtlines are lowered upon, the Top fixed by the men at the Mast head, and beat down by a Top Mall.

SETTING

The better and most usual way of rigging a fore-stay, is, the stay is fitted with an eye and seizing, Fig. 168, and both parts are passed through the inner bees of the bowsprit, (e 1), Fig. 147, led through a heart secured to the outer part of the knight-heads, set up and seized on its own part (y 1), Fig. 203, or passed around the bowsprit, and set with two eyes round the mast-head.

SETTING UP THE LOWER RIGGING.

Before the Mast is stayed, a Heart (c), Fig. 174, is turned into the lower end of the Stay, in the same manner that the Dead Eyes were for the Shrouds: left-handed if Cable-laid, right-handed if Hawser-laid: the end being whipped and capped as before. A Selvagee is clapped on the Stay at (d), and the double Block of a Luff-tackle (e), is hooked to it: The Laniard being spliced with an Eye-splice (see page 4) to the Heart (c), three or more turns are taken alternately through the Heart, on the Bowsprit (f), and the former, laying in the Scores of them. The turns being well smeared with Grease, to make them pass freely, the single Block of the Luff-tackle is attached to the Laniard by a Cat's-paw, or Black-wall Hitch (see page 8): the single Block of another Luff-tackle (g), is hooked to the Fall of that, and the double Block (h), to a Selvagee, or pair of Slings, round the Bowsprit (i), the Fall leading in on the Forecastle. The turns are then set up by the Purchase, and when sufficiently so, the parts are nippered with racking turns (see page 9), as before. Other turns are passed, the Tackle attached to the Laniard, set up in the same manner; and when it is expended, the end is whipped, and either stopped to the standing part, or hitched round the Stay, and stopped. In King's Ships and East-Indiamen, the lower Masts are generally bowsed forwards by the Runners and Tackles, before they are stayed.

The SHROUDS are next set up. The Laniard has a Matthew Walker's Knot, or two single wall Knots, one under the other, (see page 5), cast on the end, which is placed the reverse way to what the end of the Shroud is: thus in Cable-laid Shrouds, the ends on the *larboard* side lie aft; on the *starboard* side forwards; in which case the Knots will lie in the foremost holes in the Dead Eye on the larboard side; and in the aftermost, on the starboard side. Fig. 176 represents the Dead Eyes and Laniard of a Cable-laid Shroud on the *larboard* side, the end of the Shroud (k), laying aft, and the Knot of the Laniard in the foremost hole (l), of the upper Dead Eye. The lower Dead Eye is iron-bound, and fixed to the Ship's side by the Chain plate. The Knot being cast on the end, the Laniard is reeved through the foremost hole *(inside)* of the upper Dead Eye (l), then through the foremost hole *(outside)* of the lower Dead Eye, next through the middle hole of the upper Dead Eye, returning through the middle hole of the lower one, up again through the aftermost hole of the upper Dead Eye, and through the same in the lower one. The end (m), is then ready for hooking the Tackle to.

The Shroud is set up thus, Fig. 177. A Selvagee is fixed on the Shroud at (n): the *single* Block of a Luff-tackle is hooked to it, and the *double* Block to a Cat's-paw or a Black-wall Hitch (see page 8), on the Laniard (o). The Runner-tackle is over-hauled, and the *single* Block (p), hooked to the Fall of the Luff-tackle: its Fall reeves through a leading Block (q), hooked or strapped to an Eye Bolt in the Deck. The Laniard is well smeared with Grease, the Tackles are bowsed upon, and when sufficiently taught, the parts of the Laniard are nippered together with Rope-yarns (see page 9). The end of the Laniard is taken round *one* part of the Shroud above the Dead Eye, and then round *both* parts, until the whole is expended: it is then stopped to the Shroud.

LOWER RIGGING.

*Blunt gives an abbreviated method of staying the mast. Figure 174 (see Appendix 6) shows minor differences in securing the stay end.

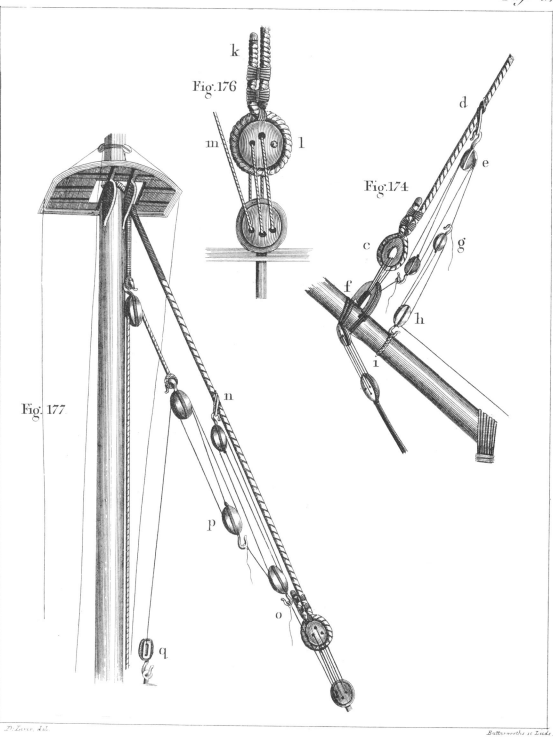

Fig. 176

Fig. 174

Fig. 177

Lower Rigging.

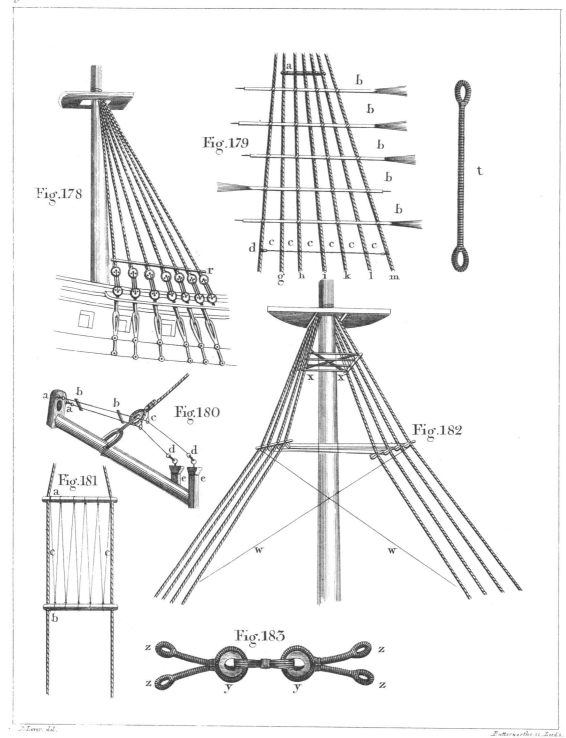

Fig.178

Fig.179

t

Fig.180

Fig.181

Fig.182

Fig.183

LOWER RIGGING.

When the whole are set up, the Shrouds on the larboard side (without board) will appear like Fig. 178. A piece of wood (r), called a *Stretcher*, or squaring Staff, is seized to the Shrouds, just above the Dead Eyes, athwart the whole of them, which keeps them from twisting, and makes the Laniards lie fairly.

The Futtock Staves may be now seized on, and the Shrouds rattled down. For the latter purpose, Fig, 179, Oars (b), or Spars are laid athwart the Shrouds without board, and seized fast at the distance of four or five feet. They are for the men to stand on to fix the RATLINES : These are seized a foot distant from each other, beginning from the Futtock Stave (a).---The Futtock Stave is sometimes made of rope, served ; and sometimes of wood; and is only seized to those Shrouds which are to be catharpined in.

The Ratlines (c) are made fast to the Shrouds in the following manner. An Eye is spliced in one end, which is seized to the foremost Shroud (d) : the remaining part is made fast round the Shrouds (g. h. i. k. l. m.), with Clove-hitches (see page 7) ; and an Eye being spliced in the other end, it is seized as before to the Shroud (m). Whilst this is doing, the Bow-sprit Horses may be fixed, Fig. 180. The end of each Horse is spliced round a Thimble, in an Eye-bolt (a), at the after side of the Bow-sprit Cap. The other ends are reeved through two Stretchers (b) ; then through Thimbles (c), in a Span, made fast above the Heart in the Fore-stay, and having Thimbles spliced in (d), are set up by hand with a Laniard to iron Stantions in the Knight-heads (e).

The Fore-Topmast Stay-sail Netting is made on these Stretchers thus, Fig. 181. A piece of Ratline Stuff is spliced round the outer Stretcher at (a), the other end is taken round the inner one at (b), and seized, the remainder being passed round each, alternately, and seized in the same manner : afterwards, the outside parts (c), are seized at different distances to the Horses, and then to each other, which forms the Netting.

The CATHARPINS are variously formed. Some go thus : They have an Eye spliced in each $*$ end (t), and are either wormed, parcelled and served, or else, wormed and leathered. Previously to these being fixed, a Spar is seized across the Shrouds on each side, Fig. 182 : and Tail-blocks are made fast round the Spar, and each Shroud, that is to be catharpined in. A rope, called a *Swifter* (w), has its ends reeved through the middle Blocks on each side, then through the others, alternately, and the fall leads across the Deck : one end being through the foremost Block on one side, and the other through the aftermost one opposite. The Shrouds are then bowsed in, and the Catharpin legs (x), seized to their respective Shrouds and Futtock Stave. The foremost Shroud formerly, was never catharpined in, on account of its being so much abreast of the Mast, that the leg would chafe it ; but it is now customary in the Merchant Service, to have both the foremost and aftermost Shrouds Cat-harpined. This is done by an additional leg on each side, (as may be seen in the Figure), one Eye seized to the aftermost Shroud on one side, and the other to the foremost one opposite, above the other legs. These are called CROSS CATHARPINS, and are of great use in keeping the lee-rigging well in, when the Ship rolls.

Another method is thus : An Eye is spliced in each end of the Catharpin Leg, as before ; it is then middled, and a small Heart, or large Thimble (y), Fig. 183, is seized in the Bight with a round Seizing (see page 9). Each Eye (z), is then seized to a Shroud, and they are set up by a Laniard, reeved alternately, through each Heart (y), frapping-turns being taken round the parts. These may be taken in at any time.

G   SWAYING

The British spelling of CATHARPINS is changed in Blunt's version to the hyphenated version CAT-HARPINS, a significant aid in pronunciation to one not familiar with the term. (The Oxford English Dictionary calls them "cat-harpings".) Blunt adds the comment, "None of the modern-rigged merchant ships have cat-harpins."

SWAYING UP THE TOPMASTS, &c.

When the Catharpin Legs go in the last-mentioned manner, and the foremost Shroud is to be catharpined in, there is neither Heart nor Thimble seized in the Bight: but a piece of copper (a), Fig. 184, being nailed round the Mast, and the Legs well leathered, the Bight is taken round it, and the ends are seized as before, to the Shrouds and Futtock Staves.

The LOWER CAP, Fig. 185,

Is a thick Block of Elm, with a round hole in the fore part, for the Topmast to enter, and a square one abaft, to fit the lower Mast-head: the round hole is generally leathered within. Underneath this Cap are Eye-bolts (b), on each side, one for the top Block, and the foremost one for the Fore Lift Block to hook to. The use of this Cap is to keep the Topmast steady on the Tressle-trees, and secure it to the lower Mast-head.

Topmasts are squared like the lower Masts above the Hounds (c), Fig. 186: and in Men of War and East Indiamen, Cheek-bolts (b), are bolted on to the square on each side, with two Sheaves, one above the other, for the Jib and Stay-sail Halliards. It is generally eight square from the Heel (d), to where the Cap fits (e). In the Heel a square hole (f), is cut, called the *Fid-hole*, and a Sheave-hole just above this in the eight square (g), leading from the after part on the *larboard* side, to the fore part on the *starboard* side; and from this hole *upwards* to the Head of the eight Square, there is a Groove for the Top-rope to lie in, that it may not be jambed between the Mast and the Tressle-trees. The part below the Heel (h), is called the *Block of the Topmast*. Some Topmasts are rounded all the way from the Hounds to the Heel.

The lower Cap and Top-block are hoisted up into the Top by the Girtlines: and another large single Block for a Hawser to reeve through.

The TOPMAST is then hoisted on board, Fig. 187. The last-mentioned Block (i), is lashed round the Head of the lower Mast, and a Hawser being reeved through it, leads down between the Tressle-trees before the Fore Mast. It is taken through the Fid-hole in the Heel (k), brought up, and hitched round the Head of the Mast, and its standing part (l), and stopped with Spun-yarn in several places (m). The Hawser is then taken through a large snatch Block to the Capstern, (or Windlass) and the Mast is hove on board. When the Head of the Topmast is above the lower Tressle-trees, the end of the Hawser is cast off, (the Mast hanging by the Stops) (m), and made fast round the lower Mast-head with a Timber Hitch (see page 8). The men in the Top then place the Cap, with the round hole over the Topmast-head, and stop it with Spun-yarn. The Hawser is hove upon, until the Cap is high enough, and the square hole is placed over the lower Mast-head: It is then beaten down with a Top-Mall.

The Top-block (n), Fig. 188, is hooked to an iron bolt under the *larboard* side of the Cap: The Top-rope (m), is reeved through it, led down between the Tressle-trees, through the Sheave-hole in the larboard aft-side of the Mast (l), up again between the Tressle-trees, and the end is made fast with two Half-hitches to the Eye-bolt under the *starboard* side of the Cap. An Eye being spliced in the other end of the Top-rope, it is thrust through the strap of the Top-tackle Block (p), and a piece of wood called a *Toggle* (o), put in. The lower Block of the Top-tackle (k), is hooked to an iron Bolt in the Deck, and the Fall (q), being reeved through a leading Block, is taken to the Capstern.

In large Ships there is a Top-block on each side of the Cap (a.b.), Fig. D, and the end of the Top-rope, instead of being hitched to the Eye-bolt on the starboard side of the Cap, reeves through the starboard Top-block (a), and is toggled or bent to another Top-tackle Block (c), which leads similarly to the larboard one.

CROSS

*Blunt defines the cap as a block of oak rather than elm.

Swaying up Topmasts &c.

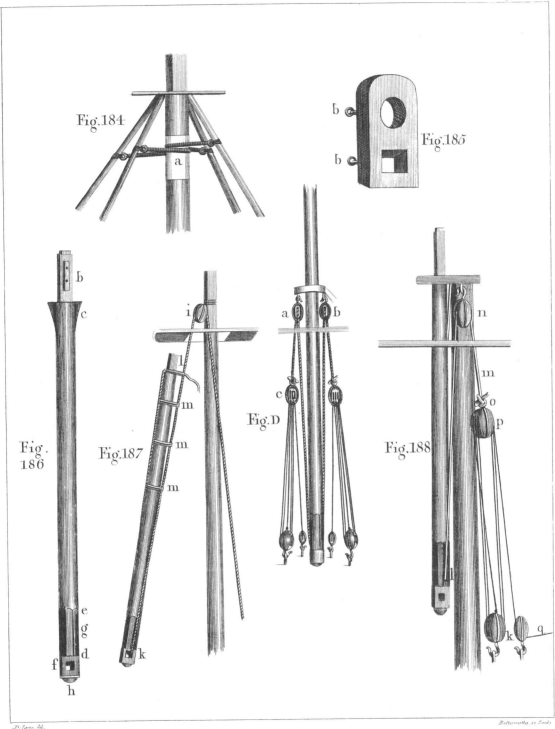

Fig. 184

Fig. 185

Fig. 186

Fig. 187

Fig. D

Fig. 188

Cross Trees_Sister Blocks, &c,

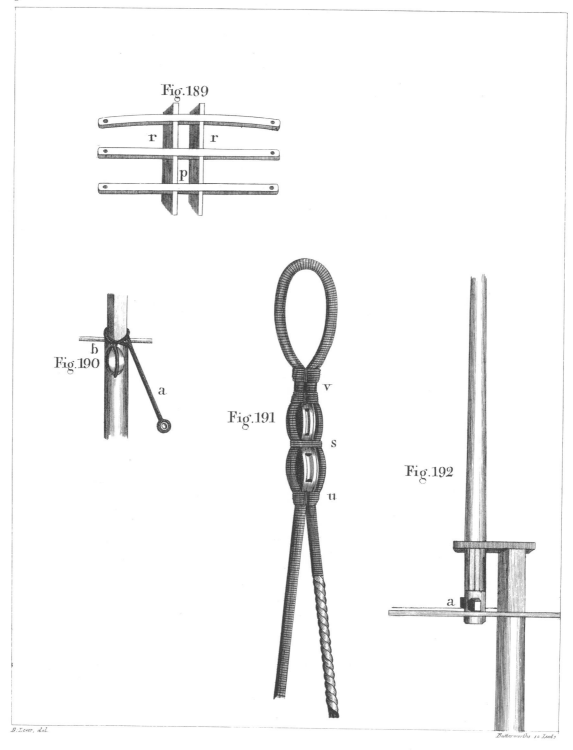

Fig.189

r   r

p

Fig.190

b

a

Fig.191

v

s

u

Fig.192

a

B. Lever, del.

Butterworths sc Leeds

CROSS TREES——SISTER BLOCKS, &c.

The Girtlines are over-hauled for the CROSS-TREES. These are pieces of Timber, Fig. 189, let into two Tressle-trees (r), like the lower ones, and bolted firm to them. At each end of the Cross-Trees, are holes for the Top-Gallant Shrouds to reeve through : and in the Merchant Service the space between the after part of the Tressle-trees is filled up with a chock, having Sheave-holes in.

The Cross-trees are laid with the after Square (p), over the round hole of the lower Cap, and the Top-mast being swayed high enough, enters with its head. The Girtlines are over-hauled down for the Topmast Rigging, which is got over in the same manner as the lower Shrouds were. A Crommet is frequently put over the Mast-head, to answer as a Bolster, to prevent the friction of the rigging against the Tressle-trees ; and sometimes a Bolster, the same as for the lower Masts. The BURTON PENDENTS are first put over, which are fitted with a Cut-splice (see page 5), the same as the Runner Pendents below, having a Thimble spliced in each end, for the purpose of hooking the Burton Tackle to.

If there be no Cheek-blocks at the Mast-head, a Span with a double Block at each end is put over in the same manner, with a Cut-splice, wormed, parcelled, and served over the Collar, which is formed by it, Fig. 190 : (a) the Burton Pendent, (b) the Span-block on the *larboard* side. These double Blocks are for the Jib Halliards, Stay, &c.

The TOPMAST SHROUDS are got over in the same manner as the lower ones, being served round the eyes, and the foremost Shroud all the length, to preserve it from being chafed by the Top-sail Yard, when braced up at different reefs. They are put over alternately, first a pair on the starboard, then a pair on the larboard side, having Dead Eyes turned into them the same as the lower ones (see page 22).

In the foremost pair of Shrouds, on each side, close under the Seizing, is seized a Sister Block, Fig. 191, having two Sheave-holes, one above the other : A Seizing (s), is clapped on between the Sheave-holes, a score being left for that purpose : another at the upper end below the Eye Seizing (v) ; and a third beneath the lower Sheave-hole (u).

The BREAST BACK-STAYS, which are also for the lateral support of the Topmast, are next put over. They are served like the Shrouds over the eye, about two feet below the Cross-trees, and in the wake of the Top-brim and lower Yard. They have either a *single* or a *double* Block turned into their lower ends, and being for temporary use, they are not set up with Dead Eyes. The method of setting them up is mentioned in page 29, with a Figure.

The STANDING BACK-STAYS go next over-head, and have Dead Eyes turned in their lower ends. They hang *abaft* the Mast, whereas the Breast Back-stays hang down the side of it.

The STAY and SPRING-STAY are then put over, (as mentioned in page 23). In large Ships they have a Mouse raised like the lower ones : sometimes instead of a Mouse an over-hand Knot is made, and a Flemish, or a Spindle Eye (see page 4), worked on the end ; but in smaller vessels, the Collar is made by splicing the end into the standing part. They are served round the Collar, and about three feet below the Mouse or Splice.

The Topmast Cap is shaped like the lower one, and placed over the Mast-head by hand ; after which the Topmast is swayed up. When the square hole in the heel is clear above the Tressle-trees, a large piece of iron (a), Fig. 192, is put through it, resting upon them. The Top-rope is then eased off, and the Mast rests upon the Fid.

SETTING

SETTING UP THE TOPMAST RIGGING.

The Futtock Plates are hauled up into the Top, and put through the Mortises in the side of it. In one end of each is a Dead Eye, to connect with those in the lower end of the Topmast Rigging; and in the other, a hole, to admit the hook of a Futtock Shroud, Fig. 193.

The FUTTOCK SHROUDS have strong Hooks and Thimbles spliced into their upper ends, Fig. 194, and Thimbles in the lower extremity: These splices are combed out, marled down, and served over with Spun-yarn. The Shrouds are wormed, and sometimes served. The hook at the upper end goes through the hole in the Futtock Plate, Fig. 195, and a Laniard being spliced in the Thimble at the other end, it is secured by passing it alternately, round the Futtock Stave (a), the lower Shroud (b), and through the Thimble; frapping the end part round the turns. Care should be taken that these Shrouds are not cut too long, to allow for stretching, otherwise the lower Splices must be drawn. They are sometimes not secured by a Laniard; but the end of the Futtock Shroud, Fig. 196, is taken over the Futtock Stave and lower Shroud, and seized down to the latter. This is not so good a method as the former, being a strain upon the Shroud, and apt to chafe it.

The FORE TOPMAST STAY and SPRING STAY, Fig. 197,

Are reeved on each side of the Bowsprit end, through the Block under the Bees. When there are no Bees, a Cheek Block (a), is bolted to that part: and in some Vessels there is a Bolt with a single Block strapped in at the Bowsprit end for that purpose.

When the Stay is reeved, either a Dead Eye, a double, or a long Tackle-block is turned into the end (b): the Fall reeves through this, and through another Dead Eye, or Block, strapped to an Eye-bolt in the Bows. The double Block of a Luff-tackle (c), is hooked to a Cat's-paw, or Black-wall Hitch (see page 8): on this Laniard or Fall, the single one to a Selvagee round a Timber-head on the Fore-castle; and by this purchase, the Mast is stayed forwards. The Laniard is nippered as those for the lower Shrouds were, and the end is taken through the Eye-bolt, over the Block, hitched round the other parts, and the end stopped; if it be long, frapping turns are taken round the other parts, like the Figure under the Bowsprit. The Bee, or Cheek-block for the SPRING STAY, should be well abaft the other, for the Topmast Stay, that the Fore Topmast Stay-sail may not be chafed by it. The Spring Stay is reeved through Hanks, (to which the Fore Topmast Stay-sail is afterwards bent), previously to its being led through the Bee, or Cheek-block.

The TOPMAST SHROUDS, Fig. 198,

Are set up thus: In large Ships, a Runner (d), having an Eye and Thimble spliced in one end, and the other end or tail being plaited or selvageed, is reeved through a single Block (e), strapped with an Eye and Thimble. The tail of the Runner is made fast round the Shroud at (f), with a Midshipman's Hitch (see page 9). The Laniard of the Shroud is Cat's-pawed to the hook, or toggled to the Thimble of the Runner Block (e): the BURTON TACKLE (g), is hooked to the Thimble in the end of the Runner: and this is the purchase by which the Shrouds are set up. In smaller Ships they are set up by the Burton singly, and frequently by a *Spanish Windlass* in the Top, as will be shewn in page 46, for the Top-gallant Shrouds. As the Top will naturally rise a little whilst the Shrouds are setting up, it is beaten down with the Top Mall.

The STANDING BACK-STAYS

Are then set up with Luff upon Luff, as mentioned for the lower Rigging, (but in small Vessels with a single Luff), being connected by their Laniards to a Dead Eye in a stool at the after part of the channel.

BREAST

Blunt adds a note on improved rigging methods for futtock shrouds, as follows. (See Appendix 12 for Blunt's figure 233.)

In the improved method of rigging, the futtock shrouds are of iron, and are hooked into the futtock plates and led down to an iron strap around the mast (a), Fig. 233, to which they are secured by bolts. Few ships have more than three futtock shrouds. (b), Fig. 233.

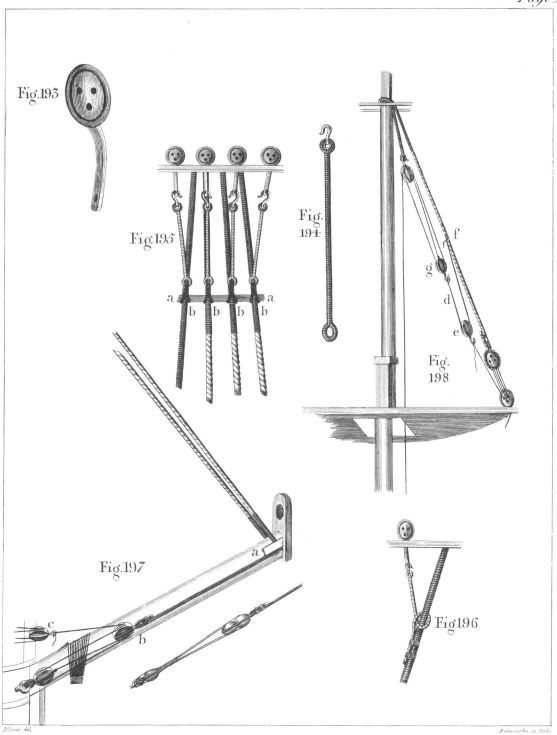

Fig.193

Fig.195

Fig. 194

Fig. 198

Fig.197

Fig 196

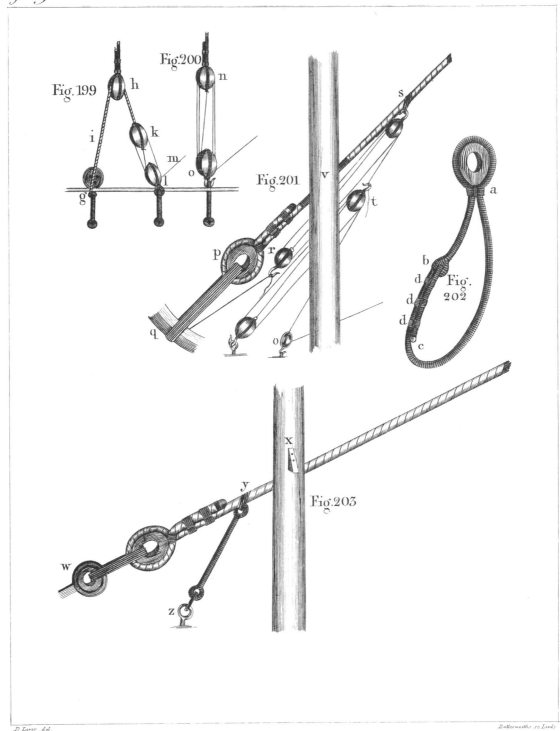

Fig. 199 Fig. 200 Fig. 201 Fig. 202 Fig. 203

D. Lever del.

Butterworth sc. Leeds

Original Erratum: *"Pages 29 and 30---in Figs. 202 and 208, the upper Seizings should be throat ones."*

BREAST BACKSTAYS——MAIN STAY.

The BREAST BACKSTAYS,

Are only set up occasionally. When they go with a Runner, Fig. 199, it leads thus: A single Block (h), is turned into the end of the Back-stay: a Runner (i), is reeved through this, hitched, and seized to one of the Chain Plates (g): and in the end of this Runner is spliced a single Block (k): a double Block (l), strapped with two Legs, having an Eye in each, is seized to the next Chain Plate. The Fall (m), reeves through a Sheave-hole in the double Block (l), then through the single one (k), through the double one again, and the end is either made fast to a Becket spliced round the Runner under the single block, with a Sheet-bend (see page 8), or hitched round the Runner above the Block: the other end of the Fall (m), leads in upon Deck.

Sometimes a *double* Block (n), Fig. 200, is turned into the Backstay, and a *treble* Block (o), strapped with a Hook and Thimble, is hooked to an additional Chain Plate: the Fall is reeved as above, first, through the lower or treble Block (o), then through the double one, alternately, and the end is made fast, as before, to a Becket under the upper, or double Block: the Fall leads in upon Deck.

The Rigging is put over the head of the *Mainmast, Main Topmast, Mizen* and *Mizen Topmast,* in the same manner that it is done forwards.

The MAIN STAY, Fig. 201, *

Is sometimes set up thus: A Heart (p), is turned into the lower end, as mentioned for the Forestay: the end seized back to the standing part, and capped: the Laniard is spliced round the Heart, led over the Breast-hook forwards (q), and through the Heart (p), alternately. The double Block of a Luff Tackle is hooked to a Selvagee on the Stay (s), and the single Block (r), to a Cat's-paw or a Blackwall Hitch (see page 8), on the Laniard. The double Block of another Luff-tackle (t), is hooked in the same manner to the Fall of this, the single Block to an Eye-bolt forwards, and the Fall through a leading Block (o), passing aft. The Laniard being well smeared with Grease, the Stay is set up by this purchase; then nippered, and stopped, like the Forestay Laniard. The Stay is served in the Wake of the Foremast (v), with small plait.

Frequently there is a Collar, Fig. 202, having a Heart seized in at (a), with a round Seizing (see page 9). This Collar is wormed, parcelled, and served: in the end of the short Leg there is an Eye spliced (b), and the long Leg being taken over the Breast-hook, or through a large ring-bolt forwards, its end (c), is reeved through the Eye (b), and seized to the standing part with one Throat, and two, or three round Seizings (d), see page 9.

Sometimes, a Heart is iron-bound, or strapped, to a large bolt (w), in the Bows, Fig. 203, and not unfrequently the Laniard is reeved through a large Ring in this bolt, well rounded with Horse-hide. When the Stay is set up, it is often lashed to the Foremast, a Cleat (x), being nailed on for that purpose: This is to keep it from chafing the Mast, which it would be apt to do by its working; but instead of this Lashing, which is a great strain on the Mast, it is often steadied thus: A Pendent called a JUMPER, has an Eye spliced in one end, and a Thimble in the other: The Eye is seized to the Stay (y), abreast of the Foremast, and the Thimble at the lower end has a Laniard spliced into it, which is reeved alternately through an Eye-bolt in the Deck (z), and the Thimble. This Eye-bolt, which is a little distant from the Mast on the starboard side, guys the Stay off, and keeps it from working too much.

H   STAYS.

---

*Blunt shows in Figures 201 and 203 (see Appendix 7) a changed method of main stay attachment and lashing.

STAYS.

There is often a Cleat A, with a large hole in, nailed to the Foremast on the starboard side: the Main Stay leads through this, which confines it, and keeps it from chafing the Mast.

In some Vessels the Heart of the Main-stay Collar lays abaft the Foremast, Fig. 204, the Collar being made sufficiently long for that purpose, and the Heart (b), is seized in the Bight. The Collar is served and leathered in the wake of the Mast: the ends (c), are spliced or turned round Thimbles in Eye-bolts, one on each side of the Bows.

When the Collar goes abaft the Foremast, it is sometimes of one piece, middled, the Bight (e), Fig. 205, laid over the Bowsprit without board, and each end reeved through holes bored for the purpose in the Knight-heads (d): then spliced, and the Heart (b), seized in as before; the Seizings being snaked in the Grooves of the Heart. This Collar acts as a *preventer Gammoning* to the Bowsprit. Sometimes it is laid over the Bowsprit *within* board, and led through holes in the Breast-Hook.

The Collar for the MAIN SPRING STAY has two Legs, with an Eye in each end. The Heart is seized in the Bight (d), laying abaft the Foremast (e), and a Seizing secures the two Eyes (f), together, *before* the Mast. It is set up with a Laniard to the Heart in the Stay as before, with Luff upon Luff. In small Ships it is often set up as the Mizen Stay in the next Page. But a more snug way for this Stay to be rigged, is to have neither Hearts, nor Collar, thus:

The Stay is first reeved through Hanks, for bending the Sail to, and then an Eye is spliced in the lower end. Fig. 206, taken round the Foremast under a Cleat, and the other end reeved through it, (g). At the upper end of the Stay (i), Fig. 207, there is another Eye; and a Pendent (h), of the same size as the Stay, having an Eye in one end, is spliced into the Stay at (k), where the Mouse would be: these are set up with a Lashing, or Laniard (l), reeving alternately through the Eyes, abaft the Mainmast Head above the Rigging, by a *Spanish Windlass*, (see page 46).

For the MAIN-TOPMAST STAY, a large single Block, Fig. 208, is strapped with a long and short Leg. The long Leg goes round the Foremast Head above the Rigging, reeves through the Eye in the short Leg, and is seized back to the standing part with a Throat and a round Seizing, (see page 9). The MAIN-TOPMAST STAY, Fig. 209, leads through this Block, down between the Tressle-trees, abaft the Foremast, and within the Catharpins. In large Ships a Dead Eye (o), is turned into this end, and the Stay is set up by the Runner Tackle hooked to the Laniard, which is reeved alternately through this, and a Dead Eye strapped, or iron-bound, to an Eye Bolt in the Deck abaft the Foremast Head. In smaller Ships, the Block for the Stay is strapped to an iron Bolt abaft the Foremast Head, and instead of the Dead Eye in the lower End there is a small Heart or large Thimble: and sometimes the Stay has a Thimble turned into the End, and sets up with a Laniard to a Thimble strapped round the Head of the Foremast above the Rigging, by a *Spanish* Windlass, as above mentioned.

The SPRING or STAYSAIL STAY, Fig. 210, being reeved through Hanks as before, leads through a Thimble seized into the Strap with two Legs, and lashed round the Foremast close under the Bibbs (n), the Thimble laying at the after part of the Mast, it sometimes leads *down* abaft the Mast, and sets up like the Topmast Stay; but more frequently it leads *up* through this Thimble, and sets up to another, strapped round the Foremast Head above the Rigging, as in the Figure, by a *Spanish* Windlass, (see page 46).

MIZEN

*Figures 204 and 205 and Blunt's text (see Appendix 8) define a different method of fitting the main top-mast stay. In Blunt's version it does not depend on the foremast.

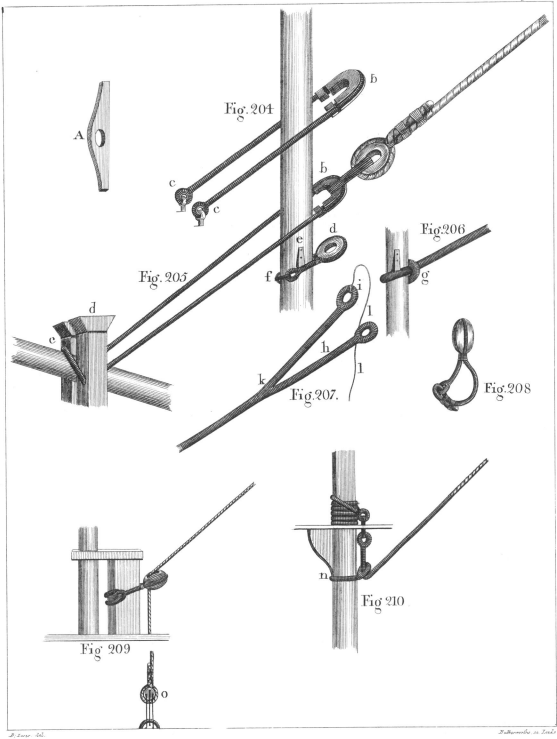

Fig. 204

Fig. 205

Fig. 206

Fig. 207.

Fig. 208

Fig. 209

Fig. 210

Original Erratum: *"Pages 29 and 30---in Figs. 202 and 208, the upper Seizings should be throat ones."*

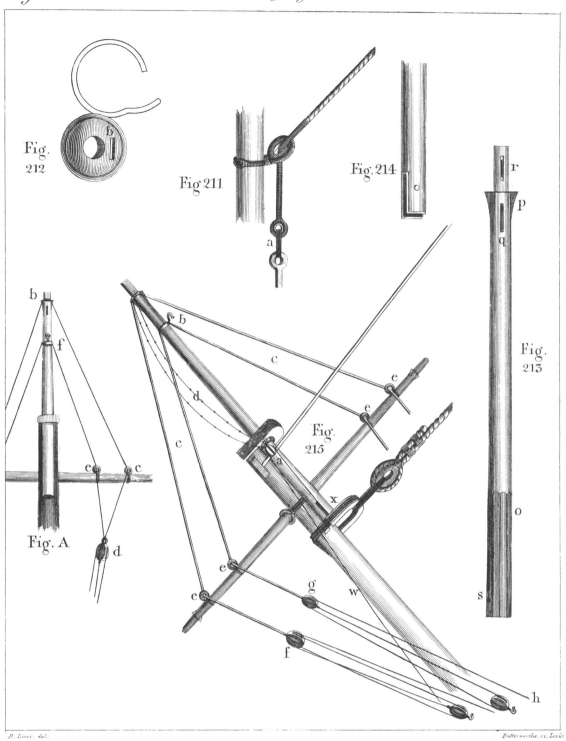

Fig. 212

Fig 211

Fig. 214

Fig. 213

Fig. 215

Fig. A

D. Lever. del.

Butterworths, sc. Leeds

MIZEN STAY——JIB BOOM.

The *MIZEN STAY*, Fig. 211,

Has a Collar with two Legs lashed round the Mainmast, and a large Thimble, or small Heart, seized in the Bight abaft it: the Stay, after the Hanks being put on, leads through this, and having a Thimble or small Heart spliced or turned into the End, a Laniard (a), is passed through this and another in an Eye-bolt on Deck, setting up with the runner Tackle like the Main Topmast Stay. In large Ships there are Dead Eyes, in the Stay and Bolt. But a neater method is to have a Heart iron-bound, and a Clasp round the Mainmast, Fig. 212. On one side of the Hole may be cut a Sheave-hole (b), for the Mizen Stay-sail Down-hauler.

The *JIB BOOM*

Runs out through the Cap of the Bowsprit, as a Topmast does through the lower Cap: it is generally rounded all the way; but in Men of War, it is eight square (o), Fig. 213, from the Heel, to the part which lies in the Bowsprit Cap. At the outer End of the Boom a Shoulder (p), is raised as a Stop to the Rigging: a little within this Shoulder, a Sheave Hole (q), is cut, and sometimes one without at (r). At the inner End in the squared Part, is a Sheave-hole (s), for the Out-hauler or Top-rope, and sometimes a Hole for a Heel-lashing; but there is frequently instead of this Sheave-hole, a *Snatch Sheave* at the Heel, like Fig. 214.

The *OUT-HAULER*, (w), Fig. 215,

Is reeved up through a Block (a), strapped to an Eye Bolt in the Bowsprit Cap, then through the Sheave Hole in the Heel (x), and the End is taken to an Eye-bolt in the other Side of the Cap and hitched; but when the Fore Stay Heart is formed like Fig. 116, (page 14), it is reeved through a Block on the aft side of the Heart, through the snatch Sheave, and the End being passed through a Hole on the other side of the Heart, an Over-hand, or a Wall Knot, (see pages 5 and 7), is cast upon it. The Boom is hauled out a little beyond the Cap, and the Rigging is put on as follows: First an iron Ring called a *Traveller* (b), is put over the Boom End, which will be mentioned particularly in page 60, when shewing the Jib Stay, &c.

The *HORSES*, (d),

For the Men to stand on, go next over with a Cut-splice, (see page 5), or a jambing hitch, and have Over-hand, or Diamond Knots (see page 6), cast on them at different distances. Their Ends are hitched round the Boom, within the Cap, when run out, and stopped with Spun-yarn to the standing Part. The GUY PENDENTS, (c), go next over the Boom End in the same manner: these are for supporting the Boom to Windward. The TRAVELLING GUYS are spliced round Thimbles on the Traveller (b).

On the Spritsail-Yard (the rigging and getting across of which will be mentioned in pages 40 and 41), two Thimbles (e), are seized on each side, through which these Guy Pendents are reeved, and in the End of each Pendent is turned a double, or single Block (f. g.) (according to the size of the Vessel), connected by their Falls with Blocks strapped to Eye-Bolts in the Bows. If a *double* Block be turned in (f), the Purchase is that of a Luff-Tackle; but if a single one (g), it is either a *single Whip*, or a *Gun-tackle Purchase*, as in the Figure, setting up to the single Block (h), in the Bows.

The rest of the Rigging belonging to the Boom will be mentioned when describing the Jib, page 60.

The two Guys are commonly set up with one Purchase, like Fig. A. having one Fall on each Side. The PENDENTS are middled over the Boom End (b), and the Ends on each Side being taken through the outer Thimble (c), on the Sprit-sail Yard, through the Thimble in the Strap of the Block (d), and through the inner Thimble (e), on the Yard, are spliced to the Thimbles on the Traveller (f).

LOWER

Significant differences in securing the mizen stay are shown and described in Blunt's version (see Figure 211 in Appendix 9). Minor differences exist in Figure 215, the Blunt version of which is also shown in Appendix 9. Blunt describes the mizen stay in different terms.
Blunt added an entirely new page after page 31, giving fore-end rigging details. The text and associated figures are shown in Appendix 10.

LOWER YARDS.

THE MAIN AND FORE YARDS,

Are large Poles, and in Men of War are of different Pieces scarfed together; but in smaller Ships they are of one Piece. The Center of the Pole (g), Fig. 216, is called the *Slings of the Yard :* from that to the first quarter on each side (h), it is eight Square, and on these Squares, Battens are frequently nailed.

On each side of the Slings there is a Cleat (i), called a *Sling Cleat :* and within the Yard-arms are two Cleats, called *Stop Cleats* (k), for the Rigging to rest against. These are often raised on the Yard.

The IRONS for the Studding Sail Booms are sometimes nailed and hooped on the Yard-arms, like (l); but in others, they are made to ship and un-ship, like (m) : and are driven on the square of the Yard-arm.

Large Ships have an *inner* Boom Iron, which is fastened round the Yard with an iron Strap (n), and nailed to it : but in smaller Vessels there is a wooden Saddle (o), for the Boom to rest on.

To get this Yard on board for rigging, Fig. 217, a Hawser is reeved through the Top-block (c); it is then bent round the Slings of the Yard with a *Fisherman's Bend* (see page 8), and stopped at different places with Spun-yarn (a). If it be got on board on the *larboard* side, the *starboard* yard-arm is the uppermost, and the Hawser of course stopped to that, as in the Figure.

The Hawser being led through a *snatch* Block (see page 13), upon Deck, it is taken to the Capstern, and the Yard is hove on board : as it rises, the outer Stops (a), are cut; and if it be large. the starboard Runner Tackle may be made fast to the first quarter, to ease it in lowering, when the Stops (a), are cut. When it is lowered, it will lie *athwart* the Fore-castle, and over the Main Stay (c), for rigging. In small Vessels, a Mat is laid over the Stay ; but in large Ships, Fig. F, the Runners (a), are hitched round the first quarter of the Yard on each side, and their lower Tackle-blocks (b), hooked to the Bights : the Yard thus hangs clear of the Main-stay (c), ready for rigging.

RIGGING

Blunt added a comment, "Yards now are fitted, as seen in Fig. 218, before they are taken on deck."

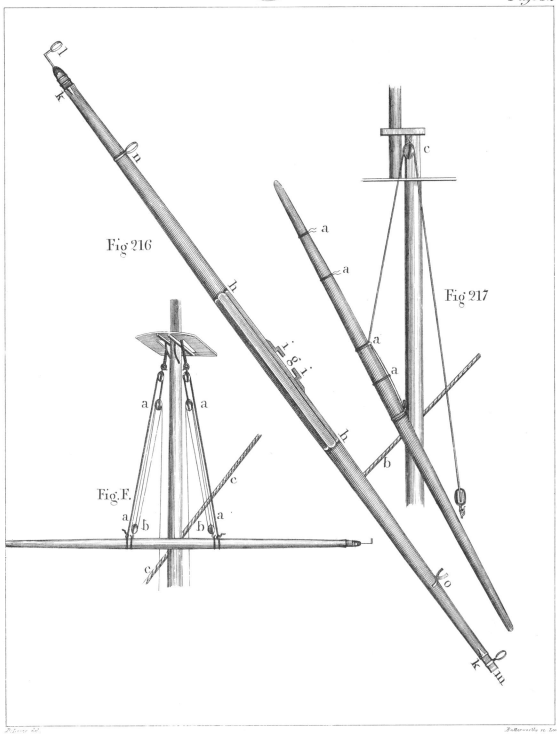

Fig. 216

Fig. 217

Fig. F.

Rigging the lower Yards.

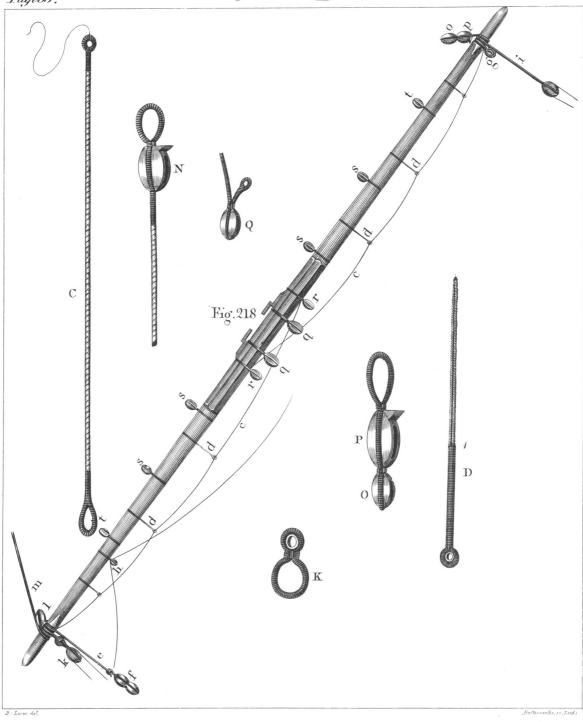

Fig. 218

C

N

Q

P

O

K

D

RIGGING THE LOWER YARDS, Fig. 218.

The HORSES (c), for the men to stand on, are first put on the Yards. They have an Eye spliced in one end, large enough to fit the Yard-arm; the other end is reeved through Thimbles, spliced into the ends of short ropes, called *Stirrups* (d). A Thimble is spliced into the other end of the Horse (c), and it is lashed round the Yard by a Laniard (spliced to the Thimble) on the opposite side of the Slings, without the quarter Block (q). They are sometimes seized to the strap of the quarter Block, and sometimes to a Thimble strapped to the strap of the Clue-Garnet Block (r), on the opposite side.

The STIRRUP, D, has an Eye spliced in one end, it is then stopped with Rope-yarn at (1), unstranded, and plaited to the end: two or three turns are then taken round the Yard (d), to which they are nailed through the plaiting.

The YARD-TACKLE PENDENTS (e), are next put over: They have an Eye spliced in one end, to fit the Yard-arm, as the Horses had; and in the other end a Thimble, to hook the double Block of a Luff, or a Long-tackle to. When these Tackles go without Pendents, a strap with a Thimble in (g), is put over the Yard-arm for the hook of the Tackle. These Tackles are used for hoisting in the boats, provisions, &c. and when not wanted, are triced up to the Yard by a line called a *Tricing Line*. This is reeved through a Block strapped round the Yard, and hanging underneath it at (h), about the distance of the Pendent's length within the Arm Cleats: When a Pendent (e), is used, there are *two* Tricing-lines, and the last-mentioned is called the *outer* one. The *inner* one is reeved through a Block seized to the Futtock Stave, and a Thimble being spliced in the end, the single Block of the Yard-tackle is hooked to it. When no Pendent is used, but merely the Strap (g), there is but one Tricing-line, which generally reeves through an iron staple under the Yard, and through a small Block strapped to the Truss Pendent at the seizing, close to the Yard, belaying to a Cleat on the Mast below.

After these, the BRACE PENDENTS (i), are put over, which are made similar to the last, except that instead of the Thimble, the Brace-block is spliced in the end. All the above-mentioned Rigging is served over the Eye splices. Brace Pendents are now seldom used; but in their stead a stout strap, with a Thimble, is seized in (K): another Thimble is placed round this, and the strap of the Brace-block lies over it, so that it keeps snug to the Yard-arm (k).

The TOPSAIL SHEET BLOCKS,

Are strapped, and placed over the Yard Arms next to the Pendents (l), after which the *Lifts* (m), having an Eye to fit the Yard Arms are placed on.

Sometimes the *Topsail Sheet Block* is spliced into the Lift (N), leaving beneath the Seizing, an Eye for the Yard Arm, which is served over. When the Lifts go *double*, the Lift Block (O), and the Topsail Sheet Block (P), are generally strapped together, the former above the latter (o. p.).

The QUARTER BLOCKS, (Q),

Are strapped with long and short Legs, having an Eye in each. These are large single Blocks hanging below the Yard on each Side the Slings within the Cleats (q), and are for the Topsail Sheets. A Lashing is spliced into one eye of the Strap, and is passed through both Eyes in the form of a Rose Lashing (see page 11).

The CLUE-GARNET BLOCKS, (r),

Strapped in the same manner, hang underneath the Yard just without the Cleats on each Side, lashed as before. There are two *Buntline-Blocks* on each Side (s), placed as in the Figure, these stand on the upper Part of the Yard: The *Leech-Line Blocks* (t), stand also above the Yard. The Lashings or Seizings of these, are passed the same as for the Quarter Blocks, except that the Lashings here are underneath the Yard.

I

LIFTS,

---

*Methods and materials used in rigging the lower yards had changed considerably by 1858. The equivalent page in the Blunt version and the different Figure 218 are shown in Appendix 11.

LIFTS, JEARS, &c.

When the LIFTS go SINGLE, Fig. 219, they reeve through Blocks hooked to Eye-bolts in the fore part of the lower Cap (v), leading down through the square, or *Lubbers* hole, in the top: at the lower end, a single block (t), is turned in; the Fall is made fast to a Becket, with a sheet bend (see page 8), spliced round the strap of another single block, which is hooked to a bolt in the Channel, just within the Foremast Dead Eye ; then reeved through the upper block (t), again through the lower one, and the Fall leads in upon the Fore-castle.   Sometimes a Span goes over the Cap, Fig. 220, having the Lift-blocks spliced in, and the Span lashing passed under the Cap.

Another way for the Lifts when single is, not to have any blocks at the Cap ; but the Lifts to lead over the top of it, like Fig. 221, and down through Lubbers Hole on the opposite side, having a *double* block (s), turned in the lower end, setting up with a Fall to a *single* block in the Channel, which leads through a block strapped to a bolt in the side within board.   This looks snug, and is found in the Merchant Service to answer very well.   The Lift must be leathered in the wake of the Cap.

DOUBLE LIFTS go thus, Fig. 222 : They are reeved up through the block at the fore part of the Cap (v), through the Lift-block (u), strapped to the strap of the Topsail Sheet Block, and the end is made fast to the Eye-bolt in the Cap (v), the lower end has either a single block turned in as before, or it is led through a block in the side.

Straps for the Slings, Fig. 223, are thus made.   A piece of rope of sufficient length is wormed, parcelled, and served, or leathered, and spliced together : a large Thimble or small Heart is seized in with a round Seizing (see page 9), at the Splice (w).   The Strap is laid under the Yard, exactly in the middle, between the Sling Cleats, the Heart or Thimble laying forwards ; the Bight (v), is then brought up *abaft* the Yard, the Thimble *before* it, and reeved through the Bight, pointing upwards.

JEARS in Men of War go thus : A large Cleat (x), is bolted on the square of the lower Mast-head on each side : two large three-fold Blocks are hoisted into the Top by the Burton Tackles.   These blocks are double strapped (see page 15).   Long lashings are spliced to the straps of these blocks. The lashing of the block (y), Fig. 224, on the *larboard* side, goes round the fore part of the Mast-head, over the Cleat on the *starboard* side, round the after part of the Mast, through the strap again, and is continued in the same manner until the whole is expended.   The block on the *starboard* side has its Lashing passed over the Cleat (x), on the *larboard* side, and through its strap in the same manner.

Two double Blocks, Fig. 225, are lashed on the Fore Yard, one on each side of the strap for the Slings, laying upon the Yard.   These are double strapped, and are secured by a Rose Lashing (see page 11), underneath.   The Jear Falls are reeved in the following manner, Fig. 226.   The end is taken up *abaft* , through the outer Sheave-hole of the *treble* or upper Block, then *before* through the outer Sheave-hole of the *double* Block (a), and so on alternately, the end being hitched or spliced to the strap of the block (a).   In small Ships in the Royal Navy, and East Indiamen, the Jears commonly go with Tyes and Falls, as in the next page.

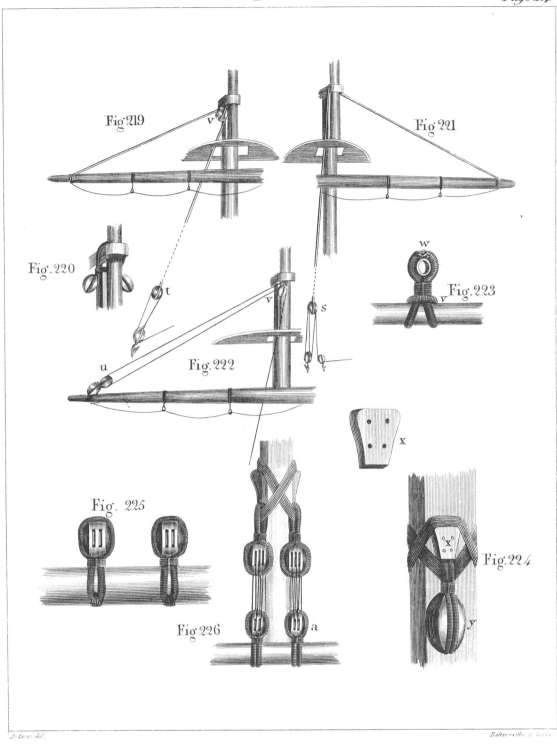

Original Erratum: *"Fig. 222, the Block of the lower Lift is hooked to the fore End of the Cap, instead of the fore Part of the Side of it."*

Jears & Slings.

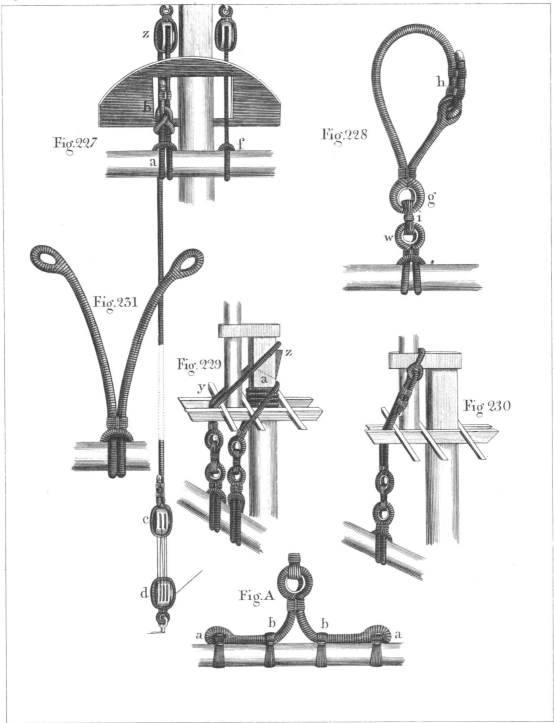

Fig.227

Fig.228

Fig.231

Fig.229

Fig.230

Fig.A

D. Lever del.

Butterworths, sc Leeds.

JEARS AND SLINGS.

For the JEAR TYES, Fig. 227, two Straps similar to the Sling Strap are sometimes put over the Yard, one on each side, within the Cleats, like (a). The Tyes are then led through the single Blocks (z), at the Mast Head, (lashed in the same manner over the Cleats that the treble Blocks were): the Ends are bent to the Straps with a Sheet Bend, and seized to the standing Part (b), with a *round* Seizing (see page 9). In the other End treble or double Blocks (c), are turned with a *Throat*, and *round* Seizings; and *treble* or *four-fold* ones (d), being strapped to Eye-bolts in the Deck, they are connected together by the Jear Falls as before; the Ends of the Falls being in this case made fast to the *upper* Blocks. The Jear Tyes sometimes go round the Yards without Straps. In this case they have Eyes spliced in their Ends, which being brought up on the after Side of the Yard, and the other Ends before it, the latter is reeved through the former (f).

When Jears are carried, their Falls are stretched aft, and the Yard is swayed up by them; but if there be no Jears, it is got up either by the Hawser which hove it on board taken to the Capstern, or otherwise by Tackles; their double Blocks being hooked one on each Side, to an Eye-bolt in the Cap, and the single Blocks to Selvagees on each Side the Slings of the Yard. The *Slings* of the Yard, and the *Trusses* which go variously, as in the next page, are then fitted on.

SLINGS

Are sometimes made thus: Fig. 228. An Eye is spliced in one End, they are then wormed, parcelled. and served, the whole Length: a large Thimble (g), is seized in with a round Seizing, so as to make a long and short Leg, the Thimble hangs before the Mast: the long Leg goes round the Mast above the Rigging, and the End is reeved through the short one: it is then seized back to the standing Part (h): when the Slings go in this manner, either the Seizing at the Thimbles (g), or the Seizing (h), should be a Throat one, (see page 9). A Laniard (i), is then spliced into the Thimble (g), which is reeved alternately through it, and the Thimble (w), in the Strap on the Yard. When sufficient Turns are taken, the End-part is frapped round the whole and stopped. The Jears or Tackles, are then eased off, and the Yard hangs by the Slings. It is kept in a horizontal Direction by the Lifts, which are hauled taught, and squared by the Braces, which will be mentioned as to their leading in page 48.

Ships which carry no Jears, have frequently two Pair of Slings, one of which is called the *preventer* Slings. In this case, the inner ones sometimes go with a long and short Leg above the Rigging, Fig 229, one Leg leading on each Side of the Tressle-trees, and before the Cross-tree close to the Fore-mast; the outer Pair (the Ship having a Grating Top) lead up between the Tressle-trees and before the foremost Cross-tree (y): the two Legs being lashed together above the Cleat (z), at the after part of the Mast. Some Ships have the Slings taken over the lower Cap, Fig. 230, with a long and short Leg. These Slings are often lashed down to the after part of the Mast, the Lashing leading in the direction of the dotted Line (a), Fig. 229. N. B. The first Seizings on the long Legs of these Slings (Figs. 228 and 230), have been drawn inadvertently with *round* Seizings instead of *Throat* ones.

In some Ships there are no Straps on the Yard for the Slings, but they being made sufficiently long, Fig. 231, the Legs are taken over the Yard and through the Bight abaft the Yard: and the two Eyes are lashed together abaft the Mast.

Sometimes the Straps for the Slings are made like Fig. A---an Eye (a), being spliced in each end, is seized to the Yard; two other Seizings are also clapped on the Bight, at (b). These give the Yards play for bracing up.

*

TRUSSES

*Blunt adds the following note: "N. B. The thimble in Fig. A, should be close to the yard. One end (a) might be first seized down: the eye in the other should be hooked to a luff-tackle, and hove well taught: then, the other seizings may be clapped on."

TRUSSES.

Sometimes in small Vessels a Strap with an Eye and Thimble (a), Fig. 232, goes round the Yard, the Slings reeve through the Eye, have a round Seizing, (see page 9), just above the Yard, and another above the foremost Cross Tree; they are set up with a Lashing through the two Eyes abaft the Mast, or with a long, and short Leg over the Cap, as in the last page.

Sometimes the lower Yards are slung with Chains like Fig. 233, for which purpose a Bolt (b), is driven into the lower Mast between the Bibbs, or hooped to it; a Link of the Chain (a), is fastened to the Bolt, reeved through an iron Strap on the Yard, and the other End is hooked to the Bolt.

In order to keep the Yard close to the Mast (when it lies square), a Rope called a *Truss* is used, the Pendents of which are made in this form: Fig. 234. An Eye and Thimble is spliced into the End of each Pendent; that on the starboard Side is put over the Yard, the End with the Eye in being uppermost (b), and seized with a throat Seizing, (see page 9), to the standing part abaft the Yard: the End of the *larboard* Pendent (d), being *uppermost*, is reeved through the Eye of the starboard one (b), and the End of the *starboard* Pendent which is *underneath*, through the Eye in the larboard one (c), which is below also; a double Block is turned, or spliced into the End of each Pendent (e), and is joined by a Fall to a single one hooked, or strapped to an Eye-bolt in the Deck close to the Mast. These Pendents are placed over the Yard within the sling Cleats, they are wormed and served, and all the Parts which lie abaft the Mast (for a sufficient Length to ease off) and round the Yard, are leathered, and well greased, that they may traverse smoothly through the Thimbles, when they are hauled upon, or let go. If only one of these Trusses be used, Fig. 235, the End goes abaft the Mast, round the Yard, abaft the Mast again, and through the Thimble (b), leading down as before. But this Method of the Truss Tackles leading below, is now generally exploded, and they lead up to the lower Tressle-trees or Topmast-Cap.

To reeve a DOUBLE TRUSS upon the BIGHT, Fig. 236,

Which shews the after Side of the lower Mast, a Thimble (a), is spliced into one End of the Truss Pendent, which is taken round the Yard, and seized to the standing Part as before, (the Eye being uppermost) with a Throat-seizing (see page 9); a Cleat with two Holes is nailed on the Mast (b). The End of the Truss Pendent is taken through the *lower* Hole in the Cleat (a), and reeved through two Thimbles (c and d): the End is next taken *round* before the Mast, reeved through the Thimble (a), led through the *upper* Hole in the Cleat (b), over and under the Yard at the dotted Line, and the End is spliced round the Thimble (c). The End (c), and the standing Part are then seized together at the dotted Line as before. A *single* Block of a Truss Tackle is strapped round the Thimble (d), and the double Block may be hooked to a Bolt in the Cap, Fig. 237, (which shews the fore Side of the Mast), when the Truss Pendent will lead as represented by the dotted Line; or the double Block of the Truss Tackle may be strapped to the Bight (d), and the single one to a Strap (e), round the Mast, laying before it; but it is always better to have the Tackle up aloft, for the reason given below. Thus there is double Truss and only a single Fall leading down on Deck, and the Pendents are easily over-hauled.

A THIRD WAY, Fig. 238.

The Pendents are made much shorter than common, having only sufficient Length to over-haul, in order to give the Yard play. A single Block being spliced or turned into the End of each Pendent (i), sets up with a Fall to a double Block (k), lashed to the Tressle-trees, or aftermost Cross-tree on each Side. Should the Slings of the Yard give way, these will act as preventer Slings, and hang the Yard until sufficiently secured.

TRUSSES

Blunt's Figure 233 (see Appendix 12) shows rigging differences. In the discussion of Trusses, Blunt replaces the second paragraph with the text in the appendix.

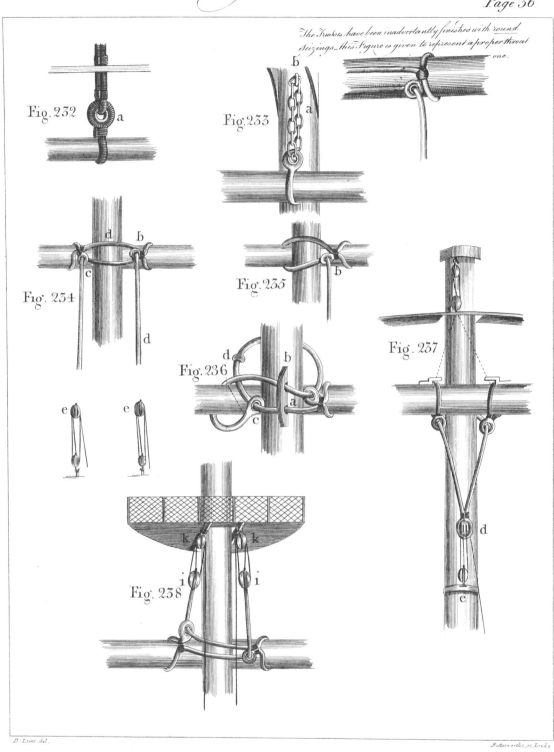

The Trusses have been inadvertantly finished with round seizings—this Figure is given to represent a proper throat one.

Fig. 232   a

Fig. 233   b   a

Fig. 234   d   b   c   d

Fig. 235   b

Fig. 236   d   b   a   c

Fig. 237   d   e

e   e

Fig. 238   k   k   i   i

D.Lever del.   Butterworth, sc. Leeds

Trusses—Cross-Jack Yard &c.

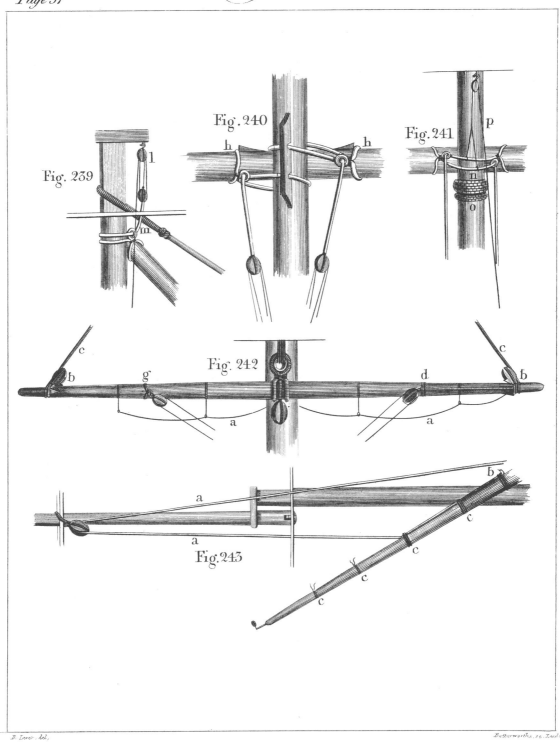

Fig. 239

Fig. 240

Fig. 241

Fig. 242

Fig. 243

D. Lever. del.

Butterworths. sc. Leeds.

TRUSSES—CROSS-JACK YARD, &c.

A FOURTH WAY, Fig. 239.

This is to answer the last-mentioned purpose. The Pendents are short, as before : a single Block is turned or spliced into the end of each, setting up by a Fall to a double one (l), hooked to an Eye-bolt in the Topmast Cap, leading down through Lubbers-hole. This leads very fair ; but the Collar of the Main-stay (m), and the Truss-pendent, must be well leathered.

A FIFTH WAY, Fig. 240.

The Pendents are reeved through the Cleat abaft the Mast, and led down below, as before ; but instead of laying round the Yard *within* the Sling-cleats, an additional Cleat (h), is nailed on the Yard farther out, on each side, to stop them from coming in. The end of each Pendent is taken round the Mast, and reeved through its own Thimble. The Fall, by these means, laying close into the Mast, each Truss acts as a *rolling Tackle*, by bowsing the Yard in.

When the Trusses lead down on Deck, and there is no Cleat to keep the Bights of the Pendents from slipping down, and to hang the Yard by, should the Slings give way, a Pudding (n), is placed round the Mast, and the ends are seized together before it, with a *Rose* Lashing, as mentioned in page 11. Under this, as a support, is placed a Dolphin (o), lashed in the same manner. To make these (see pages 10 and 11). In order to over-haul these Truss-pendents, a rope called a *Nave Line* (p), with a Span, is reeved through a Block under the after part of the Top, and the ends are spliced to Thimbles on the Pendent.

The MAIN YARD

Is rigged in the same manner as the Fore Yard.

The CROSS JACK YARD

Is slung to the Mizen Mast like the other Yards to their respective Masts. The Horses (a), Fig. 242. Topsail Sheet Blocks (b), and Lifts (c), are placed over the Yards Arms; but the Brace Pendents go on with the Blocks hanging before. As the Braces lead across (see page 49), the Bight of the Pendent close to the Block, is seized down to the Yard at (d), by which means they lead much clearer. Instead of the Pendent, some have an iron Strap round the Yard with a Block at (g). There are frequently Sheave Holes in the Yard for the Topsail Sheets.

The TOPSAIL YARDS

Are made similar to the lower ones : eight square from the Slings to the first Quarter on each side, and rounded from thence to the Yard Arms.

In some Ships there are two Sheave-holes; one within the Arm Cleats for the Top-Gallant Sheets, and another without them for the Reef Tackle Pendent; but as they are thought to weaken the Yard, the former are avoided.

In order to get this Yard on board for Rigging, a Block is taken up to the Topmast-Head, Fig. 243, and lashed there ; a Hawser (a), being reeved through it, is made fast to the Slings of the Yard (b), and stopped along the starboard Yard-arm (c), (if it be got up on the *larboard* side) with Spun-yarn. As it is hove on board the Stops are cut, and it lies athwart the Fore-castle over the Main-stay (which has a Mat placed on it to keep it from chafing) ready for Rigging. This Yard is rigged below; but I shall describe it as if it were aloft, and shew how to get it across in page 40.

K   TOPSAIL

*The newer use of chain and iron strapping is shown in Figure 242 (see Appendix 13) and in Blunt's description of the (Lower) Cross Jack Yard.

TOPSAIL YARD RIGGED—TYES.

The HORSES (a) Fig. 244.

Are reeved through the Stirrups which are previously nailed on. (To make this Rigging see that for a lower Yard, page 33). An Eye is spliced in the inner End, and they are seized either to the Yard without the Cleats on the opposite Side, or to the Straps of the quarter Blocks; when to the latter, a Span is spliced round the Strap of each Block to keep them from flying outwards, when the Top-Gallant Sheets are not hauled home. Sometimes they are seized to the Strap of the Tye Block (k).

There is an additional Horse on the Topsail Yard called a *FLEMISH HORSE* (b), having an Eye spliced in each End, one of which goes over the Bolt in the Yard Arm, and the other is seized to the Yard within the Arm Cleats (c); but frequently this Eye in the *inner* End is spliced round a Thimble in the other Horse, like (d). To the Bolt or Boom Iron in each Yard Arm, is strapped a Block (e), called a *Jewel Block*, for the Topmast Studding Sail Halliards; but sometimes this Block is seized into the Eye of the Flemish Horse like (d).

The BRACE PENDENTS (f),

Go next over the Yard Arms; but if there be no Pendents, a Block strapped like that mentioned in page 33, for the lower Yard, is attached to a Strap and Thimble which goes over the Yard Arm.

The Lifts (g), when there are Sheave-holes in the Yard for the Top-Gallant Sheets, go over with Eyes like the single lower Lifts, but when there are no Sheave-holes, then the Top-gallant Sheet Block (h), is strapped into the Lift. The Lift is reeved through the *lower* Sheave-hole of the *Sister* Block which is seized in between the two foremost Topmast Shrouds (as shewn in page 27), and sometimes large Ships have a Block turned into the lower End, setting up with a single Whip, one End of the Fall being hitched or clinched to a Chain Plate, or to one of the lower Shrouds; but more commonly they have no Block turned in, and the End of the Lift is made fast, with a Midshipman's Hitch (see page 9), round one of the lower Shrouds.

When the *TOPSAIL LIFTS* go double, Fig. 245, the Lift Block (a), is strapped with an Eye to fit the Yard Arm, the standing Part of the Lift has a Hook spliced in the End (b), which is hooked either to a Span or an Eye Bolt in the Topmast Cap, the other End leads through the Block (a), and through the *lower* Sheave-hole in the Sister Block, as before, being hitched round one of the lower Shrouds above the Dead Eye. The Top-Gallant Sheet Block is strapped in below the Lift Block, like the Topsail Sheet Block on the lower Yard, (page 33 P. O.)

The REEF TACKLE PENDENTS, (i), Fig. 244,

Are reeved through the *upper* Sheave-holes in the Sister Blocks, and through the Sheave-holes in the Yard Arms without the Stop Cleats: an overhand Knot is cast on the ends, till wanted, to prevent their unreeving: In the other End a double Block is turned, and a single one being strapped, or lashed to the lower Tressle-tree, it is hauled out when used, with a Luff Tackle purchase (n), the Fall leading down upon Deck, through a leading Block. (For the different Methods of leading REEF TACKLES in the Merchant Service, see page 55).

The TYE BLOCK (k),

Having two Buntline Blocks strapped to it, (or in small Ships in the Merchant Service two Thimbles) is double strapped like the Jear Blocks on the lower Yard, (see page 33), and is secured with Rose Lashings underneath. The Strap if single is sometimes spliced round the Yard, and the Block seized in.

When the *Tyes* go double, the Block on the Yard is a double one, and they lead thus: A large single Block (a), Fig. 246, is lashed on each side of the Topmast Head, hanging close under the Stay Collar. The ends of the Tyes (b), are reeved through them, then through the double Block on the Yard (c), and clinched or hitched round the Topmast Head, above the Rigging. The Fly-block of the Topsail Halliards (d), (being double) is turned into the end of each Tye, and they reeve through it, and a single Block in the Channel, the end of the Halliards being made fast to a Becket in the Strap of the single Block (like a Luff Tackle). For the single Block, see the next page.

TYES

Topsail Yard rigged — Tyes.

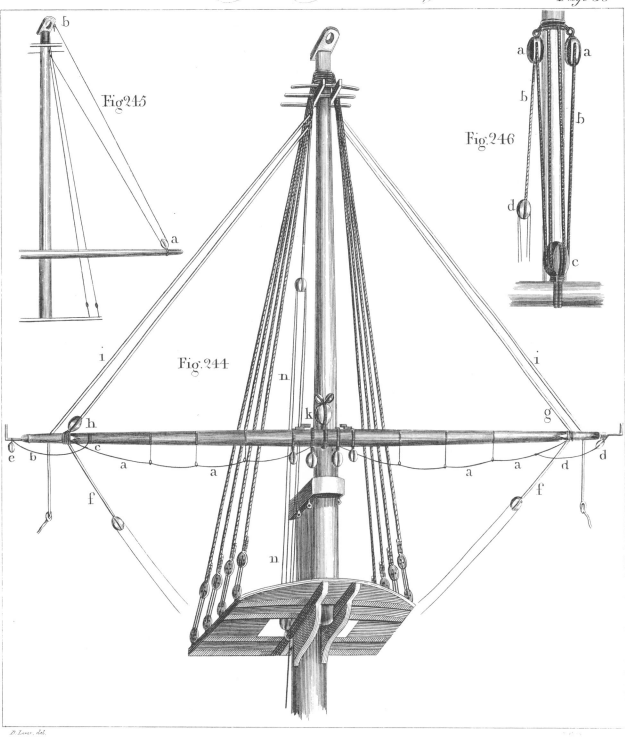

Fig.245

Fig.246

Fig.244

Tyes_Parral, &c.

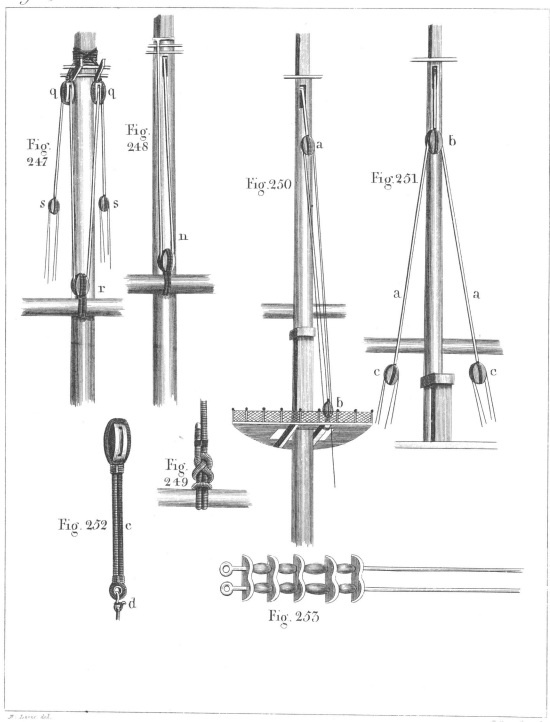

Fig. 247

Fig. 248

Fig. 250

Fig. 251

Fig. 249

Fig. 252

Fig. 253

TYES——PARRAL, &c.

When the *single* Block is used on the Yard, and two Blocks at the Mast Head, having two pair of Halliards, the TYE leads thus, Fig. 247 : The End of the Tye is reeved through one of the Blocks at the Mast Head (q), as before ; through the single Block on the Yard (r), and through the other Block (q), at the Head of the Mast. In each End is turned a Fly Block (s), the Halliards leading as before to a single Block in the Channel. This is an excellent method for a single Tye; because if the Yard remain at the Mast Head for a considerable time, (which is often the case), the Tye is liable to be chafed by continual Friction in the Blocks ; but the Service may be freshened by easing off one Pair of Halliards and hoisting on the other. The Tye is wormed, parcelled, and served about three-fourths of its Length.

The Tyes in smaller Vessels sometimes go thus, Fig. 248. The Tye (n), is reeved through the Sheave-hole in the Topmast-Head, then through the Block on the Yard, and the End is taken up and clinched round the Mast-Head. There are only one Pair of Halliards which reeve as before. If there be no Block on the Yard, a Strap, similar to the Sling Strap on the Lower Yard is put on, Fig. 249, and the Tye after reeving through the Sheave-hole at the Mast-Head, is bent to this with a Sheet-bend, and the End seized to the standing Part as in the Figure. Selvagee Straps are reckoned very snug and pliant for this purpose.

In order to avoid the Necessity of shifting the Topsail Halliards over to Windward, when there is but one Pair, they lead thus : the Fly Block (a), Fig. 250, is spliced into the End of the Tye a little below the Topmast Catharpins ; the single Block (b), instead of leading to the Channel, is hooked to a Strap round the aftermost Part of the Tressle-trees, * . This Tye, which is short, is served the whole Length, and the Fall of the Halliards leads down abaft the Mast and through a leading Block below.

An excellent Method for Tyes when there are but few Hands, is to have a short Tye, a Runner, and two Pair of Topsail Halliards like Fig. 251. The Runner (a), is reeved through a *single* Block (b), spliced or turned into the End of the short Tye, and a Fly Block (c), is turned into each End, the Falls leading as usual to a single Block in the Channel on each Side. Some Ships have only one Pair of Halliards with the Runner, in which case, one End of the Runner is hitched round the Tressle-tree on one Side, and the single Block of the Halliards lashed to the other. When the Yard is down, the Fly Block will be chock up to the Block in the Tye.

The single Block of the Topsail Halliards, Fig. 252, when hooked to the Channel, has a long Strap with two Seizings (c), to clear the Gunnel, and the Eye-bolt to which it is hooked has a Swivel ; so that if the Halliards be twisted, the Turns are easily taken out, by slueing the Block round. The Hook (d), is moused with Spunyarn, and the Strap of this Block is generally pointed over.

The TOPSAIL YARDS are retained to the Masts by PARRALS, which answer the same Purpose   **
that the Trusses do to the lower Yards. The Parral ropes have an Eye spliced in one End, and are reeved through a Set of Ribs and Trucks, Fig. 253. The Ribs are flat Pieces of Wood, with Holes in each End for the Ropes to reeve through : the Trucks which lie between them, are round, and have Holes for the same Purpose.

One Eye of the Parral Rope goes over the Yard, and the other under ; they are then seized together : the other Ends are taken over and under the Yard alternately, passing round the Back of the Ribs and Trucks till the whole is expended ; the Parts are then all marled together. Sufficient play, must be left for the Yards to brace sharp up when occasion requires it. These Ribs and Trucks are seldom used in the Merchant Service, except in the largest Ships. In smaller Ships they are fitted as follows :

Getting

* *The Topmast Catharpins lead across, and if the two foremost Shrouds be abreast of the Mast, they may be catharpin'd round it, as mentioned for the lower Catharpins (see page 26) : by these Means the Tye will be in no danger of chafing against them.*

Ed. Notes:
**Blunt's description of parrals differs and relates to the changed Figure 253 and added Figure 253a, shown in Appendix 14.*

Getting the TOPSAIL YARDS ACROSS—SPRITSAIL YARD.

The **Parral Rope** is put on the Stretch, wormed, parcelled, and served, or leathered, Fig. 254. An Eye (f), is spliced in each end; then a round Seizing (g), forming the Bight which goes over the Yard on one side is clapped on, and the Bight (h), put over the Yard-arm, and driven taught on to the Slings of the Yard, previously to its being rigged, and the Sling Cleats nailed on. The quarter Seizing is clapped on close to the upper Eye (i): the Eye at the lower end is taken *under* and *over* the Yard, a Seizing clapped on close to the Yard, and the two Eyes seized together. N.B. The quarter Seizing (i), must be clapped on first, or it could not be crossed. In smaller Vessels the Parrals are made like those for the Top Gallant Yards.

If the TOPSAIL YARD be got across before the lower Yard, it may be done with the Lifts and Braces reeved, ropes being bent to the ends of the Lifts, to lengthen them for overhauling; but if not, the Braces, &c. are coiled on the Bunt of the Yard. The Hawser (a), Fig. 256, being bent to the Slings of the Yard, it is stopped to the starboard Yard-arm (b), in different places. The Hawser is then hove upon, and as the Yard rises, the Stops are cut: when high enough above the lower Cap, the last Stop is cut, which crosses it. The Braces are thrown down, taken up, and reeved through their proper Blocks at the Stays or Mast Heads (for which see pages 48 and 49). In small Merchant Men, the Topsail Yards may be got across like the Top Gallant Yards, the upper Yard-arms being rigged up aloft.

The SPRITSAIL YARD, which is rounded all the way, is laid *fore* and *aft* on the Fore-castle for rigging, the *starboard* Yard-arm laying forwards, if it be on the *larboard* side. It is described here as rigged across (to get it across, see the next page). The Horses (a), Fig. 255, are first put over the Yard-arms, reeving through the Stirrups, and seized as before: the Brace Pendents or Straps (c), are next put over. The Lifts (f), if single, go over the Yard-arms, with Eyes, and are either hitched to the Eye-bolts in the Bowsprit Cap, or led through Blocks seized to the Bolts, and belay to a Timber-head on the Fore-castle. If double, a Block (e), is strapped to fit the Yard-arm, and put over after the Brace-block or Pendent on each side. The Lift is reeved through the Block at the Cap (d), then through the Block at the Yard-arm (e), and the end is hitched to an Eye-bolt in the Cap. Sometimes there is a Hook and Thimble spliced in the end of the Lift, and this is hooked to the Eye-bolt in the Cap. This occasionally serves as a Spritsail Topsail Sheet, by being hooked to a Thimble in the Clue of that Sail.

*   The PARRAL, which goes over the Saddle on the Bowsprit, is sometimes made like the Parral for the Topsail Yard, Fig, 254; but more commonly thus: Fig 257, an Eye and Thimble is spliced in one end (g); this Eye is passed underneath the Yard, taken up again, and the two parts are seized together with a round Seizing, a little below it at (h). The other end is then taken *over* the Saddle, under the Spritsail Yard, *over* the Saddle again, reeved through the Thimble which is spliced in the end (g), and seized back to the standing part with a *Throat* and round Seizing (see page 9): a round Seizing (k), is clapped on the two parts on the opposite side, *above* the Yard. This Parral is frequently leathered.

The BRACES, Figure 255,

Are led up through one of the Sheaves of a double Block (m), under the *after* part of the Fore-Top, and through another under the *fore* part; next through the Block in the Brace-Pendent, or Strap (c), and the ends are made fast round the Collar of the Fore-stay (o): the leading part (p), is belayed to a Pin or Cleat on the Fore-castle. When the Braces go single, as in small Ships, they have an Eye to fit the Yard-arm, and are led through Blocks under the Top, as before.

Getting

*Blunt omits this paragraph.

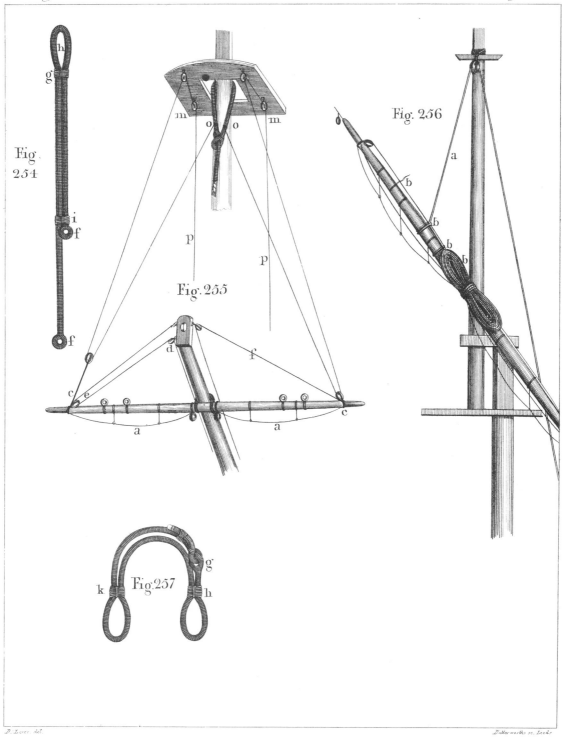

Fig. 254

Fig. 255

Fig. 256

Fig. 257

Getting across the Spritsail Yard &c.

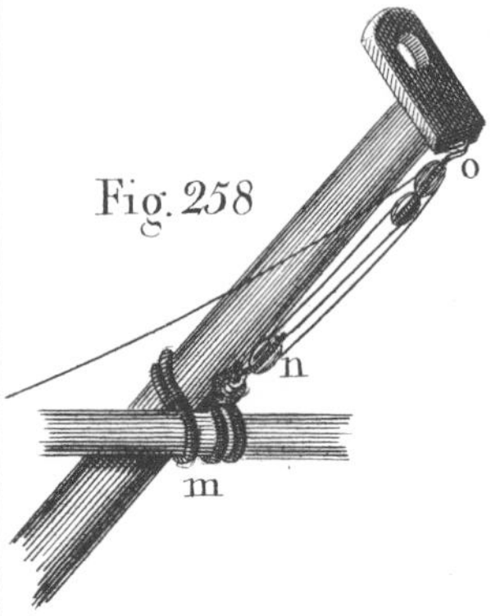

Fig. 258

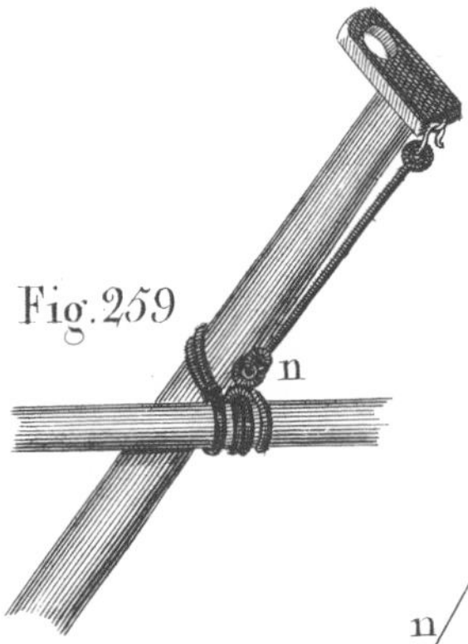

o

n

m

Fig. 259

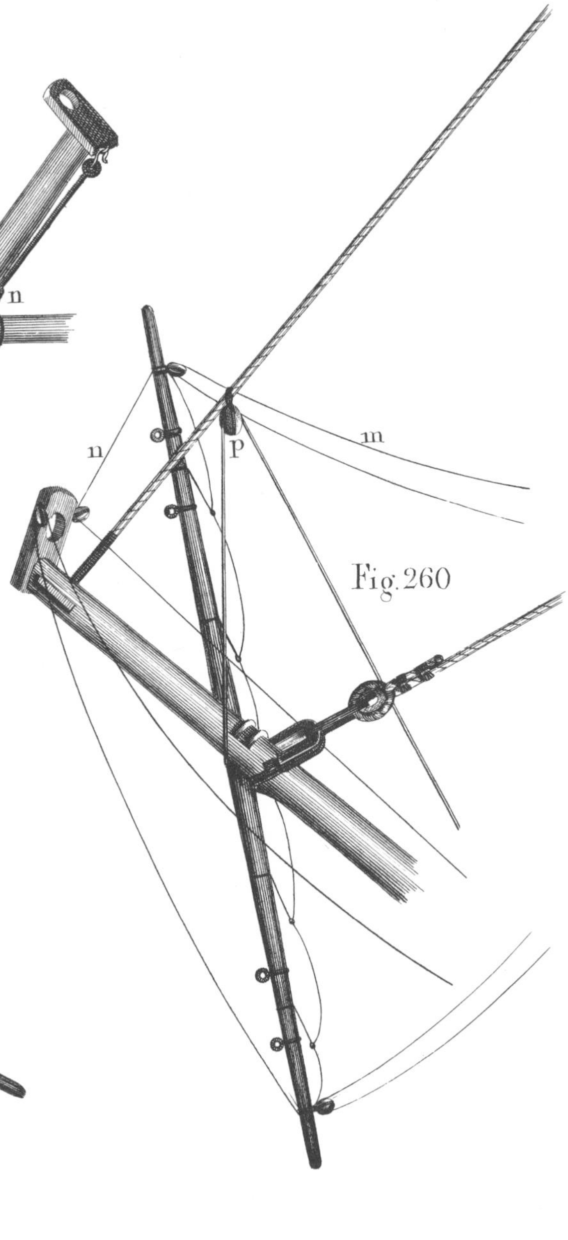

n

Fig. 260

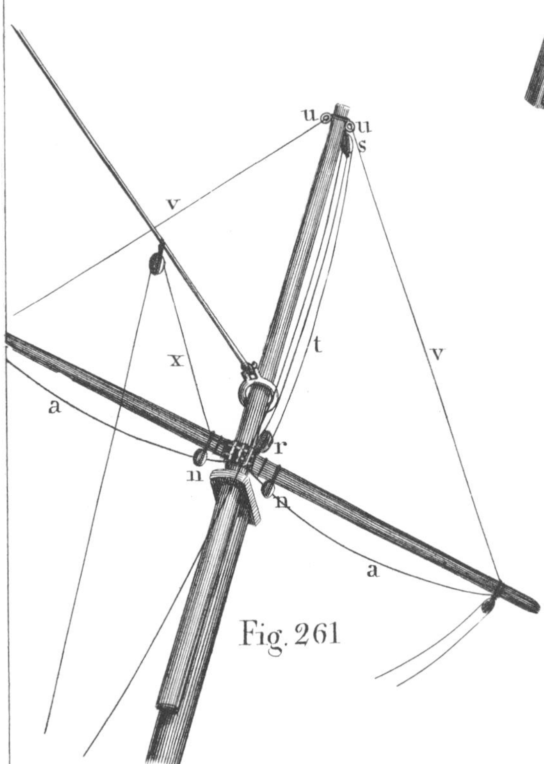

n

p

m

u   u
      s

v

v

t

x

a

r

n

n

a

Fig. 261

D. Lever, del.

Battersworth sc. Leeds

GETTING ACROSS THE SPRITSAIL YARD, &c.

Some Ships have Halliards to the Spritsail Yard, Fig. 258. A Strap (m), is spliced round the Slings of the Yard, having a Thimble seized in, and the Splice laying on the Thimble. The single Block of the Halliards (n), is hooked to this, and moused with Spun-yarn: the double Block (which is long Tackle Fashion) is hooked to an Eye Bolt (o), in the under part of the Bowsprit Cap. These Halliards are now generally left off, and in the Merchant Service are never used: when this is the case the Yard is slung like Fig. 259. The lower End of the Sling is spliced through the Eye of the Strap on the Yard (n), over a second Thimble. In the upper End is spliced a Hook and Thimble, and it is hooked to the Bolt in the Bowsprit Cap.

When the Yard is rigged, the *starboard* Brace (m), and Lift (n), Fig. 260, are taken underneath the Bowsprit, as it lies on the *larboard* Side of the Forecastle, and it is got across by a Yard Rope (or Top Rope) reeved through a Tail Block (p), lashed on the Fore Topmast Stay, and is squared by the Lifts and Braces. When the Sling is hooked, and the Parral passed over the Saddle, the Top Rope is taken off.

In small Ships in the Merchant Service, it is got across by the Lifts and Braces, without the Top Rope. When these Vessels carry no Spritsail Yard, the Jib-Boom is made proportionally strong, having no Support from Guys; but a Guy might be led from the Boom End to the Cat-Head on each Side.

The SPRITSAIL TOPSAIL YARD, Fig. 261,

Is rigged as follows: The Horses (a), are put over the Yard Arms like the others, and seized to the Yard on the opposite Sides of the Slings. The Clue-line Blocks (n), are seized in the Straps, which sometimes go round the Yard; but frequently have an Eye in each End, and are seized together like the Blocks on the other Yards: and often there are Thimbles instead of Blocks.

A single Block (r), is strapped round the Slings of the Yard, resting upon the fore, or upper Part of it: another single Block (s), is strapped with an Eye, and put over the Jib-boom End.

The *HALLIARDS* (t), are reeved through the Block (s), then through the Block (r), on the Yard, and the End is clinched round the Jib-boom End above the Strap, or bent to a Becket in the Strap of the Block (s), making a Gun-Tackle Purchase. The Lifts (v), go single, with Eyes to fit the Yard Arms, and they are reeved through Thimbles (u), strapped with a Span round the Jib-boom End.

The Braces are led like the Spritsail Braces, under the Fore-Top.

This Yard is got across by the same means as the Spritsail Yard was. A Top, or Yard-Rope (x), being reeved through a Tail-Block on the Jib Stay for that purpose. The Parral goes with Ribs and Trucks like that mentioned in page 39, for the Topsail Yard.

The *MIZEN YARD* is rounded all the way, and is hoisted on board by a Hawser reeved through the Mizen Top-block. It is laid fore and aft on the starboard Side for rigging, the larboard Yard Arm being forwards.

L.   MIZEN

*Blunt omits this paragraph.

MIZEN YARD.

Between the Cleats (m), Fig. 262, a large double Block for the Jears (a), is double strapped, wormed, parcelled and served. This Block lies above the Yard, and one Bight of the Strap being on the starboard and another on the larboard Side, it is lashed underneath like the Block on the lower Yards, Rose-fashion, (see page 11), and hove well taught by a Heaver. Another double Block (b), is lashed round the Head of the Mizen Mast, the Lashing being past over a Cleat on the larboard Side of the Mizen Mast-head, like the upper Jear Blocks for the lower Yards, (see Page 34).

The *JEAR FALL* is reeved first through the upper Block (b), then through the lower one (a), alternately, and the End is hitched either round the Mast Head above the Rigging, or round the Strap of the upper Block (b); the Fall leading down on the starboard Side. Two small Blocks (c), are strapped with a Span just above the Cleats, and seized together, hanging underneath the Yard, for the Throat Brails: two others at (d), in the same manner by the Derrick Block (f), for the middle Brails: and two others a few Feet within the Peak (e), for the Peak Brails.

The DERRICK BLOCK, (f),

Is sometimes strapped with two Legs having an Eye in each, and in some Ships double strapped like the Jear Block, being lashed under the Yard in the same Manner, half way between the Slings and the Peak.

The Double Block for the Derrick Fall is often hooked to a Bolt hooped round the Mizen Mast Head, but if there be no Bolt, it is strapped with two long Legs, having an Eye in each. The Block then rests on the Mizen Cap (g), and the Legs being taken underneath, are brought upon the opposite Sides, and lashed together.

The Derrick Fall (n), has an Eye spliced in one End to fit the upper Yard Arm or Peak, and rests against the Stop-cleats: the other End is reeved *down* through the upper Block (g), *up* through the single Block (f), on the Yard, and down again through the double Block (g), leading through Lubbers Hole on the larboard Side. This is belayed in the Mizen Chains on the *larboard* Side, and the Jear-Fall on the *starboard* Side, and they are coiled up there.

The *VANG* Pendents (h), are doubled, and they go over the Peak End with a Cut-splice, see Page 5), or with a jambing Hitch, the Parts being stopped together: a double Block (i), is turned or spliced into each end of the Pendent, and a single Block (o), being strapped to an Eye-Bolt in the quarter Piece on each Side, they are connected together by the Fall, (p), making a Luff Tackle Purchase.

A Double Block (j), (or two single ones), is strapped on each Side of the Peak, one Sheave-hole of which is for the Mizen Topsail, and the other for the Mizen Top-Gallant Braces. A Block is also strapped to the Eye-Bolt (k), in the upper Yard Arm for the Ensign Halliards. In the Eye-bolt at the lower Yard-arm are strapped two bowline Blocks (l). One end of each Bowline is spliced round a Thimble in an Eye-bolt at the Side (n), and the other End is reeved through the Bowline Block (l), and belayed to a Cleat bolted to the other Side. These Yards are now seldom used.

MIZEN

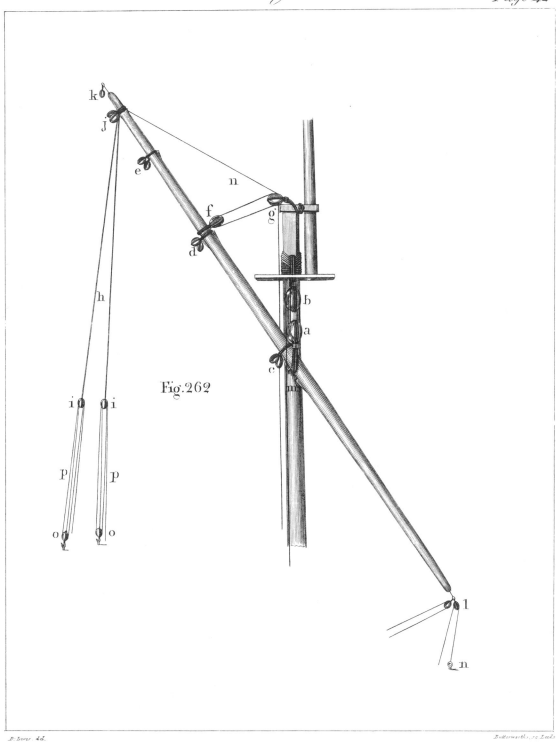

Fig. 262

D. Lever del.

Butterworth, sc Leeds

Mizen Gaff.

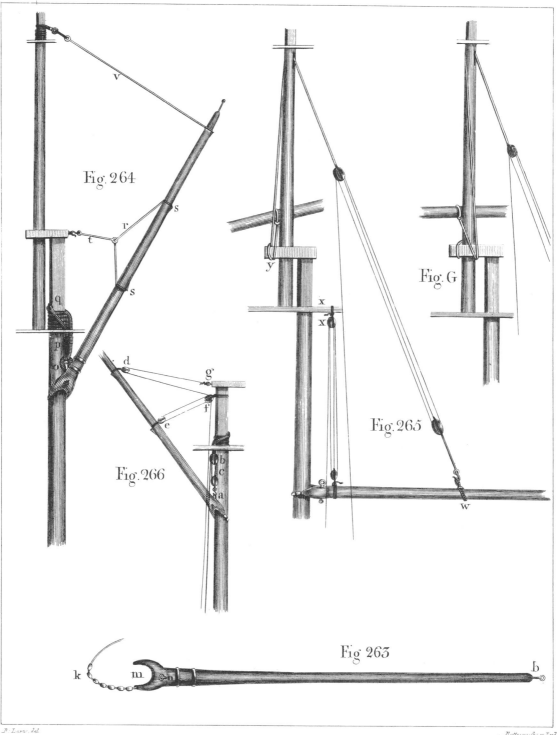

Fig. 264

Fig. 266

Fig. G

Fig. 265

Fig 263

MIZEN GAFF.

At the inner End or Throat of the Gaff, Fig. 263, Jaws (m), are made to receive the after Part of the Mizen Mast, with a bevel proportionable to the Stiving of the Gaff. To these Jaws is fixed a Parral with Trucks (k). An Eye Bolt (n), is driven in the upper Part of them, and a small one underneath. It is there scarfed and hooped. There is an Eye Bolt (b), also fitted to the Peak end, like the Mizen Yard. The Gaff is sometimes slung; and often hoisted like a Brig's Main-Gaff. It is slung thus, Fig. 264.

The Bolt in the upper Part of the Jaws having a Thimble in the Eye (o), the Slings (p), are wormed, parcelled and served; they are reeved through the Bolt (o), over the Thimble, and an Eye is spliced in each End. Just above the Bolt, a Throat Seizing is clapped on (see page 9), and a Round one a little higher up; the two Ends with the Eyes are taken up between the Tressle-trees abaft the Mizen Mast, and being passed on each Side of the Mast-Head (q), above the Rigging, the Eyes are lashed together before it; or being made with a long and short Leg, the End of the long one is reeved through an Eye in the short one, and seized back to its own Part with one Throat, and two round Seizings, like the Slings for the lower Yards, as described in page 35, Fig. 228. It is also often slung at the Throat, like the lower Yards, having a Strap with a large Thimble in, and a Laniard setting up to the Thimble in the Slings, as shewn in the same Figure.

A SPAN (r), being served and leathered, is reeved through a Thimble spliced in the End of a Pendent (t), and in each End of this Span is spliced an Eye to fit the Gaff: they are driven on, each a certain Distance from the Center of the Gaff, and stop Cleats (s), if necessary, are nailed on to prevent their moving. A Hook and Thimble is spliced into the other End of the Pendent (t), which is hooked to an Eye-bolt in the after Part of the Mizen Cap.

Another Pendent (v), which is called the *Peak Tye*, goes round the Peak End with an Eye; and a Thimble being spliced in the other End, it is connected by a Laniard to a Strap with a Thimble in it, at the Mizen Topmast Head above the Rigging. The Brail Blocks are strapped on, as before described for the Mizen Yard.

To get this Gaff up for rigging, Fig. 265, the lower Block of the Mizen Topsail Halliards is hooked to a Selvagee (w), in the Middle of it: a Tail-Tackle is made fast with the double Block to the Mizen Tressle-tree (x), and the Tail of the single one is hitched round the Throat. In some Vessels the Mizen Topsail Yard is lashed down to the Cap; but where the fore Part of the Cap projects out sufficiently, the Bight of the Tye (y), is taken with a Hitch round it; or the Bight of the Tye may be taken under the Cap between the Masts, and put over the fore Part of it like Fig. G. The Gaff is hoisted up by the Tail Tackle and Topsail Halliards, and slung as before described.

When the Gaff traverses up and down the Mast, Fig. 266, a double or single Block, according to the Size of it, is strapped with a Hook and Thimble, and hooked to the Eye Bolt in the Throat (a): another double Block (b), is double strapped; the Bights of the Strap are taken up between the Tressle-trees, and being placed on each Side of the Mizen Mast Head, are lashed together before it. The Fall (c), is reeved alternately through these Blocks and called the THROAT HALLIARDS. In some Ships the upper Block (b), is hooked to an iron Strap round the Mizen Mast Head.

The PEAK HALLIARDS are commonly reeved like the Derrick Fall (see the former Page); but frequently an additional Block (d), is lashed about one fifth within the Peak, the other (e), is lashed on like the Derrick Block. The End of the Halliards is then taken up through Lubbers-hole, reeved through a double Block (f), at the Mast Head, down through the Block (e), up again through the Block (f), up through the Block (d), and the End is hitched round the Head of the Mizen Mast, or to an Eye Bolt in the Cap (g).

GAFF

Blunt's significant differences in treatment of the Mizen Gaff may be seen in Appendix 15, where close examination of Figures 264 and 266 will be of help.

GAFF—SPANKER BOOM.

In large Ships there are sometimes Peak, and Throat *Tyes*, Fig. 267 ; but these are more commonly used for the Main Gaffs of Brigs, or of Ships which carry fore and aft Mainsails (see page 66). A large single Block (g), is strapped, and lashed round the Head of the Mast above the Rigging, hanging down abaft, like the double one in the former page, below the Tressle-trees.

The THROAT TYE (f), is spliced round a Thimble in the Bolt, at the upper part of the Jaws, the other end is reeved through the Block (g), and has a double Block (e), turned into it : this is connected by the Halliards (d), to a single Block (c), hooked to an Eye-bolt in the Deck, reeving like a Luff Tackle.

The PEAK-TYE (h), is spliced round a Thimble on the Span (b), reeved through the Block at the Mast-head (a), led down through Lubbers-hole on the larboard side, and has a double Block (i), turned into the lower end, the Halliards reeving as before.

When the Gaff is rigged to hoist, there are no Vangs, nor Blocks, for the Mizen Topmast and Mizen Top-Gallant Braces, which then lead forwards ; but there is a Block (k), strapped to the Bolt in the Peak end, through which the Peak *Down-hauler* (l), is reeved.

Ships which have their Gaffs traverse, carry Mizen Booms, which are rigged like the Spanker Boom.

The SPANKER BOOM, Fig. 268,

Has sometimes a large Bolt and Hook, called *Goose-Neck* (l), nailed and hooped on its inner end. This is hooked to an Eye which is hooped round the Mizen Mast ; but in some Ships, the inner end of the Boom is fitted up with Jaws, as described on the Gaff, and has a Shoulder bolted on the Mizen Mast, for it to rest upon.

The TOPPING LIFTS (m), are doubled, go over the Mizen Topmast-head, with a Hitch above the Rigging, and are there seized together. They are served round the Bight, and about three or four feet below the Cross-Trees on each side. A single Block (n), is spliced into the end of each, and a double Block (o), strapped with an Eye over the Boom end, resting against the Shoulder or Stop Cleat. The *Bight* of the Fall is middled, and hitched over the Boom end without the Block (o) : the ends are reeved through the single Blocks (n), then through the double one (o), leading through a Thimble fastened by a Staple (p), to the upper part of the Boom on each side, just without the inner ends of the Horses (q), and are belayed to Cleats (d), on each end of the Boom within board.

The HORSES (q), are spliced to Thimbles on the Bolt at the Boom end : Diamond, or over-hand Knots (see pages 6 and 7), are cast on them, and Eyes being spliced in the ends, they are seized to the Boom just above the Taffarel. When there is no Bolt in the Boom end, they are middled, and seized without the Shoulder, or Stop Cleats, round the Boom end.

The SHEET BLOCK (r), is double strapped : the Bights of the Strap are put over the inner end of the Boom, and placed between two Cleats on the Boom, over the Horse on Deck : a round Seizing is then clapped on underneath : sometimes the Bights of the Strap are lashed together above the Boom, like the Blocks on the Yards. The end of the Sheet (s), is bent to a Becket in the Strap of the upper Sheet Block (r), with a Sheet Bend (see page 8), reeved alternately through the upper Block (r), and the lower one, which is also double, and the end is led in upon Deck. The lower Block (i), is strapped to a Thimble on an iron Horse (h).

On the Topping Lifts (t), are worked two Turks Heads (see page 12) : a small Block is strapped on each part between them : through each of these is reeved a Crane Line (u) : a double Wall-knot (see page 5), is cast on one end of each, and fastened by a Staple driven into the Fife-Rail : the other end is belayed on Deck. These are for over-hauling the Lee Topping Lift.

Another method (more common), Fig. 269, is to have the Topping Lift middled, and the Bight hitched and seized round the Boom end. A single Block (v), is lashed on each side of the Mizen Mast Head, through which the ends of the Topping Lifts are reeved. A double Block (w), is spliced into the end of each, which is connected by its Fall to a single one (u), hooked to an Eye-bolt in the Deck.---
The Hooks are moused with Spun-yarn.   SPANKER

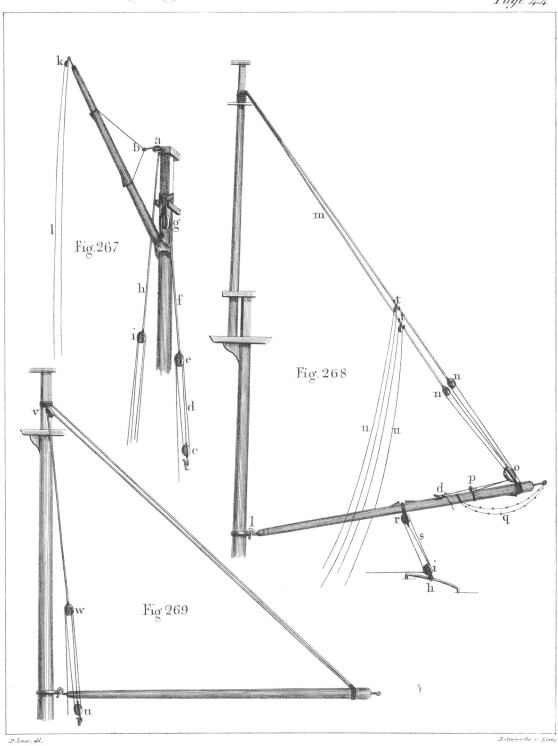

Fig. 267

Fig. 268

Fig 269

D. Lowe, del.

Butterworths r. Leeds

Spanker Boom — Top-Gallant Mast,

Fig. 270

Fig. 271

Fig. 272

Fig. 273

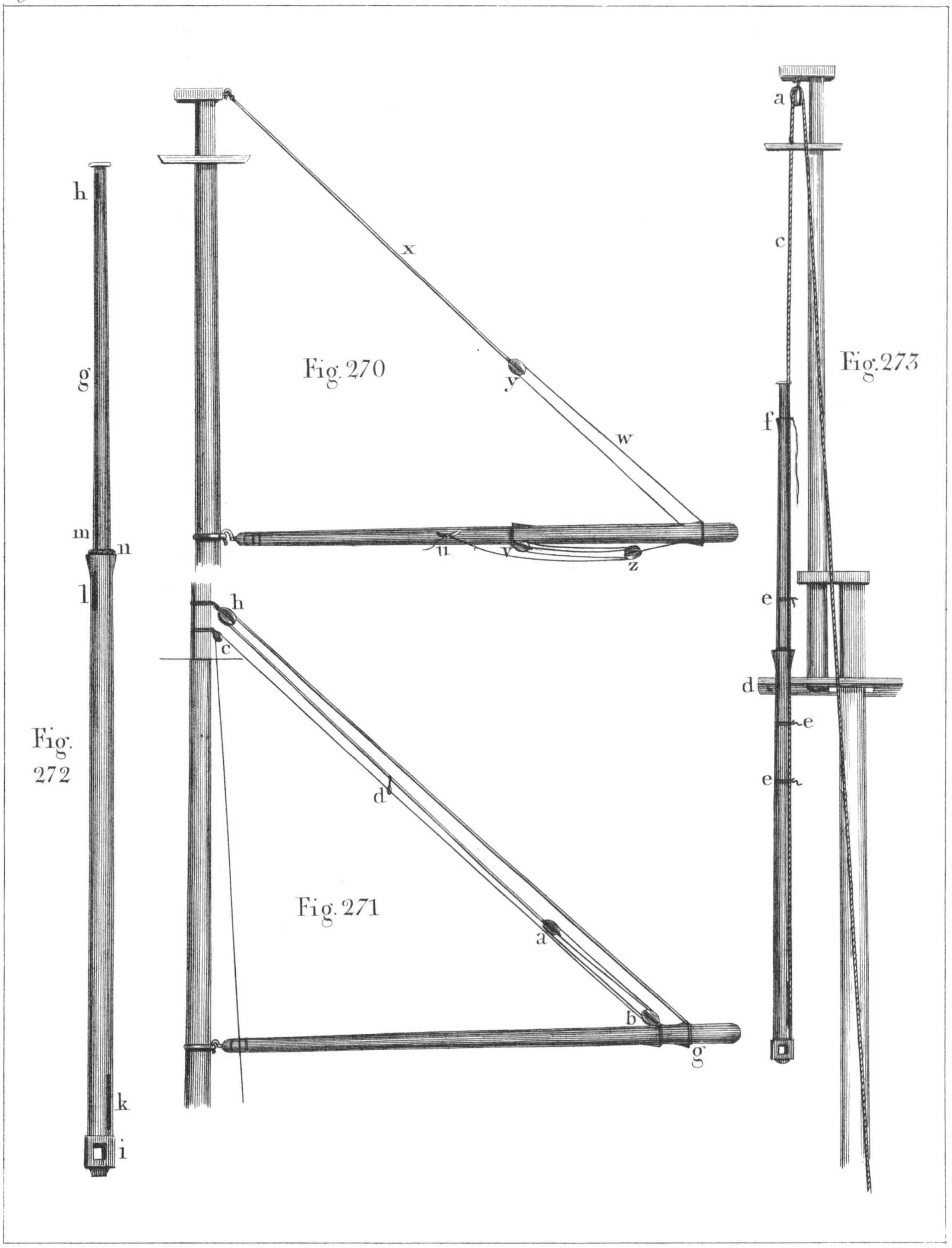

SPANKER BOOM—TOP GALLANT MAST.

A THIRD METHOD, Fig. 270,

Is to have a Pendent (x), with a Hook and Thimble spliced into one end, and a single Block (y), into the other: The Hook is put through an Eye-bolt in the after part of the Mizen Cap. A Runner (w), having a double Block (z), spliced in its end, is reeved up through a Sheave-hole in the Boom, through the Block (y), and an Eye being spliced in the end, it is put over the Boom end, resting against the Shoulder. A single Block (v), is strapped on the middle of the Boom, and the end of the Fall being spliced round the Strap, is led alternately through the two Blocks (z) and (v), and belayed to a Cleat (u), farther in on the Boom.

A FOURTH METHOD, Fig. 271.

The end (g) is put over the Boom end with an Eye, as before mentioned, or clinched round it; the other is led through a single Block (h), at the after part of the Mizen Mast Head, and a single Block (a), is spliced or turned into it. A double Block (b), is lashed on the Boom, or strapped round it, resting against a Stop Cleat. The end of the Fall is bent to a Becket put over the end of the Topping Lift, before the Block (a), is spliced in, and being reeved alternately through the Blocks (b and a), is belayed to a Cleat on the Boom, as before; but in some Ships a Bull's-Eye or Thimble (d), is seized to the Topping Lift, and the end of the Fall being led through it, is reeved through a Block (c), at the Mizen Mast Head, and belayed to a Cleat on the Mast below. The two first plans are the' best, because there is a Topping Lift to Windward and to Leeward; and therefore no occasion to dip the Peak on either Tack.

For the Guy belonging to this Boom (see the Mizen Boom, page 66).

The Booms of BRIGS, SLOOPS, and CUTTERS, are rigged in some of these methods.

TOP GALLANT MASTS, Fig. 272,

Are rounded all the way, from the Heel to the Hounds: above them there is a long Pole (g), rounded to the Truck. In the Heel (i), which is square, there is a hole for the Fid, and above it a Sheave-hole, for the Top-rope, is cut (k), from the after part of the larboard, to the fore part of the starboard side, with a Groove for the Rope to lie in, that it may not be jambed in the Topmast Tressle-Trees. In the Head of the Mast (l), there is a Sheave-hole for the Top Gallant Tye; and in the Main Top Gallant Mast another (m), in the Pole, just above the Hounds, for the Main Top Gallant Staysail Halliards. A Gromet of Rope (n), (see page 11), is driven over the Pole close to the Hounds, to keep the Rigging from chafing. There is a Sheave-hole also near the Head of the Pole (h), for the Royal Halliards.

TO GET THIS MAST UP, Fig. 273,

A small Top-block (a), is hooked to the Eye-bolt in the Topmast Cap, on the larboard side, and the Top-rope (c), is reeved through it: the fore part of it is over-hauled down between the Topmast Tressle-trees and the two foremost Cross-trees, and before the Top (d). It is reeved through the Sheave-hole in the larboard side, and the end hitched round the Pole and standing part at (f), leaving a sufficient length to cast off, when the Mast has entered the Tressle-trees and Topmast Cap. The Bights are then well stopped with Spun-yarn (e), at different places.

The Mast is swayed up by the Top-rope, being guyed off the Rim of the Top by the Men there; and when the Pole Head is sufficiently entered through the Cap, the end is cast off (the Mast hanging by the Stops), and hitched to the Eye-bolt in the starboard side of the Cap. The Stops are then cut, and the Mast hangs by the Top-rope, ready for Rigging. The Rigging is hoisted up by the Girtlines, like the Topmast Rigging.

M   TOP

TOP GALLANT MAST RIGGED.

A Pair of Shrouds (n), Fig. 274, are put over on the *starboard* Side, then a Pair on the larboard, and as there is an odd Shroud on each side, the Leg of the last Pair (o), is led down as a Backstay, and set up in the Channel or in the Stool for the Topmast Backstay, with Dead Eyes; or in small Vessels, with Thimbles. Men of War have two Top Gallant Backstays on each side.

The Shrouds are seized with Eyes like the Topmast ones, and they are served round the Eyes, and in the Wake of the Holes in the Cross-Trees. In the foremost Pair, just below the Eye-seizing, a Thimble is seized for the Top-Gallant Lifts to reeve through.

The *STAY* (m), instead of a Mouse being raised, has the End spliced in the standing Part, forming a Collar, and is served over as before-mentioned for the Topmast Stay. Sometimes the Stay has no Collar; but the End is spliced round a Thimble on an iron Traveller, Fig. M, which is placed over the Pole Head after the Rigging is put over; but in this Case the Pole should be made very strong, particularly that of the Main Top Gallant Mast, for the Stay going up with the Royal Yard, the Strain of it and the Top Gallant Staysail (the Halliards of which must reeve through a Block on the Traveller), will be entirely on it.

The *ROYAL BACKSTAYS* (q), and Stay (s), are next put over the Head of the Pole, and are stopped from coming down, by Cleats nailed on for that purpose; after which the Truck (P p), which has a Sheave-hole on each Side, for the Pennant Halliards, is placed on the Tenon at the Pole Head, having a Mortise cut in for that purpose.

The Mast is then swayed up by the Top or Mast Rope; the Fid thrust through the square Hole in the Heel, the Top-rope eased, and then unreeved, and the Top-Gallant Top Block unhooked and lowered down below.

Previously to the Rigging being set up, a Futtock-stave similar to the lower one, is seized on the Topmast Shrouds (a), and they are catharpined in, as mentioned in page 39.

The *SHROUDS* are then reeved through the Holes in the outer End of the Cross Trees (b), and leading down over the Futtock Stave, a Thimble is turned into the End of each.

A *STRAP* or *SPAN*, Fig. 275, with three Thimbles or small Blocks is placed over the End of the Jib Boom; and through the middle Thimble or Block, the Fore Top-Gallant Stay is reeved: a small Heart, Dead Eye, or Thimble is turned into the end, (and when the Stay goes with a Traveller, sometimes a Block) and a Laniard being spliced to it, it is set up to a Heart, Dead Eye, or Eye-Bolt in the Bows. Sometimes instead of the Thimble, a small three-fold Block is strapped over the Jib-Boom End. The Stay is set up with a Jigger Tackle.

A Laniard is spliced round the Thimble in the End of the Top-Gallant Shroud (r), Fig. T, which connects it to another Thimble (t), seized in a Strap round the Futtock Plate. The Top-Burton Tackle being over-hauled, the Laniard of each Shroud is cat's-pawed to the Hook of its single Block, and they are set up by the People in the Top. Or a SPANISH WINDLASS, Fig. 276, being made by laying one End of a Handspike (b), over the iron Rail of the Top, and the other in a Becket on the Shroud, the Laniard (c), is taken round it, and set up by a Heaver (d).

Sometimes the TOP-GALLANT SHROUDS are led across like, Fig. 277, (which shews the aft side of the Topmast), and are set up to Thimbles in the opposite Futtock Plates: this is a great ease to the Futtock Stave and Topmast Rigging, and the lee Rigging by these Means is kept taught, as they act like Bentick Shrouds below.

The FORE TOP-GALLANT BACK-STAY (o), Fig. 274, in some Ships has a Thimble turned into the lower end, and is set up to another, strapped round the Chain Plate of the Topmast Backstay (like the Thimble of the Top-Gallant Shrouds to the Futtock Plate). In larger Ships, it has a Dead Eye turned into the lower end, and is set up to another Dead Eye in a Chain Plate for that purpose, a Jigger-Tackle being clapped on the Backstay with a Midshipman's Hitch (see page 9), and the Hook of the lower Block cat's-pawed to the Laniard.

FORE

*Top-Gallant Mast rigging differs somewhat in the Blunt edition. See the lower half of the page in Appendix 16 for the Blunt version, together with the changed Figure 275.

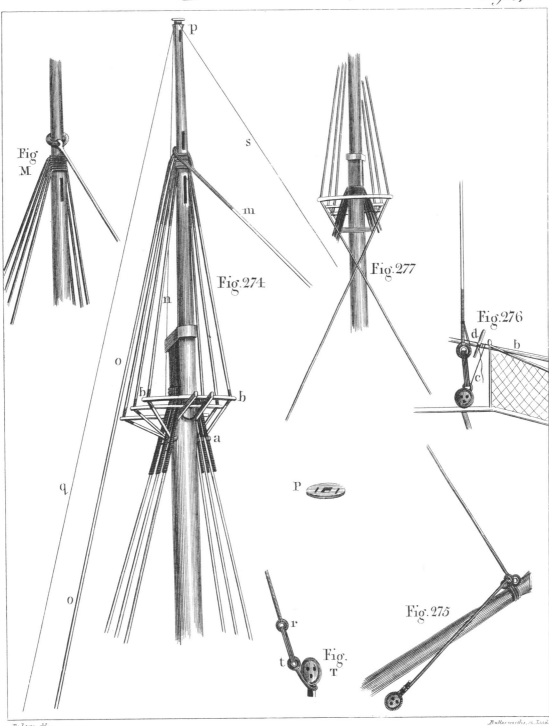

Fig.
M

Fig. 274

Fig.277

Fig.276

Fig. 275

Fig.
T

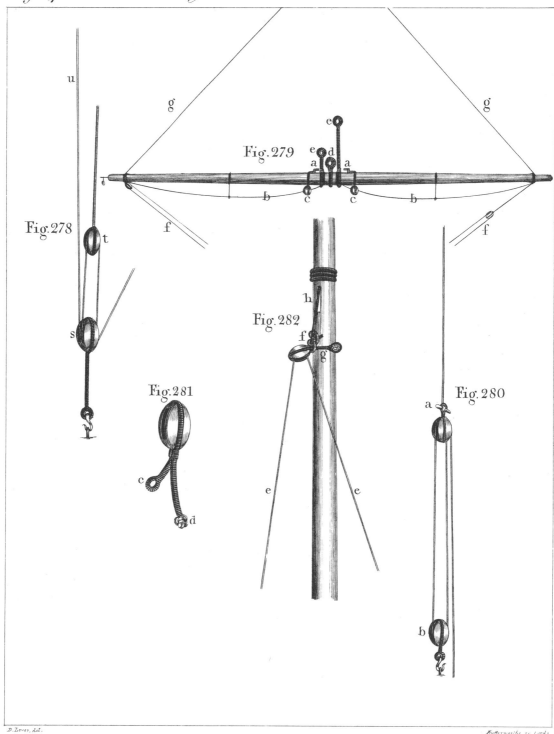

Fig. 279

Fig. 278

Fig. 281

Fig. 282

Fig. 280

FORE TOP-GALLANT YARD——JACK BLOCK, &c.

In the Merchant Service the Top-Gallant Backstay is sometimes led thus, Fig. 278. A double Block (s), is strapped with a long Strap, like that for the single or lower Block of the Topsail Halliards: a single Block (t), is spliced or turned into the end of the Backstay; the end of the Fall (u), is clinched round the Pole Head of the Top-Gallant Mast above the Cleats, the other End is reeved through one of the Sheaves of the double Block (s), then through the single one (t), and again through the Sheave of the lower one (s), leading in upon Deck. Thus the Fall of the Top-Gallant Backstay (u), acts as a ROYAL BACKSTAY. One Fall (if there be a Coil long enough) will do for the Backstay on each Side: the Fall is middled, put over the Pole Head with a Clove Hitch, (see page 7), and reeved on each Side as before.

The TOP-GALLANT YARDS are rounded all the way, Fig. 279. Cleats (a), are nailed on the Slings and Yard Arms, like the Topsail Yards. The HORSES (b), go over the Yard Arms in the same manner: *Clew-line Blocks* (c), are strapped on the Yard just within the Cleats as before. In some Vessels a Strap with a Thimble (d), is placed round the Yard for the Top-Gallant Tye to bend to; but the Tye is frequently bent to the Yard with a Fisherman's Bend, (see page 8).

Two Straps (e), with Eyes, one long the other short, are spliced, or seized, round the Yard for the PARRAL; but sometimes the Parral is made like that for the Topsail Yard, page 40, Fig. 254.

The BRACES and SINGLE LIFTS as before: these and the Clew-lines are made fast to the Topmast Cross-Trees, to be in readiness when the Yard is sent up, it being rigged aloft. The Lifts are reeved through a Thimble seized in between the two foremost Top-Gallant Shrouds, just below the Eye seizing.

The TOP-GALLANT TYE is reeved through the Sheave-hole in the Top-Gallant Mast, and hitched round the Cross-trees till wanted. In the other end a double Block is turned or spliced, and a single one is strapped to the lower Tressle Tree, the Halliards are reeved like the Topsail Halliards in page 39, Fig. 250. Sometimes the lower Block is strapped to an Eye Bolt in the Deck abaft the Mast.

Frequently the Tye and Halliards are in one, like Fig. 280: the Tye (a), being hitched round the Strap of the upper (single) Block and toggled, to reeve alternately through the lower Block (b), at the Tressle-tree, and the Block (a). When the Tye leads thus, the Toggle being taken out and the Fall unreeved, it answers for a Top-rope to send the Yard up and down by; but when the Tye and Halliards are in two Parts, the Top-Gallant Yards are got up as follows:

A Block called a JACK BLOCK, Fig. 281, is strapped with a long and short Leg: the short one (c), has an Eye spliced in the End of it, and a double Wall Knot, (see page 5), cast on the End of the long one (d). The former is called the *Loop* and the latter the *Button*. The Strap is placed round the Top-Gallant Mast, the Block lying before, and the Knot (d), is thrust through the Eye (e).

The TOP-ROPE for the Yard (e), Fig. 282, is reeved through the Block, and overhauled down upon Deck before the Top, the leading part through Lubber's-hole. The Tye (f), is hitched round the Strap of the Block (g), and the Men below hoisting upon the Halliards, trice it up: the Halliards are then belayed.

The Top-rope is made fast to the Slings of the Yard with a Fisherman's-bend, (see page 8), and stopped to the second Quarter on the *starboard* Side with Spun-yarn, if the Yard be got up on the *larboard* Side, and vice versa.

Getting

Getting the Top Gallant Yards across—Leading the Braces.

A Man (e), Fig. 283, stands on the Cross-trees, to put the starboard Brace (b), and Lift (d), over the Yard-arm : the larboard Lift (g), has the end of the Clew-line bent to it (not being long enough to overhaul down below), and the Man (f), stands in the larboard Topmast Shrouds, to place the larboard Brace (a), and Lift over the larboard Yard-arm. The Yard is then swayed up by the Top-rope *(or Yard-rope)* ; and when high enough, the Men put the Rigging on, before mentioned ; the larboard Clew-line is gathered in. The Top-rope is again swayed upon, and as the Yard advances, the Man in the Cross-trees cuts the Stops (h). When the Bunt, or Slings of the Yard, is sufficiently above the Topmast Cap, the last Stop is cut, and the larboard Clew-line being hauled upon, the Yard falls across, and is squared by the Lifts and Braces. The ends of the Lifts are made fast round the Cross-trees, the Clew-lines reeved through the Blocks on the Yard, and an overhand Knot is cast on the end : the Eyes of the Parral are seized together.

B R A C E S.

The FORE BRACE is sometimes reeved through a Block (a), lashed to the Collar of the Mainstay, Fig. 284, under the Top, then through the Block in the Pendent or *Strap*, at the Yard-arm (b), and the end is taken back and hitched round the Collar of the Stay, below the Block (a). The leading part goes down by the Mainmast, and is reeved through a leading Block (z), strapped to an Eye-bolt in the Deck ; but in the Merchant Service, the Block (a), is more commonly a *double* one (one Sheave-hole being for the Fore Topsail Brace), and is strapped to an Eye-bolt hooped round the Mainmast Head, two or three Feet below the Tressle-trees, the standing part being made fast just below the Mouse of the Stay.

The FORE TOPSAIL BRACE is reeved through a Block (n), on the Mainstay, just above the fore Hatchway, then through the Block (c), on the Collar above the Mouse, through the Block in the Pendent or Strap (d), on the Yard-arm ; and the end is hitched, or clinched round the Collar of the Mainstay, above the Block.

A better method for the Fore Topsail Brace to lead is this, Fig. 285. The end of the standing part (after reeving through the Blocks (g, f, and d), on the Mainmast Head, Stay, and the Yard-arm), is made fast to the *Main Topmast Stay* (e). The two parts of the Brace being thus divided, it does not pull the Yard so much down, when it is hoisted up to the Head of the Fore Topmast.

The FORE TOP GALLANT BRACE (when double), in large Ships, is reeved through a Block seized to the after part of the Fore Top (h), through a Block seized to the Collar of the Main Topmast Stay (i), then through the Brace-block at the Yard-arm (k), and the end is hitched to the Stay Collar. When this Brace goes single, Fig. 286, with an Eye over the Yard-arm, it is led through a Block on the Main Topmast Stay, just below the Splice, and through a Block seized to the upper part of the foremost Main Topmast Shroud, close under the Rigging.

In the MERCHANT SERVICE, the Fore, Fore Topsail, and Fore Top Gallant Braces are generally led down by the Mainmast, and belayed together there : and in small vessels through a *treble* Block, seized to the foremost Main Shroud, and belayed to a Pin in the Block. So that in " *hauling off all*," they are let go together.

BRACES.

Fig. 286

Fig. 283

Fig. 284

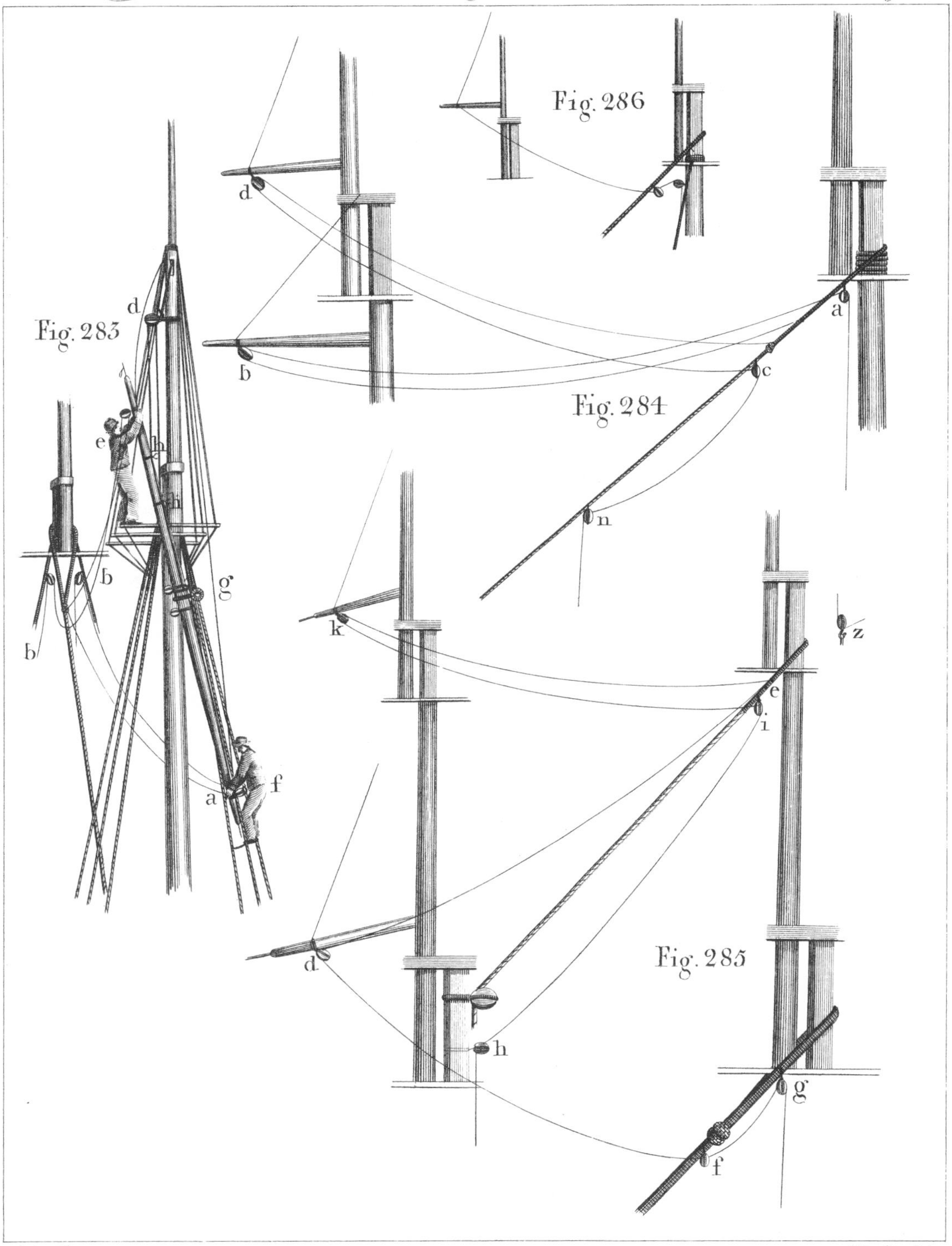

Fig. 285

Braces.

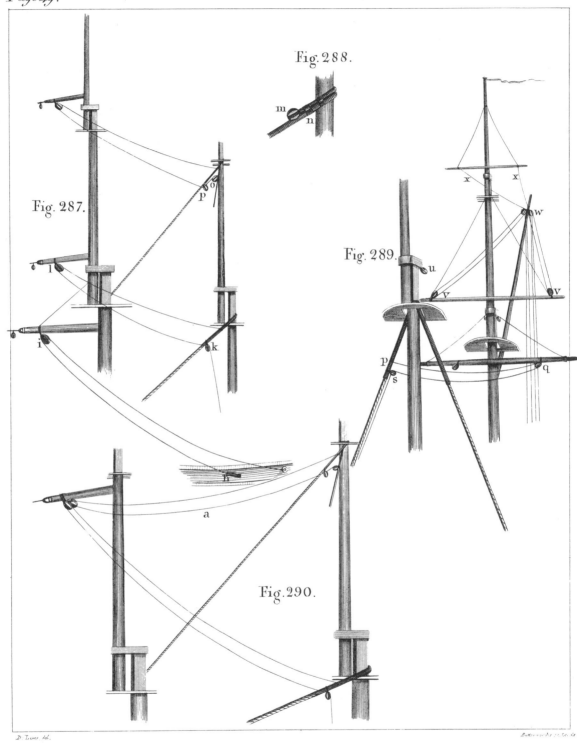

Fig. 288.

Fig. 287.

Fig. 289.

Fig. 290.

BRACES.

The MAIN BRACE, Fig. 287,

Is reeved out through a Sheave-hole (h), in the Side of the **Quarter Deck**, through the Block in the Strap or Pendent at the Yard Arm (i), and the End of the standing Part is clinched to an Eye Bolt in the Quarter Piece.

The MAIN TOPSAIL BRACE is led through a Block at the Mizen Stay Collar (k), or to a Block strapped to a Bolt hooped round the Mizen Mast Head, then through the Block in the Strap or Pendent (l), and the End is hitched to the Stay Collar. But more frequently the Brace Blocks (m), at the Mizen Mast, Fig. 288, are spliced in each End of a Pendent, which lies with its Bight abaft the Mizen Mast, and is seized to the Mizen Stay Collar (n).

This leading of the Main Topsail Braces to the Mizen Mast Head, has the effect of canting the Yard when up at the Mast Head, particularly if the Main Tack be not on board, of course prevents the Sail standing well.

In the Merchant Service they often have, on this account, the Mizen Topmast made stouter than usual, and lead the Main Topsail Brace to the Mizen Topmast Head, which causes it to traverse in a more horizontal Direction; an additional Backstay is also frequently used. At all Events it would perhaps be better for the standing Part of the Brace to be taken to the Mizen Topmast Head, like that of the Fore Topsail Brace to the Main Topmast Head, mentioned in the former page.

The MAIN TOP GALLANT BRACE, Fig. 287, is reeved up through a Block (o), seized to the upper Part of the foremost Mizen Topmast Shroud, through another at the Mizen Topmast Stay Collar (p), then through the Pendent or Block at the Yard Arm, and the End is hitched round the Stay Collar.

In Coasters which carry few Hands, the Main, Main Topsail, and Main Top Gallant Braces lead forwards, for the Convenience of working.

The CROSS JACK BRACES, Fig. 289,

When there are Pendents, have them frapped round the outer Quarter of the Yard. When there are none, the Brace Block (q), is strapped round a Thimble in an Eye, which goes round the Yard with an iron Strap. The Cross Jack Braces are led across *forwards*: the standing Part of the larboard Brace (p), is hitched to the after Main Shroud on the starboard Side, upon the Service, the leading Part through the Block on the Yard, and through another on the Main Shroud (s), seized close under the standing Part, being led through a double or treble Block on the Shroud below, and belayed to a Cleat on the Shroud or fife Rail.

When the Gaff hoists up and down, the Mizen Topsail and Top Gallant Braces are also led forwards, and commonly go single: the Topsail Brace is reeved through a double Block (u), strapped to an Eye Bolt in the after Part of the Main Cap, and the Top Gallant Brace through a Block seized to the aftermost Main Topmast Shroud; but when the Gaff or Mizen Yard is slung (as mentioned in pages 42 and 43), the Mizen Topsail Braces are reeved through one of the Sheaves of a double Block (or a single Block) at the Mizen Peak (w), then through the Block at the Yard Arm (v), and the Ends are clinched round the Peak. The Top Gallant Braces (x), are reeved through the other Sheave-hole, or through another single Block (w), at the Peak.

French Men of War have sometimes two Pair of Topsail Braces, which are a great Security to the Yard, the upper Brace (a) Fig. 290, acting in a more horizontal Direction when the Yard is at the Mast Head, and when the Topsail is reefed, (of course blowing fresh) an equal Strain lies on the upper and lower Brace. This would not answer in the Merchant Service, where there are few Hands, as the over-hauling of two Pair of Braces would impede the working of the Ship. The best Substitute is to lead the Topsail Braces, as shewn in Fig. 285.

N

SAILS

SAILS.

The Names of the Sails are derived from the Masts to which they are attached : thus the Foresail is named from the Fore Mast, the Mainsail from the Main Mast, the Main Topsail from the Main Top Mast, &c.

The SQUARE SAILS, Fig. 291 and 292, are

(a) *The Fore Sail.*
(b) *The Fore Topsail.*
(c) *The Fore Top Gallant Sail.*
(d) *The Fore Top Gallant Royal.*
(e) *The Fore Studding Sail.*
(f) *The Fore Topmast Studding Sail.*
(g) *The Fore Top-Gallant Studding Sail.*
(h) *The Mainsail.*
(i) *The Main Topsail.*

(k) *The Main Top Gallant Sail.*
(l) *The Main Top Gallant Royal.*
(m) *The Main Topmast Studding Sail.*
(n) *The Main Top Gallant Studding Sail.*
(o) *The Mizen Topsail.*
(p) *The Mizen Top Gallant Sail.*
(q) *The Mizen Top Gallant Royal.*
(r) *The Spritsail.*
(s) *The Spritsail Topsail.*

The FORE *and* AFT SAILS, are

(t) *The Jib.*
(u) *The Fore Topmast Staysail.*
(v) *The Fore Staysail.*
(w) *The Main Staysail.*
(x) *The Main Topmast Staysail.*
(y) *The Middle Staysail.*

(z) *The Main Top Gallant Staysail.*
(a a) *The Mizen Staysail.*
(a b) *The Mizen Topmast Staysail.*
(a c) *The Mizen Top Gallant Staysail.*
(a d) *The Driver or Spanker with the Mizen brailed up.*

Sails are made of Canvas, the number and strength of which is determined by the size or use of the Sail. The strongest Canvas is called *No.* 1, and it decreases gradually to *No.* 8. Sails are surrounded by a Rope called a *Bolt Rope;* but this is of different denominations according as it is sewn to the Head, Foot or Leech. Thus that at the Head is called the *Head Rope,* that at the Side the *Leech Rope,* and that at the Foot the *Foot Rope.* The Foot Rope is the strongest, the Leech Rope somewhat less, and the Head Rope the least.

Square Sails are not so called from their Shape; but because they are suspended to Yards, their Heads hanging parallel to their Feet; which distinguishes them from the Staysails or Fore and Aft Sails. They are made of Pieces of Canvas, called *Cloths,* each Piece being two Feet in breadth, having *generally* more of these in the Foot than in the Head. These laying parallel to each other, and perpendicular to the Head, the Breadth of the Sail is diminished by being cut from the lower Corners or Clews (a), Fig. 293, diagonally towards the Head (b). This is called *goring* a Sail.

Sails are frequently gored more or less in the Foot, some going with an entire Sweep or Hollow : others are gored from a certain Cloth on each Side to the Clew as (1. 2. 3. 4. 5. 6.) : and others again have the Foot parallel to the Head.

The FORESAIL is attached to the Fore Yard, and is in form as represented by Figure 294. When the Mast stands well aft, it is sometimes of equal Breadth at the Head and Foot ; but more frequently, particularly if the Mast be forward, it is a Cloth broader at the Head than at the Foot : that is, a Cloth on each Side is gored, or cut sloping, from the Head to the Foot, so that it is half a Cloth broader on each Side. Sometimes instead of this half Cloth on each Side, the Sail is made broader at the Head, by decreasing the Breadth of the Seams towards the Foot. The Shape of the Sail must be regulated by the Height of the Mast and the squareness of the Yard. Ships in the Merchant Service vary as to these proportions, some having taunt lower Masts and narrow Yards, others short Masts and square Yards, and others again in a Medium between the two former.

FORESAIL

An article on Canvas can be found in Appendix 26.

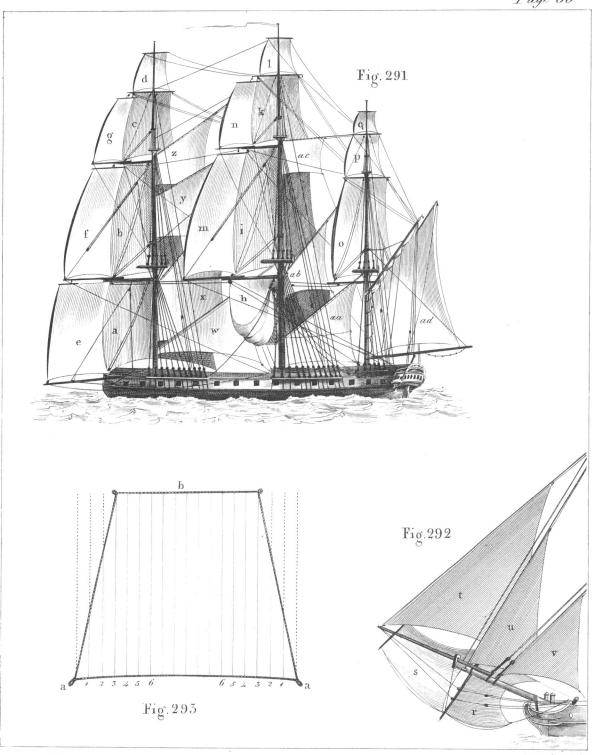

Fig. 291

Fig. 292

Fig. 293

D. Lever del.

Butterworths, sc. Leeds.

Fore-sail

Fig. 294

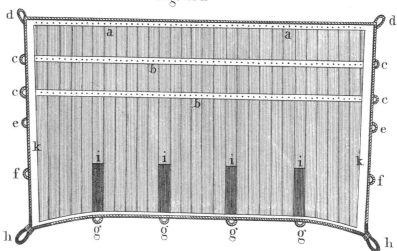

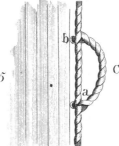

Fig. 295

FORESAIL.

The Cloths have one Side laid over the other, and are sewn together in the Royal Navy with waxed Twine: but in the Merchant Service the Twine is generally dipped in Tar, softened with Oil. Previously to the Sail being stitched to the Bolt Rope, it is hemmed pretty broad, by doubling it down, and this is called *Tabling* (a), Fig. 294. Holes are cut through the Tabling at the Head of the Sail, and small Gromets made to the Size of them, are worked with Log-line: These are fitted to the Holes and worked round with Twine.

A REEF BAND (b), which is a Piece of Canvas one third or one fourth of the Breadth of the Cloth, is sewn across the Sail at a proper Distance, according to the Depth of it. Holes similar to those in the Head of the Sail, and small Gromets fitted to the Size of them, are worked into this Band for the Points to reeve through. Some Sail-makers put two Holes in each Cloth; but others place one in each Cloth and one in each Seam.

Opposite to the Reef Band on each Side, in the Leech Rope, a Gromet (e), called a *Cringle*, is worked thus: a Strand of good Rope (C), is taken out, of a sufficient length: a Hole being made in the Tabling in the Band, this Strand is reeved through it, and through two of the Strands in the Leech Rope (a), Fig. 295, then through the Hole (b), in the same manner, and one Part is laid over till it resembles the Rope (as described in making a Gromet, (page 11), the Ends being pushed through between the Strands of the Leech Rope, as in splicing.

The Earing Cringle (d), Fig. 294, is made by the Leech Rope being spliced into itself.

In the middle of the Sail, a Cringle, called the *Upper Bowline Cringle* (e), is passed through the Strands and laid up as before, but not put through the Tabling. Half way between this and the Foot, another is worked in the same manner, called the *Lower Bowline Cringle* (f): and at equal Distances in the Foot are two or more Cringles (g), called BUNTLINE CRINGLES. All these Cringles are now generally worked round Thimbles.

The CLEWS (h), or lower corner of the Sails are made of larger Rope than the Bolt-rope in the Royal Navy; but in the Merchant Service it is generally omitted as unnecessary, being heavy and unhandy: The Clew is now a Continuation of the Foot Rope, and if it be thought necessary to strengthen it, a Strand of the same sized Rope is opened and laid round it.

The Clews are wormed, parcelled and served, and Holes being made in the Tabling, the Sail is marled down to it, because the Service is too strong for the sail Needle to enter: the two Parts are seized together with a round Seizing. It was found by experience that the large Clews generally necked at the Seizing, and not uncommonly were the cause of splitting the Sail.

Bolt Ropes in the *Merchant Service* are generally one third less than those formerly used, and were they still less it might be found to answer the purpose. The Sails would be thus light and handy, which is a matter of great consequence where Ships are so lightly manned: and to shew the insufficiency of shose very large Bolt Ropes, we need only observe a Dutchman's Jib, which is in the opposite extreme; being frequently not much stronger than Hambro' Line.

In the Wake of the Buntline Cringles additional Canvas (i), is stuck on; these are called *Buntline Cloths*.

Additional Canvas (k), called the *Lining*, is also stitched on the Leeches, the Breadth of a Cloth; these and the Buntline Cloths are placed on the fore Part of the Sail, and when half worn, an additional Cloth called a *middle Band*, is sewn across the Sail between the Bowline Cringles.

FORESAIL

A change in material in the clew from hemp to iron is shown in Blunt's Figure 294 and added Figure K (see Appendix 17). Mentioned, but not shown, is the change of cringles from plain hemp to being worked around thimbles. The Royal Navy had more spare manpower than the merchant vessels, so could bend new cringles more often. Strangely, this change isn't shown in Figure 308, the Royal Topsail, perhaps because of less stress on the royals.

FORESAIL GEER.

When this sail is to be bent to the Yard, it is brought upon the Fore-castle, and laid athwart over the Mainstay, for that purpose.

The CLEW-GARNET BLOCK (l), Fig. 296, is put through the Clew, and seized. This Block, Fig. 298, is strapped with two Legs, which are reeved through the holes in the Shoulder of the Block, and the round Seizing clapped on. An Eye is spliced in the end of each Leg : these are put through the Clew on the after side, brought round it up again, and they are then seized together, as represented in the Figure.

A large single Block, called the *Fore Sheet Block*, (m), Fig. 296, has its Strap put over the Clew : the Block laying aft for the Fore Sheet (p), to reeve through.

The FORE TACK (n), if single, is a Cable-laid rope, generally tapered in the making ; and on the thick end, a double-walled Knot, double crowned, (see page 5), is cast. The small end being put through the Clew, (the Knot laying aft), is reeved through the Block at the Boomkin end, and led in upon the Fore-castle. The Tack is served sufficiently for lying in the Block, when it is either eased off or hauled close down. In small Vessels in the Merchant Service, the Tack is often *slack-laid* with four Strands, having a Spindle Eye (see page 4), worked in the end, which is reeved through the Clew, and a Toggle put in : and as they carry no Boomkin, the Tack is taken under the after side of the Cat-head, and belayed to the Timber-head before it.

When the Fore Tack goes double, the Block is sometimes seized into the Clew, like Fig. 300 (a) ; but frequently a Spritsail Sheet Knot (see page 6), is made on the two ends of the Strap of the Block (i), Fig. 297, and thrust through it, laying aft. *For the leading in of the Tacks and Sheets, see page 57.*

The BUNTLINE LEGS, in Men of War, are reeved through a Shoe-block (p), Fig. 299. One end is reeved through the *inner* Sheave-hole of a double Block (q), seized to the after part of the Top, through another at the fore part (r), then through the *outer* Buntline-block on the Yard (s), leading down before the Sail, and is bent to the outer Cringle on the Foot : the outer Sheaves of these Blocks are left for the Leech-line. The other Leg is reeved through the outer Sheave-holes of the Blocks (o and p), through the inner Buntline-block on the Yard (v), and bent to the inner Cringle at the Foot of the Sail. The inner Sheave-holes of the Blocks (o and p), are left for the Spritsail Braces. The Buntlines are led in the same manner on the starboard side. The FALL (w), is led through the lower Sheave-hole of the Block (p), and one end is hitched to an Eye-bolt in the Deck.

In the Merchant Service, two single Buntlines are preferred to the Leg and Fall ; the Shoe-block scarcely permitting the Foot of the Sail to be hauled close up, and the weight of it preventing the Buntline from overhauling, and hanging slack before the Sail.

The BOWLINE BRIDLE (x), Fig. 300, is clinched to the upper Cringle (y), reeved through a Thimble spliced in the end of the Bowline (z), and then clinched to the lower Bowline Cringle. The Bowline is for hauling the weather Leech of the Sail forward. For the leading of it, see page 57. In the Merchant Service, if Fore-bowlines went with Toggles, they would be found to answer in wear and tear ; because, when going long on one Tack, the Lee-bowline might be cast off, by which means the Sail would not be chafed by its flapping against it, which in wet weather is often found to be the case.

The SLAB-LINE is reeved through Block (b), which hangs underneath the Yard, abaft the Sail, and which is sometimes strapped to the Strap of one of the quarter Blocks ; another piece is spliced into it, forming the Span (c), one Leg of which is bent to the inner Buntline Cringle on each side.

The Clew-Garnet (d), is reeved through its Block on the Yard (e), through the Block at the Clew, and the end is hitched round the Yard.

BENDING

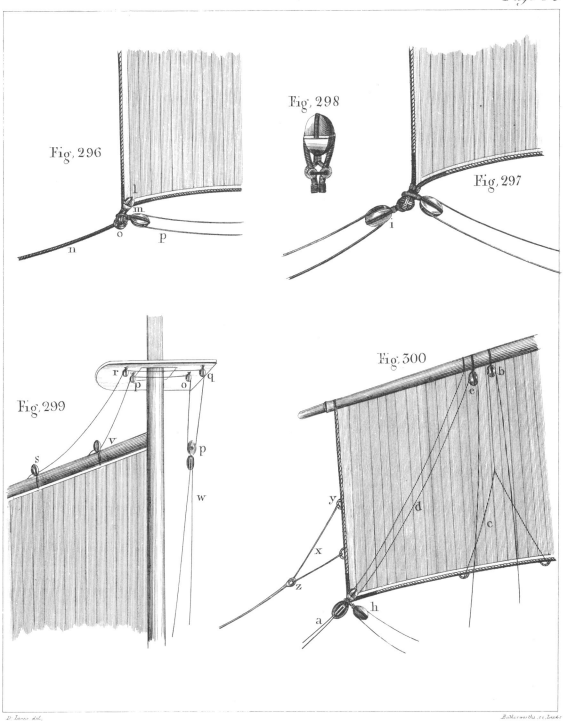

Fig. 296

Fig. 298

Fig. 297

Fig. 299

Fig. 300

D. Lever del.

Butterworths sc, Leeds.

Bending the Foresail, &c.

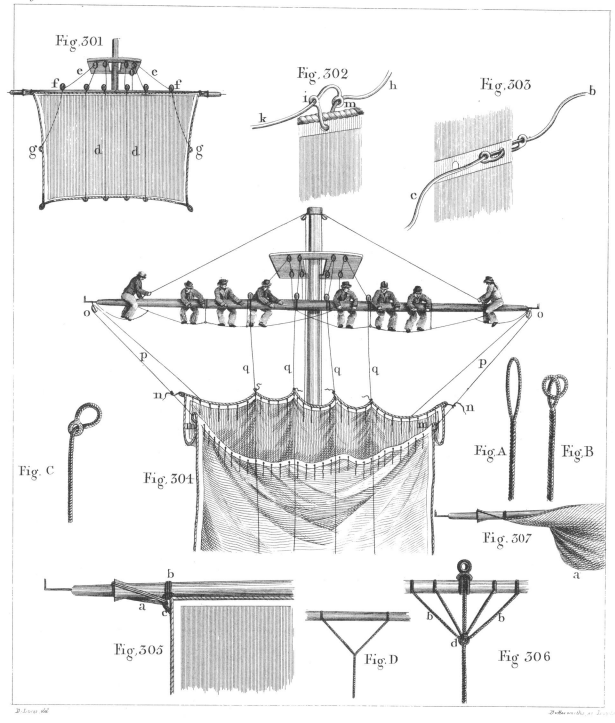

Fig. 301

Fig. 302

Fig. 303

Fig. C

Fig. 304

Fig. A

Fig. B

Fig. 307

Fig. 305

Fig. D

Fig. 306

BENDING THE FORESAIL.

The LEECH-LINES, Fig. 301,

Are reeved through the outer Sheave-holes of the outer Blocks, under the Top. The Leech-lines (e), are reeved through the Blocks (f), then through the Blocks on the Yard, and the ends are clinched to   * the upper Bow-line Cringles (g).---(d), the Bunt-lines.

The ROPE-BANDS and POINTS are put into the Sail thus : There is a long and short Rope-band, with an Eye in each, to every Eyelet hole in the Head of the Sail, Fig. 302. The end of the short Leg (h), goes through the hole in the Sail, the Eye (i), being before it : the end of the long Leg (k), is reeved through the Eye of the short one (i), and the end of the short one (h), through the Eye of the long one (m).

The POINTS are frequently of one piece, and being reeved through the Eyelet-holes in the Reef-band, an overhand Knot is cast on, on each side of the Sail : but they are frequently made with two Legs, having each an Eye in one end, Fig. A, but made much longer than those in the Rope-bands, which will admit a turn to be taken in them, (like Fig. B), when put through the Sail, making them double the Thickness. The Eye of one Point is put through the hole in the Reef-band, Fig. 303, on one side of the Sail, and the other through the same hole on the other side : the Eye of the Point (c), having a turn taken in it, as before mentioned, the end of the Point (b), is put through it, and the end of the Point (c), through the Eye of the Point (b), in the same manner : and commonly the Eyes are made the usual size : the end of the Point, Fig. C, is put through its own Eye, forming a larger Bight ; and the ends of each Point being reeved through the Eyelet-hole, are then put through the Eyes of each other.

A Line, called an *Earing* (n), Fig. 304, is spliced into the Head Cringle, on each side. When the Geer is bent, a Tail Block (o), is lashed on each Boom Iron, at the Yard-arm ; and a Rope (p), called a *Yard Rope*, is reeved through it, and bent to the Reef Cringle (m). The Bunt-lines (q), are stopped to the Head of the Sail, by hitching a Rope-band round each. The Head Earings (n), are hitched to the Yard-rope (p), for the Men at the Yard-arms to reach it more conveniently. The Men go on the Yard, and the Sail is hauled up to it by the Yard-ropes, Bunt-lines, and Clew-garnets.

The Men at the Yard-arms haul the Head of the Sail to an equal distance on each side : taking *two* Turns with the Earing (a), Fig. 305, round the Yard without the Stop-cleats, and through the Cringle (c) ; then as many turns (b), within the Cleats as will expend the whole Earing. The two *outer* Turns (a), are sufficient, being merely for the purpose of keeping the Head of the Sail on the stretch ; whereas the *inner* Turns (b), have the weight of the Tack, Sheet, and Bow-line, to sustain.

The Head of the Sail is then hauled well upon the Yard ; the *long* Legs of the Rope-bands (being *before* the Sail) are taken over and under the Yard with a round Turn ; and the *short* ones being brought up *abaft* it, they are made fast together by a Reef-Knot (see page 7). The Yard Ropes (p), are then cast off, unreeved, and the Tail Blocks taken from the Boom Irons. The Sail is now let fall : the Bunt-lines and Leech-lines overhauled, to see that every thing is bent clear, and the Gaskets (see page 11) made fast to the Yard. The BUNT-GASKET is generally made with three Legs, like Fig. D ; but if a long Leg be worked with an Eye in the Bight, Fig. 306, having a Thimble (d), seized in it, other Legs (b), may be reeved through it, and their ends made fast to the Yard.

When the Sail is to be furled, the Men on the Yard haul it up, leaving enough of the Head part (a), Fig. 307, hanging in a Bight, (which is called a *Skin)* to cover the folds. When it is all gathered up, this part (a), is brought over the rest, and all the Men exerting themselves at the same time, toss it well on the Top of the Yard. The Gaskets are then passed, being brought up before the Sail, and taken round the Yard and Sail. Care must be taken that both Rope-bands and Gaskets be taken clear of the Topsail Sheets. The Bunt Gasket, Fig. 306, is passed thus : the Middle Leg is taken round the Strap of the Slings, and the end reeved through the Thimble (d), by which a good purchase is got, to lift the Sail well on the Yard.

The FORE TOPSAIL

Is bent to the Fore Topsail Yard, and its shape depends on the squareness of that and the Fore Yard, to which the Clew or lower Corners are extended ; for which purpose the Cloths at the Leech are gored.

O   FORE

---

*Although original Erratum reads *"in line 4 from the top, for 'are reeved through these Blocks, then through the Blocks (f) on the Yard,' read 'are reeved through the Blocks (f), then through the Blocks on the Yard.'"*, it should be *"in line 4 from the top, for 'are reeved through the Blocks (f), then through the Blocks on the Yard,' read 'are reeved through these Blocks, then through the Blocks (f) on the Yard.'"*

FORE TOPSAIL.

This Sail, Fig. 308, has two, three, or four Reef-bands (a), at equal distances, with Cringles (b), the same as the Foresail. There are three Bow-line Cringles (c), the upper one of which is in the middle of the Sail: and a Cringle for the Reef-tackle Pendent (d), between the lower Reef and upper Bow-line Cringle. In the Merchant Service, the Reef-bands are not always placed at equal distances, some Masters chusing to have a greater space between the second and third Reef. On the *aft* side of the Sail, there is a Lining sometimes cut in steps, (which will be shewn in page 56, Fig. 317), called a *Top Lining*, to prevent the Sail's chafing when flapping against the Top; and sometimes the middle part of this Lining is carried up to the lower Reef-band, and called a *Mast Lining*. In the Merchant Service, these Linings are generally objected to; for it has been found by experience, that rain water lodging between the two parts of the Canvas, is apt to rot the Sail. This Sail is marled to the Clews as the Foresail was, which are served two feet or more on each side, and also at the foot, in the Wake of the Top-lining. Rope-bands are put in at the Head, and Points, in all the Reef-bands, as those in the Foresail were (see page 53).

In the Merchant Service, Patches (g), are frequently clapped on in the Wake of the Reef-tackle and Bowline Cringles; the strain on the first being very powerful when hauled out to reef the Sail, and on the last, when going by the Wind.

The Geer for this Sail is bent in the Top, except the *Bowline Bridles* and *Earings*, which are generally put in upon Deck. When it is brought on Deck to be bent, the Sail is opened out, to see that it has received no damage from Rats or Water; also that no Points, or Rope-bands be wanting. The Earings are spliced into the Head and Reef Cringles, Fig. 309. The end of the first Reef-earing (g), is hitched to the Head Cringle: the end of the second (h), to the first Reef Cringle; and the end of the third Reef-earing (i), to the second Reef Cringle.

As there are *three* Bowline Cringles, so there are two Bridles, the longest of which has an Eye spliced in one end. The upper end of the short Bridle (k), is clinched to the upper Cringle; the other end is reeved through the Thimble in the lower Bridle (l), and clinched to the middle Cringle (m). The long Bridle (l), is reeved through a Thimble spliced in the end of the Bow-line (n), and clinched to the lower Cringle (o). N.B. *The long Bridle is left to be reeved through the Thimble in the Bowline, when the Sail is in the Top.*

The Sail is then made up again, and the Clews laid out. A pair of Slings are laid upon Deck, and the Sail placed on them in Fakes, Fig. 310, with the *starboard* side uppermost, if it be sent up on the *larboard* side, as in the Figure, and vice versa. The Topsail Tye (p), is sometimes stopped, and racked to the aftermost Topmast Shroud; but as this is reckoned by some a great strain on the Shroud, the Bight of the Tye is often taken round the Topmast Cap (as mentioned in page 43). The lower Block of the Topsail Halliards (q), is hooked to the Slings, and the Sail is hoisted into the Top (r), taken round the fore part of the Mast, and opened out: The Stop of the Tye is then cast off, and the lower Block of the Halliards hooked to the Channel, as before.

The CLEW-LINE BLOCKS, which are strapped with two Legs, like the Clew Garnet Blocks of the Foresail, are put through the Clews, and seized in the same manner (see page 52).

The Clew-Lines, Fig. 311, on each side are reeved through the Blocks on the Topsail Yards, then through the Blocks at the Clew (r), and the ends hitched round the Yard without the Blocks: the leading parts (t), go through Lubber's Hole.

The TOPSAIL SHEET having a double walled Knot, double crowned (see page 5) on the end, is thrust through the Clew, the Knot (u), lying aft. The Sheet is served, to prevent its chafing in the Blocks, and against the lower Yard: it is reeved through the Shoulder Block at the lower Yard-arm (w), then through the quarter Block (x), lying under the Yard at the Sling Cleats, and through a Sheave-hole in the Topsail Sheet Bitts.

The Reef Tackle Pendent is clinched to the Cringle, and leads, as described in page 38.

TOPSAIL

Blunt's Figures 311 and 313 (see Appendix 18) appear to dispense with one of the clew-line blocks. His description differs, in that it mentions use of chain for sheets, perhaps indicative of the trend to lower maintenance.

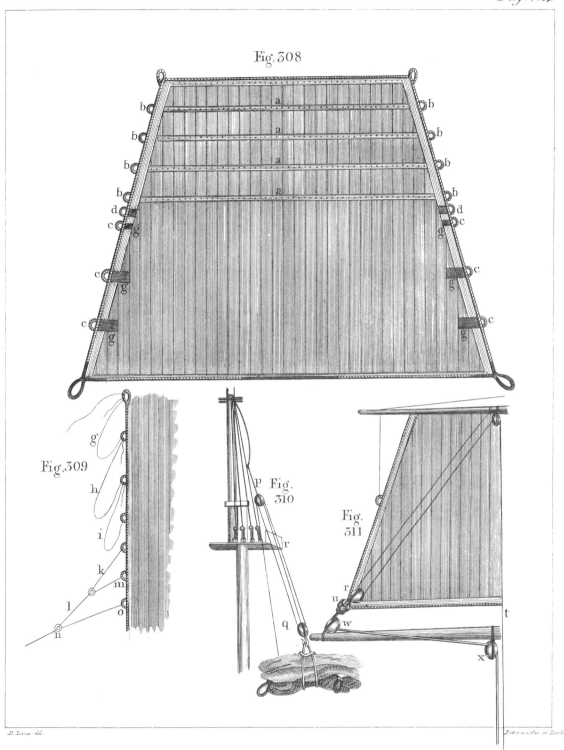

Fig. 308

Fig. 309

Fig. 310

Fig. 311

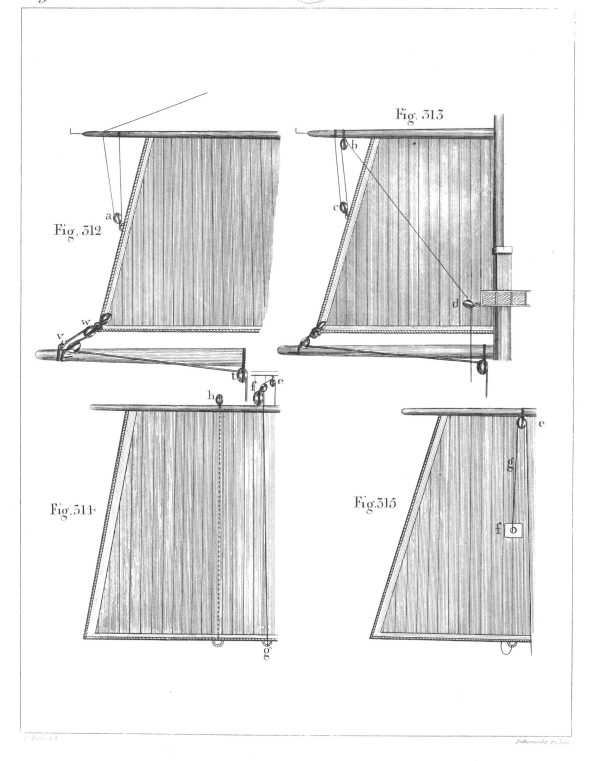

Fig. 312

Fig. 313

Fig. 314

Fig. 315

FORE TOPSAIL GEER.

The Topsail Sheet Knot is not generally used in the Merchant Service; but a small Clinch is cast on the End of the Topsail Sheet, which is not so apt to neck as the Knot.

The TOPSAIL SHEETS,

Sometimes lead double, Fig. 312: and when this is the case, there is frequently no Shoulder-block on the Yard Arm; but a Strap, with a Thimble seized in, is put over it. The Sheet on this account is smaller, and has a Hook and Thimble (v), spliced in its lower End: this is hooked to the Strap on the Yard Arm; the other End is reeved through a Block (w), which is seized in the Clew of the Sail, then through a Sheave-hole (or Block) in the Yard Arm, and through the quarter Block (t), leading down as before.

The REEF TACKLE PENDENTS,

Also often go double, Fig. 312. The Pendent is reeved through the Sheave-hole in the Yard Arm as before, then through a Block (a), which is seized to the Cringle, and the End is clinched round the Yard Arm: and in Merchant Ships where there are few Hands, a Block (b), Fig. 313, is strapped round the Yard Arm, another (c), to the Cringle, and a third (d), to the Top. The Pendent reeves through the Block (d), at the Top, the Block (b), at the Yard Arm, the Block (c), at the Cringle, and the End is clinched round the Yard Arm as before. When the Sail (after being close reefed) is handed, the weather Reef-Tackle being boused taught, acts as a rolling Tackle.

The BUNT-LINE, Fig. 314,

Is reeved through the Block (e), lashed on each Side under the Cross Trees, the Block (f), at the Strap of the Tye-Block, and (leading before the Sail) is clinched to the Cringle (g), at the Foot. In the Merchant Service, Monkey-Blocks (see page 14), are often nailed on the Yard (h): the Bunt-lines in this case are not taken to the Mast-Head; but are reeved through these Blocks, and bent to the Cringles in the Foot of the Sail, like the dotted Line. In the former Method, it is thought they prevent the Yard coming down readily; but in the latter Mode, they act as down-haul Tackles, and have equally the Effect of spilling the Sail. The principal Objection to the Monkey-blocks are, * that the Bunt-lines do not overhaul so well; for when the Yard is at the Mast-Head their Weight lies directly from the Yard to the Deck.

Another Way is to lead the Bunt-lines like Fig. 315. A Block strapped with two Legs (e), is lashed on the Yard, hanging underneath it, abaft the Sail. An Eyelet Hole with a Brass Thimble is worked in a Patch (f), just below the third Reef and the Bunt-line (g), is led through the Block (e), the Thimble (f), and bent to the Foot Cringle as before. The Sail may thus be easily spilled for handing, and the Bunt-line cannot chafe it, except in the Wake of the Bunt-line Cloth.

The Sail is hauled up to the Yard by the Reef-Tackles, (as the Foresail was by the Yard-Ropes), the Bunt-lines, and Clew-lines. The Bunt-lines are stopped to the Head of the Sail by the Rope-bands, and the Earings passed like those of the Foresail (see page 53), taking care to pass the Rope-bands clear of the Top-Gallant Sheets.

The

*Although original Erratum reads *"in line 26, for 'the principal Objection is,' read 'the principal Objection are.'"*, it should be *"in line 26, for 'The principal Objection to the Monkey-blocks are,' read 'The principal Objection to the Monkey-blocks is.'"*

FORE TOPSAIL—FORE TOP GALLANT SAIL.

The Clew-lines and Bunt-lines being eased off, the Sheets are hauled home to the Yard Arms: the Sail is then hoisted up by the Halliards to see if all be bent clear. When hoisted, the fore Part will appear like Fig. 316, and the after Part like Fig. 317.

Fig. 316.	Fig. 317.
(a) *The Bunt-lines.*	(i) *The Clew-lines.*
(b) *The Bunt-line Cloths.*	(k) *The Braces.*
(c) *The Leech-Linings.*	(l) *The Mast and Top-linings.*
(d) *The Reef-bands with Points.*	(m) *The Topsail Sheets.*
(e) *The Bow-lines and Bridles.*	(o) *The Top.*
(f) *The Topsail Sheet Blocks,*	
(g) *The Reef-tackle Pendents.*	(q) *The Lower Lifts.*
(h) *The Jewel Blocks.*	

Topsails in Men of War are square at the Foot, like Fig. 316; but in Merchantmen, they are often gored. The gored Foot is made to prevent its chafing against the lower Stay; but a deal of Wind is lost by it. If the squared Foot, and also the lower Stay be well leathered, in light Winds when the Sail is liable to flap, the Foot resting every Time against the Stay, will not permit the Sail to come with any Violence against the Top-rim. The Sail is lowered down, clewed up, and handed as the Foresail was. (See page 53, where also see Points and Gaskets.)

The FORE TOP-GALLANT SAIL, Fig. 318,

Is bent to the Fore Top-Gallant Yard. The Leeches are gored to spread at the Foot to the Top-Gallant Sheet Blocks (g), (or Sheave-holes) at the Topsail Yard Arms: the Foot is squared in the Royal Navy; but in the Merchant Service gored as the Topsail was.

This Sail is often bent on Deck before the Yard is sent up; but if not, the Clew-lines (h), Fig. 319, (having Ropes bent to them to give them length), are over-hauled down, and it is hoisted by them into the Cross-trees, where the Men lay it fair for bending. This Sail, Fig. 318, has two Bowline Cringles on each Side, (the upper one being in the middle of the Leech-rope), to which the Bridles (a), are bent, having an Eye seized in the Bight: the Bowline (b), has a Toggle in the End, which is thrust through it.

The BUNT-LINE (c),

Is reeved through a Block (d), at the Top-Gallant Mast Head, and through a Thimble seized to the Strap of the Top-Gallant Tye; another Piece being spliced into it, forms a Span (e), each Leg of which is clinched to the Cringles (f), at the Foot.

The TOP-GALLANT SHEET, Fig. 320,

Having a double Wall Knot cast on the End, is thrust through the Clew (a); but in the Merchant Service, it either goes with a Clinch as before mentioned for the Topsail Sheet, or is made fast to the Clew with a Sheet Bend, (see page 8), and the End stopped to the standing Part. If the CLEW-LINE is led double, a Block (b), is seized to the Clew: the Clew-line is reeved through the Block on the Yard (c), through the Block (b), and the End is made fast round the Yard without the Block (c). The *single* Clew-line is taken up through the Top, reeved through the Block (d), and bent to the Clew.

The Geer being bent, a couple of Rope-bands are hitched round the Bunt-line Legs as before: the Men go on the Yard, and pass the Earings and Rope-bands as they did those on the Topsail. The Sail is then handed, having one long Gasket on each Side, and another shorter in the Bunt.

BOW-LINES.

*Blunt mentions that the Top-Gallant Sheet may be chain.

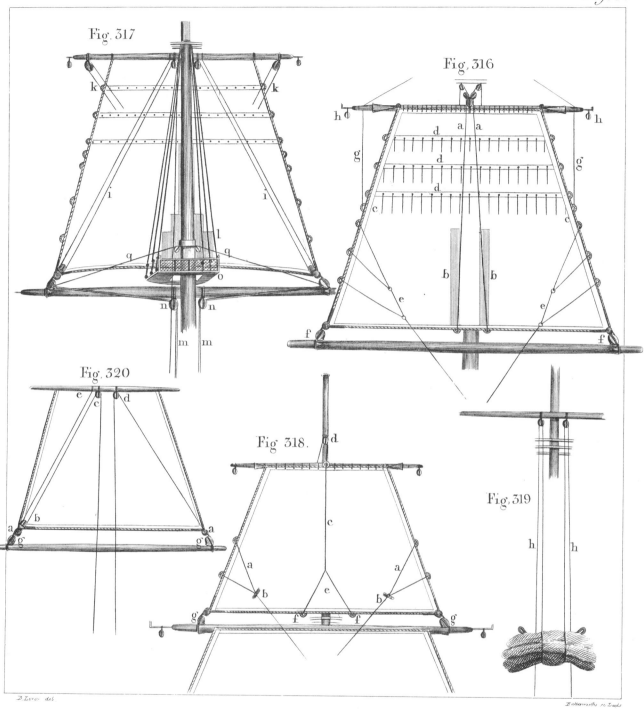

Fig. 317

Fig. 316

Fig. 320

Fig. 318.

Fig. 319

D. Lever del.

Butterworths & Leeds

Bowlines — Sheets &c.

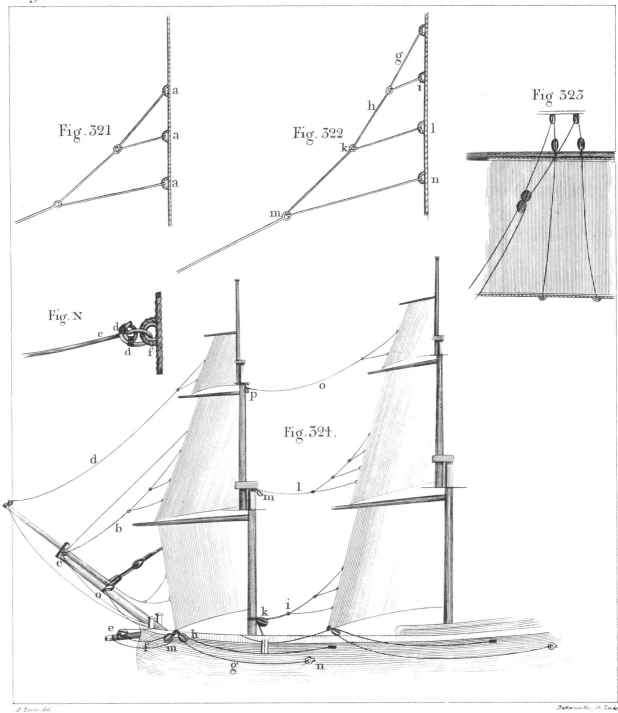

Fig. 321

Fig. 322

Fig 323

Fig. N

Fig. 324.

BOW - LINES, SHEETS, &c.

The MAINSAIL has its Geer bent like the Foresail: it is larger than the latter, and wider at the Foot than the Head; having a Cloth on each side gored for that purpose. It has three Bow-line Cringles (a), Fig. 321.

The MAIN TOPSAIL is bent and rigged like the Fore Topsail (see page 54); but has sometimes *four* Reefs, and in Men of War and East Indiamen *four* Bow-line Cringles, consequently *three* Bridles; the middle and lower one having an Eye and Thimble spliced in the end of each, leading thus :--- The *upper* Bridle (g), Fig. 322, is clinched to the *upper* Cringle, reeved through the Thimble in the end of the *middle* Bridle (h), and clinched to the second Cringle (i): the middle Bridle (h), is reeved through the Thimble in the end of the *lower* Bridle (k), and clinched to the third Cringle (l): the *lower* Bridle (k), is reeved through a Thimble in the end of the Bow-line (m), and clinched to the *fourth* Cringle (n).

The Clinch is made like Fig. N, the End of the Bridle is reeved through the Cringle (f), taken round the standing Part (e), forming a Circle; two round Seizings (d), are then clapped on.--- N.B. *The Clinch is always made less than the Cringle, &c. through which it is reeved.*

The MIZEN TOPSAIL has only two Reefs, and three, and sometimes two Bow-line Cringles. The Main and Mizen Top Gallant Sails are rigged like the Fore Top Gallant Sail.

In Men of War, where the Main Bunt-lines go with Shoe-blocks, they lead forwards like Fig. 323.

In order to shew how the *Bow-lines, Tacks,* and *Sheets* of these Sails lead, their Profiles or Leeches are given, Figure 324.

The FORE BOW-LINE is reeved through a Block (o), which is lashed to the Fore Stay Collar, or sometimes strapped to an Eye-bolt in the Bowsprit close to it, leading in upon the Fore-castle. The Fore Bow-line in the Merchant Service frequently goes with a Toggle, as before mentioned; so that when going long on one Tack, the lee one is cast off, which prevents it from chafing the Sail.

The FORE TOP BOW-LINE (b), is reeved through a Block (c), strapped to an Eye-bolt in the Bowsprit Cap, leading in on the Fore-castle, as before.

The FORE TOP GALLANT BOW-LINE (d), is reeved through a Thimble strapped to the Jib Boom End.

The FORE TACK (f), is led through the Block (e), strapped round the Boomkin end, through the Block (m), at the Clew, and the end is clinched round the Boomkin end: the other end is taken in on the Fore-castle.

The FORE SHEET (g), is reeved through a Sheave-hole in the side, at the after part of the Waist, (or in the Coasting Trade through a Snatch Block lashed there for that purpose); then through the Block (h), at the Clew of the Sail, and the end is clinched round an Eye-bolt in the side (n).

The MAIN BOW-LINE (i), is reeved through a double Block (k), lashed to the after side of the Foremast: the *starboard* Bow-line is belayed on the *larboard* side, and the larboard Bow-line on the starboard side. In small Ships in the Merchant Service, a Thimble is seized into the lower Bow-line Bridle: one end of the Bow-line is made fast to the Cross Piece or Bellfry, and the other being reeved through the Thimble in the Bridle, is belayed to the Cross Piece, so that it is unreeved every Tack.

The MAIN TOP BOW-LINE (l), is reeved through a Block (m), seized to an Eye-bolt in the after part of the Fore Cap, (or lashed round the Foremast Head above the Rigging) leading down through the Top.

The MAIN TOP GALLANT BOW-LINE (o), is reeved through a Block (p), lashed to the Fore Topmast Cross Trees: sometimes the space between the after part of the Fore Topmast Tressle-trees is filled up with a Chock, having four Sheave-holes, two for the Main Top Gallant Bow-lines, and two for the Braces, when they lead *forward*.

P

ROYALS

ROYALS—SPRITSAIL, &c.

The MIZEN BOWLINE, when a Mizen Yard is carried, Fig. 325, is reeved through a Block (p), strapped to the Eye Bolt in the lower Yard Arm : one End is clinched to an Eye Bolt in the Side, and the other is belayed to a Cleat there.

The MIZEN TOP-BOWLINE (q), is reeved through a Block (r), seized to the aftermost Main Shroud under the Futtock Stave, and through another (s), seized to the same about six Feet from the Deck. It is sometimes reeved through a Block seized to the Main Tressle-tree, or after Part of the Main Top.

The MIZEN TOP-GALLANT BOWLINE (t), (seldom used in small Vessels), is reeved through a Sheave-hole in the aftermost Main Topmast Cross-tree, or through a small Block or Thimble seized there.

* The ROYAL YARDS are seldom rigged across. When they are, they have a Royal Mast fidded on the Tressle-trees at the Top Gallant Mast Heads ; and the Masts and Yards are rigged like the Top-Gallant ones.

When these Masts are not stepped, the Royals, Fig. 326, are set flying ; that is, they are not rigged across, having neither Lifts nor Braces, (through sometimes the latter) ; but the Sail being bent to the Yard with Rope-bands made of Sennit, the Halliards which are reeved through the Sheave-hole in the Pole Head of the Top-gallant Mast are overhauled down on Deck, hitched to the Slings of the Yard, and stopped to the *starboard* Yard Arm (if the Yard be sent up on the *larboard* side), like the Top-Gallant Yard (see page 47), and it is hoisted up by them. The Boy at the Mast Head having cut the Stops, secures it to the Top-Gallant Yard by a Becket for that purpose, and the Clews are lashed to the Top-Gallant Yard Arms. If it be not set at the Time it is got up, the Halliards are unbent and made fast to the Top-Gallant Stay, that they may not impede the Top-Gallant Yard, when lowering down ; but if it be set and the Fore Top Gallant Stay (b), go with a Traveller, the Stay is let go and the Halliards being hoisted on, it traverses up with the Royal Yard by the Traveller (c), to which it is spliced. When the Sail is up, the Stay is set hand taught. If the Stay do not go with a Traveller, the Royal Yard and of course one of the Sheets must be shifted over it.

The SPRITSAIL, Fig. 327, is bent to the Spritsail Yard with Earings, and Rope-bands, as the other Square-Sails were. This Sail is neither gored at the Foot nor the Leeches : the Reef-bands (a), are not sewed athwart parallel to the head Tabling, but diagonally from the Leech to the Head. There are two Buntline Cringles (c), at the Foot ; and as this Sail, from its Situation under the Bowsprit, is liable to be immersed in the Water, there is a Hole (d), called a *Water-hole*, cut and stitched round in each Side, to let the Water off, that it may not lodge in the Bag of the Sail.

The SPRITSAIL SHEET (e), when double, has a *strap-bound* Block (like a Clew-line Block), the Ends of the Strap are thrust through the Holes in the Cheeks, and a Spritsail Sheet Knot, (see page 6), cast on the two ends : a round Seizing is clapped on between the Block and the Knot ; and the Knot is thrust through the Clew. The Sheet (e), is reeved through this Block, and the standing Part made fast to an Eye-bolt in the Bows. When the SHEET is single (f), it has a double walled Knot double crowned (see page 5), cast on one End, which is thrust through the Clew (i), or otherwise it is bent to the Clew with a Sheet-bend (see page 8), and the End stopped to the standing Part, leading in on the Forecastle.

The CLEW-LINE BLOCKS (g), if the Clew-lines be double), are seized to the Clews like those of the other square Sails (see Clew Garnet Block page 52). The Clew-line is reeved through the Block on the Yard (h), through the Block at the Clew (g), and the End is hitched round the Yard without the Block (h), leading in on the Forecastle. If they lead single, they are reeved through the Blocks on the Yard, and bent to the Clews (i).

The BUNT-LINES are reeved through small Blocks (k), strapped on each Side of the Bowsprit, then through Thimbles or Blocks (l), on the Yard, and the Ends are clinched to the Cringles (c), at the Foot. When going by the Wind, the Spritsail Yard is topped up by the lee Brace, (suppose the larboard one) : the Sail is then obliged to be reefed to prevent it dragging in the Water : when reefed, it will appear like Fig. 328, which shews the fore Side.

SPRITSAIL

Blunt describes changes in rigging the Royal Yards, as follows.

The ROYAL YARDS are now rigged across. The sails are bent to the yards before the yards are sent aloft for sea service. Ships which carry pole top-gallant masts, as shown in Fig. 274, have frequently in addition what is called sliding gunter sky-sail masts, which are small spars secured to the royal-mast head by a boom iron, and resting in an iron heel on the after part of the top-gallant mast: the heel is also lashed.

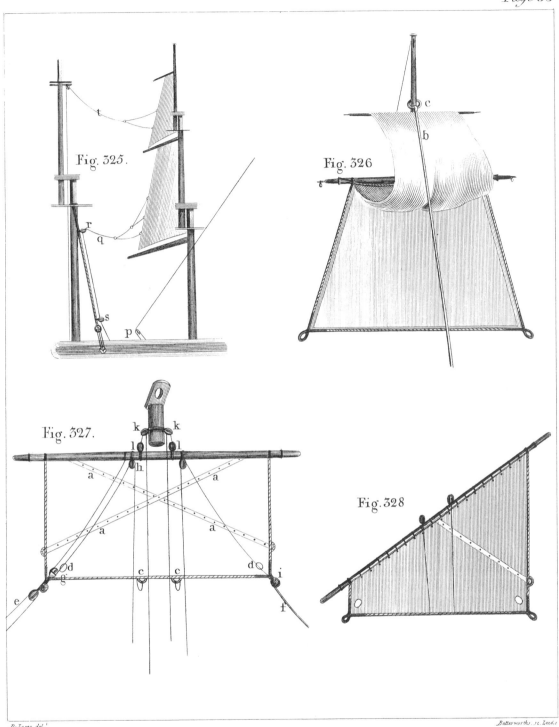

Fig. 325.

Fig. 326

Fig. 327.

Fig. 328.

D: Lever del.

Butterworths sc. Leeds

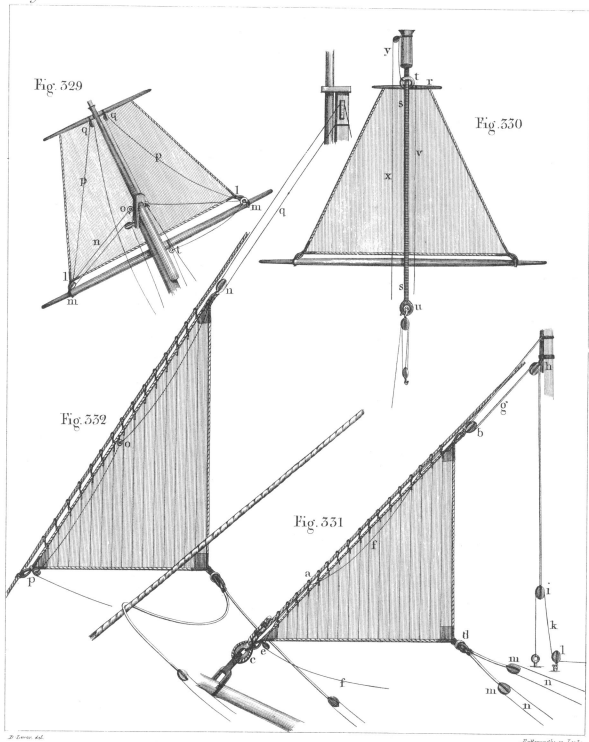

Fig. 329

Fig. 330

Fig. 332

Fig. 331

D. Lever, del.

Butterworths sc. Leeds

SPRITSAIL - TOPSAILS—STAYSAILS.

The SPRITSAIL TOPSAIL depends in shape on the Spritsail Topsail Yard, and is gored sufficiently to spread the Clews to the Spritsail Yard Arms. This Sail, Fig. 329, is bent with Rope Bands and Earings; but has no Reef Bands. Sometimes when the *Spritsail* Lifts go double, they have Hooks in the ends, which when this Sail is not set are hooked to Eye-bolts (o), in the Bowsprit Cap; but when the Spritsail Topsail is set, they are hooked to Thimbles in the Clews (l), and act as Spritsail Topsail Sheets. When the Lifts (n), go single, a Thimble is strapped on the Spritsail Yard Arm (m), another at the Slings of the Yard (t), and a Sheet is reeved like a Top Gallant Sheet.

The Clew-lines (p), are reeved through Thimbles, or Blocks (q), without the Slings of the Yard, and bent to the Clews, as before.

This Sail in East Indiamen is often set flying with a very short Yard (r), Fig. 330; for this purpose, a Horse or Jack Stay (s), is clinched round the end of the Jib Boom, having an iron Traveller on it (t), and set up with a Luff Tackle hooked to a Thimble (u), spliced in the inner end, leading in on the Fore-castle. The Yard (r), is seized to the Traveller, and the Clews to the Spritsail Yard Arms. When the Sail is taken in, it is furled in with the Spritsail, as the Royal is with the Top Gallant Sail. The Halliards (x), are single; they are led through a Block (y), at the Jib Boom end, and belayed on the Fore-castle. An In-hauler (v), is bent to the Yard, and is also led on the Fore-castle.

The FORE STAYSAIL, Fig. 331, is triangular, and holes being worked in the Tabling of the Head or Stay part, it is bent to Hanks on the Fore Spring Stay (a), made of ash or iron, and sometimes of Rope. This Sail is regularly gored on the Stay part; the after Leech and Foot are not gored. At the upper Clew, which is called the *Peak*, a Block (b), is seized for the Halliards. To the foremost Clew, which is called the *Tack*, a Laniard is spliced, which is made fast, by passing it alternately through the Heart (c), and the foremost Clew. At the Tack (c), Clue (d), and Peak (b), a Patch of additional Canvas is sewn.

The Down-hauler (f), is reeved through a Block (e), seized to the Tack Clew, through a few Hanks at the lower Clew, and through a few at the Head, bending to the Peak: and sometimes like that in the next Figure.
The Halliards (g), are reeved through a Block (h), which is lashed round the Foremast Head above the Rigging, or under the Collar of the Fore Stay, through the Block (b), at the Peak, and the end is clinched round the Mast Head. A single Block (i), is turned into the other end, and a Fall (k), is reeved through a leading Block (l), through the Block (i), and the end is clinched to an Eye-bolt in the side. This Sail is seldom used in any Ships but Men of War.

The SHEETS are made with a Pendent, the Bight of which is put through the Clew, and the ends through the Bight; this has the same appearance as a Reef Knot; the two parts are then seized together with a *throat* Seizing (see page 9). Sometimes they are made fast with a *Sheet Bend* to the Clew (see page 8), and the parts seized together, as before. A single Block (m), is spliced into the end of each Pendent: a Sheet (n), is reeved through each of these, one end of which is clinched to an Eye-bolt in the side, and the other taken through a leading Block belaying to a Cleat in the side.

The FORE-TOPMAST STAYSAIL, Fig, 332,
Is seized to Hanks on the Fore Topmast *Spring Stay*. The Halliards (q), in large Ships, are reeved through a Cheek-block on the *larboard* side of the Fore Topmast Head, and are either bent to the Peak, or reeved through a Block (n), seized to it, the end being clinched round the Mast Head. In the other end a single Block is turned, the Fall reeving like that abovementioned for the Fore Staysail. In the Merchant Service, when there are no Cheek-blocks at the Mast Head, the Halliards are reeved through one of the Sheave-holes of the double Blocks, which hang on each side of the Mast Head, under the Rigging (see page 27, Fig. 190), or through Blocks lashed for that purpose under the fore part of the Fore Topmast Tressle-trees. They go single, leading through a Block in the side, as before.

The Sheets go with Pendents like the Fore-Staysail Sheets, leading clear over the Fore Stay; but in smaller Vessels they lead single, being reeved through a Block on the Forecastle.

The Down-hauler is led through a Block (p), strapped to the Tack Clew, and either through a few Hanks like the Fore-Staysail Down-hauler, or through a Thimble (o), strapped to the Head Rope.

JIB,

Blunt's version of Figure 331 shows simpler rigging at the fore foot of the Fore Staysail (see Appendix 19).

J I B, &c.

The *JIB STAY* leads according to the form of the Traveller on the Boom. If it be made like Fig. 333, having a Shackle (p), with a Roller in it at the Top, the Stay is clinched round the Mast Head, or put over it with an Eye : the other End is reeved through the Shackle in the Traveller (p), Fig. 334, and through the Sheave-hole in the End of the Jib Boom (o) : a double or a long Tackle Block (q), is turned into the End, which is connected by its Fall (r), to a single Block (n), strapped to an Eye Bolt in the fore Part of the Bowsprit Cap, or to a Bolt in the Bows, leading it upon the Forecastle. In this Case there is no occasion for an *Out-hauler*, it answering the Purpose of both Stay and Out-hauler.

When the Traveller is made like Fig. 335, having a Shackle (s), without a Roller, a Hook (t), within the Shackle and a Thimble (u), between the Hook and Shackle, then the Stay is reeved through the upper Cheek Block on the *starboard* Side of the Fore Topmast Head, (or in the Merchant Service through the Sheave of a double Block, hanging under the Rigging, (see page 27), or lashed to the Tressle-Tree), and is clinched to the Thimble (u), on the Traveller, Fig. 336. In the other End a single or double Block is turned, connected by a Fall to a single one, strapped to the lower Tressel-tree, leading down through the Top. In smaller Vessels it goes with a single Whip, one End being made fast to the Tressle-tree.

An *Out-Hauler* (v), is reeved through the Sheave-hole in the Boom End, clinched to the Shackle on the Traveller, and set up with a long Tackle-block, as above mentioned, to the Bowsprit Cap or Bows.

The *JIB*, Fig. 337,

Is a triangular Sail, bent to the Hanks on the Jib Stay. This Sail in the Royal Navy is generally gored at the Foot upwards from the Tack to the Clew; but in the Merchant Service it is often cut with a Gore downwards (a), at the Foot, and this is called a *roach Gore*. If there be a Hook on the Traveller, a Thimble is seized in the *Tack* Clew, and the Hook put through it. The *DOWN-HAULER* is reeved through a small Block (b), seized to the Traveller, up through a *few* Hanks at the Head and Foot, or Thimbles (w), seized to the Head-rope, and made fast to the Peak; the other End leading in on the Forecastle. The *IN-HAULER* (c), is reeved through another Block (d), seized to the Traveller, and the end made fast to an Eye-bolt in the Bowsprit Cap; the other end leading in on the Forecastle. Small Ships have no In-hauler, the Down-hauler answering both purposes.

The *SHEETS* go with Pendents, which are bent to the Clew as before mentioned for the Fore-staysail : single Blocks (f), are spliced in the Ends; the Sheets (g), are reeved through these, one End of each being clinched to an Eye Bolt in the Bows, and the other led through a leading Block, or a Hole in a Timber Head on the Forecastle. These Sheets are passed clear over the Fore-Topmast Stay (h).

The *HALLIARDS* are reeved through the *lower* cheek Block at the *starboard* Side of the Fore-Topmast Head (or in the Merchant Service through a Block put over the Mast Head under the Rigging, or otherwise seized to the Fore Topmast Tressle-trees), and in large Ships through a Block (i), seized to the Peak Clue: the End is clinched round the Mast Head. The other End leading down abaft the Top is reeved through a Block strapped to an Eye Bolt in the Side.

Although the Jib Boom is secured by the Guys, leading over the Spritsail Yard, (see page 31), yet as the tendency of the Jib when set, is to lift the Boom *upwards*, it is steadied down thus : two large iron Staples or Caps are driven into the fore Side of the Bowsprit Cap, and a Bar (k), called a *Dolphin-striker* is stepped in them : in this, there are two Sheave-holes for the Martingale Stays. The *outer MARTINGALE STAY* (n), is clinched round the Boom end, or goes over it with an Eye, reeved through the lower Sheave-hole in the Dolphin-Striker, through a Block (m), strapped in a Span on the Bowsprit just within the Fore Stay Collar on the *larboard* Side, leading in on the Forecastle ; and sometimes having a Block turned in the end, setting up either with a Gun-tackle Purchase, or a single Whip (see page 16). The *inner* one (l), is clinched to the Traveller, reeved through the *upper* Sheave-hole in the Dolphin-striker, through the Block in the Span on the opposite Side, and is set up as before. In some Ships there are two Dolphin-strikers (having a Sheave in each), which project rather outwards on each Side. Many Vessels have only the outer Martingale-Stay ; but the inner one is very serviceable when the Jib is a third, or half in, as it acts immediately under the Stay.   MAIN

---

*Although original Erratum reads *"line 6 from the top, for 'leading in,' read 'leading it.'"*, it should be *"line 6 from the top, for 'leading it,' read 'leading in.'"*

**Blunt shows changes in rigging aft of the Jib in Figure 337 (see Appendix 20).*

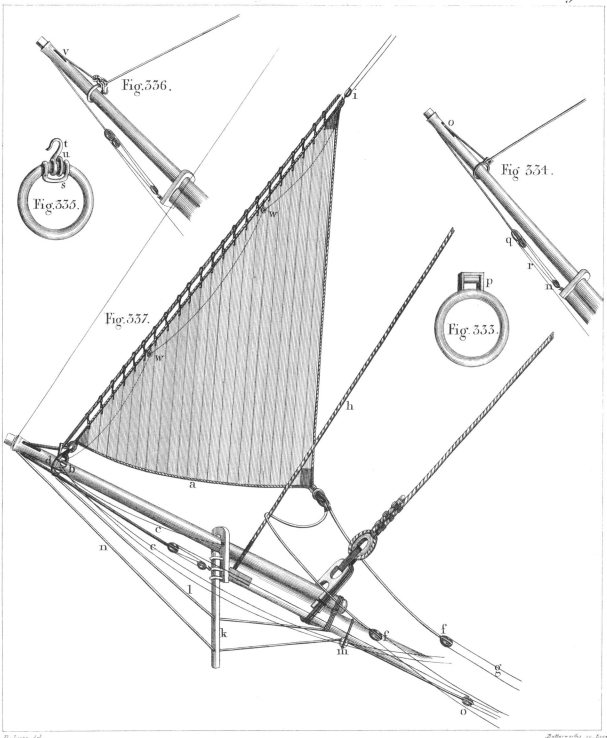

Fig. 336.

Fig. 335.

Fig. 337.

Fig. 334.

Fig. 333.

Fig. K

Fig. 338

Fig. H

Fig. 339

Fig. 340

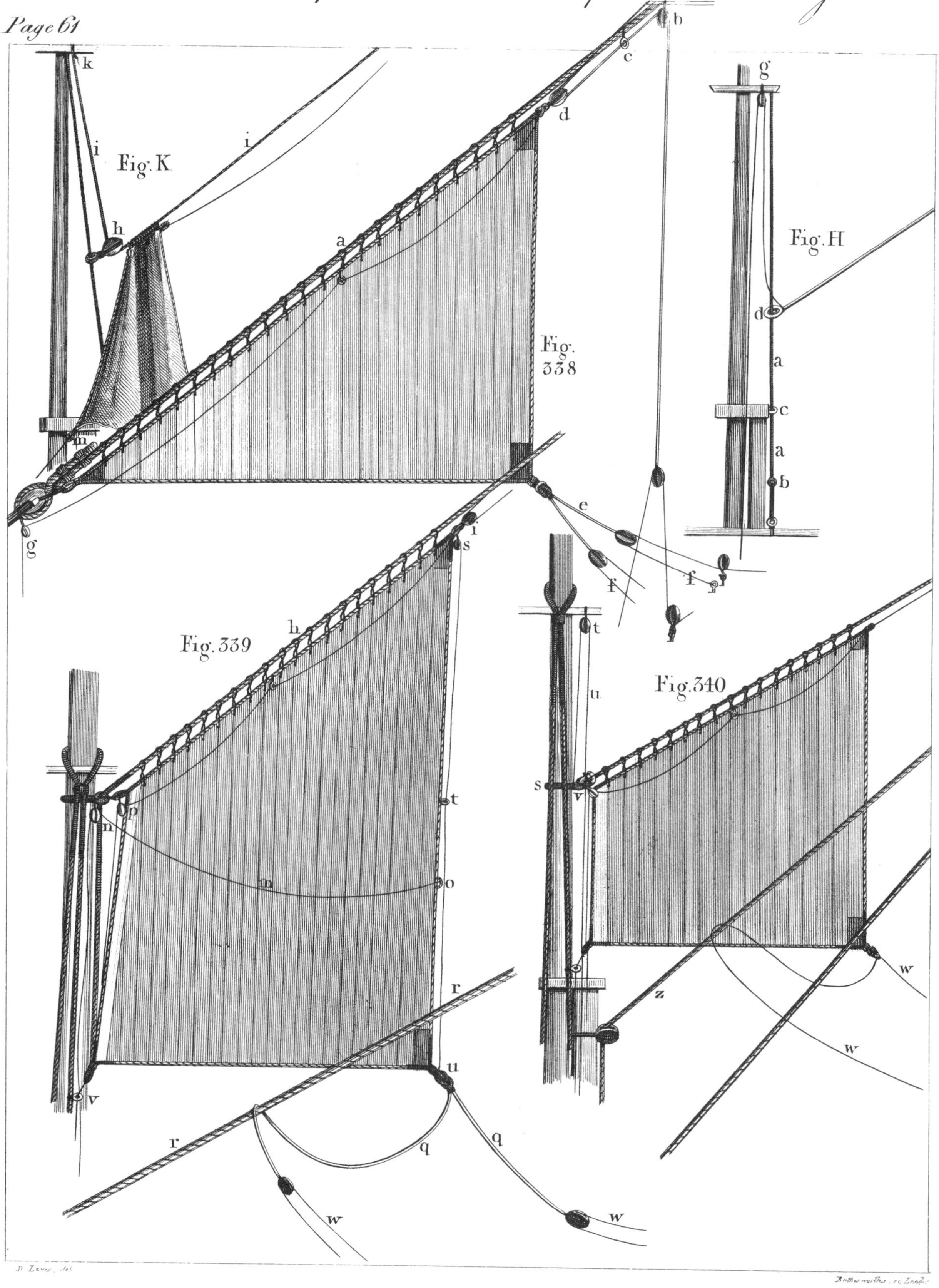

Main----Main Topmast, and Middle Staysails----Jack Stay. &c.

The MAIN STAYSAIL is seldom used, unless for laying to under; except by Brigs, and Ships which carry fore and aft Mainsails, in which Fashion many are now rigged. It is triangular, and traverses by its Hanks on the Main *Spring* Stay (a), Fig. 338. The Tack is made fast to the Stay Collar. The *Halliards* are double; they are reeved through a Block (b), lashed round the Main Mast Head, or hanging at the fore Part of the Main Tressle-tree, through a Block or Thimble seized to the Stay (c), then through a Block (d), at the Peak, and the End is clinched round the Mast Head above the Rigging.

The SHEETS have Pendents (e), which are bent to the Clew as before: one End of the Sheet (f) is clinched to an Eye-bolt or Timber Head near the Gangway, the other is reeved through the Block in the Pendent (e), and through another at the Gangway. The DOWN-HAULER (g), is reeved through a Block on the Stay Collar, and either through a few Hanks near the Tack and Peak, or through a Thimble strapped to the Head of the Sail, as before.

The MAIN TOPMAST STAYSAIL, Fig. 339, and all the Staysails abaft the Fore-Mast (except the Main Staysail), have a fore Leech which is called the *Bunt*, lined with an additional Cloth; but in the Merchant Service, a Cloth of stronger Canvas is put in at the Bunt, which answers the same purpose. This Sail traverses by its Hanks on the Main Topmast Spring Stay (h). The HALLIARDS in Men of War are reeved through the Cheek-Blocks on the starboard Side of the Main Topmast Head; but in Merchant-men through a Block, which goes with a Span round the Main Topmast Head, before the Rigging is put over: then through the Block (i), seized to the Peak, and the End is clinched (see page 57), round the Main Topmast Head. The Fall is reeved through a leading Block, strapped to an Eye Bolt in the Side.

The BRAILS (m), are reeved through the Sheave-holes of a double Block (n), seized to the Collar on the Fore Mast, and bent to the Cringle (o), on each Side.

The DOWN-HAULER leads up through a Block (p), seized to the upper Tack of the Sail, through the Thimble strapped to the Head Rope (or through a few Hanks at the Tack and Peak), through a small Block (s) at the Peak, and through the Thimble (t), in the Middle of the after Leech, the end being bent to the Clew (u). This Method answers very well for the Down-hauler. These Sails are now cut so deep, that it is sometimes difficult in working, to get the Sheets (q), over the Main Stay (r); but by hauling on this Down-hauler, it trices the Clew up, so that they are easily shifted: and by this, and the Brails (m), when the Sail is taken in, it is gathered well for the Men in the Catharpins to stow it away. The upper Tack is made fast to the Thimble in the Strap round the Foremast. The lower Tack being middled, is reeved on each Side through a Block (v), seized to one of the Fore Shrouds.

The SHEETS (w), have Pendents as before, one End being made fast to a Timber-head abaft the Gangway, the other reeved through the Block in the Pendent (q), and through a leading Block at the Gangway. The Pendents are led clear over the Main Stay (r).

The MIDDLE STAYSAIL STAY, Fig. 340, is reeved through the upper Sheave of the Cheek-Block on the *larboard* Side of the Main Topmast Head; and a Gromet (s), with an Eye and Thimble in it, being worked round the Foremast, it is led through the Hanks, and clinched to the Thimble. A Block (t), is seized to the Fore Topmast Cross-Trees, and a Rope called a *Tricing-Line* (u), is reeved through and bent to the Gromets (s). Instead of this Tricing-Line (u), the Stay is frequently put with an Eye over the Main Topmast Head, reeved through the Thimble in the Gromet (s), through the Block at the Cross Trees (t), and led down through Lubber's Hole, tricing itself up. The Gromet round the Fore Topmast is now seldom used, but a JACK STAY (a), Fig. H. having a thimble (b), spliced or turned into its lower end, is reeved through a thimble (c), in an Eye-bolt at the aft Side of the Fore Cap, through another (d), and is either clinched round the Mast Head, or one of the Tressle-trees. The Middle Staysail Stay is reeved as before, and clinched round the Thimble (d): a Block (g), is seized to the Fore Topmast Cross Trees, and a tricing Line reeved through it, being hitched to the Stay, just above the Thimble (d): this trices the Stay up to its proper height. The DOWN-HAULER is reeved as before. The upper Tack (v), Fig. 340, is made fast to the Jack Stay or Gromet; and the lower Tack being middled and bent, one End is reeved through a Thimble strapped to a Topmast Shroud on the larboard, and the other on the starboard Side. The SHEETS (w), go singly, leading clear over the Main Topmast Stay (z): they are reeved on each Side through Blocks lashed at the Gangway for that purpose. This Sail is lined, or has a Piece of Canvas in lieu of it, at the Bunt.

Sometimes there is no tricing Line to the Stay, but a Block or Thimble (h), Fig. K, is strapped to the Thimble on the Jack Stay, the Stay (i), is reeved through this, and clinched round the Fore Topmast Head, or to the Tressle-tree (k), the lower Tack (m), being taken to the Topmast Shrouds to Windward, the Stay is hoisted on, which thus trices itself up, and is checked when at its proper height by the Tack.

Q
MAIN

Main Top Gallant, Mizen, and Mizen Topmast Staysails.

The MAIN TOP GALLANT STAYSAIL STAY, Fig. 341,

Is generally spliced into the Main Top Gallant Stay, a little below the Collar; but sometimes it is put over the Mast Head, like the other Spring Stays. The Stay leading through the Hanks, is reeved through a Block, or Thimble (a), seized or strapped to the Fore Topmast Cross-trees, and led down upon Deck, being sufficiently long for the Bight to overhaul into the Top.

The Halliards (b), are reeved through the Sheave-hole in the Pole of the Main Top Gallant Mast, above the Rigging; and bent to the Peak Clew (h), with a *Sheet Bend* (see page 8).

The LOWER TACK (e), is middled, and bent to the Tack, as mentioned for the Sheet Pendents of the Fore Staysail, having a Throat-seizing clapped on both parts, and is made fast to a Fore Topmast Shroud on each side. The upper Tack, when the Sail is triced up, is seized to the Strap of the Thimble or Block (a), through which the Stay is reeved.

The DOWN-HAULER (g), is reeved up through a Thimble, or a small Block, strapped to the upper Tack of the Sail, through a few Hanks, or a Thimble seized to the Head Rope, and bent to the Peak (h).

The SHEETS (d), are middled, bent to the Clew as before, and led clear over the Middle Staysail Stay (k), belaying to a Pin in the Fife Rail.

When this Sail is hauled down, Fig. 342, the Halliards are let go, the Sheet eased off, and the Down-hauler is hauled upon, till the Peak comes to the Thimble or Block (e), through which the Stay is reeved; the upper Tack is then cast off, the Stay (f), eased away, and the Down-hauler being again hauled upon, brings the Sail and the Bight of the Stay (f), into the Top, where it is stowed away.

Some Ships in the East Country Trade carry no Middle Staysail; but have this Sail considerably larger, coming low down the Fore Topmast Rigging, and the Main Top Gallant Mast made stouter than is commonly the case.

The MIZEN STAYSAIL, Fig. 343, (if there be no Spring-stay) is seized to the Hanks on the Mizen Stay.

A strong Cloth, or an additional one for a Lining, is sewn to the Bunt or Fore Leech. Sometimes a Patch (h), is stuck on the middle of the Sail, having an Eyelet-hole worked in it: through this, a short span is reeved, a Thimble being spliced in each end; but it is now seldom used. A Cringle (i), is worked in the after Leech.

The HALLIARDS are reeved through a Block lashed round the Mizen Mast Head, or to the Mizen Tressle-trees, through the Block (k), at the Peak, and the end is clinched (see page 57, Fig. N) round the Head of the Mizen Mast. The upper Tack is lashed to the Collar which goes round the Main Mast, and the lower one to an Eye-bolt (l), in the Deck, abaft the Mast.

The DOWN-HAULER is reeved through a Block (f), strapped to the Mizen Stay Collar, or to the upper Tack of the Sail; and sometimes through a Sheave-hole in the Heart (see page 34, Fig. 212), then through a few Hanks at the Tack and Peak, or through a Thimble at the Head of the Sail, and bent to the Peak Clew (k).

The BRAILS (n), are reeved up through the Sheave of a double Block, strapped to the Collar on the Main Mast, (or a single one on each side) through the Thimble in the Patch (h), (when used) and bent to the Cringle (i).

The *SHEETS* go with a long and short Leg, which are bent to the Clew, as before: the short Leg (m), has a block or thimble spliced in its end: the long one is reeved through a block (p), strapped to an Eye-bolt in the side, through the block (m), and is belayed to a Cleat bolted to the side.

The MIZEN TOPMAST STAYSAIL. Fig. 344,

Is bent to Hanks on the Mizen Topmast Stay, and has a Lining or a strong Cloth on the Mast Leech. The *Halliards* which go single, are reeved through a Block at the Mizen Topmast Tressle-trees, and bent to the Peak (s). The Down-hauler leads through a thimble or small block (t), strapped to the upper Tack, is reeved as before, and bent to the Peak (s).

The *UPPER TACK* is lashed to the Collar (q), which goes round the Main Mast; and the lower one (u), is reeved through a thimble strapped to one of the Main Shrouds, leading down below. The Sheets (v), are middled, bent as before, and reeved through a thimble or block lashed to the foremost Mizen Shroud on each side, leading clear over the Mizen Stay.

MIZEN

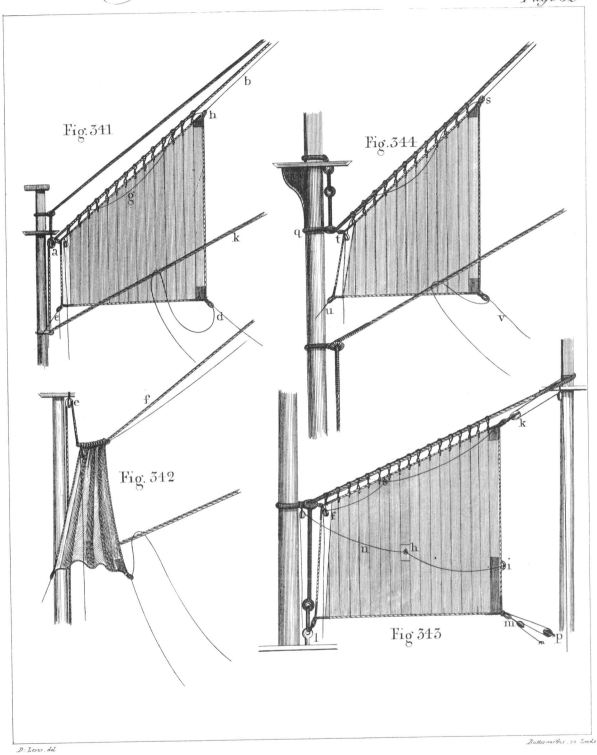

Fig. 341

Fig. 342

Fig. 344

Fig 343

D. Lever. del.

Butterworths. sc. Leeds.

Mizen Top Gallant Staysail — Mizen,

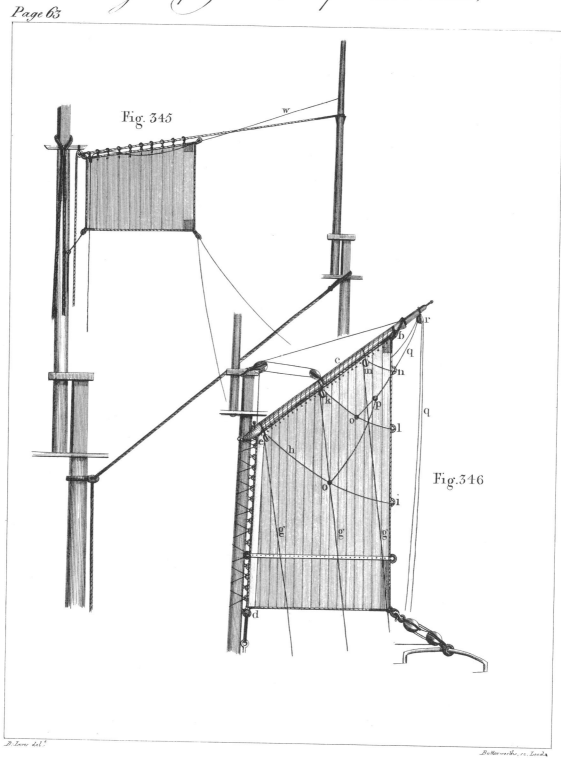

Fig. 345

Fig. 346

D. Lever del.ᵗ

Butterworths, sc. Lond.

MIZEN TOP GALLANT STAYSAIL-----MIZEN.

The *MIZEN TOP GALLANT STAYSAIL*, Fig. 345,

Is bent to the Hanks on the Mizen Top-Gallant Staysail Stay, which leads like the Main one through a Block or Thimble strapped to the Main Topmast Head : and is hauled down into the Main Top like the Main Top-gallant Staysail into the Fore Top ; and sometimes it is triced up on a Jack Stay, like the Middle Staysail (see page 61). The Shape of this Sail depends on which of the above Methods it is carried.

The HALLIARDS (w), are reeved through the Sheave-hole in the Pole of the Mizen Top-Gallant Mast, just above the Rigging, or through a Block lashed there, and bent to the Peak with a Sheet Bend (see page 8). The Down-hauler is reeved as before, and the Sheets are middled and bent to the Clew, like those of the Mizen Topmast Staysail, leading clear over the Mizen Topmast Stay, and belaying to the foremost Mizen Shroud, or to the Fife Rail, on each Side.

It is in practise in the Merchant Service to *seam prick* the Staysails (i. e. to sew them in a zig-zag manner) when they are made, because the Strain of the Sheets lies directly across the Seams from the Clew to the Tack.

The *MIZEN*, Fig. 346,

Is bent to the Mizen Yard or Gaff. It is made with a Mast Leech, which is lined with an additional Cloth, and the Gaff or Yard extends the Head instead of a Stay. If the Gaff be slung, Cringles are worked in the Mast Leech at equal distances ; but if the Gaff traverse, then Eyelet Holes are worked in.

The Earing at the Peak (b), is hauled out, as before, with two *outer* turns without the Stop Cleats, and through the Cringle ; and the *inner* turns, which bear the strain of the after Leech, are passed, till the whole is expended.

The throat Earing is spliced to the Cringle in the Throat of the Sail, and passed alternately through that and an Eye-bolt underneath the Gaff at the Jaws. The Lacing for the Head is spliced to the Cringle at the Peak (b), and reeved through the Eyelet Holes in the Head, passing over the Yard or Gaff (c).

The Lacing for the Mast Leech is spliced into the throat Cringle (e), goes round the Mast, and through the Cringles in the Mast Leech, backwards and forwards, hitching to the Tack (d). When the Gaff traverses up and down, the Eyelet Holes in the Mast Leech are fastened to Hoops which go round the Mast.

The *BRAILS* (g), are reeved through Blocks spanned on the Yard or Gaff, at the same Distance from the Peak that the Cringles on the after Leech are.

The *THROAT BRAILS* (h), are reeved through Blocks on each side of the Gaff at the Throat, through a Thimble in a Span (o), and clinched to the lower Cringle (i), in the after Leech. The *MIDDLE BRAILS* are reeved through a Block (k), in the middle of the Gaff, through the Thimble (o), in the upper Leg of the Span, and bend to the second Cringle (l), in the after Leech. The *PEAK BRAILS* are reeved through the Block (m), farther out, and clinched to the upper Cringle (n).

In order to overhaul these Brails when the Mizen is hauled out, a Fancy Line (q), having a thimble (p), spliced in one end, is reeved through the Block (r), at the Peak end : a span is reeved through this thimble, and each end spliced round the thimbles (o), on the *Throat* and Middle Brails.

The *TACK* (d), is lashed to an Eye-bolt in the Deck, abaft the Mizen Mast.

The *STUDDING SAILS* and *DRIVER* are for temporary Use. These Sails, like the others, derive their Names from the Masts to which they belong. Thus the lower Studding Sails from the lower Masts, the Topmast Studding Sails from the Topmasts, and the Top-Gallant Studding Sails from the Top-Gallant Masts.

The *LOWER STUDDING SAILS* are square at the Head, Foot and Leech, and pieced at the Earings and Clews.

STUDDING

Blunt replaces the seven paragraphs under "The MIZEN" with the text in Appendix 21, and provides a different Figure 346. The changes in rigging of the gaff and placement of the brails will be of significance to model makers.

STUDDING SAIL BOOMS—LOWER STUDDING SAIL.

Previously to these Sails being set, the Topmast Studding Sail Boom (a), Fig, 347, which rests in the Boom iron, on the lower Yard, is launched out, and the Heel secured by a Lashing. At the outer end of the Boom is strapped a Block (b), which rests upon the upper side, and through it is reeved the Topmast Studding Sail Tack (c), one part leading aft to the Gangway, and the other either before or abaft the Boom, as occasion may require. Another Block (d), is put over the Boom end, or is lashed to it, hanging underneath, for the outer Halliards of the lower Studding Sail (e). In Merchant Ships, when this Sail is gored, having more Cloths at the Foot than the Head, this Block has a short Pendent, which is retained to the Boom farther in by a Selvagee strap. Over the Boom end there is a Pendent (f), with a Block spliced in for a Brace (g), to reeve through, for the better security of the Boom when it blows fresh. After this, another Pendent, called a *Topping-lift Pendent,* is put over, having a Thimble spliced in the end: The Top-Burton Tackle being overhauled, the Hook of its lower Block (h), is put through this Thimble, and bowsed taught. This answers the same purpose that the Lifts do to the lower Yards.

The TOPMAST STUDDING SAIL BOOM is often got on the Yard by the lower Studding-sail Halliards, and sometimes one of the fore Bunt-lines is cast off from the Foot of the Sail, and made fast to it. When the Rigging abovementioned is put on, the Boom, in Men of War, is launched out by a Boom-tackle; but in small Ships in the Navy, and East Indiamen, the Yard Sheet (i), which is reeved through a Block in the inner Quarter of the lower Yard, and through another at the outer one (k), is made fast to the Heel-lashing of the Boom, and the Men on Deck hauling upon it, launch it out. When the Boom is small, it is launched out by Hand.

The *TOP GALLANT STUDDING SAIL BOOM*, Fig. 348,

Rests in the Iron (a), in the Topsail Yard Arm, and the Heel is secured to the Yard with a Lashing: there is no Rigging to this Boom; but a Thimble (b), which is strapped to the end of it, for the Top Gallant Studding Sail Tack.

The *LOWER STUDDING SAIL BOOM*, Fig. 349,

Has a large iron Hook (l), called a *Goose Neck,* driven into the inner end, which is hooked to an Eye-bolt in the side, between the fore Chains and the Cat-head. At the outer end, a Block (m), is strapped, for the lower Studding Sail Tack (n), to reeve through, one end of which is led through a Block at the Gangway. In the middle of the Boom are two Straps (o), with Thimbles seized in them; one of these lies above, and the other below the Boom.

The TOPPING LIFT (p), is reeved through a Block (q), spliced in a long Span, which goes round the lower Mast-head, and the end is clinched to the upper Strap (o), in the middle of the Boom. In order to keep the Boom from flying up, which is often the case when a Ship rolls in going large, a Block (r), is lashed to an Eye-bolt in the Bends, and a Rope called a *Martingale* (s), being reeved through it, is bent to the other Strap (o), in the middle of the Boom: it is set taught on the Forecastle, and belayed to a Timber Head. Men of War have a Tackle hooked to the Boom, to keep it down. A Block (t), is lashed on the outer quarter of the Spritsail Yard, and the FORE GUY (u), it reeved through it, and clinched to the middle of the Boom, just without the Strap: the AFTER GUY (v), is clinched close to it, and reeved through a Block lashed round a Timber-head at the Gangway. To get this Boom out and in, see pages 81 and 82.

The *LOWER STUDDING SAIL*, Fig. 350,

Is bent to a short Yard (w). The OUTER HALLIARDS (x), are reeved through a Block in a Span, which goes round the lower Cap, through the Block (y), at the Topmast Studding Sail Boom end, and are hitched round the Yard (w), with a Fisherman's Bend (see page 8). In the Merchant Service there is frequently a Pendent (a), having a large Eye spliced in one end, and a Block in the other: the Eye is taken round the Topmast Head above the Rigging, and the Block being put through the Eye, the outer Halliards are reeved through it, as before. When the lower Studding Sail is taken in, and the Halliards are unreeved, this Block is stopped to the Topmast Shrouds. In small Ships, where no Topping-lift is used to the Topmast Studding Sail Boom, a single Block is hooked to the Top-Burton Pendent, and the Halliards are reeved through it.

The INNER HALLIARDS are reeved through a Block (z), at the inner quarter of the lower Yard, through another at the outer quarter, and bent to the inner head Cringle. The *Tack* is reeved through the Block (c), and bent to the outer Clew. The *Sheet* (d), is middled, and the Bight bent to the inner Clew. STUDDING

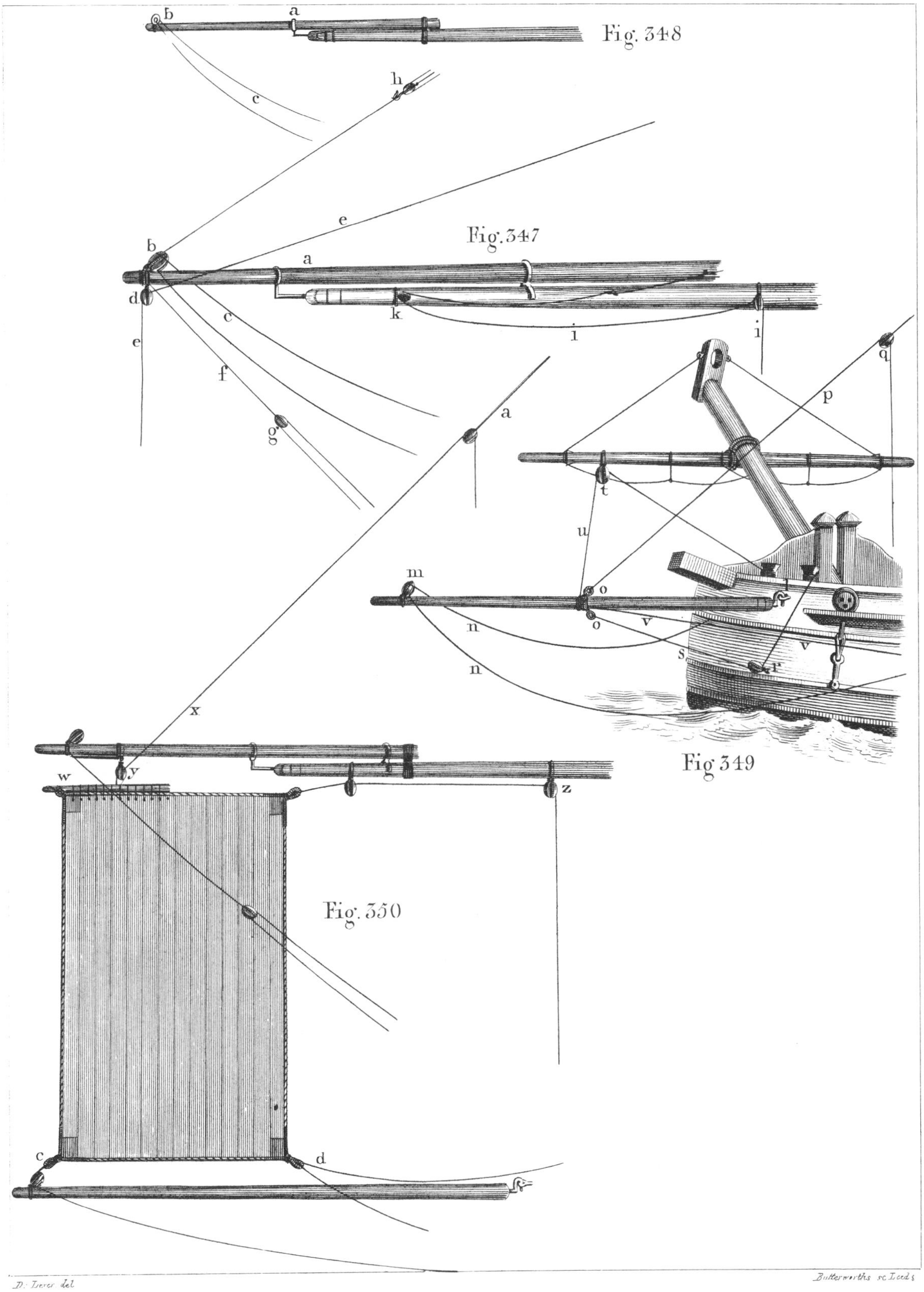

Fig. 348

Fig. 347

Fig 349

Fig. 350

D. Steel del.

Butterworths sc Leeds

Studding Sails.

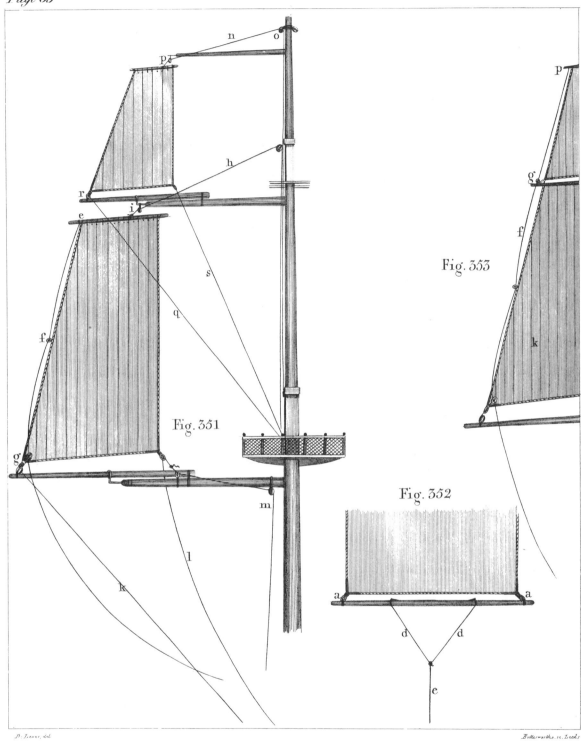

Fig. 351

Fig. 352

Fig. 353

D. Lever, del.   Butterworths, sc, Leeds.

STUDDING SAILS.

The *TOPMAST STUDDING SAIL*, Fig. 351.

Is bent to a Yard (e), with Knittles and Earings, and frequently laced to it. This Sail has sometimes a Reef-band in it. It is gored in the outer Leech according to the Length of the Boom, and the Squareness of the Yard, and also at the Head from the outer to the inner Earing. The Foot of the Sail is generally parallel to the Head. This Sail is more gored in the Merchant Service than in the Royal Navy, because there is a greater disproportion in the Squareness of the lower and topsail Yards in the former, than in the latter. Half way up the outer Leech, a Cringle (f), is worked. The *DOWN-HAULER* is reeved through the Block (g), seized to the Tack Clew, through the Cringle (f), and bent to the outer Yard Arm. The Halliards (h), are reeved through a Block hooked to an Eye-bolt in the Topmast Cap, through the Jewel Block (i), at the Topsail Yard Arm, and bent to the Yard about one third from the inner Arm, with a Fisherman's Bend, (see page 8).

The *TACK* (k), is reeved through the Block at the Topmast Studding Sail Boom End, and is led through a Block lashed to a imber Head in the Waist. The *SHEET* (l), is bent with a long and short Leg: the long Leg leads down before the lower Yard; the short one has a Thimble spliced in its End, and the Yard Sheet (m), mentioned in the former Page, is bent to it.

The *TOP-GALLANT STUDDING SAIL* is gored at the Head, Foot, and outer Leech, and bent to the Yard in the same Manner. The Halliards (n), are reeved through a Block (o), strapped in a Span round the Top Gallant Mast Head above the Rigging, then through the Jewel Block (p), at the Yard Arm, and bent to the Top Gallant Studding Sail Yard, about one third from the inner Arm. The *TACK* (q), is reeved through the Thimble (r), at the Boom End, bent to the Tack Clew, and belayed in the Top. The *SHEET* (s), is middled and bent to the inner Clew: one End is led into the Top, and the other made fast to the Topsail Yard. There is seldom any Down-hauler to this Sail; but if there be, it is bent like that of the Topmast Studding Sail.

The *MAIN STUDDING SAIL BOOM* is hooked to an Eye Bolt in the fore End of the Main Channel, and rigged like the Fore one. The Tack is reeved through a Block lashed to a Timber Head well aft on the Quarter Deck. The after Guy is reeved through a Block lashed to an Eye-bolt in the quarter Piece: the fore Guy is led through a Block lashed to the fore Chains. The *MAIN TOPMAST*, and *MAIN TOP-GALLANT* Studding Sail Booms are rigged as the Fore ones. The Topmast Studding Sail Tack is reeved through a Block on the Quarter, and the Top-Gallant one is belayed in the Main Top.

The lower Studding-sail is often set flying: that is, without a Boom. When this is the case, Fig. 352, the Sail is spread at the Foot by lashing the Clews (a), to a small Yard: a Span (d), is made fast to the Yard, and the Guy (e), bent to it.

The Top-Gallant Studding Sail is also frequently set flying, in the Merchant Service, like Fig. 353.

The two Clews are lashed to the Topmast Studding Sail Yard Arms; the Topmast Studding Sail Down-hauler (f), is reeved through a Thimble (g), on the Topmast Studding Sail Yard, and bent to the Top-Gallant Studding Sail Yard (p), which is made fast to the Topmast Studding Sail Yard with a Rope-yarn before it is sent up.

The Topmast Studding Sail Halliards are hoisted on, and the slack of the Top-Gallant ones gathered in, and when the Topmast Studding Sail (k), is up, the Top-Gallant Studding Sail Halliards are hoisted on, which breaks the Rope Yarn, and lets the Sail go up. If these Sails be set *abaft* the Topsail and Top Gallant Sail, the Topmast Studding Sail Yard must be lashed to the Topsail Yard, (which may be of bad Consequence in a sudden Squall), otherwise the weather Yard Arm will fly forward: and if they be set *before* these Sails, the lee Yard Arms may injure the Topsail and Top-Gallant Sail by pressing against them. It is therefore more secure to have a Top-Gallant Studding Sail Boom, which is light, and soon got down into the Top.

R   DRIVER

Blunt adds at the bottom of the page the comment, "The royal studding-sails are set the same as the top-gallant studding-sails."

DRIVER, SPANKER, FORE and AFT MAINSAIL.

The DRIVER is a temporary Sail, and in the Merchant Service, is sometimes cut like a Topmast Studding Sail: it is hoisted up to the Mizen Peak, like Fig. 354. The HALLIARDS are reeved through a Block at the Peak, and the Sail (which is gored sufficiently at the Head) being bent to the Yard (o), they are made fast to the third of it, with a Fisherman's Bend (see page 8). The TACK (p), is made fast to the Fife Rail to windward, and the Sheet (q), is reeved through a Block, lashed to a Pole (r), run out over the Tafferel. In the Fore Leech there are two Bowline Cringles, the Bridle (s), is reeved through the Thimble in the Bowline (t), and each end is clinched to a Cringle.

The DRIVER or SPANKER is now cut Mainsail Fashion, and in this case it is spread by a Boom, rigged as mentioned in pages 44 and 45.

The Spanker acts as a large Mizen, Fig. 355; but as the Gaff is not of sufficient squareness to spread the Head, the after part of it is bent to a Yard (a). The Tack goes with a Luff Tackle purchase, the double Block (m), hooking to a Thimble in the Tack Clew, and the single one to an Eye-bolt in the Deck. But if the Boom be made with Jaws, resting on a Shoulder bolted to the Mast, then the lower Block is often hooked to an Eye-bolt on the Boom.

The OUTER HALLIARDS (c), are reeved through a Block (d), at the end of the Gaff, and bent to the Yard (a), about one-third from the inner Arm.

The MIDDLE HALLIARDS (e), are reeved through a Block (f), and bent to a Cringle at the Head, at one-third of the distance between the Yard and the Throat.

The INNER HALLIARDS (g), are reeved through a Block (h), and bent to a Cringle half way between the Middle and Throat Halliards.

The THROAT HALLIARDS are generally reeved through a Block lashed at the Mizen Mast Head; but when the Sail is large, the lower Block of a Luff Tackle (i), is hooked to a Thimble in the Throat Cringle or Nock, and the upper one (k), to a Strap round the Mizen Mast Head. The Sheet Rope (n), is reeved through a Sheave-hole in the Boom, and clinched to an iron Traveller: in the other end a Thimble is spliced; the outer Block of a Luff Tackle (o), is hooked to it, and the inner one (p), to a bolt on the Boom.

It is more common in the Merchant Service to have a Driver Yard to spread the Head of the Sail from the Peak to the Nock, bending with Rope-bands and Earings, and it is proved by these means to stand better; the Head being so much taughter, and not liable to bag, which it naturally will, when the strain of the different Halliards lies more immediately on those Cloths, in the Wake of the Cringles. This Sail is sometimes cut square at the Foot and Mast Leech; but more frequently with a Roach Gore, as in the Figure. In the Mast Leech there are Cringles for a Lacing, like the Mizen, and sometimes Eyelet Holes: when the latter, there is often a JACK STAY, Fig. K, which is reeved through Thimbles or Hanks, acting as Travellers; and the Mast Leech is seized to these at the Eyelet Holes. The Jack Stay goes with a running Eye round the Mizen Mast Head, and is set up with a Laniard and Thimbles to an Eye-bolt in the Deck, abaft the Mizen Mast. For the different methods of rigging the Boom (see pages 44 and 45).

Ships in the Baltic and Coasting Trade, which carry fore and aft Mainsails, have the Mizen Mast as taunt as the Mainmast, and seldom carry any Mizen Topmast, Fig. 356; but a Flag Staff (m), to hoist the Ensign, &c. this is sometimes made strong enough to hoist a small Topsail with a Gaff, or Yard slung by the third; the Clew hauling out to the Mizen Peak. They carry no Cross Jack Yard, consequently no square Topsail; but the Mizen is very large in proportion.

The MIZEN STAY (o), is taken to the Mainmast Head, and reeved through a Block (p), strapped to an Eye-bolt just under the Main Cap. The Topping Lift (q), instead of leading to the *Main*, is taken to the *Mizen* Mast Head. A double Block (r), is strapped to an Eye-bolt hooped round the Mizen Mast, the single Block (s), is strapped with a Hook and Thimble, and connected by the Topping Lift Fall (t), with the double one (r). The Pendent (q), has a Thimble spliced in the *upper* end, to which the single Block is hooked; and the *lower* end is spliced to a Thimble in the Eye-bolt (g), in the Boom end. The Peak and Throat Tyes, or Halliards, reeve as mentioned for the Gaff, which traverses (see pages 43 and 44). The Sheet hooks to an Eye-bolt a-midships, and if the Sail be large, there are double Sheets, one on each side.

The Guy Pendent (f), is hooked to a Strap round the Middle of the Boom, the double Block (w), of a Luff Tackle is hooked to it, and the single one to the Main Chains. Gaffs which traverse have a Throat Down-hauler.---the lower Block (v), is hooked to a Strap round the Mast, and the upper one to an Eye-bolt under the Jaws of the Gaff.

ANCHORS,

*The original shows a more complex rigging than Blunt's text and figures, which are reproduced in Appendix 22.

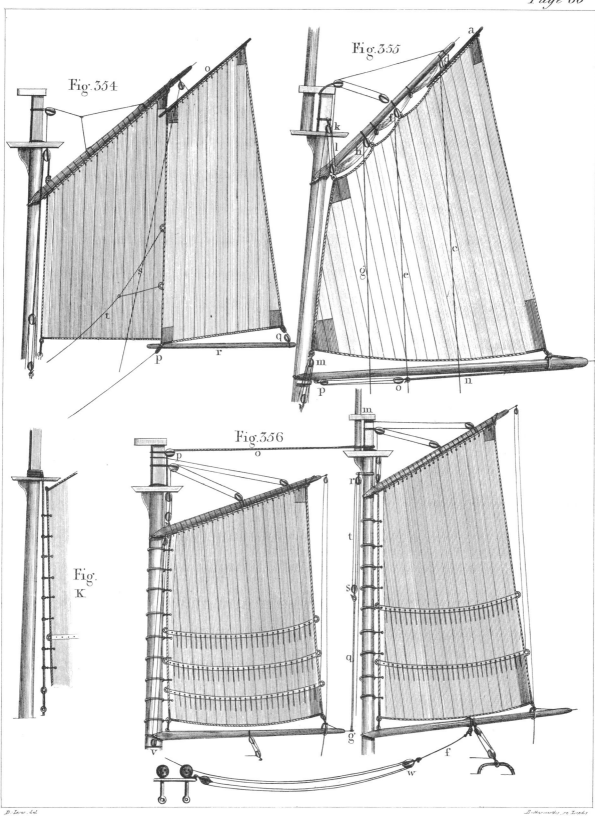

Fig.354

Fig.355

Fig.356

Fig. K

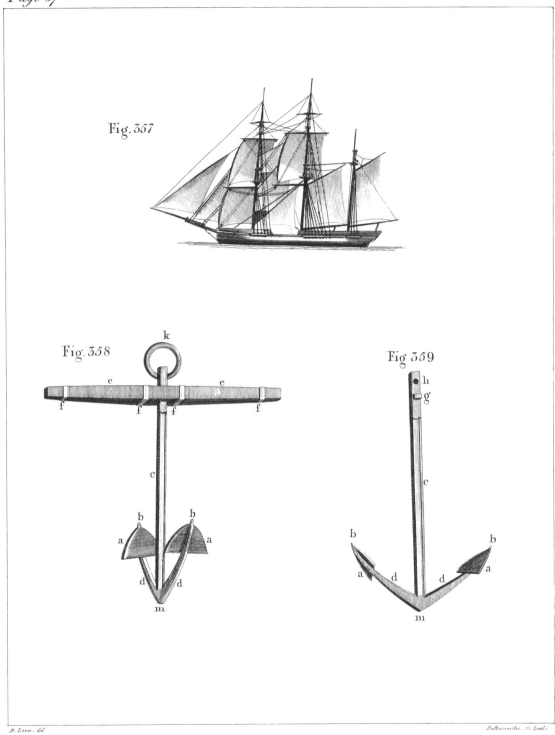

Fig. 357

Fig. 358

Fig 359

D. Lever. del.

Butterworths. sc. Leeds.

67

ANCHORS, &c.

Ships rigged in this Manner can sail with a Hand or two less, and answer very well for working through Narrows, there being no after Sail to brace about, but the Main Topsail and Main Top-Gallant Sail, and *their* Braces lead forwards.

The Main or Cross Jack Brace Fig. 357, leads through a Block at the aftermost Fore Shroud, and the Main Topsail Brace, through a Block strapped to an Eye-Bolt in the after Part of the Fore Cap, the standing Part being hitched round the Foremast Head : and the Top-Gallant Brace, to the after Part of the Fore Topmast Cross-Tree.

The aftermost Shroud of any Mast rigged with a Boom, and Gaff which traverses, the Sail having Reefs in, should be served the whole Length : and the aftermost Topmast Backstay go with a Block and Runner, as mentioned for the Breast Backstay. The former, that it may not be chafed when going large, and the latter to make room for the Boom to be guyed forwards.

Men of War, East Indiamen, and large Ships in the Southern Trade, carry one Sheet Anchor, one Spare Anchor, two Bower Anchors, one Stream Anchor, and one Kedge.

An *ANCHOR* is a large Instrument of Iron, shaped like Figures 358 and 359, (a), the Flukes or Palms, (b), the Bills, (c), the Shanks, (d), the Arms, (e), the Stock made of Oak, bolted together, hooped, and farther secured by the Nut (g), (f), the iron Hoops, (h), the Eye for the Ring, (k), the Ring, and (m), the Crown of the Anchor. In the Royal Navy, the two Bower and Sheet Anchors are of the same Size, as are their Cables.

On the Channel and Home Service there are generally three Cables on the best Bower, two on the small Bower, and the Sheet's Cable ; and on Foreign Service three on the small Bower. In the Merchant Service the Anchors and Cables sometimes differ in Size and Number.

East Indiamen have, in general, two Cables on the Sheet Anchor, two on the best Bower, which is on the larboard Side, one on the small Bower on the starboard Side, and one on the Stream Anchor. When they want to veer on the small Bower, the Stream Cable is spliced to it.

In Coasters, and particularly in the Coal Trade from the North to London, they have their Anchors and Cables as follows :

Two *BOWER* Anchors, and in Vessels of two hundred Tons and upwards, a spare or waist Anchor. Three Cables of *eighty-five* Fathoms each are spliced together, and the Bight seized to the Main or Foremast. Thus they have plenty of Scope on the Anchor which they ride by, to veer away, and as they never moor, the Cables are kept spliced, they having no Hawse to clear. The working Cable has always its Services kept on, of which there are three : viz. the short or windward Service at about forty-five Fathoms, the second Service at seventy-five Fathoms from the Anchor, and the long or leeward Service clapped on, so as to leave a Fake in the Tier, to freshen Hawse with. From the Anchor to the short Service, the Cable is wormed with twice-laid Stuff, sufficiently large to project above it, which is a great Preservative against its being damaged by foul Ground. It is then keckled and rounded with Plait. The long Service is only rounded. Men of War and East Indiamen have about seven Fathom of Keckling, four of Rounding, and four of Plait.

PUDDENING

---

*Blunt's text differs considerably. He mentions Porter's anchor and shows it in figure 364a. Text and figure are in Appendix 23.
**Although original Erratum reads *"line 18 from the bottom, for 'Sheet Cable,' read 'Sheet's Cable.'"*, it should be *"line 18 from the bottom, for 'Sheet's Cable,' read 'Sheet Cable.'"*

PUDDENING the RINGS—BUOY, &c.

The Rings of the Anchors are well parcelled with tarred Canvas, and then wrapped round with twice-laid Stuff, which is called *Puddening the Anchors*. It is done thus---

A number of lengths are cut, each three times the diameter of the Ring. These are laid on the Ring, and stopped by a temporary Seizing in the middle (a), Fig. 360. They are laid by hand as far as (b), when a turn or two of Ratline Stuff is taken round, and a Heaver (b), being put through it, it is hove well round, which stretches all the turns of the Pudding or Wreath, making them lie taught and even. A Seizing is clapped on within the Heaver, and snaked (see page 10), and the Heaver is then taken off.

The parts are then laid and hove in the same manner to (c), Fig. 361, where another Seizing is clapped on. The same operation is performed on the other side to (d and e), when it will appear like the Figure, the temporary Seizing being taken off. The ends of the Pudding are then opened out (f), and well tarred.

The BUOY is a kind of cask, made in the form of Figure 362. It is slung, for the purpose of bending one end of the Buoy Rope to, the other end being fixed to the Crown of the Anchor. Nine times the length of the Buoy will make the Slings and Hoops.

These are hove out, parcelled, and served. The Slings have an Eye spliced in each end. The lower Hoop (g), is reeved through the Eyes of the upper Slings (h), which are taken under the upper Hoop (i) : this is reeved through the Eyes of the lower Slings (k), which are taken under the lower Hoop (g). The Hoops are spliced together. A Tackle is hooked to the Bights of one pair of Slings, and the Bights of the other being put over a Timber Head : they are bowsed well out, and the Hoops beat down : the Bights at each end are then seized with a round Seizing (see page 9), and double crossed. There is often a Thimble (m), seized in the Bights, round which is another Thimble, and to it the Buoy Rope is bent. A Laniard (l), is spliced to the upper Eye of the Slings.

The Buoy Rope is unstranded for two or three Feet, and a Buoy Rope Knot (see page 7), is cast on the end, which is bent to the Crown of the Anchor, Fig. 363. It is made fast with a Clove Hitch round the Arms, close to the Crown (l), and the end part stopped to the Shank with Seizings : one just within the Throat (m), and the other close to the Knot (n). The other end is spliced to the Thimble in the Bight of the Buoy Slings. The Buoy Rope is seventeen or eighteen Fathoms in length, and sometimes longer, where the Anchorage is deep.

In the Merchant Service they have often a Chain, Fig. 364, seven or eight feet long, which is bent to the Anchor, and the end seized to the Shank : the Link in the upper end having a Thimble in it, for the Buoy Rope to be spliced round. This will be very little additional expense, and prevent the bad consequences likely to result from the want of a Chain ; for the Buoy Rope is apt to be chafed where it is bent ; if it be much injured, (should the Cable part) the Anchor cannot be well weighed ; and should it break, there is no chance of recovering the Anchor, but by sweeping for it with Boats and a Hawser, which is very precarious.

CATTING

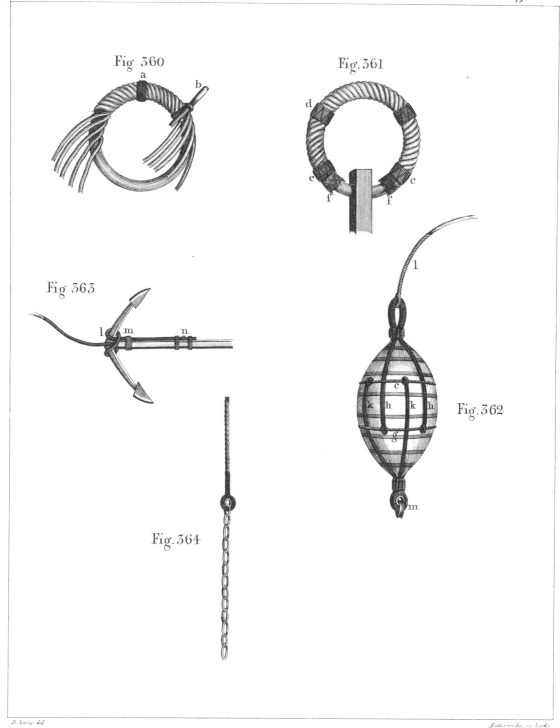

Fig. 360

Fig. 361

Fig 363

Fig. 362

Fig. 364

Catting and Fishing the Anchors.

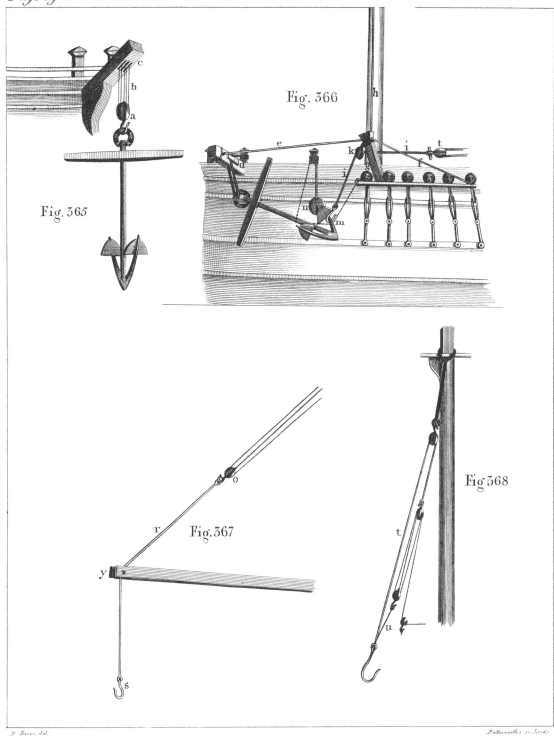

Fig. 366

Fig. 365

Fig. 367

Fig 368

CATTING and FISHING the ANCHORS.

When the Anchors are brought along side, the two Bowers are *catted*, *fished*, and the *Stoppers* and *Shank Painters* passed; the other Anchors are got on board by the Runners and Tackles, Yard and Stay Tackles.

The Hook of the Cat Block (a), Fig. 365, is put through the Ring of the Anchor and the Cat Fall (b), which is reeved alternately through the Sheave-holes in the Cat Head (c), and those in the Cat Block, being swayed upon, the Anchor is thus brought up to the Cat Head : this is called *Catting the Anchor*. A Stopper, one end of which is hitched and seized round the Cat Head, (or reeved through a hole in it, having a double walled Knot, double crowned (see page 5), cast on one end), is taken through the Ring of the Anchor, over a Cleat (d), Fig. 366, bolted on the Cat Head for that purpose, hauled taught, belayed to Timber-heads, and stopped.

In Men of War, East Indiamen, and large Ships in the Merchant Service, there is a Davit (g). This is placed in the fore part of the Fore Chains, and is rigged with three Guys. The Fore Guy (e), is taken round the Cat Head, the After Guy (f), to the after part of the Fore Channel, and the Guy (h), is hitched round the Foremast Head : the Cat Fall is eased off, and the Block unhooked.

The FISH PENDENT (i), is reeved through a large single Block (k), (having a large Hook and Thimble turned in the lower end), and placed with its Strap over the Davit end. In the other end an Eye is spliced, and the Strap of a double Block (t), being put through it, a Toggle is thrust in it. The double Block (t), is connected to a single one (by its fall), which is hooked to an Eye-bolt aft.--- Sometimes a Thimble is spliced in the inner end of the Pendent (i), and the double Block of a Luff Tackle is hooked to it : and frequently the Pendent has no Tackle attached to it; but it is made longer, and the end taken to the Capstern. The Fish Hook is taken to the inner Arm of the Anchor (m), and the Tackle Fall being stretched along, the Men sway it up. When high enough, (supposing the Cable to be bent, for which see page 94), a wooden Fender, called a *Shoe* (n), having a Laniard to it, is placed over the side, for the inner Bill of the Anchor to rest against; and the Shank Painter, which is a Stopper, with an Iron Chain, is passed under the inner Arm and Shank, (as represented by the dotted line) belayed to Timber Heads, hitched and stopped. The Anchor Stock is bowsed to with a Tackle, to make the Arms lie square. The Fish Tackle is then eased off, and the Fish unhooked. When the Anchors are stowed, the inner Arms rest on the Gunnel.

Smaller Ships, which carry Davits, have them run out over the Gunnel athwart-Ships, the inner end resting on the Forecastle, Fig. 367. In the inner end (y), is a Snatch-sheave, in which the Bight of a short Pendent (r), is placed, having the Fish Hook (s), spliced in one end, and a Thimble in the other, to which is hooked the lower Block of the Runner Tackle (o).   *

Some Ships have no Davits. The Anchors are then fished by the Runners and Tackles.

The Runner (t), Fig. 368, is bent to the Fish Hook, and a piece of short Rope, called a *Lizard* (u), being spliced into the Runner a little above the Hook, the lower Block of the Runner Tackle is hooked to it; and thus the Power of the Runner and Tackle is applied.

S   Bentick

*Although original Erratum reads *"line 7 from the bottom, for 'outer End,' read 'inner End.'"*, it should be *"line 7 from the bottom, for 'inner end,' read 'outer end.'"*

Bentick Shrouds---Getting in the Bowsprit by the Fore Yard.

BENTICK SHROUDS are generally set up at Sea ; but as some Ships have them constantly rigged, particularly when they lead like Fig. 371, it will be proper to describe them in this page.

The Bentick Shrouds do not lead down on the Side they are meant to act upon ; but are taken across, the upper End being on the starboard and the lower End on the larboard Side, and vice versa.

In the upper End of the Bentick Shroud, Fig. 370, a large Thimble (p), is spliced : through this a Span (q), is reeved, which has also a Thimble spliced in each End (r) : and through each of these Thimbles another Span (s), is reeved, having a Thimble in each Leg. These Legs are seized to the Futtock Stave and lower Shroud, each one opposite to a Futtock Shroud (t).

In the other End of the BENTICK Shroud a Dead-eye (o), is turned, which is set up by a Laniard to another Dead-eye in the Channel. Another is led across in the same Manner on the opposite Side.

An UPRIGHT BENTICK, Fig. 371, has only one Shroud or Pendent, and acts by its Legs on each Side, as before. The Shroud (a), has a large Thimble (b), spliced in as before, with two Spans (c), and Thimbles leading on each Side. Two other Spans (d), with their Thimbles, are reeved through these, and seized to the Shrouds and Futtock Staves, as in the former Figure. The Dead-Eye (e), in the lower End of the Shroud, is set up with a Laniard to another (f), which is strapped in an iron Bolt in the Deck, abaft the lower Mast.

These Shrouds ease the Futtock Staves and lower Rigging, the strain of the Topmast Shrouds laying a good deal on them ; so that when the Ship rolls to leeward, the Rigging is kept taught, and when she rolls again to windward, does not come to with that sudden Jerk, which it is liable to without their Aid.

When a new Bowsprit is to be stepped, it is generally (in the Merchant Service) got in without Sheers, by the Fore Yard, Fig. 372, the Slings being cast off.

The Fore Yard is lowered down one third, or any other Distance, according to its Squareness, by the Jears, if they be carried, or otherwise by Tackles from the lower Cap. The single Block of the starboard Yard Tackle is brought to the Cathead (g), hooked to a Pair of Slings, and the Fall taken through a leading Block (h). By bowsing on that Tackle, and gathering in the larboard Lift (i), the Yard is got fore and aft within the Rigging : and if the Bowsprit be stepped between Decks it will require to be carried very forward, and the Yard Arm may be lowered or topped by the Lift as occasion requires. A strong Lashing is passed round the Mast at (k), and a large single Block at (l). A Hawser (m), is reeved through the Top Block (n), (or through a Block lashed to the Foremast Head above the Rigging) through the Block (l), and the End is hitched round the Foremast. The other End of the Hawser is hove taught and belayed, which secures the Yard against the Strain of the Purchase. The Purchase Block (o), is lashed round the Yard, and the lower Block (p), is toggled to a stout Selvagee on the Bowsprit, like that mentioned for the lower Masts. A Back Rope or Guy (q), is reeved through a Block lashed round the Fore Cap, and hitched round the Bowsprit End, which guys it in the Direction required, whether it be more horizontal or perpendicular.

ELEMENTS

Bentick Shrouds &c.

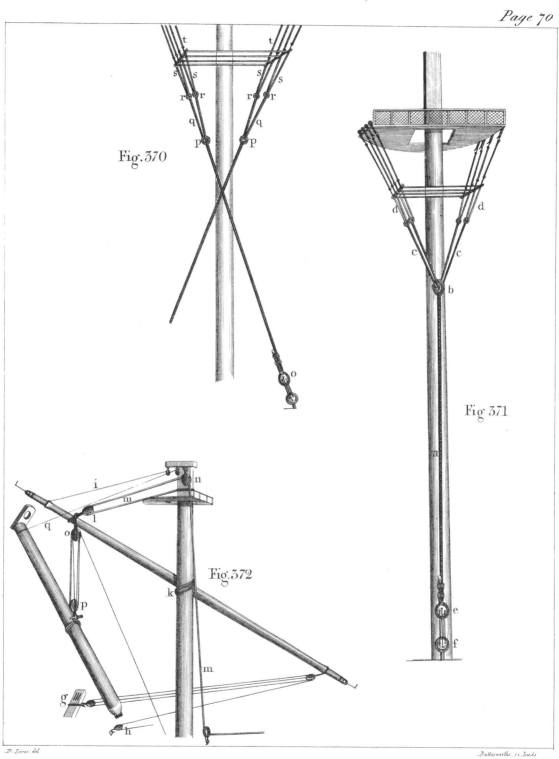

Fig. 370

Fig 371

Fig. 372

D. Lover. del.

Butterworths. sc. Leeds

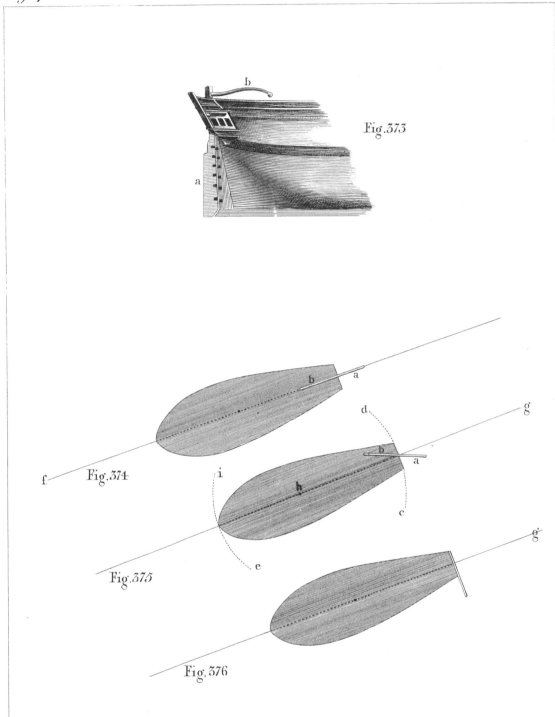

Fig.373

Fig.374

Fig.375

Fig.376

D.r Lever del.   Butterworths, sc., Leeds.

ELEMENTS of PRACTICAL SEAMANSHIP.

The Rudder of a Ship (a), Fig. 373, is a Machine attached to the Stern-post, for the Purpose of governing her Movements. It is turned by a lever of Wood, called a *Tiller* (b), which is also denominated the *Helm*, so as to expose either Side occasionally to the Shock of the Water : and it is immaterial whether the Rudder be acted upon by the Water, or the Water by the Rudder, the Effect being the same. This Tiller in large Ships is moved by a Wheel, attached to it by the Tiller Rope.

Let Fig. 374, represent the Surface of a Vessel, and (a) the Rudder and the Tiller, in the direction of her Keel. If she be pushed forward through the Water, she will go in the Course of the dotted Line towards (f), without any resistance or hindrance from the Rudder ; which proves that it can have no Effect on the Ship in that Position, the Helm (b), being a midships, and the nearer it is kept to that Position, the more rapid will be the Progress of the Vessel through the Water.

If the Ship, Fig. 375, be pushed forward in the Direction of the Keel, and the Rudder (a), be put over from its original Position towards (c), then will her Way be in some Degree checked, and the larboard or left side of the Rudder being forced against the Water, will drive her Stern towards (d), and her Head towards (e) ; the Ship turning on her Center of Gravity (h). The Tiller or Helm (b), which puts the Rudder over to Port or to the left, goes itself over to starboard, or to the right : therefore in this Position the Helm is said to be a-starboard. If the same Vessel were pushed Stern foremost towards (g), with the helm (b), in the same position (*a-starboard*) ; then the after or starboard Side of the Rudder being forced against the Water, would turn her Stern towards (c), consequently her Head towards (i), and whether the Rudder be forced against the Water, or the Water against the Rudder, the Effect will be the same.

If the Rudder could be so far put over as to lie athwart, or be perpendicular to the Keel, like Fig. 376, then the Water acting a direct Line against its Surface, would only tend to check the Ship's way, * and afterwards force her astern in the Direction of her Keel towards (g), without affecting her turning Motion. From this it is evident that the less the Rudder is put over the better ; for as the smallest Deviation from its first Position, Fig. 374, will act in some Degree as a check to the Ship's Way, the more it is kept in that Direction, the more rapid will be her Velocity through the Water.

The following Rule being retained in the Memory, will render the Description of the Vessel's Evolutions easy and familiar.

In going a-head, *if the Helm be put a-starboard, it will turn the Ship's Head* } to { *Port, or to the Left,* *and her Stern - - -* } { *Starboard.*

But in going a-stern, *if the Helm be put a-starboard, it will turn the Ship's Head* } to { *Starboard.* *and her Stern - - -* } { *Port.*

In going a-head, *if the Helm be put a-port, it will turn the Ship's Head--* { to { *Starboard.* *and her Stern - - -* { { *Port.*

But in going a-stern, *if the Helm be put a-port, it will turn the Ship's Head -* } to { *Port.* *and her Stern - - -* } { *Starboard.*

From the foregoing Rule it appears that in going a-head, the Helm must be put the *contrary* Way to that which the Bow is to approach ; and that in going a-stern, it must be put the *same* way that her Head is intended to be turned.

The Current or Tide running *a-stern* will have the same effect on the Rudder as if the Vessel were going a-head ; and when it runs forward or a-head, it will be the same as though the Ship were going a-stern.

If the Rudder, when hard over, make an Angle of between thirty-three and thirty-five Degrees, it is found by Experience to be sufficient.

ELEMENTS

---

*Although original Erratum reads *"line 23 from the top, for 'in a direct Line,' read 'a direct Line.'"*, it should be *"line 23 from the top, for 'a direct Line,' read 'in a direct Line.'"*

ELEMENTS of PRACTICAL SEAMANSHIP.

It will now be expedient to shew how the Sails act upon the Ship, with respect to her Center of Gravity or Rotation.

Let Fig. 377 represent a Vane on a Spindle, or Center, in a perfect Calm. If a light Breeze spring up, and blow from (l), the broad part (n), will be moved from its station to (m), and the point consequently come to (l). But if there be a flat surface of equal dimensions, instead of the point, on the opposite side, then it will remain stationary; because both Blades being acted upon, the one will counterpoise the other. Upon this principle may be deduced the effects of all the Sails before and abaft the Center of Gravity or Rotation, like the effect of the Blades on one or both sides of the Spindle or Axis.

For if a Model of a Vessel, Fig. 378, having three Masts, with three square Sails to hoist on them, be placed in the water, and an imaginary Axis described by the dotted line (n), pass vertically through the Center of Gravity or Rotation, (which is here supposed to be in the Center of the Model) it will appear by the annexed Figures, that the effect will be similar.

As the larboard or left side of the Vessel is presented, suppose the wind blow right on her side, then it will be what Seamen term, *on the Beam;* therefore the larboard, or left, will be the *windward or weather side;* and the starboard, or right, the *lee* one. So any thing on this side is called being to *windward,* and on the other to *leeward.*

Let the Foresail (a), be hoisted up by the Halliards (b), the Clew to windward (d), fastened down by its Tack, the lee Clew (e), hauled aft by its Sheet, and the Yard braced up by the starboard or lee Brace (f); the Sail will then stand fair. The Tacks always keeping down the Clews to windward, is the reason that when the wind is on the starboard or larboard side, the Ship is said to be on the starboard or larboard Tack.

The effect of the Sail (a), will be, as it lies before the imaginary Spindle or Center of Gravity (m), to turn the Ship's Head to starboard, and at the same time to drive her a-head in the direction of her Keel.

If there be added to this Vessel a Boom, Fig. 379, with a Jib (c), set upon it, having its Tack made fast to the Boom end, and its Sheet (d), hauled aft, as before; then great power will be given to turn the Ship's Head to starboard or leeward; because this Boom extending out so far from the Center of Gravity (m), its power is increased in proportion to its distance from that Center.

Now if the Center of Gravity (m), be in the middle of the Ship, or where the Mainmast stands, (which we will suppose in this case) then it will appear by Fig. 380, that the Jib (c), Fore Topmast Staysail (b), Spritsail (a), Spritsail Topsail (d), Foresail (e), Fore Topsail (f), Fore Top Gallant Sail (g), Fore Top Gallant Royal (h), Main Staysail (i), Main Topmast Staysail (k), Middle Staysail (l), and Main Top Gallant Staysail (n), act before the Center of Gravity (m), and that their endeavour is to pay the Ship's Head off to leeward, or make her ware, at the same time they drive her a-head in the direction of her Keel, like the single Sail, Fig. 378.

ELEMENTS

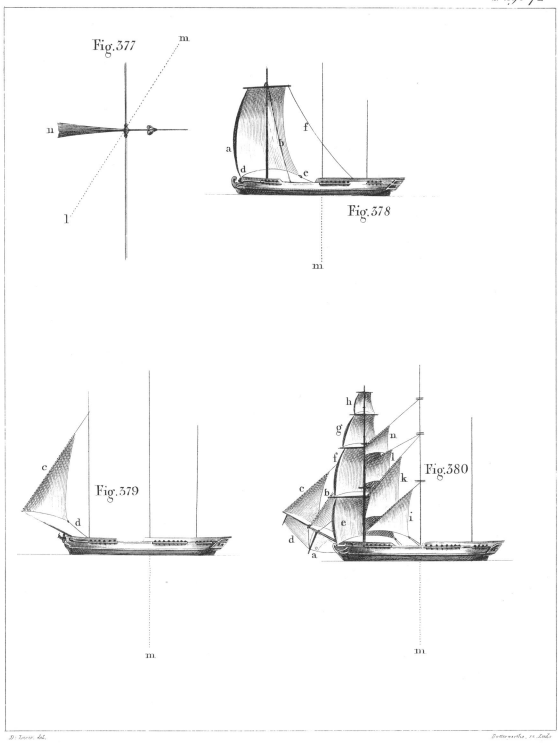

Fig. 377

Fig. 378

Fig. 379

Fig. 380

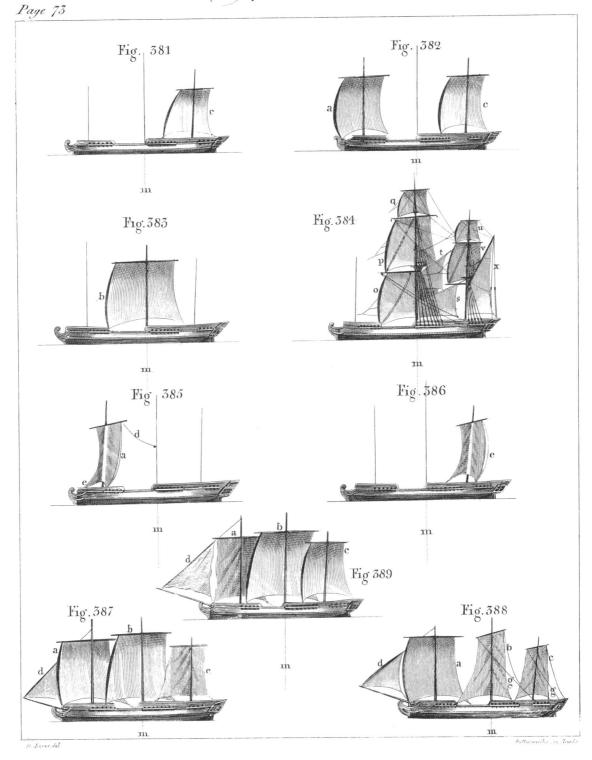

Fig. 381

Fig. 382

Fig. 383

Fig. 384

Fig. 385

Fig. 386

Fig 389

Fig. 387

Fig. 388

ELEMENTS of PRACTICAL SEAMANSHIP.

If the Sail (c), Fig. 381, which we will call the Mizen, be set as before, with the larboard Tack down to windward, and the starboard Sheet aft, it will force her *stern* to leeward, or starboard, consequently bring her Head up to the Wind, and drive her forward in the Direction of her Keel; because it is set abaft the imaginary Axis or Center of Gravity: by which it is evident that any Sail set abaft this Center, tends to make a Ship stay, or come to the Wind, and all before it, to make her fly off from the Wind, and ware, or veer.

If both the Sails (a and c), Fig. 382, be set at the same time, and be of equal Dimensions, then their united Power will force the Vessel with greater Velocity through the Water; and at the same Time keep her in her original Position; because the one acting before, and the other abaft the Center of Gravity, or imaginary Axis (m), they counter-balance each other, like the two Blades of the Vane before-mentioned.

If the Sail (b), Fig. 383, (the Mainsail) be set, the Tack acting before, and the Sheet abaft the imaginary Axis or Center of Gravity (m), will also retain her in her original Position, and impel her a-head in the Direction of her Keel.

From the Effect of these Sails, it appears (allowing the Center of Rotation to be a-midships), that the *lee* Sides of the Mainsail (o), Fig. 384, Main Topsail (p), Main Top Gallant Sail (q), the Whole of the Mizen Staysail (s), Mizen Topmast Staysail (t), Mizen Topsail (v), Mizen Top Gallant Sail (u), and Mizen (x), act abaft the Center of Gravity, consequently force her Stern to leeward or starboard, and at the same Time send her a-head in the Direction of her Keel.

If the Sail (a), Fig. 385, be braced *a-back* with the larboard or weather Brace (d), the lee Tack (e), being hauled forward, and the weather Sheet aft, its Effect will then be to pay her Head off rapidly to leeward or to starboard, and at the same time to force her a-stern in the Direction of her Keel. For the Sail laying flat against the Mast, having its forward Surface exposed to the Wind, must have a contrary Effect to what it has when full, and its power when braced aback, (the Wind being forward), is much greater to pay her Head off to leeward, as it acts directly against its Surface.

If the Sail (c), Fig. 386, be braced aback, having its forward Surface exposed to the Wind, its Action will be to force her a-stern in the Direction of her Keel, and also to drive her Stern to leeward or starboard.

If this Vessel, having these three square Sails and a Jib, be to ware, or recede from the Wind, it appears that the Power of the Sails abaft the Center of Gravity, or imaginary Axis (m), must be considerably diminished, or taken away, because their Tendency is to bring her Head *towards* the Wind, by impelling her Stern to leeward. Therefore if the Sheet of the Sail (c), Fig. 387, be let go, it will shake, and lose its Power abaft the Center (m), and consequently give more Effort to the Sails (a d), and the windward Part of (b), to turn her Head from the Wind. If the Sheet of the Sail (b), were also let go, and the Yards of the Sails (b and c), Fig. 388, pointed to the Wind, by letting go the lee Braces, and hauling in the larboard or weather ones (g), their Effort abaft the Center (m), would be entirely destroyed, the Wind not acting on their Surfaces, but only on their Extremities or Leeches: the greatest impulse will then be given to the Foresail (a), and Jib (d), that they can possibly receive, without the after Yards being lowered down. On the contrary, if the Vessel be to approach the Wind, or Stay; the Sheets of the Sails (a and d), Fig. 389, must be let go, and the Power being thus given to the Sails (b and c), abaft the Center (m), the Stern will recede from, consequently her Head approach to the Wind.

T

ELEMENTS

ELEMENTS of PRACTICAL SEAMANSHIP.

If the Power of the Sails (b and c), Fig. 390, be continued to bring the Vessel's Head to the Wind, till the Sail (a), be a-back, that Sail will then have its Effort more powerful to bring her Head to: and if she persevere in her head-way until her Bow pass the Direction of the Wind, she will then come round and recede from the Wind again to Port or to the left.

Suppose the Ship retain her Velocity through the Water, and by the action of the Sails (b and c), in the first instance, and the Sail (a), when a-back in the second, bring the Wind right a-head like Fig. 391 : the Sails (b and c), are becalmed by the Sail (a), which receives all the Force on its forward Surface. These Sails (b and c), being changed by bracing them about like the Figure, are prepared when she has passed the line of the wind about four Points by the falling off, to again receive it, and renew her head-way, which will be nearly exhausted, by the great Power of the Sail (a), being kept so long a-back, the Ship keeping her rotary Motion to Port or to the Left; which Aid will be then no longer necessary, as she will have brought the Wind on the *starboard* Side : therefore the Sail (a), Fig. 392, must be also changed, by bracing it about with the *larboard* Brace, getting the starboard Tack aboard, and hauling aft the larboard Sheet. She will then be on the starboard Tack, that is, she will have the Wind on the starboard Side, with the starboard Clews or lower Corners of the Sails, hauled forwards by their Tacks.

This Method of bringing the Ship round against the Wind is termed TACKING ; and has great Advantage, as will be shewn when speaking of WARING, or making a Rotation from the Wind.

The Effect of the Sails both before and abaft the Center of Gravity, may be greatly assisted by the Rudder ; but when the Vessel is to go in a direct Course a-head, the more the Sails can be set to counteract each other, and keep the Ship in Equilibrio the better, that there may be as little Occasion as possible for the Rudder to be put over from its fore and aft Position : every Inclination from that Direction checking the Ship in her Way through the Water.

The Effect of the Sails has been given as if the Center of Gravity were in the Center of the Ship ; but the Center of Rotation in many Ships, as they now are built, may not be much abaft the Chess-tree to which the Main Tack is hauled; for the main Breadth or dead Flat being there, the greatest Cavity will be there also, and of course the principal Weight of the Cargo or Materials in the Hold should center near that Part, being the strongest. Therefore the Center of Rotation will greatly depend on proper Stowage. If the Ship be much by the Head or Stern, the Center will be carried more forwards, or aft, as may be seen by a Ship's taking the Ground. If the Vessel, Fig. 393, take the Ground aft, with the Sails (a. b. c and d.) set as before, her after Part, or Heel, being fixed, and her fore Part having no lateral Resistance but the Water, her Head will fly round off to leeward, the after Sails having lost their Power : and if she take the Ground forward, like Fig. 394, her Stern will fly round off, for the same Reason. Thus if a Ship be much by the Stern, she cannot keep her Wind well, (because her Head will fly off) without assistance from the Rudder, and if she be by the Head, she cannot easily ware, on account of the great Resistance under her Bows to leeward. So a difference in the Situation of the Center of Gravity, may cause a difference in the Effect of the Sails : and as Ships vary so much in Construction and Trim, these must be first known, before the proper Effect can be found.

The Ship, Fig. 395, is represented sailing on the starboard Tack, the Yards braced sharp up with the larboard Braces, and the weather or starboard Leeches of the square Sails hauled forward by the Bowlines. It is soon known if the Ship be kept in Equilibrio by the Sails before and abaft the Center of Gravity; for if she be, the Helm may be kept nearly a-midships in smooth Water; but if she gripe, or carry her Helm much to windward or starboard, it may proceed from having too much Sail set abaft the Center, in which case, the Mizen Top Gallant Sail, Top Gallant, and Topmast Staysails may be taken in, and if not sufficient, the Mizen also; for these Sails being set, instead of encreasing, check her Head-way, by causing her to drag the flat Part of the Rudder after her. But her griping may possibly proceed from having too much head Sail ; for when a Ship lies much over on a Wind, the square Sails forward have a tendency to press her downwards, and raise her proportionably abaft, so that she meets the same lateral resistance under her Bows to leeward, as if she were so much by the Head, which must considerably impair her head-way; for her after Part flying off to leeward, the Helm is obliged to be carried a-starboard, or a-weather in some degree, in order to keep her to. When the Griping proceeds from this cause, the Royal and Top Gallant Sail forward, may be taken in, which will probably bring her to her proper Steerage again.

COMPASS

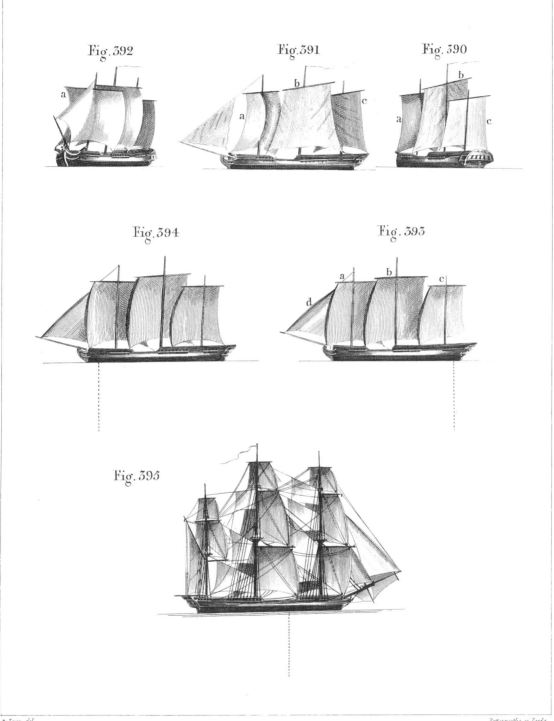

Fig. 392   Fig. 391   Fig. 390

Fig. 394   Fig. 393

Fig. 395

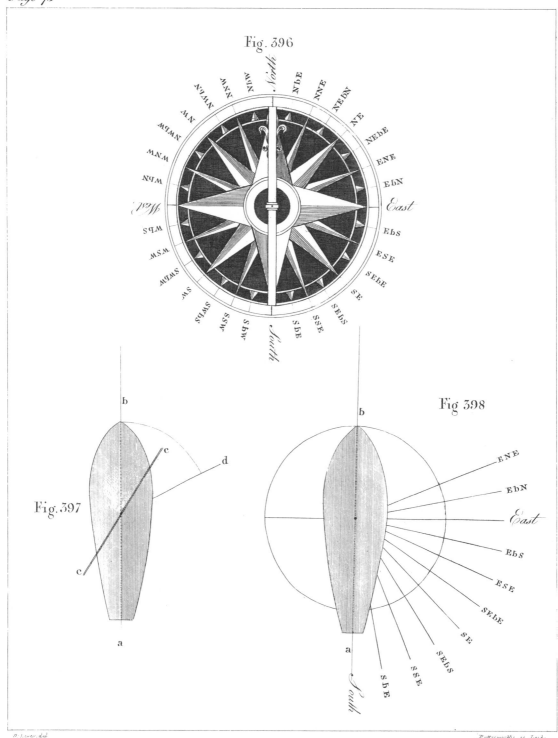

Fig. 396

Fig. 397

Fig 398

COMPASS, &c.

A square rigged Vessel when close hauled, (i. e. as close to the Wind as she can possibly lie), can approach no nearer to it than six Points: to the perfect undertaking of which, the Young Sea Officer must make himself thoroughly acquainted with the Mariner's Compass, which should be diligently got by art, that he may refer to it in his Memory on all Occasions.

The Compass is described on a Card like Fig. 396, divided into several Points; and this Card being fixed on a Piece of Steel called the *Needle*, which has been touched by a Loadstone, acquires the Property when resting on a Pivot fixed vertically in the Compass Box, of pointing to the North.— The North Point of the Compass then pointing to the North, the others will of course point to their respective Parts of the Horizon. The Variation of the Compass is not here noticed, as it may be referred to in any Book of Navigation.

The Compass has eight Points in each Quarter, equal to ninety Degrees, making in the Whole thirty two, equal to three hundred and sixty degrees of the Horizon. A square rigged Ship, when close-hauled (as before mentioned), can lie no nearer to the Wind than six Points: therefore if a Ship be close-hauled on the starboard Tack, and her Head at North, count six Points from thence to the right Hand, or towards the East, and you will find the Wind must be at E. N. E. The wind then forms an Angle with the Keel of six Points, or sixty three Degrees forty five Minutes: so that if the Line (a. b.) Fig. 397, represent the Ship's Keel, (c) will be the Yard when braced up, and (d) the Direction of the Wind. In practice the Yard is braced up sharper, to make the Sail stand to the most advantage.

When the Wind is at E. b N. Fig. 398, she has then one Point free; because she is seven Points from the Wind. When at East, which is eight Points from North, it is said to be on the Beam. It then blows on the Ends of the Ship's Beams, which lie athwart her, and in Lines perpendicular to the Keel, (a. b). E. b S. is one Point abaft the Beam, E. S. E. two Points, S. E. b E. three Points abaft the Beam.

When the Wind is at S. E. it is termed being on the Quarter, when at S. E. b S. one Point on the Quarter, S. S. E. two Points, S. b E. three Points on the Quarter, and when at South, it is right aft, for the Ship is then before the Wind.

When the Ship is on the larboard Tack with her Head North, the Points are counted on the opposite or West Side: and if the Ship's Head be put to any Point of the Compass, the Distances will be the same; for by looking at the Compass, Fig. 396, and counting the Points to the right or left Hand, according as the Ship is on the starboard or larboard Tack, the young Mariner may always find how the Wind is with respect to the Ship's Keel.

The Ship may now be supposed at Sea, close hauled on the starboard Tack, as described in the former page. She is placed at Sea in the first Instance, because her Movements there must be previously understood, in order to comprehend the Management of her at Anchor, casting for a weather Tide, getting under Way, &c. and that all may be made *progressively* clear to the Young Officer.

As all Vessels differ so materially in their working on account of the difference in their Construction, or Trim, there can be no one Method recommended as certain till these be known.

SEAMANSHIP.

*Although original Erratum reads *"line 3 from the top, for 'perfect understanding,' read 'perfect undertaking.'"*, it should be *"line 3 from the top, for 'perfect undertaking,' read 'perfect understanding.'"*

SEAMANSHIP.

TACKING BY THE METHOD FORMERLY PRACTISED.

The system of tacking formerly practised, and which was commonly used as a general rule, will best define the principles, and tend to elucidate the other evolutions more clearly to the young Sea Officer: although the sudden putting down of the Helm, &c. is erroneous.

The Ship, Fig. 399, is now on the *starboard* Tack, with the wind at E N E, and it is found necessary to put about, and stand on the *larboard* Tack. Now, with the wind at E N E, she will lie with her Head North, which is six points from it: therefore when she brings the wind right a-head, she will of course lie E N E; and when she is close hauled on the *larboard* Tack, she will lie with her Head S E, which is also six points from the wind, as may be seen by the Compass, Fig. 403.

When every thing was ready, such as the Weather Braces stretched along, the *lee* Tacks, *weather* Sheets, and *lee* Bowlines hauled through the slack, it was the custom to put the Helm hard over to leeward, and then the word was given---" THE HELM'S A-LEE, FORE SHEET, FORE TOP-BOWLINE, JIB AND STAYSAIL SHEETS LET GO!" *(The Helm was put a-lee, to bring the Ship's Head towards the wind, the Fore, Jib, and Fore Topmast Staysail Sheets let go, to take away the power of those Sails which lie before the Center of Gravity, and give all the effort to those which lie abaft it, and the Fore Top Bowline let go, that the Fore Topsail might the sooner CATCH aback ; and to assist it still more, as soon as that Sail began to touch, the Weather Fore Topsail Brace was hauled on, and as she came to, the Yard was braced up again).*

Suppose this word to have been given, as above, in the Ship, Fig. 399, which had her Head North, as per Compass, and that in consequence she was coming round gradually to the Eastward, and approaching the wind: when she arrived at the position of the Ship, Fig. 400, her Head would be N E by N, (see Compass) within three points of the wind, which blowing on the Leeches or Extremities of the after Sails, made them shake; at this moment the word was given, " OFF TACKS AND SHEETS !" when the Main Tack, Sheet, and all the Staysail Tacks and Sheets were let go, because they were of no farther use in bringing the Ship to the wind; it having no effect upon them but to make them shake. *(at this time the Tacks and Sheets of the Staysails were shifted over the Stays, to be ready for the other Tack ; and the Main Clew-Garnet hauled a little up, that the Yard might come about the easier).*

During this, she was coming rapidly to, and when in the position of the Ship, Fig. 401, (being then Head to wind, E N E, as per Compass) the word was given, " MAINSAIL HAUL !" *(The Mainsail, Main Topsail, Main Top Gallant Sail, Mizen Topsail, and Mizen Top Gallant Sail, having their Bowlines and lee Braces let go, and being quite becalmed by the Head Sails, were braced about, as in the Figure : the larboard Main Tack got down to the Chesstree, and the Sheet gathered aft. The Ship then being liable to sternway, the Helm was shifted over to starboard (see Rudder, page 71), that the starboard side of the Rudder acting against the water might send her Stern to port, consequently her Head to starboard : the Spritsail Yard was topped the contrary way by the starboard Brace, and the larboard Jib Guys set up).*

She was then falling off rapidly, and when so much so that the after Sails were full, the word was given, " LET GO AND HAUL !" the Fore Tack and Bowline were raised, and the Head Yards braced about, the larboard Fore Tack got on board, and the Sheet gathered aft; but the Head Yards were not braced sharp up, that she might come to. *(for after hauling the Head Yards, her falling off would be rapid ; but as she would soon get head-way, the Helm which was a-starboard assisted in bringing her to again, and it was eased as she approached the wind).*

The Yards were then braced sharp up, and the Bowlines hauled, when she would be in the situation of the Ship, Fig. 402, on the larboard Tack, with the wind as before, close hauled, and her Head S E, as per Compass. The principal errors in this mode of tacking a Ship, are as follow :

TACKING

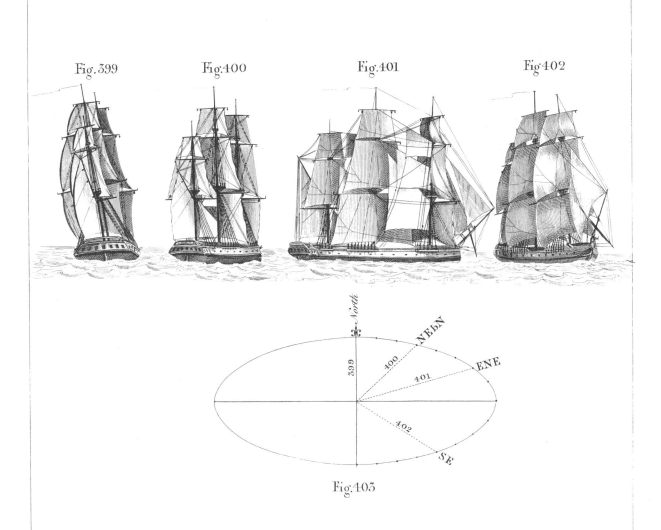

Fig. 399   Fig. 400   Fig. 401   Fig. 402

Fig. 403

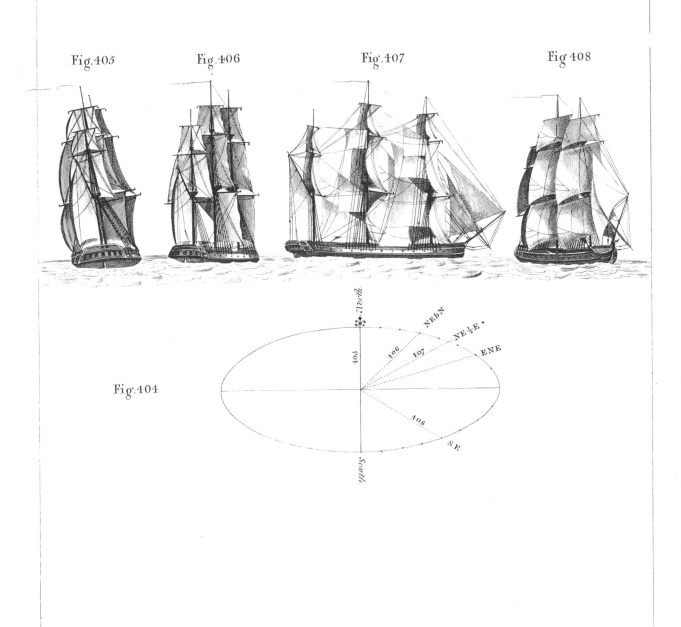

Fig. 405   Fig. 406   Fig. 407   Fig 408

Fig. 404

TACKING EXPEDITIOUSLY.

Firstly.—By the putting of the Helm suddenly over, and at the same time, hard a-lee : by which, though the Ship was brought quickly to the Wind, yet having the flat Part of the starboard Side of the Rudder to drag after her, the Velocity was considerably diminished, and sometimes so much so, as not to bring her past the Point where she would be Head to Wind ; in which case she was sure to miss Stays, and fall off again.

Secondly.—By the bracing to of the Fore Topsail,* which augmented the Defect in the Head-way.

Thirdly.—By not hauling the Mainsail, till the Wind was right a-head ; for the after Sails being becalmed by the Head ones, and laying dead against the Mast, came heavily about, and frequently so much so, as by the Ship's falling off, to get full before the Main Tack could be got on Board, which with a strong Breeze, in Ships weakly manned, could not be done without a Purchase.

Fourthly.—By the Jib and Fore Topmast Staysail Sheets being shifted over the Stays at the same Time with the others ; by which means they caught a-back the wrong way, and prevented the Ship coming to.

And Fifthly.—By the Ground lost to leeward, owing to the falling off before the Sails could be trimmed : all which are much against quick working.

TACKING EXPEDITIOUSLY.

Suppose the Ship, Fig. 405, be on the *starboard* Tack, close hauled, her Head North, of course the Wind at E.N.E. per Compass, Fig. 404, the Water tolerably smooth, and it is thought necessary to put about and stand on the *larboard* Tack, every thing being ready as before. The first Precaution is (as indeed it should be at all times in steering by the Wind), to have her so suited with Sail as nearly to steer herself, with little assistance from the Rudder : by which her way will be more powerful through the Water : she will be brought to the Wind with a small Helm (the Water making little Resistance against it), and probably not have any Stern-way through the whole Rotation.

Every thing being ready, the Ship is luffed *gradually* up with as little Helm as necessary from her known Trim, and the Word, " The Helm's a-lee !" &c. is given as before, when the Fore Sheet, Fore Topmast Staysail, and Jib Sheets, are let go ; *(their Power being taken away before the Center of Rotation, give Effort to the Mizen and other Staysails, to bring her up to the Wind).* When she comes round to the Position of the Ship, Fig. 406, her Head being about N.E. by N. the Wind will blow directly on the Leeches of the square Sails, and the Word is given, " Off Tacks and Sheets !" *The Main Tack and Sheet, and all the Staysail Tacks and Sheets abaft the Fore Mast are let go, and the latter shifted over the Stays.* As soon as she brings the Wind about a Point and a half on the weather Bow (her Head being N.E. ½ E. per Compass), like Fig. 407, the Word is given, " Mainsail Haul !" *The Ship is in the Act of hauling the Mainsail, and it appears by the Figure that the after Yards will nearly fly round of themselves, by the weather Leeches of those Sails catching strongly a-back when the Bowlines and lee Braces are let go, and the Wind having more Power on the weather Side of the Sail to swing the Yard round. After the Mainsail is hauled, she will be nearly Head to Wind, and the after Sails being becalmed by the Head ones, the Main Tack may be got down, and the Sheet aft, with ease, there being little more to do than to gather in the Slack ; the Helm is righted, and afterwards used as her coming to, or falling off requires. Having past the Direction of the Wind, the Jib and Fore Topmast Staysail Sheets are shifted over the Stays. The Breast Backstays should also now be set up. The Spritsail Yard is topped up with the starboard Brace, and the Jib Guys set up as before.* When she brings the Wind about four Points before the larboard Beam, (or sooner if her falling off be rapid) the Word is given, " Let go and Haul !" *The Fore Tack and Head Bowlines are raised, and the Yards braced smartly about with the starboard Braces ; but the weather Braces are checked, that she may come to ; the Yards are braced sharp up, the Bowlines hauled, the weather Braces set taught, and the Geer coiled up.* She will then be in the Position of the Ship, Fig. 408, close hauled on the larboard Tack, her Head S.E. as per Compass.

U

FLATTING

---

* *In working up a River or narrow Channel, the Fore Topsail is commonly braced to, that the Ship may not shoot too far a-head while in Stays.*

FLATTING IN----BOXING OFF.

The Ship is now on the larboard Tack, with the same Sail set as before, the Wind at E.N.E. consequently her Head at S.E. as per Compass, Fig. 409. If the Man at the Helm through neglect, let the Ship, Fig. 410, come up in the Wind *(which is often the case when the weather Helm is not attended to: her Head approaching to the Eastward, brings the Yards in to the Wind's Eye, they being, when full, not much more than three points from it, so that the square Sails shaking forward, lose their Power to pay her Head off to leeward again)*, the Helm is put a-weather, *(or to Port)* the Mizen is hauled up, and the Mizen Staysail down, like Fig. 411, and some hands on the Forecastle, flat in the Jib, and Fore Topmast Staysail Sheets, by hauling the Bights of them over to windward. This will often be effectual, for the Mizen and Mizen Staysail laying abaft the Center of Rotation, and which caused her (particularly the former) to fly up in the Wind, are now taken in, and the Bights of the Sheets forward being hauled over, give additional Power to the Jib, and Fore Topmast Staysail, with the weather Helm, to pay her Head off again.

The effect of flatting in may be seen by Fig. 412; for the Bight of the Sheet which the Man hauls to him, brings the Clew of the Sail more towards the Center of the Ship, which gives it the effect to pay her Head off again, though not so much so (as when the Sail is a-back with the Sheet hauled over to windward) as to considerably impede her Head-way.

If the Ship be too far gone for this to recover her, and she continue coming round to the Eastward, the Fore Tack, Sheet, Head Bowlines and lee Braces are let go, and the Head Yards are braced rapidly about by the larboard Braces, the larboard or weather Jib and Fore Topmast Staysail Sheets hauled aft, and the starboard or lee bowlines forward, like Fig. 413. She will be then sure to pay off again; for the Jib and Fore Topmast Staysail, as well as the *Head Sails*, all laying a-back, have the greatest power given them they can possibly receive, to act before the Center of Rotation, and turn her Head to leeward; at the same time they receive no check from the after Sails, which are shivering, and are of course without effort to effect her. If she have Stern-way, and it be thought necessary to help her with the Helm, it may be put a-lee, or a-starboard. *(the starboard side of the Rudder being pressed against the Water, will force her Stern to windward, which assists the Head Sails to pay her Head off to starboard).* If it be not thought adviseable to assist her with the Helm, it may be righted, and used as her falling off, or coming to requires. See Note at the bottom of page 79.

When danger is discovered to *windward*, it is avoided by the Ship's Head *receding from* the Wind; and if it be necessary to stand on the other Tack, she *wares* or *veers*; but it is only on such occasions in fine weather that Ships ever ware, the disadvantage being so great in losing ground. For by the Compass, Fig. 414, it will be seen, that in tacking and going round to the Eastward from N. to S.E. she had only to move twelve points from her first position, and that till she came Head to Wind, she was gaining considerably to windward, and allowing the falling off before she is trimmed again, to be equal to this, (which if she be well managed it will not be) she has then performed her Evolution, and is in the same situation as before, having at least, lost nothing by the manœuvre.

VEERING

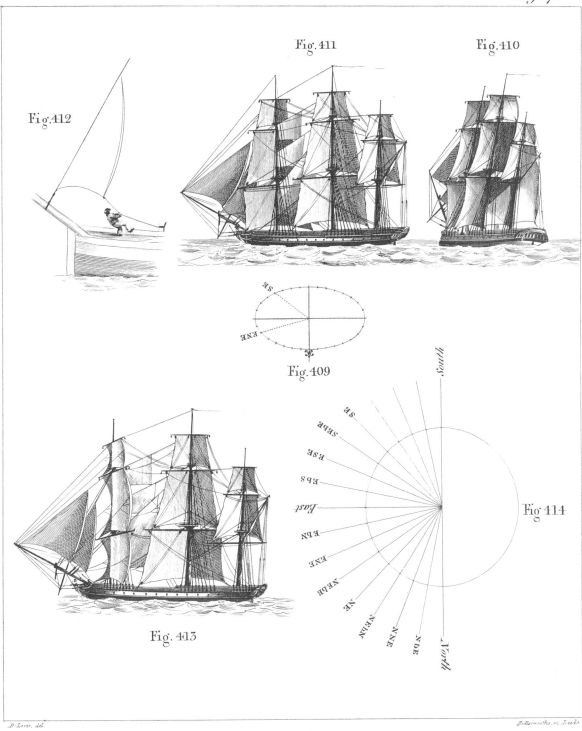

Fig. 412

Fig. 411

Fig. 410

Fig. 409

Fig. 413

Fig. 414

Fig. 416   Fig 417   Fig. 418   Fig. 419

Fig.415

Fig. 420   Fig. 421

D. Lever del.

Butterworths sc. Leeds

VEERING or WARING---TAKEN A-BACK.

In the Compass, Fig. 415, which describes her Waring distance, the disadvantage of this movement is evident: for in the mere turning motion, she must go from S. E. to North, which is twenty points, being eight points (or one-fourth) of the Compass more than she had to go in tacking; but the principal defect is, that during this movement, whilst she is receding from the wind, she is forced rapidly through the water, and making all her way to leeward. However, in the present instance, all this is supposed to be necessary.

The Ship, Fig. 416, perceiving danger to windward, puts the Helm to *port*, (or *a-weather)* hauls up the Mizen, down the Mizen Staysail, and shivers the Mizen Topsail, *(by letting go the Bowline and lee Brace, and hauling in the Weather one)* and sometimes hauls up the Mainsail; but if not, the Main Sheet is eased off. *(The Helm being a-weather, and the Power being taken from the Sails, which are at the after extremity of the Ship, effort is given to the Head Sails, which lie before the Center of Gravity, to pay her head off to leeward)*. The Main, Main Top, and Main Top Gallant Bowlines are let go; and when her Head is South, (as per Compass) the wind being then two points abaft the Beam, like Fig. 417, the Main Tack is raised, and the Weather Braces are rounded in. When she has fallen off so as to bring her Head W.S.W. (as per Compass) she will be before the wind, and in the position of the Ship, Fig. 418: the Yards are then squared, and the starboard Main and Fore Tacks got on board: *(the Head Sails, as may be seen in the Figure, will be at this time becalmed by the after ones)* the Jib, and Staysail Sheets are shifted over the Stays, the Spritsail Yard topped up with the larboard Brace, and the Starboad Jib Guys set up. When her Head is W.N.W. (as per Compass) she will have the wind on the starboard quarter, at which time the Mizen is hauled out, the Mizen Staysail hoisted, and the Sheet hauled aft, like Fig. 419. *(these acting abaft the Center of Gravity, help to bring her rapidly to)*. When she has come round so as to bring the wind on the Beam, *(her Head being N.N.W.)* or before, if required, the Helm is righted, to moderate her coming to; the Yards are then braced sharp up, the Sheets hauled aft, the Bowlines hauled, and the Geer coiled up. She will then be on the starboard Tack, again close hauled, her Head North, and the wind at E.N.E. as before.

Suppose the Ship, Fig. 420, to be on the starboard Tack, and that the wind shift suddenly a-head. *(when she is taken with the wind a-head, the Head Sails lie flat a-back, and the after ones are becalmed by them, as in the Figure)*. In this case, the Main Tack is raised, the Main Sheet, after Bowlines, and lee Braces let go; the after Yards braced about like Fig. 421, the larboard Main Tack got on board, and the starboard Sheet aft: the Jib and Staysail Sheets shifted over the Stays, *(the Jib and Fore Topmast Staysail Sheets are not hauled aft, if her falling off be rapid)* the Spritsail Yard topped, and the Helm righted.* When she has brought the wind about four points before the Beam, (or before, if she fall off fast) the Fore Tack, Sheet, Head Bowlines, and lee Braces are let go, the Head Yards braced about, the larboard Fore Tack got on board, the Sheet aft, and all trimmed sharp when come to, as described in " *letting go and hauling*". (see Tacking, page 76). She will be then on the larboard Tack again.

Wind

* *It is often a custom to put the Helm a-starboard in this case, if the Ship have Stern-way, that the starboard side of the Rudder being forced against the water, by sending her Stern to Port, may assist her falling off. However, the Ship's particular Trim must be attended to in this, as in all other Cases.---Most Ships will fall off fast enough, having Stern-way, and the Head Sails being a-back, with the Helm a-midships; and many Seamen object to the Helm being put over when going a-stern, as a dangerous pressure against the Rudder. This can only be objected to when it is blowing fresh: for in many situations, such as Boxhauling a Ship when near a lee Shore, making a-stern-board, &c. it is absolutely necessary to use the Helm in Stern-way.*

Wind abaft the Beam-----Setting Topmast Studding Sails.

Suppose the Ship to be on the larboard Tack close hauled, and to have had the Wind at W N W, her Head laying North; but that it is now come round to W b S; (see Compass, Fig. 422), it is then one Point abaft the Beam, and nine from the Direction of her Keel; so that when she was close-hauled, it was W N W, or six Points from her Keel; but now she has it three Points free, as may be seen by the Compass.

When this is the case, as in Fig. 423, the Sheets are eased off, the Bowlines let go, the lee Braces eased and the weather ones hauled in a little; the Fore Tack eased off, the Sheet hauled a little aft, and the weather Clew got down to the Cat-head by a Rope called a *Passaree*. The Trusses are set taught, and as it is fine Weather, if it be thought necessary to make sail, Hands are sent up to bend the Royal Halliards, unbecket the Royals, and shift their Sheets over the Top Gallant Stays. The Royals are then hoisted up, the Spritsail and Spritsail Topsail set, and the Studding Sail Booms run out as in the Figure.

The Topmast and Top Gallant Studding Sail Halliards, (a and b), Fig. 424, are reeved through the Span-Blocks at the Mast Heads (c and d), and through the Jewel Blocks at the Yard Arms (e and f): the Topmast Studding Sail Tack (g), through the Block at the Boom End, and the lower Studding Sail Halliards (h), through the Span-Block at the lower Cap, and through the Block (k), on the Top-mast Studding Sail Boom. The Yard Sheet (l), Fig. 425, is bent to the Heel Lashing (m), of the Boom, and the Men bowsing upon it, launch the Boom out. In large Ships a Tackle is used instead of the Yard Sheet.

One of the Burton Tackles (o), Fig. 426, is hooked to a Selvagee on the Topsail Yard at the second Quarter (p), the double Block to an Eye Bolt in the Topmast Cap (q): the other Burton Tackle (r), is hooked to its own Pendent by the double Block, and to the Topping Lift Pendent on the Topmast Studding Sail Boom (s), by its single one. The former of these Burtons (o), acts as a Preventer Lift, and keeps the Topsail Yard from sagging down by the Weight of the Topmast Studding Sail, and the latter (r), supports the Topmast Studding Sail Boom against the weight of the lower Studding Sail.

The Fore Topmast Studding Sail is brought on the Forecastle and bent to its Yard, Fig. 427. The Halliards (t), are made fast with a Fisherman's Bend (see page 8), one third from the inner Yard Arm (s): the Tack (u), is bent to the Clew (v), and the Down-hauler is reeved through the Block at the Clew (w), through the Thimble in the Middle of the outer Leech (x), and made fast to the outer Yard Arm (y). The Sheet (z), is bent to the inner Clew with a long and short Leg, the short Leg having a Thimble in it. The Sail is made up, and stopped to its Yard with Rope Yarns; the Halliards (a), Fig. 428, are also stopped to the outer Yard Arm. The Halliards are hoisted on, and the Man (b), on the Fore Yard, having bent the Yard Sheet (c), to the Thimble in the short Leg of the Sheet (d), cuts the Stops. The Tack (m), is then hauled out to the Boom End (n), the Sail hoisted up, and the Man on the Yard keeps it abaft the Leech of the Topsail. *(A Topmast Studding Sail is set abaft the Topsail when to windward, and before it when to leeward, because to windward the outer Yard Arm must incline rather forwards, to make the Sail stand fair; which could not be the case if the Sail were set before the Topsail, for the Pressure of the inner Yard Arm would prevent it, and might injure the Topsail. When a Topmast Studding Sail is set before the Topsail to leeward, the Deck Sheet is then hauled forward, and the Yard Sheet let go).*

When the Sail is up, the Yard Sheet is hauled out. The Sail when hoisted will appear like Fig. 429.--- (e) the Tack, (f) the Deck Sheet, (g) the Yard Sheet, (h) the Down-hauler, (i) the Halliards, (k) the Leech of the Topsail, (l) the Boom Brace and Pendent.

SETTING

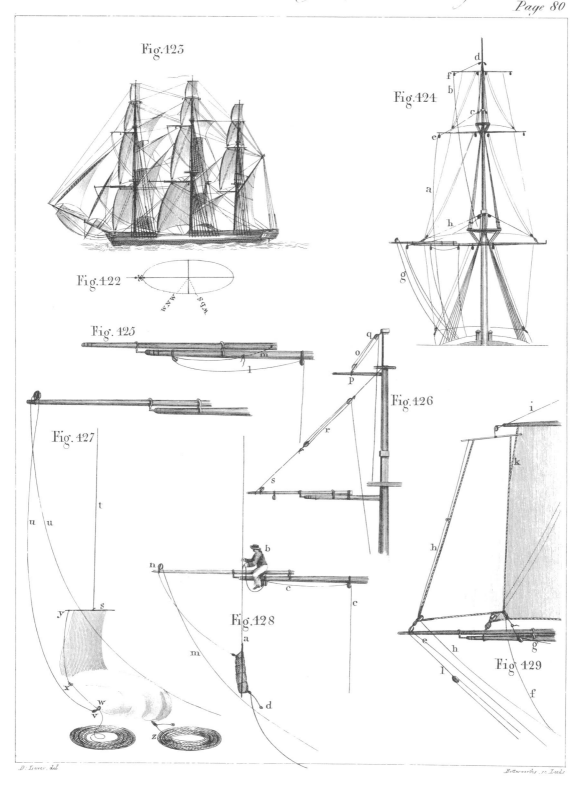

Fig.423

Fig.422

Fig.424

Fig.425

Fig.426

Fig.427

Fig.428

Fig.429

D. Inver. del.

Butterworths. sc. Leeds.

Setting Studding Sails.

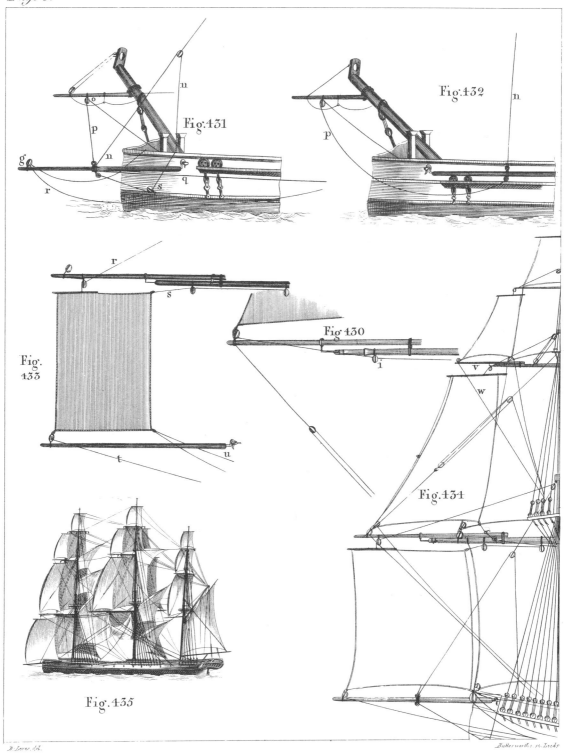

Fig. 431

Fig. 432

Fig. 430

Fig. 433

Fig. 434

Fig. 435

D. Lever. del.

Butterworth. sc. Leeds.

SETTING STUDDING SAILS.

It is sometimes the Practice to lead the Topmast Sudding Sail Tacks like Topsail Sheets, Fig. 430, through a Block (i), on the lower Yard, and through another farther in, instead of its being taken to the Gangway; for in going large, (these Sails, particularly in East Indiamen, being carried when it blows fresh), should the Wind come suddenly forward, and require the weather Braces to be eased off, it is not always that the Tack can be eased in Proportion: if it be too much so, it is difficult to haul out again, and if not enough, the Boom is liable to be carried away by the Strain: therefore in Ships which go long Voyages, where this Sail is of such constant use, it is good to have a stout Brace always reeved, and the Tack to lead as before mentioned, as there will then be no risk in bracing forward, of carrying away the Boom.

Before the lower Studding Sail Boom is rigged out, the Topping Lift (n), Fig. 431, is hooked to the Thimble in the Strap on the Middle of the Boom, and a Block (o), being lashed on the Spritsail Yard, the fore Guy (p), is reeved through it, and made fast to the Boom a-midships: the after Guy (q), is also bent to the Boom a-midships, and the other End reeved through a Block lashed to a Timber Head at the Gangway. The Martingale (s), is reeved through a Block lashed to a Bolt in the Bends, and clinched to a Thimble in a Strap at the Middle of the Boom. The Tack (r), is reeved through the Block (g), at the Boom End leading on the Forecastle, the other is reeved through a Block at the Gangway.

To rig the Boom out, Fig. 432,—Hoist upon the Topping Lift (n), haul out the fore Guy (p), and ease the after one, when it will come across, and appear like Fig. 431.

The lower Studding Sail may now be set, Fig. 433, the outer Halliards (r), are bent to the Yard with a Fisherman's Bend, (see page 8): the inner ones (s), to the inner Cringle at the Head of the Sail, with a Sheet Bend (see page 8): the Tack (t), to the outer Clew, the Sheet (u), to the inner Clew. First, haul out the Tack (t), then hoist up the Yard with the outer Halliards (r), and when they are belayed, hoist on the inner ones, (which stretch the Head of the Sail), and haul taught the Sheet (u).

The Top Gallant Studding Sail Boom (v), Fig. 434, is rigged out by Hand, by Men on the Topsail Yard. The Tack (w), which is reeved through a Thimble at the Boom End, is over-hauled into the Top, and there, with the Halliards, bent. In large Ships the Sail is stopped and hoisted up, and a Man on the Topsail Yard, guys it abaft the Top Gallant Sail, as the Topmast Studding Sail was set abaft the Topsail. This Figure shews the lower, Topmast, and Top Gallant Studding Sails when set, with their Geer. The Main Studding Sails are set in the same Manner.

(To set the lower, and Top Gallant Studding Sails flying, see page 65).

The Spanker is set like a lower Studding Sail, by hauling out the Sheet Rope to the Boom End, hoisting on the outer Halliards, then the inner and Throat ones, and hauling the Tack forwards, or to Windward, (see Spanker, page 66).

If the Wind come to two Points on the Quarter, like Fig. 435, the weather Skirt of the Mainsail is hauled up, that it may not becalm the Sails forward, the *lee* Main Topmast and Main Top Gallant Studding Sails may be set *before* the Topsails, as in the Figure. Preventer Backstays should be now got up; as the Strain on the Masts comes from abaft. The Runners hitched round the Topmast Heads will answer this Purpose.

W   Before

Before the Wind---Wind abaft the Beam---Taking in Studding Sails.

If the Wind come round to South, which is right aft, (as per Compass, Fig. 438), the Driver, Jib, and Staysails are hauled down, the Mizen Topsail lowered down on the Cap, or handed : the Mainsail hauled up, the Topmast and Top Gallant Studding Sails hauled down forwards : the Fore Topsail and Fore Top Gallant Sail, lowered down, clewed up and handed, like Fig. 436.

The Driver is taken in because it will not stand well, or if it did, being so far aft, it would cause the Ship to steer wild ; and the Rudder on that account, having one Side or the other continually opposed to the Water, must check the Ship's way considerably. The Mizen Topsail is taken in, because it would in some measure take the Wind out of the Main Topsail, and also cause bad Steerage, by being so far aft : the Staysails are hauled down, for they will not stand in that Direction, and the Fore Topsail and Fore Top Gallant Sail are clewed up, on account of their being becalmed by the Main ones : these two Sails are furled, to prevent their being injured by flapping against the Masts as the Ship rolls. (To take in a Topsail, see page 89).

The Mainsail is hauled up to let the wind into the Foresail, the Spritsail is kept set, as it will catch Wind under the Foot of the Foresail. The Studding Sails are sometimes set as in the Figure ; two Topmast and two Top Gallant Studding Sails aft, and two lower Studding Sails forward : the Power of the Sails is thus tolerably divided ; but in this, as in all cases of setting Sail, the Management must be left to the Judgment of the Officer, knowing the Trim of the Ship : some Vessels sailing better with more Sail forward, others with more aft, according as they are by the Stern or Head.--- Sometimes in order to divide the Effect of the Sails, as in Fig. 437, the Topmast and lower Studding Sails are set forward, the Fore Topsail being furled, and the Yard hoisted up to the Mast-head : the Top Gallant Studding Sails aft : this in the common Cant of Seamen is termed *scandalizing the Fore Topsail Yard.* Ships which answer their Helm well, will often Sail a Knot faster by having both Main Sheets aft before the Wind, the Foresail being in the Brails.

Suppose the Wind come forward again to W. b S. (as per Compass, Fig. 439), one Point abaft the Beam, the Ship steering North with the Studding Sails and Staysails set, like Fig. 440, and the Wind encreasing so, that it is prudent to take in Sail. The Royals, Top Gallant Studding Sails, Spritsail Topsail, and Driver, are taken in : the latter will have great Power in a strong Breeze, and may occasion her to gripe, and carry weather Helm.

The Top Gallant Studding Sails are taken in by lowering the Halliards (a), Fig. 441, hauling down upon the Sheet (b), and easing off the Tack (c) : when in the Top, they are made up, the Booms run in and lashed to the Topsail Yards by the Heel Lashing, or lowered down on Deck. The Halliards (a), are unreeved from the Jewel Blocks at the Yard Arms (d), and a Figure of Eight Knot, (see page 7), being cast on the End, they are rounded up to the Span Block (e), at the Top Gallant Mast Head, that they may not impede the lowering of the Top Gallant Yard (f). The Royals when lowered, must be becketted, the Halliards unbent, and hitched round the Top Gallant Stay, for the same Reason.

If the Wind encrease, and it be thought proper to take in the lower Studding Sail, the Sheet (g), is stretched aft, Fig. 442, the outer Halliards (h), are lowered, the Tack (i), eased off, the Sail is gathered in on the Forecastle, and the inner Halliards lowered. The Boom is then swung fore and aft, by easing off the fore Guy (m), Fig. 443, and hauling in upon the after one (n) : it is then lashed in the Chains, the Geer coiled upon it, and secured. The Block (p), is taken off the Spritsail Yard.

TAKING.

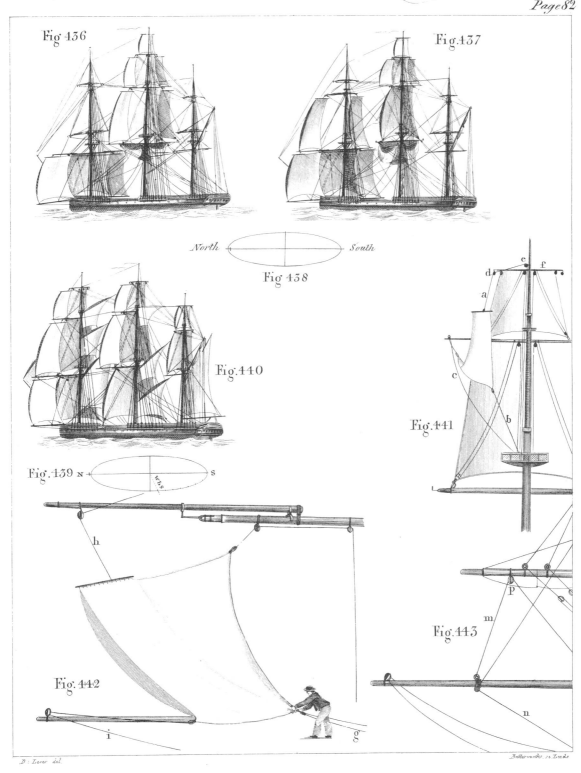

Fig.436

Fig.437

North ————— South

Fig 438

Fig.440

Fig.441

Fig.439 N ————— S

Fig.442

Fig.443

D: Lever del.

Butterworth re Leeds.

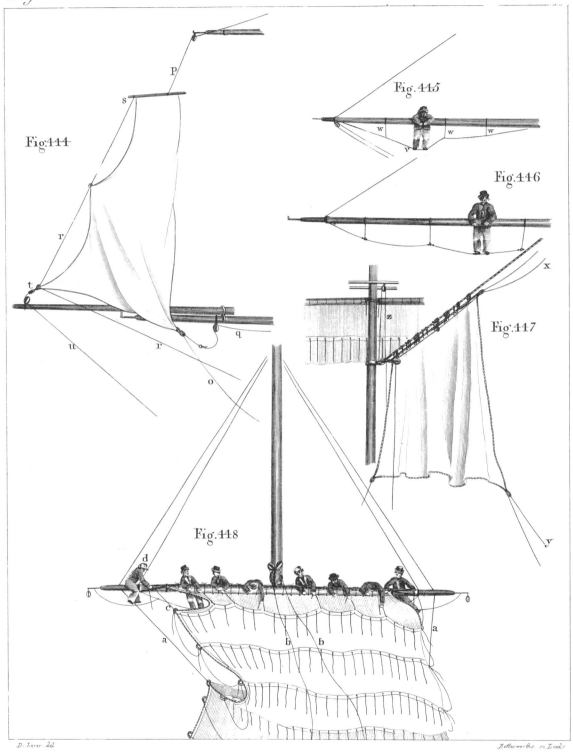

Fig: 444

Fig: 445

Fig: 446

Fig: 447

Fig: 448

TAKING IN STUDDING SAILS---REEFING TOPSAILS, &c.

If the wind come forward, the Yards are braced up, and the Fore Topmast Studding Sail hauled down. A hand is sent on the Fore Yard to pass the Deck Sheet (o), Fig. 444, a-baft the Yard: the Down-hauler (r), is then manned, the Halliards (p), are lowered, the Yard Sheet (q), eased, and the Down-hauler (r), hauled on, till the Yard Arm (s), comes down to the Tack Clew (t): the Tack (u), is then eased off, and the Sail hauled down, gathering it in on the Forecastle by the Deck Sheet (o). When this Sail is taken in with the wind very large, it is hauled down forward, the Deck Sheet and Down-hauler being passed before the Yard. The Yards are braced up, the Fore Tack got on board, the Sheets aft, and the Bowlines hauled. The Spritsail is reefed, (see Spritsail, page 58) the Spritsail Yard topped up with the lee Brace, the Jib Guy set up, and the Mizen hauled out: she is then close hauled on the larboard Tack again, the wind at W.N.W. her Head consequently North.

The Topmast Studding Sail Boom is rigged in; the Geer coiled, and stopped on the Yard Arm; the Halliards are unreeved from the Jewel Blocks, a Figure of Eight Knot cast on the end, and rounded up to the Span Block at the Topmast Cap, (as mentioned in the former page for the Top Galiant Studding Sail Halliards) that they may not prevent the Topsail Yard's coming down. The Burton Pendents (mentioned page 80, Fig. 426) are taken off the Topsail Yard, and Topping Lift Pendent.   *

If the wind freshen, the Main Top Gallant Staysail is hauled down into the Fore Top, and the Mizen Topmast Staysail into the Main Catharpins. (to haul down the Main Top Gallant Staysail, see page 62, Fig. 342). The Jib is hauled one-third in, and a Reef taken in the Topsails. The Horses on the Yards (in large Ships particularly) should be moused; for by Fig. 445, it appears that the Horse (v), gives way through the Stirrups (w), with the Man who first goes on the Yard; and a Boy going on occasionally, is often dangerously situated, as he can have but little hold, and certainly do nothing in that state. Now by the Horses being moused at proper distances, like Fig. 446, the Men may lie out on the Yard with twice the expedition; and it is much handier for a Man or two to go on to let out a Reef, &c. for by this, they stand as securely on the Yard, as if it were full manned.--- Instead of mousing, the Stirrups may be *tailed* into the Horses, for neatness.

Before the Topsails are reefed, the Top Gallant Sails are lowered and clewed up, or clewed up at the Mast Head: and if the Middle Staysail have no Jack Stay, and go with a Gromet round the Mast, it may be hauled down into the Fore Top, otherwise the Fore Topsail Yard cannot come down. The Halliards (x), Fig. 447, are let go, the Down-hauler hauled on, the Sheet (y), eased off; and when the Sail is down to the Gromet, the Stay is eased off, the tricing Line (z), let go, and it comes down into the Top.

In reefing a Topsail, the Halliards are let fly, the Clew-lines hauled on, and the Weather Braces rounded in, to spill the Sail. The Reef Tackles (a), Fig. 448, are hauled out, and the Men go on the Yard. *(if the Buntlines (b), be kept fast when the Halliards are let go, they assist in spilling the Sail).* The Weather Earing (c), is first hauled out by the Man (d), at the Yard Arm; because the lee one is easily got out by the Sail blowing over to leeward. The Men therefore haul the Reef over to the Man (d), and when at a proper distance from the Yard Arm, he takes two *outer* turns, and expends the remainder of the Earing in *inner* ones. The *lee* Earing is then passed in the same manner, the Sail hauled well on the Yard, and the Points made fast with Reef Knots (see page 7).

It is plain that *two outer* turns are sufficient, (as shewn in page 53, Fig. 305) their use being only to keep the Head of the Sail on the Stretch; whereas the *inner* turns have the whole strain of the Leech to bear when the Sail is hoisted, and the Bowline hauled.

Setting

---

*Although original Erratum reads *"line 15 from the top, for 'Burton Tackles, read 'Burton Pendents.'"*, it should be *"line 15 from the top, for 'Burton Pendents,' read 'Burton Tackles.'"*

Setting and Taking in Top Gallant Sails---Taking in the Jib, &c.

Care must be taken that the Sails be hauled well upon the Yards, and that the Points be passed clear of the Top Gallant Sheets. When the Men are off the Yard, the Halliards are stretched along, the Reef Tackle let go, and the Topsails hoisted up, keeping them shaking by the Weather Braces, (the Men in the Tops overhauling the Clew-lines, Buntlines, and Reef Tackles) and when they are up with a taught Leech, the Halliards are belayed, the Yards braced up, the Bowlines hauled, and the Geer coiled up.

The Top Gallant Sails are sheeted home, and hoisted. The *lee* Sheets of either Topsails or Top-Gallant Sails, are always hauled home first, (except when going very large) Fig. 449, because the wind blowing the Sail over to leeward, the *lee* Sheet (i), will almost come home of itself; and then the Sail being kept shaking by the Weather Brace, the Weather Sheet (k), is easily hauled home. She is then like Fig 450, the Topsails reefed, the Top Gallant Sails set over them, (except the Mizen Top Gallant Sail, which is furled) the Jib a third in, Fore Topmast Staysail, Main Topmast Staysail, Mizen Staysail and Mizen.

When a ship gripes or carries her Helm too much to windward, it is commonly the rule to haul up the Mizen, and if that be not sufficient, to take in the Mizen Staysail also; but it should be well considered, what is the occasion of her requiring so much Weather Helm, otherwise the taking in of these Sails, instead of remedying, may greatly encrease the defect; for a Ship is as likely to gripe by having too much Sail set forward as abaft, the consequence of which is, that she meets with great lateral resistance against her Bows to leeward, for the Head Sails may press her down forward, and raise her proportionably abaft, and then the Rudder loses a deal of its power to make her ware, by being lifted so much out of the water. Thus the Ship is in the same situation as if she were trimmed by the Head, which is well known to be much against either sailing or steerage. Therefore when the Ship gripes from this cause, instead of the Mizen and Mizen Staysail being taken in, the Fore Top Gallant Sail is handed, Fig. 451, which eases her forward: she then slackens her Helm, consequently makes her way better through the water, by not having the flat part of the Rudder to drag after her.

In taking in the Fore Top Gallant Sail, let go the Halliards, round in the Weather Brace, and clew up to windward first (see taking in the Fore Topsail, Figs. 458 and 459, page 86), then to leeward, and haul up the Buntline.

As many Vessels in the Coasting Trade have no Buntlines to their Top Gallant Sails, it would be well if the necessity of carrying them were strongly enforced. When it blows fresh, these Sails (generally left to the management of boys) are very heavy to hand, and if there be no Buntlines to spill them, the result may be fatal to those on the *lee* Yard Arm, by the Sail's blowing over to leeward, as may be seen by Fig. 452. Surely the saving of a few Fathoms of small Rope should not be put in competition with the life of a fellow-creature!

If it blow so fresh that it is necessary to take in the Jib, Fig. 453, the Halliards (l), are let go, the Down-hauler (m), hauled upon, the Sheet (n), eased off, and when it is close down on the Boom, if the wind be likely to encrease, the Stay or Out-hauler (o), (according as it is rigged, see Jib, page 60), is let go: it is hauled in close to the Bowsprit Cap (p), and stowed away in the Fore Topmast Staysail Netting (q).

Hauling

Fig.449

Fig.450

Fig.451

Fig.452

Fig.453

D: Lever. del.

Butterworths. sc. Leeds.

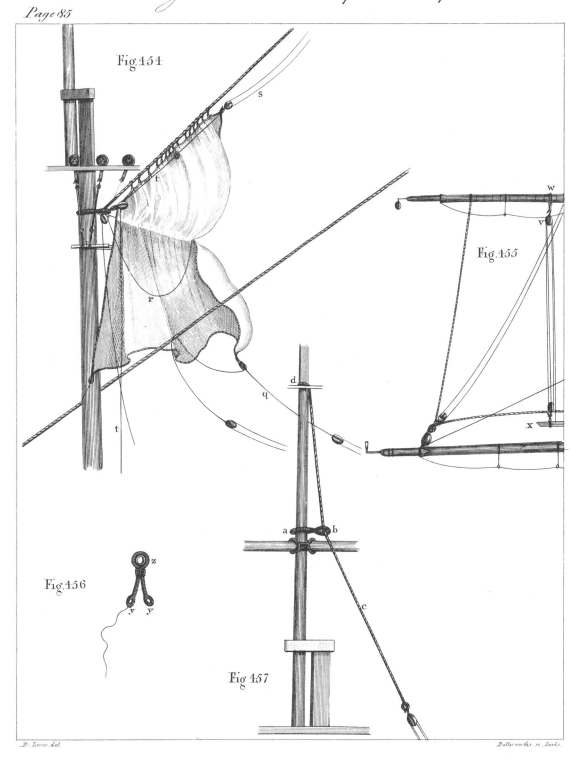

Fig. 454

Fig. 455

Fig. 456

Fig 457

D: Lever. del.   *Butterworths. sc. Leeds.*

85

Hauling down the Main Topmast Staysail---Travelling Backstay, &c.

The Wind being now pretty fresh, it may be necessary to take in the Main Top Gallant Sail, and the Main Topmast Staysail.—*(for the former see taking in the Fore Topsail, Fig. 458, page 86).* The latter is now cut so deep, that it is generally thought to bear as much Strain on the Mast as the Main Topsail.

The Sheet (q), Fig. 454, is eased off, and the *lee* Brail only hauled up, gathering in the Slack of the Weather one (r); *(if the Weather one were hauled up first, the Sail catching a-back would hold so much Wind, as in a heavy Squall, to prevent its being taken in; its flying out, and flapping violently up and down, might also split or damage it)*: the Halliards (s) are let go, and it is hauled down by the Down hauler (t). If it be likely to blow hard, it is hauled up on the fore Catharpins, and stowed away there, having a Gasket passed round it. In many Ships there are Nettings stretched from the Futtock Shrouds on each side, to secure it the better.

The Burton Tackles may be clapped on the Topsail Yards, as follows, Fig. 455. The double Block (v), is hooked to a Strap or Selvagee, passed round the inner Quarter of the Yard (w), and the single Block to a Strap round the lower Tressle-tree (x): this will act as a Down-haul Tackle, to haul the Yard down by, when the Ship heels over in a Squall; the Tendency of the Topsail being then to fly up to the Mast Head. In Merchant Ships where the Buntlines go with Monkey Blocks, (see page 55), they serve as Down-haulers. As the Wind increases, the second Reefs may be taken in the Topsails, which is done in the same Manner as mentioned for the first Reef, (see page 83), taking care to haul the Sail well upon the Yard over the first Reef.

When a Topsail is double reefed, the Strain is taken considerably from the Mast Head where it lay before, and where the Rigging immediately counteracted it: on this account, a Preventer, or Travelling Backstay is used as a Support to the Mast, just above the Topsail Yard, for which purpose a strong Gromet is often worked round the Topmast, or else a Strap, Fig. 456, with an Eye in each Leg, (y), and a large Thimble (z), seized in the Bight. This Strap (a), Fig. 457, is taken round the Mast, the two Eyes are seized together before it, the Thimble (b), laying aft. One of the Runners (c), is reeved through this Thimble, and clinched or hitched round the Mast Head (d), the lower Block of the runner Tackle is hooked to an Eye Bolt in the Stool of the Topmast Backstay: the Fall is taken through a leading Block on Deck.

When the Topsail is hoisted, it may be kept shaking by the weather Brace, and the Strap being slid down just above the Yard, the Travelling Backstay is set up: the Sail is then filled, the Bowline hauled, the weather Brace set taught, and the Geer coiled up.

If the Sea run high, particularly on the Beam, caution must be had what Sail is set that may cause her to gripe: This must entirely depend on the Trim of the Ship, as some carry their Helms very differently from others, with the same Sail set. If she carry much weather Helm, the Mizen may be hauled up, and the third Reef taken in the Fore Topsail, which will ease her forward, as her being pressed down in the Water will prevent her receding from the Wind in a sudden Squall, or answering the Helm when put up to avoid a heavy Sea, and make it pass aft. In taking in the Mizen when the Sheet is eased off, the lee throat Brail is well manned and hauled up, then the other Brails, and the weather ones gathered in.

If the Weather look angry, and there be reason to expect a heavy Gale, the Guns must be secured, Preventer Breechings clapped on, and the Ports well lashed in: the Booms, if there be many on Deck, must be confined by additional Lashings, passed through the Span Shackles on each Side, and frapped.

X   Taking

Taking in a Topsail---Getting down Top Gallant Yards.

The third Reef may be taken in the Main Topsail, (for which purpose the Sail must be clewed up) and the Mizen Topsail handed, and if the wind increase, the Fore Topsail also.   To take in the Fore Topsail, the Clew-lines, Down-haul Tackle and Weather Brace are well manned, the Halliards are let go, the Weather Brace hauled in, the Weather Sheet started, and the Clew-line hauled up: the Bowline is then let go, the lee Sheet started and clewed up, and the Buntlines hauled up. The Rolling Tackle is clapped on, and the Men go on the Yard to furl the Sail.

In taking in a Topsail, Fig. 458, the Weather Sheet (f), is first clewed up, because the Sail naturally flies to leeward, and keeps full : then the Bowline (e), and lee Sheet (d), being let go, the Sail catches aback, like Figure 459, and is taken in almost without a Shake ; for if the lee Sheet were eased off first, the Sail might shake so violently as to split.   However, it is sometimes necessary when a Vessel is weakly manned, to haul the Clew-line a little up, in order to get the weather Brace in.

The Rolling Tackle is clapped on to windward, Fig. 460 : the single Block of a Luff-tackle is hooked to a Strap or a Selvagee round the Yard, at (g), and the double one (h), to an Eye-bolt at the lower Cap, the Fall leading down upon Deck : when the Ship rolls over to leeward, this Tackle is bowsed taught and belayed, which confines the Yard so that it has not play to chafe the Mast by the Ship's rolling.   The Ship will now be under the Main Sail, Fore Sail, close reefed Main Topsail, Fore Topmast and Mizen Staysails, like Fig. 461; but if she gripe, the Mizen Staysail is brailed up and hauled down ; as the Main Topmast Staysail was, (see page 85).

The Top Gallant Yards may now be got down ; for which purpose the Jack Block (i), Fig. 462, is taken aloft, and buttoned round the Top Gallant Mast: the Tye (k), must be cast off the Yard, and hitched to the Strap of the Jack Block (i), and the Top Rope (l), being reeved through it, the Block is triced up by the Halliards (m).   The Sheets (n), Bowlines, Buntlines, and Clew-lines, are cast off, and made fast to the Cross-trees (o) : the *Top* or *Yard Rope* is bent to the Slings of the Yard by a Fisherman's Bend (see page 8), and the Bight (q), carried to leeward and stopped : (or it may be hitched there, and the end bent to the Slings of the Yard, as before) the weather Clew-line is bent to the weather Lift, (if the latter be not long enough to lower upon) and the Parral cast off.   The *Top* or *Yard* Rope is then swayed upon, and being stopped at (q), it cants the Yard : the weather Clew-line is eased, the Yard Rope lowered away a little, and the Yard stopped to the Traveller (w), Fig. 463, on the weather Topmast Backstay.   The Man (s), in the Topmast Shrouds unrigs the lower or weather Yard Arm, and he on the Cross-trees the upper one.   The Yard is then lowered down on Deck, being kept to windward by the Traveller on the Backstay (w).   The Braces and Lifts are made fast to the Cross-trees, the Yard Rope is cast off when the Yard is down, unreeved from the Jack Block, which is unbuttoned, and sent down, and the Tye hitched to the Cross-trees.

The Top Gallant Top Block (t), Fig. 464, being hooked to the Eye-bolt in the larboard side of the Topmast Cap ; the Top Rope is reeved through it, through the Sheave Hole in the Top Gallant Mast, and the end is hitched to the Eye-bolt in the starboard side of the Cap (u).

If the Top Gallant Masts are to be struck, the Stays and Rigging are eased off; the Top Rope is swayed upon, the Fid. (v), taken out, and the Mast lowered down : when low enough, the Top Rope is belayed, and a Heel lashing passed through the Fid Hole and round the Topmast ; but it is preferable to lower the Masts down on Deck.

Close

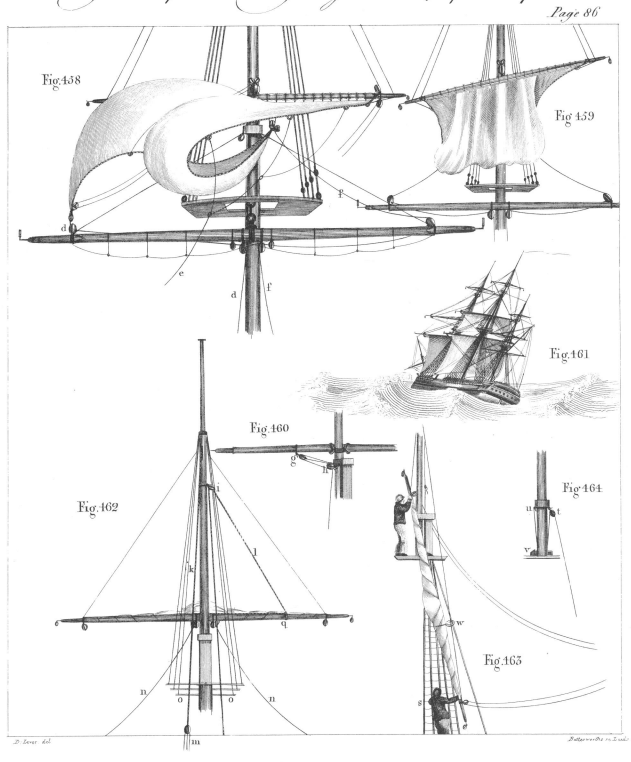

Fig. 458

Fig. 459

Fig. 461

Fig. 460

Fig. 464

Fig. 462

Fig. 463

D. Lever del.

Butterworths sc. Leeds

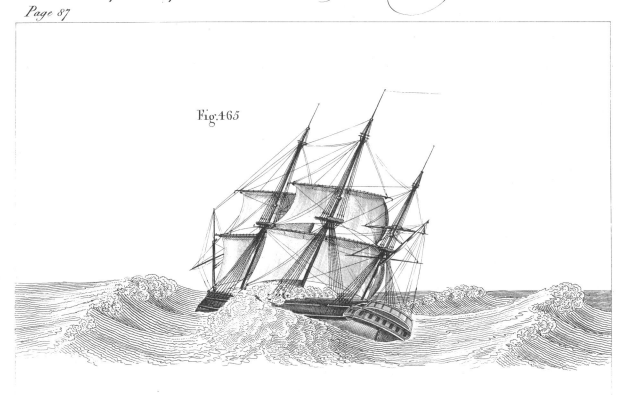

Fig. 465

Fig. 466   Fig. 467   Fig. 468   Fig. 469

D. Lever del.   Butterworth sc. Leeds.

Close reefed Topsails over reefed Courses---Waring under Courses.

The Main Topsail is taken in as the Fore Topsail was; but this Sail is of so much consequence in a heavy Sea in waring and scudding, that when a Ship is thought to have too much Canvas, it is frequently judged to be more advantageous to keep the Topsails set, close reefed, and to reef the Courses. The Tacks may be got close down, even then, by bowsing well on the lee Lift, and canting the Yard; and the lee part of the Sail being elevated, the Sea may pass under; but in double-reefed Courses, this could not be done without settling the Yard, and the Topsails prevent that.

It will perhaps be an objection that the Main and Fore Tacks cannot be got close down without the lower Yards being settled, by casting off the Slings and easing the Jears; but this circumstance is attended with convenience; for when a Ship is reduced to such small Canvas, there is generally a heavy Sea running, which in breaking, often strikes the Bellies of the Main and Fore Sails: whereas when these Sails are reefed, as represented by Fig. 465, the Tacks not being close down, consequently the Feet of the Sails elevated, the Sea passes under them, and this may prevent their splitting---a not uncommon occurrence when the Yards are settled.

Close reefed Topsails over *double* reefed Courses, are frequently carried in the Coasting Trade, which are found to answer remarkably well, particularly with a few Hands; for if the Gale increase, the close reefed Topsails are soon handed, and the Ship is then reduced to very small Canvas, viz. *double* reefed Courses, which may be also soon taken in, when obliged to lie to under any of the lower Staysails.

Let it be supposed that the Main Topsail is handed as before mentioned, and the Fore Topmast Staysail hauled down (see taking in the Jib, page 84), and stowed away in the Netting. The Ship will then be under Courses: it will be necessary to bring the Yard Tackles aft, for Preventer Braces, and Preventer Sheets may be also reeved.---Bentick Shrouds (see page 70), should be always rigged preparatory to an expected Gale, and indeed they are of such general use, that it would be well in certain Latitudes to have them constantly set up.

A Fore Staysail is frequently bent in Men of War and East Indiamen, hoisting to the Foremast Head on the Spring Stay (see page 59).

The Ship is now on the larboard Tack: if it be thought expedient to get her on the starboard one, it is done by waring; for which purpose the Main Clew Garnets are well manned: when every thing is ready, Fig. 466, the Mizen Topsail and Cross Jack Yards are squared, the Main Tack and Bowline eased off, and the *weather* Clew-garnet hauled up, for the reason before-mentioned in starting the weather Sheet of the Topsail (see page 86): the Main Sheet is then eased off, the *lee* Clew-garnet hauled up, and the Buntlines and Leechlines: the Main and Main Topsail Yards are squared, and the Helm put a-weather.

As she falls off, like Fig. 467, the Fore Bowline is let go, the Fore Sheet eased off, and the weather or larboard Braces gathered in forward: when she is before the wind, Fig. 468, the starboard Tacks are got on board, and the Main Sheet hauled aft; but the Weather Braces are kept in forward. When the Main Tack is difficult to be got down, a Luff-tackle is hooked to the lower Bowline Cringle, or to a Lizard spliced into the Bowline Bridle for that purpose: as she comes to, like Fig. 469, the Helm is eased, that she may not fly up too rapidly, the Fore Sheet is hauled flat aft, the Yards braced sharp up, the Bowlines hauled, the Weather Braces set taught, and the Rolling Tackles (see page 86), shifted to the starboard side, and the Geer coiled up.

Getting

Getting in the Spritsail Yard.---Waring under a Mainsail.

The JIB BOOM may be now run in to ease her in her 'scending Motions. The SPRITSAIL YARD may be also got fore and aft; for which purpose a Block (c), Fig. 470, is hooked to a Selvagee on the Fore Topmast Stay, with the Top or Yard Rope (d), reeved through it. This is bent to the Slings of the Yard to windward of the Bowsprit, and hove taught; the Parral and Slings are then cast off, (if Halliards (b), be carried, they are eased as the Yard is got in) the *starboard Lift* (c), and the *larboard Brace* (a), are eased off, the *larboard Lift* (f), and the *starboard Brace* (g), are hauled upon, the Yard Rope (d), eased, and the Yard is thus got fore and aft, and may either be lashed alongside of the Bowsprit, or got in upon Deck.

If the Gale increase so that she must be laid to under a Mainsail, the weather Fore Clew-garnet is manned, the Tack and Bowline eased off, and the Clew-garnet hauled up, then the lee one, &c. as before. The Yard is pointed to the wind by the weather Brace, the Trusses hauled taught, the Rolling Tackle (see page 86), clapped on, and the Hands sent on the Yard to furl the Sail. It is furled as mentioned in page 53.---N.B. The Foresail might be taken whilst waring, as in the former page. The Helm is put sufficiently a-lee, to keep her to the wind.

Ships which have to ware when lying to under this Sail, generally do it by hoisting the Fore or Fore Topmast Staysails, as shewn in the next page when lying to under a Mizen Staysail; but if these should be carried away, the Mizen Topsail and Cross Jack Yards are got down, the Gaff lowered, and the Mizen Topmast struck, like Fig. 471; all these lying so far abaft the Center of Gravity, are a hindrance to a Ship's waring, particularly in the present situation. The Head Yards are filled, and the opportunity taken of her falling off, and getting headway, to put the Helm a-weather : the Main Sheet is eased off, and as she falls off, the Weather Brace is gathered in, and when she brings the wind abaft the Beam, like Fig. 472, the Main Tack is raised : when before the wind, the larboard Tack is got on board; when the wind is on the larboard quarter, the Helm is eased, as her coming to will be rapid : then the Sheet is hauled aft, the Yards are braced up as in waring under Courses; the Helm is to leeward, and she is lying to as before, on the *larboard* Tack. If the Jib Boom were run out at the time of her falling off, it might assist her in waring, the Weather Fore Shrouds might also be manned with as many Hands as can lie on them.

If she will not ware by the above method the Foresail is loosed, and she is wore as under Courses ; or if there be any risk in loosing the Foresail, a Hawser is veered over the lee Quarter, as mentioned in page 90, which will be certain to pay her off. Merchant Ships formerly carried a Span, called a *Quick Saver :* this was hauled taught when waring under Courses, to keep them from bellying so much forward when from the wind, and the Sheets eased off.

This Span was also of great use in waring a Ship under a Mainsail. The ends were made fast to the Main Yard, as in Fig. 473, and a Thimble (a), being worked in the Middle Leg, a Laniard (having one end made fast to the Topsail Sheet Bitts) was reeved through it, and then hauled taught, when the Ship came to ; and when the Main Sheet was eased off, this kept the Weather side of the Main Sail full, and gave it all its power to act before the Center, and assist her in waring.

If the Mainsail should split, it is hauled up as before directed ; but before it is taken in, the Mizen Staysail is hoisted, and the Sheet got aft with a Luff-tackle. The Mainsail is handed, as mentioned in page 53. When the Sail is furled, the Rope-bands are cast off, made fast round the Sail, and one hitched to each Buntline (n), Fig. 474 : the Gaskets are then cast off, the lee Earing (o), eased away, and the Sail lowered by the lee Buntlines, Leech-line, &c. When the lee part is on Deck, the Weather Earing (p), is eased, and the Sail lowered to windward.

Lying

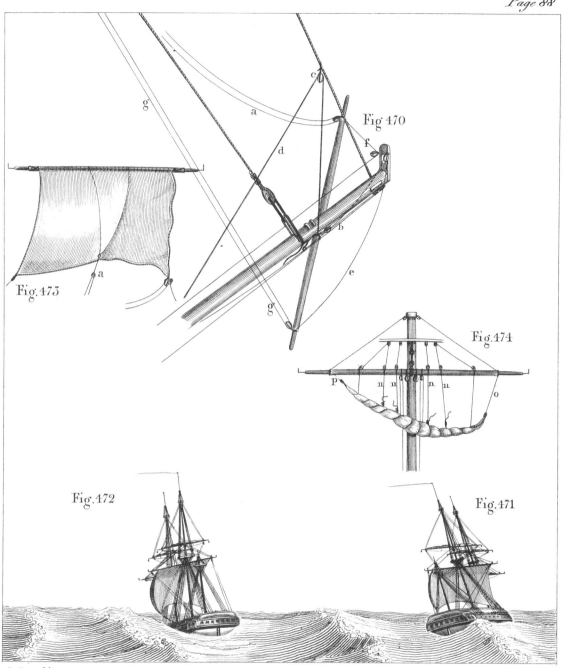

Fig 470

Fig.473

Fig.474

Fig.472

Fig.471

D. Lever, del.

Butterworths sc. Leeds.

Fig. 475

Fig. 476

Fig. 477

Fig. 478

Fig. 479

Fig. 480

Fig. 481

Fig. 482

D. Dover. del.

Butterworth. sc. Leeds.

Lying to under different SAILS---WARING.

When the Sail is on Deck the Geer is cast off, and if the weather permit, another is bent, as described by the Figure in bending the Foresail, page 53.

The Ship is now lying to under the Mizen Staysail, like Fig. 475, which being so far aft keeps her well to the wind ; but she cannot ware without the Fore, or Fore Topmast Staysail. When this is done, the opportunity is taken of her falling off, to haul down the Mizen Staysail, put the Helm up, fill the Head Yards, and hoist the Fore Topmast Staysail, like Fig. 476. The Weather Braces are gathered in as before. When she is before the wind, the Fore Topmast Staysail is hauled down, and when she comes round, like Fig. 477, so as to bring the wind on the starboard Quarter, the Mizen Staysail is again hoisted, and the larboard Sheet got aft. The Helm is eased according to her coming to ; the Yards are pointed to the wind, the Helm put to leeward, and she lies to again under the Mizen Staysail.

Some Ships are laid to under this Sail and the Mizen ; others under a Mizen only, like Fig. 478, in order to keep her well to the wind ; but the disadvantage of laying to under a Mizen is very great ; for however well it may keep her to, she is liable to receive much injury by it ; as it is evident, that the whole Strain of laying the Ship down is now placed on the weakest part. The Main Breadth and greatest Cavity being so far forward, the pressure that is to force that Cavity down in the water, to ease the rolling, ought to be as near to it as possible ; whereas, here it is the reverse. The impropriety of laying a stiff Ship to under this Sail, cannot be better exemplified, than by considering what would be the probable consequence of heaving her down (would the Mast bear it) by the Mizen Mast alone.

A heavy rolling Ship, whose Center of Gravity lies low, will require a lofty Sail to keep her steady in the water, and lay her down for that purpose. A close reefed Main Topsail, Fig. 479, is generally used for such a Ship to lie to under.

For Ships which are not so stiff, of course easier in the Sea, a Main Staysail, Fig. 480, is reckoned the most eligible of any *single* Sail, as it strains the Ship less than any other, by lying immediately over the greatest Cavity, and its power is divided between the Main and Fore Masts.

When the weather and circumstances permit, it is judged better to divide the pressure amongst the three lower Staysails and Mizen, like Fig. 481. Under these Sails she will fall less to leeward, her way being kept up, and she may be easily wore by taking in the Mizen and Mizen Staysail, filling the Head Yards, and clapping the Helm a-weather.

Many Ships which are much by the Stern, will lie best to under the Foresail, like Fig. 482 ; because they require to be pressed down forward : for when a Ship in this Trim endeavours to lie to under any after Sail, she has all the lateral resistance aft, and little forward, to prevent her falling off. The Breadth being now so forward, and the Foremast stepped well aft, the strain on the Ship is not so injurious under this Sail as it formerly was, and it is immediately on the strongest part.

Y   WARING

WARING under bare POLES---SCUDDING.

Suppose the Ship to be in that distressed condition, as to have lost all her lower Canvas, and that lying to under bare Poles, she has no Sail to ware by. Ships which are much by the Stern, and do not lie to well, will often ware under bare Poles, by filling the Head Yards; but Vessels in a proper Trim will seldom do it. It is the custom in this case, to veer a good Scope of a Hawser or Cablet over the lee Quarter, like Fig. 483, with a Buoy, &c. attached to the end, to keep it from sinking, and to make Stopwaters. The effect of the Hawser (q), may be there seen; for being veered away out of one of the *lee* or starboard quarter Quarter Ports, the Ship drops to leeward, and the effort of the Hawser, lying so far to windward, moves the Center of Rotation (by the check her Stern receives) so far aft, as to turn her nearly round upon her Heel. *(Thus it is commonly known when a Ship takes the Ground a-stern, as mentioned in page* 74 ; *the turning Center being there fixed, she falls round off from the Wind).* When before the wind, the Hawser is immediately roused in.

If the Vessel (being as above, without lower Canvas) lie to under bare Poles, and from some unexpected cause, such as a Ship being discovered at day-light so close upon her to windward, that she must by any means be wore, to avoid the dreadful consequence of the other's falling on board, (and there is not a moment's time to lose in veering a Hawser out, which may not be immediately at hand) the only expedient appears to be (which would not be attempted but to avoid such a disaster, when every Risk must be run) to *boxhaul* her by the Yards. *(Boxhauling is described in page* 93).

Keep the Helm hard a-lee, and if the Top Gallant Masts be down on deck, run the Topsail Yards half or two-thirds up, brace the Head Yards sharp aback with the *larboard* Braces, and lay the after ones square, like Fig. 484; this will give her powerful Sternway, and the *after* or *starboard* side of the Rudder being pressed against the water, will check the Stern, something like the effect of the Hawser, consequently help the Head Yards to box her off rapidly: when she has fallen off, fill the Head Yards to give her Head-way, put the Helm a-weather (or to Port), gathering in the weather Braces, as in waring: when the wind is on the *larboard* Quarter, Fig. 485, keep the Topsail Yards still up, to avoid the Stern-board of the Sea, as described below in Scudding, for in this situation the way lost to leeward is not to be considered, provided there be Sea Room. Proceed as in waring, (see page 88), and as she comes to, right the Helm, and haul down the Topsail Yards, by the Clew-lines and down-haul Tackles: point the Yards to the wind, &c. as before.---This is mentioned merely as a resource in case of emergency, as the Sea might break over the Ship, and the Rudder might be endangered by the powerful Sternway.

Suppose the Ship to be laying to under the three lower Staysails and Mizen, or without the latter, like Fig. 486, and that it be thought prudent to bear away and scud; then the close reefed Main Topsail must be loosed and sheeted home, the Foresail loosed, the *larboard* Tack got down, and the *starboard* Sheet aft. The Mizen must be hauled up, if set, the Mizen and Main Staysails down, the Fore Staysail may be kept up as an *off* Sail, and to assist in waring; the Main and Topsail Braces *hauled* in to shiver the Topsail, and the Helm put up: when she is before the wind, the Yards are squared, and both Fore Sheets hauled aft.

The use of the close reefed Main Topsail, Fig. 487, will now be evident, for *without* it, when the Ship is in the Trough of a Sea, the lower part of the Foresail may be becalmed, and her Head-way by this so diminished, that she may be pooped by the following Sea, and the violence of it against the Counter be fatal; but with the close reefed Main Topsail set like the Figure, she will have so much way that it can never reach her to do much injury. If the Main Topsail should by any accident be split, it will be still necessary to have a lofty Sail set in such a Sea, and the close reefed Fore Topsail singly will be the best to scud under.

Brought

Fig.183

Fig.484

Fig.485

Fig.486

Fig 487

D. Lever. dd.

Butterworth sc. Leeds

Fig. 488

Fig. 489

Fig. 490

Fig. 491

D. Steel. del.

Butterworths sc. Leeds.

Brought by the Lee---Striking Topmasts---Topsail Yards kept across.

In scudding under a close reefed Main Topsail and Foresail, many Ships are apt to steer wild, and to broach to ; on which account the Fore or Fore Topmast Staysail is kept set, which in case of flying to, will act as an off Sail, and as the Braces must be always attended to in any Ship which steers rather wild, she may be managed without much danger. Care must be taken to have a good Helms-man on this occasion, and to see that he be well relieved. A Cablet or Hawser towed over the Stern is sometimes used, to prevent a Ship from broaching to.

Steering with these Sails with the Wind on the Quarter, Vessels are more liable to be brought by the lee, than to be broached to. This generally happens from the neglect of the Helms-man : the Sails lying against the Masts, she is in a dangerous Situation, exposed to the Sea, which may break over her, by her laying dead in the water, (the Sails catching aback) till the Yards are braced about. The Ship, Fig. 488, sailing with the Wind on the Quarter, under a close reefed Main Topsail and Foresail, flies off, and brings the Wind on the starboard side, which takes the Sails aback, and she lies exposed to the Sea, like Fig. 489 ; therefore to guard against an Accident of this nature (in a Ship with few Hands), it is usual to keep a Tackle hooked to the lee Clew of the Foresail, the double Block being carried to the Cat-Head, and the Fall stretched aft, in order to get the Tack down, as the Yards must be braced about immediately ; and when she gets Headway, she may be brought gradually round with the Wind on the larboard Quarter as before. Should this happen in the Night, it would perhaps be best to clew up the Foresail, brace about the Main Topsail, and lay her to under that Sail upon the starboard Tack till day light ; for before the Yards could be braced about (except in a Man of War, or other Ship stoutly manned), in the Confusion which sometimes unavoidably occurs in the Night, a Sea might break upon her, and lodging in the Belly of the Foresail, split it : at the same Time (if the Rigging were bad) the Snock laying upon the Fore Stay, might spring or carry away the Foremast.

It is proved however from Experience, that when steering in a heavy Sea with the Wind on the Quarter, a Ship is under more command without the Foresail and Main Topsail : instead of which the close reefed Fore Topsail, and Main Topmast Staysail are carried like Fig. 490. The Fore Topmast Staysail may be also hoisted---if the Ship fly off, the Fore Topsail is soon braced about, and the larboard Main Topmast Staysail Sheet gathered aft, so that her Headway would be scarcely impeded.

It is possible, that a Ship may be obliged from particular Circumstances, (such as being very crank, &c. to strike her Topmasts at Sea. In a heavy rolling Ship, this would only increase the defect, by moving the Center of Gravity lower down. At all events, when this is done, the Topsail Yards should be kept across, like Fig. 491, because it may happen, from damage done to the Bowsprit, on which the Masts so much depend, she may be obliged to loose the Foresail and bear away, and the close reefed Main Topsail may be carried on the Main Topmast, above the lower Cap with safety, the Backstays being sheep-shanked (see page 12), and set up. A Preventer Top-rope may be taken through the Fid-Hole of the Topmasts, and led through a Block lashed round the lower Mast Head. If the Topsail Yards were down, in this Situation, the Ship having no lofty Sail set to give her sufficient Way from a high following Sea, the Consequences might be serious ; but with these Yards across, should even the Foresail split in setting, the close reefed Fore Topsail is an excellent Sail to scud under, set in the same Manner.

STAYING

STAYING against a HEAD SEA, &c.

Suppose the weather to be now more moderate, and the Ship under the Mainsail, Foresail, close reefed Topsails, Mizen, and Fore Topmast Staysail : as the wind slackens, the second Reefs are shook out of the Fore and Main Topsails : for which purpose, the Yards are settled a little, to ease the strain in casting off the Points ; the Reef Tackles may also be bowsed taught.   Care is taken that all the Points are let go before the Earings are eased, otherwise a Point being left fast, like (r), Fig. 492, may split the Sail, by the whole strain of the Canvas being upon it

Whilst this is doing, the Top Gallant Masts may be swayed up and fidded, the Mizen Topmast swayed up, the Gaff hoisted, and the Rigging set up by a Spanish Windlass, (see page 46), except in large Ships where they use a Burton.   When the Reefs are out of the Topsails, they are hoisted up with a taught Leech, being kept shaking by the weather Brace.   The Mizen Topsail Yard is got across (by a Top or Yard Rope reeved through the Block or Sheave-hole at the Mast Head), like the Top Gallant Yard.   (see pages 47 and 48).   The Cross Jack Yard is swayed up by a Tackle hooked to an Eye-bolt in the Mizen Cap, and slung.   The Jib Boom is run out, and the Spritsail Yard got across, as mentioned in page 41.   The other Reefs are shook out of the Topsails, the Mizen Topsail and Mizen set ; and if the wind come forward, the Yards are braced sharp up, the Tacks got on board, and the Bowlines hauled.

The Ship is on the starboard Tack, close hauled, Fig. 493, under the three Topsails, Fore Topmast Staysail, Foresail, Mainsail, Mizen Staysail, and Mizen.

When it is thought proper to get her on the other Tack, every attention will be necessary to make her stay, as from the blowing weather she has had, there will of course be a heavy Sea, which will continue to strike on the weather Bow on every attempt to tack, and tend to pay her Head off again. The Fore Topmast Staysail, on this account, is hauled down.

When every thing is ready, taking advantage of the smoothest water, the Ship, Fig. 493, is gradually luffed up with as little Helm as necessary from the known trim, and the word, the HELM'S A-LEE! is given, the Fore Sheet being let go.   When she is come up to the position of Fig. 494, the Sails will shake.   As soon as she brings the wind a Point on the weather Bow, like Fig. 495, the word is given, MAINSAIL HAUL! The Main Tack, Sheet, after Bowlines, and lee Braces, being let go, the after Yards will nearly fly round of themselves, by the wind acting aback on their starboard or weather Leeches ; and when the wind is right a-head, the after Sails being becalmed, the Main Tack is easily got down : the Mizen Staysail Sheet may be now shifted.   *(If the Head-way cease at this time, the Helm is put a starboard, that the starboard or after side of the Rudder being pressed against the water by the Sternway, which she will immediately have, may cast her Stern to Port, consequently her Head to starboard).*

As soon as she brings the wind on the larboard or weather Bow, her falling off will be very rapid by the Sternway *(the Helm on that account is shifted to Port or a-weather, that the larboard side of the Rudder being opposed to the water may moderate the falling off)*, and the word is immediately given, to LET GO AND HAUL! The Fore Tack and Head Bowlines are raised, and the Head Yards braced about ; but the weather Braces are kept in.   When she gets Head-way, the Helm is righted ; and as she comes to, the Yards are braced sharp up, and the Bowlines hauled ; she will be then on the larboard Tack, like Fig. 496.   The Fore Topmast Staysail is hoisted again.----N.B. If the Headway cease before she brings the wind a-head, she is certain to miss stays, and fall off again.

Missing

* *See Note at the Bottom of page* 79.

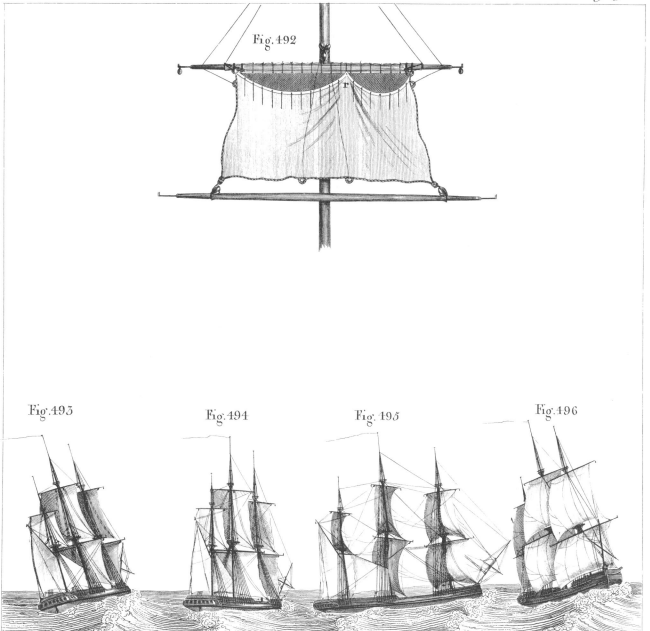

Fig. 492

Fig. 493   Fig. 494   Fig. 495   Fig. 496

D. Lever. del.   Butterworths. sc. Leeds

Fig.500   Fig.499   Fig.498   Fig.497

Fig.501

D. Lever del.   Butterworths sc. Leeds

Missing Stays---Waring Short Round---Box-hauling.

Suppose the Ship, Fig. 497, be on the starboard Tack, as before, that in attempting to tack, she has missed Stays, and that all being trimmed sharp again, it is intended to try her a second time. In a Merchant Vessel where there are few hands, she is luffed up as before, and the Fore Sheet let go; but as her staying is doubtful, the principal object is to get the Mainsail hauled, and if she fall off, the Mizen and Mizen Staysail are brailed up, and the Fore Sheet hauled aft again, like Fig. 498.

The cause of her missing Stays is the Sea (a), which boxes her Head off again; therefore when the Mainsail is hauled, the after Sails lying a-back, give her Sternway; and the Fore Sheet being hauled aft again, the Head Sails being full, pay her round off, and the Helm being kept a-lee, assists them by the Sternway, by having the after or larboard side of the Rudder forced against the Water. If hands can be spared the Mainsail may be hauled up. When she has fallen off so as to bring the wind on the Quarter, like Fig. 499. The Main Tack is easily got down, the after Sails shaking by the wind blowing on their Leeches. At the time she gets Headway, the Helm is put a starboard. When she is before the wind, like Fig. 500, the Head Yards are braced about, and the larboard Fore Tack got on board; and when the wind comes on the larboard Quarter, the Mizen is hauled out, the Mizen Staysail hoisted, and the weather Braces kept in forward, to let her come to; as she comes to, the Helm is righted, as in waring (see page 79), and the Yards are braced sharp up, hauling the Bowlines, &c. as before.

When a Man of War, or other Ship, having plenty of hands on board, will not stay, she is box-hauled as follows:---The Ship, Fig. 497, being on the starboard Tack as before, and refusing Stays, the Helm is kept a-lee, the Mainsail and Mizen hauled up, and the Mizen Staysail down; the after Yards are squared, the Fore Tack and Head Bowlines raised, the Head Yards braced sharp a-back; and if the Fore Topmast Staysail be set, the weather Sheet is hauled over, like Fig. 501. *(The Main and Mizen Topsails lying a-back with the Yards square, will give her Sternway, and the Helm* being a-lee or to Port, the larboard side of the Rudder meeting with such resistance, helps her Head to cast to Port, the Fore Sail and Fore Topsail laying against the Masts with the starboard Braces hauled sharp up, and the lee Bowlines forward, with the Fore Topmast Staysail, paying her round, and rapidly off).* When she has fallen off so as to bring the wind on the starboard Quarter, like Fig. 499, *(the starboard after Braces having been gathered in as she fell off),* the larboard Main and Fore Tacks may be got on board with ease, because the Yard Arms being in the wind's eye at that time, the Sails are shaking: when she gets Headway (which by this management she will not do much before she brings the wind aft), the Helm is shifted to starboard; and when the wind comes on the larboard Quarter, as in waring, (see page 79), the Mizen is hauled out, the Mizen Staysail hoisted, the weather Braces kept in forward, the Fore Topmast Staysail Sheet kept flying, and as she comes to, the Helm is righted, and all trimmed sharp.

As the wind becomes less powerful, the Jib is hauled out, the Spritsail Yard topped, the Jib Guys set up, the Dolphin Striker rigged, and the Martingale Stays set up (see Jib, page 60). The Main Topmast Staysail is cast out of the Fore Catharpins, and set, as also the Middle Staysail (see these Sails, page 61). The Top Gallant Yards are got ready for sending up. The Sails are made well up on the Yards, leaving the Buntline Cringles, Bowline Bridles and Clews out; and the Yards are got across, as described in pages 47 and 48. The Seizings are clapped on the Parral, the Sheets, Clew-lines, Buntlines, and Bowlines bent. The Sails are loosed, the lee Sheets hauled home, then the weather ones (as described in page 84), the Sails hoisted, the Yards braced up, and the Bowlines hauled.

Z   HEAVING.

* *See the Note at the Bottom of Page 79, concerning Helm and Sternway.*

HEAVING TO---SOUNDING.

When two Ships heave to, to speak, the Jib and Fore Topmast Staysails are hauled down, the Courses braiied up, the Top Gallant Sails lowered, and sometimes clewed up, the Helm a -lee, and one of the Topsails laid a-back. The Ship, Fig. 502. being to windward, is hove to by laying the *Main* Topsail a-back, that she may the more readily fill, without falling off so as to risk running on board the Ship, Fig. 503 ; but the latter Ship being to leeward, is hove to with the *Fore* Topsail to the Mast, that she may box her head off, and keep clear of the Ship which is to windward ; for she will only have to haul up the Mizen, run up the Jib and Fore Topmast Staysail, keeping the after Sails shivering by the weather Braces, and she will fall off.

If the *weather* Ship, Fig. 502, by accident come too near the *lee* one, and the latter do not wear in time to clear her, as she may be becalmed by the weather one ; then the weather Ship braces her Mizen Topsail sharp a-back, squares the Head Yards, drops her Mainsail, and claps her Helm hard a Port or a weather, like Fig. 504. The Head Yards being square, drive her a-stern ; the after ones, with the assistance of the Mainsail, greatly add to the Sternway, and keep her Head to ; and the larboard or after side of the Rudder meeting with such great resistance, forces her Stern to starboard, consequently prevents her falling off ; but if she be inclined to lose her wind, the Fore Topsail is kept shaking.

When Land is expected to be made, the BOWER CABLES are bent : these Cables are run out of the Hawse Holes, having a Hawse Rope bent to their Ends, of a sufficient length, and reeved through the Rings of their respective Anchors ; the Bights are then hauled up. The End of each Cable (a), Fig. 505, is taken over and under the Bight (b), forming the Shape of the Clinch, which must not be larger than the Ring of the Anchor (d). The Seizings (c), which are called the BENDS, are then clapped on and crossed. The Anchors are got over the side by the Runner and Yard Tackles, and hung by the Stoppers and Shank Painters (see page 69). A long Range of the Cables is hauled up, the Tiers are all clear for running, and the Stoppers and Ring Ropes got ready---see page 109.

When Soundings are tried for, it is done by the deep Sea Lead, on the Bottom of which is put a Composition of Tallow : this is called *arming* the Lead : so that when it touches the Ground, it brings up some of that substance which lies on the Surface, such as Sand, Corral, Shells, Oaze, &c. and by these (from repeated trials being made and marked in the Charts), the bearings of certain Headlands, Rocks, Buoys, Sands, &c. are generally known.

If a Ship be going free with a light Breeze, Soundings may be got by passing the Lead to windward from the Quarter along the Waist to the Cat-head ; or if that be not sufficient, a Hand is sent out to the Spritsail Yard Arm (a), Fig. 506 ; and another (carrying the Bight of the Line) to the Jib Boom End (b). The Man (a), heaves the Lead from him, and the Man (b), swings it forward : as the Ship advances, the Line being veered away from a Reel, a Hand in the Mizen Chains (d), gets the Soundings. The Bight of the Line is then put into a small snatch Block made fast to the Mizen Shrouds, hauled in, and reeled up.

SOUNDING

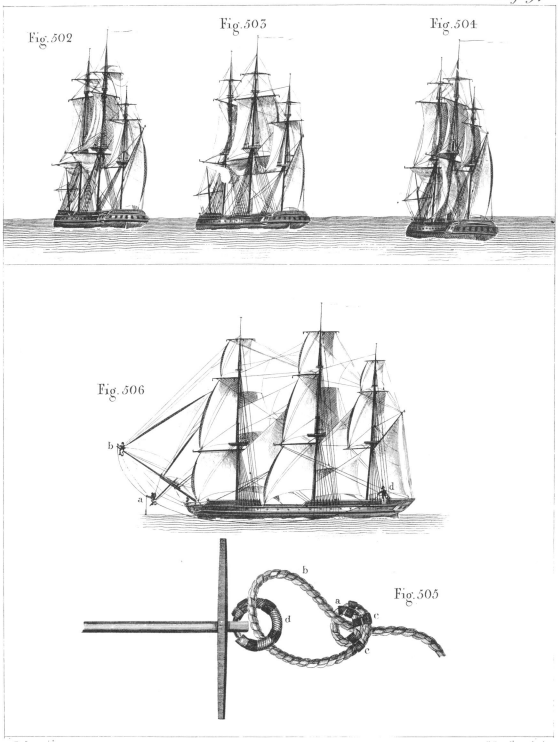

Fig. 502

Fig. 503

Fig. 504

Fig. 506

Fig. 505

Sounding — Box and Club-hauling,

Fig.508   Fig.507   Fig.509   Fig.510

Fig.513   Fig.512   Fig.511

D. Lever. del.   Butterworths. sc. Leeds

SOUNDING---BOX and CLUB-HAULING.

If the Ship have too much way, she may be stopped by bringing her gradually to the wind, brailing up the Mizen and Mizen Staysail, and squaring a-back the Mizen Topsail, like Fig. 507. When it blows rather brisk, the Ship is hove to by either the Main or Fore Topsails, laying those Yards square: when with the former, the Bight of the Lead Line is taken up from the weather Quarter to the lee Main Yard Arm, like Fig. 508, and the Main Yard laid square, the Helm being put a-lee: when she comes to, the Lead is hove from the Lee Gangway, and swung out by the Man on the Main Yard (d). The Ship being hove in the wind, her way is stopped, and she then drops to leeward by her Sternway, near to the place where the Lead was hove. When she is brought to by the *Fore* Topsail, the Line being passed to windward, as in the former page, the Head Yards are braced sharp a-back, like Fig. 509, the Helm put down, and the Lead being hove according to her Way, she brings her Stern over it, when the Soundings are got as before, the Head Yards as she falls off, are then filled again.

If the two Ships, Figs. 508 and 507, be near the Land, and sailing close hauled on the larboard Tack to keep the weather Shore on board, and the former suddenly see danger a-head and to windward, so that she cannot tack, and if she ware she will be foul of Fig. 511, she is Box-hauled, as before mentioned in page 93. She therefore claps the Helm a-lee, hauls up the Mainsail, brails up the Mizen and Mizen Staysail, squares the after Yards, lets go the Fore Tack, Sheet, Bowlines and lee Braces, braces the Head Yards sharp a-back, like Fig. 509, and hauls over the weather Jib and Fore Topmast Staysail Sheets: she will then pay round off on her Heel. When the Ship to leeward sees her Companion a-back, she puts her Helm a-weather, hauls up the Mainsail, Mizen, and Mizen Staysail, lets go the after Bowlines and lee Braces, shivering the after Sails, and bearing away, like Fig. 510; but if the Ship to windward be rather too much a-head, then she acts as described in the former page by Fig. 504.

When two Ships on different Tacks are in danger of running foul of each other, it is always expected by Seamen, that the Vessel on the *larboard* Tack accommodates the other by putting her Helm up or down, as Occasion may require.

If a Ship by accident be so near a lee Shore with a head Sea, as to make it certain that she will not stay, she is Box-hauled; putting her Helm gradually down as if she were going about, and then proceeding as mentioned in one of the methods according to her strength of Hands, in page 93; but if she be too near even to venture on that, she puts down her Helm, and when the Headway is stopped, lets go the lee Anchor, which brings her Head to wind, and then casts on the other Tack by the Sails (as in heaving up the Anchor), and cuts the Cable. This is called CLUB-HAULING.

The Ship, Fig. 511, being on the starboard Tack, and close in Shore, luffs up, lets fly the Fore, and Fore Topmast Staysail Sheets, and as she comes in the wind, lets go the lee or larboard Anchor, which brings her Head to wind, like Fig. 512, she then raises the Main Tack, Sheet, after Bowlines and lee Braces, hauls the Mainsail as in Tacking, and rights the Helm; when the Main Tack is on board she cuts the Cable; the Head Sails being a-back, pay her off. As she is certain to have Sternway, the Helm may (if she fall off too rapidly) be put a little a-weather; the after or larboard side of the Rudder being pressed against the water, checks her Stern from coming to windward, consequently prevents her Head from falling too rapidly off. As she falls off, the Head Yards are braced about: when she gets Headway the Helm is righted, and all trimmed sharp, and she is then on the larboard Tack, like Fig. 513. If there be time, a Hawser (a), may be bent to the larboard Anchor or Cable, Fig. 512, as a Spring, and led out of one of the Quarter Ports to leeward, which being hauled upon when the Cable is cut, will help to cast her, by bringing her Stern to windward.

A SHIP

*Although original Erratum reads *"line 16 from the top, for 'Fig. 507,' read 'Fig. 512.'"*, it should be *"line 16 from the top, for 'Fig. 511,' read 'Fig. 507.'"*
**Blunt comments, *"The Courts have decided that such is the usage.—Am.Ed."*

A SHIP on her BEAM ENDS.

In carrying a press of Sail, if by a sudden Squall, canting the Ballast, &c. a Ship be laid on her Beam Ends, the method of righting her without cutting away the Masts, (which is to be avoided if possible) is by a Hawser, having strong Stop-waters to it, such as Spars, Hen Coops, &c. veered out over the lee Quarter, as mentioned in Waring under bare Poles.

When a Ship is laid down in this manner, the Sails lose much of their power by the horizontal Position of the Masts, and are in a great measure becalmed by the Hull, as may be seen by Fig. 514. The Hawser has the effect shewn in Fig. 483, page 90. The wind acting powerfully against the Hull of the Ship thus laid over, gives her great drift to leeward, and the Spars, &c. having such hold in the water to windward, draw her Stern towards the wind when hauled upon, and will certainly ware her so as to bring the wind aft; but then losing its power, it must be cut, and whether the Ship will turn so far as to bring the wind on the starboard Quarter, is doubtful; but if a Spring (a), Fig. 515, could be brought aft from the starboard side of the Forecastle, or from the Foremast which lies out over the side like a Lever, made fast to the Hawser (b), and hauled on when she brings the wind aft, and is sure to have Headway, this check to her forwards might cause her Stern to fall off to Port, and bring the wind on the starboard Quarter, which will then have the flat part of the Deck to act against, and give more power to the Spring; the Sails may then be trimmed to assist in righting her; but this would be impracticable, on account of the after Masts, Yards, Rigging, &c. laying also over to leeward. The Figure is drawn without the Masts, to render it more distinct.

When there is anchoring Ground, the practice is to let go the lee Anchor, which brings the Vessel head to wind, like Fig. 516: in this case, the strongest part of the Ship is exposed to the Sea, and the wind catching the Sails a-back, she may be cast on the starboard Tack as in Club-hauling, when the Ballast or other Materials may be shifted.

If a Ship at Sea, where no ground is to be got, could be brought head to wind, instead of waring her with the Hawser, it would be much better. A stout Spar, like Fig. 517, with a Span (a), of sufficient length, and a Hawser (b), bent to it, will keep a Ship's Head to the Sea, which will not lie to under any of the lower Sails; and a similar aid might be applied to a Ship overset, which would be certain to have the effect of bringing her to the wind. The end of the Hawser (b), Fig. 514, being brought from the Bows without board, to windward, and taken aft, the Spar might be there bent and launched overboard, veering away a good scope, as the Ship drifts to leeward; and being belayed when far enough, her Head would be checked, her Stern fly off, and she would fall Wind-rode; and might be cast as before mentioned.

Every method should be tried in preference to cutting away the Masts, which should never be resorted to but to prevent foundering. If the Ballast have shifted, the cutting away of the Masts will not right, though it may lighten her; and many instances have occurred besides the under-mentioned, (a remarkable one), of Vessels remaining a long time in this state, after being dismasted, without being able to right them.----A letter from Portsmouth, dated September the 19th, 1797, mentioned, " that the *Joanna* of *Embden*, *Capt. Renhaut*, fell in with the *Recovery Schooner, John Fluin, Master*, laden with Fish. She was laid on her Beam Ends, the Masts and Rigging were cut away, and they had been in that state for *seventeen* days, without any means of recovering her: three of the Men died for want, and the Master and two Seamen subsisted on a favorite *Newfoundland Dog*, which they were obliged to kill."

Vessels crossing the Ocean in Ballast, should be prepared for this disaster, and a Spar above-mentioned, with a Hawser bent, might be kept ready for that purpose.

COMING

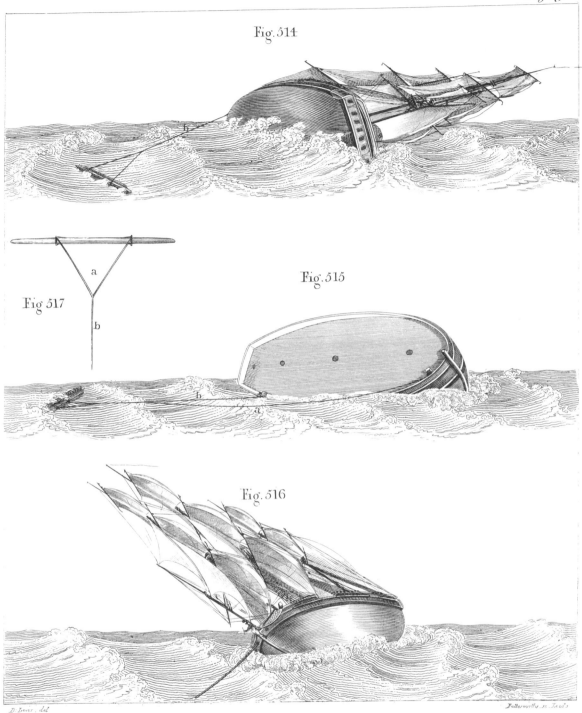

Fig. 514

Fig. 517

Fig. 515

a

b

a

b

b

a

Fig. 516

D. Lever, del.

Butterworth, sc. Leeds

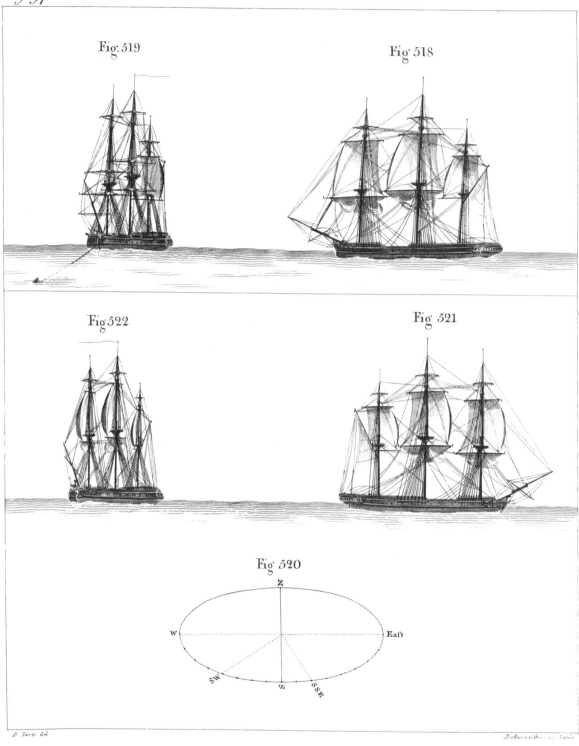

Coming to an Anchor,

Fig. 519

Fig. 518

Fig. 522

Fig. 521

Fig. 520

N

W — East

SW S SSE

D. Lever del

Butterworth sc. London

COMING to an ANCHOR.

If the Land be made near the destined Port, the Ship being close hauled (suppose on the larboard Tack), and she can fetch a place of safety to remain in till the wind comes round, there being no Tide to check her, the Top Gallant Sails, Courses, Jib and Staysails are taken in: then, with the Fore Topmast Staysail, Mizen, and three Topsails, like Fig. 518, she stands on till near her Birth: the Buoy is streamed, (having Hands stationed at the Stopper and Shank Painter, and every thing clear of the Range of the Cable) the Fore Topmast Staysail hauled down, and the Helm is put down to leeward; when she is in the wind, the Main and Fore Topsail Halliards are let fly, the weather Braces are hauled in, the Sheets started, and the Sails clewed up: the Mizen Topsail is hove a-back, and when she gets Sternway the Helm is righted, and the Anchor let go: Fig. 519. the proper Scope of Cable is veered away according to the strength of the wind, the Stopper is clapped on forwards, the Bight of the Cable thrown over the Bitts, and the Stoppers are clapped on aft (see page 109). The Hands are then sent on the Yards to furl the Sails.

If there be so little wind that it is necessary to continue the Mizen Topsail set, to keep her a-stern of her Anchor, the short Service only is veered out; because the Ship not having power to keep it taught, the Cable may be injured by being dragged on the Ground. If the wind be pretty strong when she is brought up, the Mizen Topsail may be taken in with the others; the Mizen will bring her head to wind, she will get Sternway, and the Anchor may be let go, veering away the proper Scope of Cable.

When a Vessel comes to an Anchor, (particularly in a Tide-way) it is always prudent to take three Reefs in the Topsails before they are handed, as they will be ready should a sudden Gale arise, if there be a necessity for running out to Sea.

If there be a Tide, the Ship is put on that Tack by which she can stem it. Thus if the Tide run from East, and the wind be at S.S.E. it is plain by the Compass, Fig. 520, that she must be got on the starboard Tack; when being close hauled, like Fig. 521, she just stems it: whereas were she on the larboard Tack, like Fig. 522, she would only lie S.W. as per Compass; so that she would drive out again with the Tide, her Course being only four Points from West, its absolute direction.

When a Ship therefore intends to anchor, and stems the Tide, like Fig. 521, she gets under an easy Sail, taking in the Top Gallant Sails and Courses, &c. according to the strength of the wind; and when near enough, (having streamed the Buoy, &c. as before) clews up the Topsails, the Tide then checking her Way, she lets go the Anchor. When she has sufficient Cable, and the proper Service in the Hawse, she rides by the Tide with the wind almost across. How to sheer will be mentioned when treating on the Single Anchor.

Thus in coming to an Anchor the Ship's Head must be always put to the Stream. If it come from leeward, there is nothing to do but to shorten Sail, and when the Topsails are clewed up, let go the Anchor: If from windward, she must be luffed up, hauling out the Mizen, and when she meets the Stream, and her Headway is stopped, the Anchor is let go.

A a

ANCHORING

ANCHORING---DRIFTING.

If the wind be large, or right aft, like Fig. 522, and the Stream from windward, or what is called *a leeward Tide*, then all the Sails are handed, except the Fore Topsail, and the Cable is bitted : the Ship is hauled up sooner, the Helm put a-lee, the Fore Topsail clewed up, the Mizen hauled out, the Mizen Staysail Sheet aft, to bring her to the wind, like Fig. 523 ; and when she comes head to wind, like Fig. 524, she loses her Headway, at which time the Anchor is let go, and according to the strength of the wind and Tide, a long Scope of Cable is veered out.

When the wind is right out of a River, and the Ship is to go up, she waits till there is water enough, and the Flood sufficiently strong to drive by against the wind : she then drifts in, either Stern foremost, or Broadside to it, having sufficient Sail set to determine the Rate of driving. When there is Room enough, the first of these is preferred, as she will answer her Helm by the Tide acting against the sides of the Rudder, as if she were going a-head.

The Ship, Fig. 525, is driving with the Tide setting to the Southward, against the wind, which is on the Quarter : this is called a *Weather Tide.* Proportioning her Sail according to the strength of it, she sometimes sets her Top Gallant Sails, by which she remains stationary, and sometimes as occasion may require lets fall the Foresail, by which she shoots a little a-head ; so that she is under every Command that can be wished ; but in drifting to the Southward, when she gets to a certain depth of water, *(which is found by the Hand Lead (see page 12), or some particular object, by the bearing of which it is known ; or by two Marks, such as the Church and Perch in the Figure being in one)*, in order to avoid a Rock or Shoal (d), a-stern, the Helm is put down to leeward, or a starboard, the Mizen hauled out, the Yards braced up, and she stands over to the Westward, like Fig. 526.

When she was driving Stern foremost, like Fig. 525, her Head was North, with the wind at S.W. on the larboard Quarter, as per Compass, Fig. 527 ; and now she is hauled close to the wind, like Fig. 526, her Head is W.N.W. so that as she drifts with the Tide to the Southward, she is reaching across it towards the weather Shore.

Thus she may proceed driving with her Broadside to windward, and when she wants to get over to the weather Shore, and shoot quicker a-head in case of danger, she has only to drop the Courses, and set Top Gallant Sails, &c : and if she find it necessary to stand over to the Eastward, she may either stay, or Box-haul round on the other Tack, when she will lie S.S.E. (see Compass), close hauled on the starboard Tack.

When it is wished to drive with the Broadside exposed to the Tide, and not to advance a-head, the Main and Mizen Topsails are laid a-back, and the Fore Topsail kept shivering or a-back, as occasion may require ; but as her falling off will be very rapid, (on account of the Rake forward, as mentioned in the next page, except the Ship be by the Head and deep laden), the Fore Topsail is seldom laid a-back, but kept shivering, because its power is very great to pay the Ship's Head off.

DRIFTING.

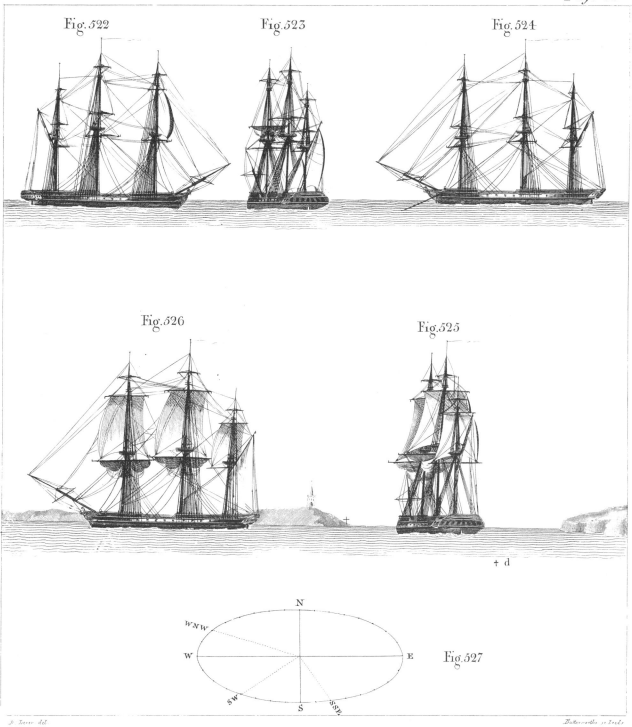

Fig. 522   Fig. 523   Fig. 524

Fig. 526   Fig. 525

+ d

Fig. 527

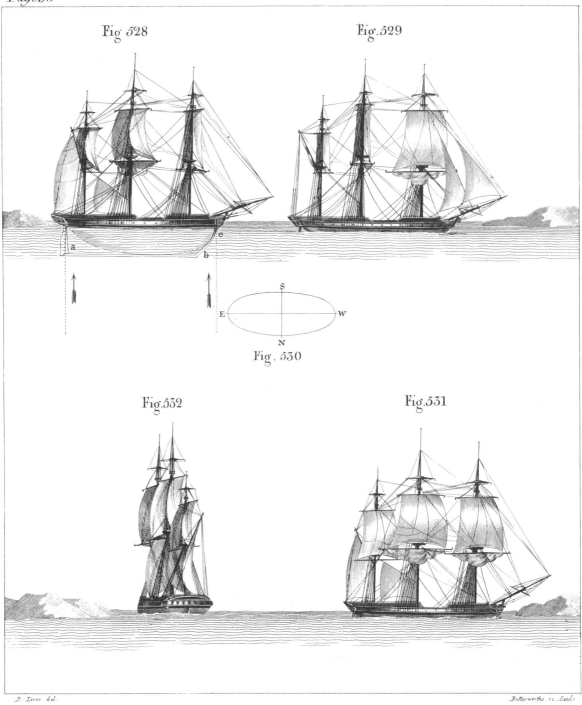

Drifting,

Page 99

Fig 528

Fig. 529

Fig. 530

Fig. 532

Fig. 531

D. Lever del.

Butterworths sc. Leeds.

DRIFTING.

This falling off is caused by the Rake forward, where she does not meet with that resistance which she finds abaft. The Tide also acts powerfully against her lee Side; and has so much more effect abaft than forward, as to throw her Stern up in the wind, which gives every effort to the Fore Topsail to pay her Head off, and make her recede from it.

Thus by Fig. 528, if the Tide run in the direction of the Arrows to the Southward, as per Compass, Fig. 530, against the starboard side of the Ship, it will have more effect against the Stern Post, which is nearly perpendicular, and the Run (a), than it can have forward against the Gripe (b), and Cutwater (c): on the contrary the after Sails, which should force her Stern to leeward, or to the Northward, and keep her Head to the wind, are resisted by the Tide; but the Fore Topsail (if it were a-back), would pay her Head off to leeward, on account of the *Stem* being so little acted on, in proportion by the Stream. It is this continual falling off, which renders it difficult to give her Sternway, because she brings the wind farther aft by it, and gets Headway till she comes to again. As she sometimes drives with the Sails full, and sometimes a-back, this method of going up a River, or Channel, is called *backing and filling*.

When it is necessary to drive on the other Tack, she is either wared, Box-hauled, or put in Stays. If the Ship be light, one of the former methods is taken to bring her round. If she be to ware: then when she falls off by the Sternway to the Northward, the Mizen is hauled up, the Mizen Staysail down, like Fig. 529, the Main and Mizen Topsails shivered by the starboard Braces, the Fore Topsail braced sharp about with the same, the Jib and Fore Topmast Staysail hoisted, and the Helm put a-weather or to Port: when she proceeds gathering in the Braces, as in waring, page 79.

If she be Box-hauled, the Ship, Fig. 528, has nothing to do but to haul up the Mizen and down the Mizen Staysail, brace sharp a-back the Fore Topsail; and if necessary hoist the Jib and Fore Topmast Staysail hauling aft the weather Sheets, and then to proceed as in Box-hauling (see page 93); but Ships which are deeply laden will generally stay: therefore when the Ship, Fig. 528, is to be put in Stays, the Yards are all braced about full, and the after ones trimmed sharp, like Fig. 531; and when she has sufficient Way, the Helm is put down to leeward---if it be thought necessary to make a Stern Board, when she has passed the direction of the wind, and brought it on the weather Bow, like Fig. 532, the Helm and Yards are kept as they were, the former being before a-lee (or *a-starboard)*, is now a-weather; and the Sails being all a-back, will send her a-stern towards the Western Shore, the water assisting the after or starboard side of the Rudder, sends her Stern to the Northward, and prevents her Head from immediately falling off. If necessary, she drops the Mainsail, which gives her more powerful Sternway, as in the Figure. When she falls off, the Fore Topsail must be shivered as before; and when she gets Headway the Helm is put a-lee, or to Port. She will then drift to the Southward with the Sails a-back as before, her Head to the Eastern Shore.

In very rapid Tides, as in the River *Garrone*, in *France*, where there are a number of Ships crowded together, it would not be possible to manage a Ship by backing and filling: it is therefore the custom to club the Ship, which is driving with the Anchor up and down, heaving in, or veering away the Cable as the water shoals, or deepens, or as it is wanted to drift or bring up.

Merchant Ships, which at Sea carry their Main Braces aft, have often working Braces fixed to the Yards, to lead forward when coming into a Tide-way. A Tail-block is made fast to each Yard-Arm, a temporary Brace reeved through it, and carried forward to the after Fore Shrouds: the after Braces are overhauled sufficiently to let the Yards work, and hang (by the Bights) in Beckets made fast to the Main Topmast Backstays.

SINGLE

SINGLE ANCHOR.

It may be easily conceived that a Ship riding at Anchor, like Fig. 533, with the Tide running from the South, must consequently be to the Northward of her Anchor, and that at the Change of the Tide, she must be swung or got round to the Southward of it, when the Tide will run from the North: and that if the Cable be taught (which it must be) she will in this Swing describe a Semicirle (a b, or a c), of which it will be the Radius. The Cable is kept on the Stretch to avoid fouling the Anchor, which is done by its getting, when slack, round the upper Fluke (b), Fig. 534, or the Stock (a), and sometimes round both, in which case she is in no Security. Great Caution and Skill must be therefore used to avoid this Disaster: and it is reckoned a particular Disgrace in the Coasting Trade, to heave up an Anchor thus entangled.

Suppose a Ship be riding leeward Tide, that is with the Wind and Tide both a-head: she has then the united Power of the Tide against her Body under Water, and of the Wind against her Masts and Yards bearing upon the Cable. Therefore if the Wind be strong, she will in this case require a greater Scope of Cable than in any other.

Now the Cable is veered away, because the Anchor, lying in the Ground in the Position described by Fig. 534, the lower Arm (c), having deep hold with its Fluke in the Bottom, and the Stock (a), laying transversely upon it, it is brought into a more horizontal State, and the Strain being placed in that Line of Direction, tends the more to fix the lower Fluke in the Ground. Whereas when a shorter Scope is out, the Ship is nearer to her Anchor, the Angle between the Cable and the Surface of the Bottom is rendered more obtuse, the former pointing in the Prolongation of the dotted Line (e). The Strain being imparted to it in that Line, its Effort is to lift the Anchor upwards, and of course to make it insecure to ride by, turning the lower Fluke from its holding Direction: so that with this combined Force of Wind and Tide against the Anchor, it is necessary to veer away to the *long* or *leeward* Service. *(For the Services, see page 67.)*

When it is low Water (supposing the Ebb to be the leeward Tide), the Ship must of course be got to the Southward or *windward* of her Anchor, that she may ride with her Head to the Flood. Now if she were left to herself, she would naturally swing to windward when the Flood began to set to the Southward; but then she would probably go over her Anchor, and the Cable lying Slack on the Ground, would have its Bight dragged round the Stock and Fluke; the Consequence of which would be that it would no longer hold her, and she would drive at the mercy of the Tide: and if she did not by chance foul her Anchor, the great Scope of Cable being dragged after her over foul Ground, &c. would infallibly so cut and chafe it, as to render it incapable of bearing sufficient Strain to ride by. It is therefore evidently of the utmost consequence to keep a clear Anchor, and also in swinging from one side to the other, to have the Cable so taught that it may not drag on the Bottom.

TENDING

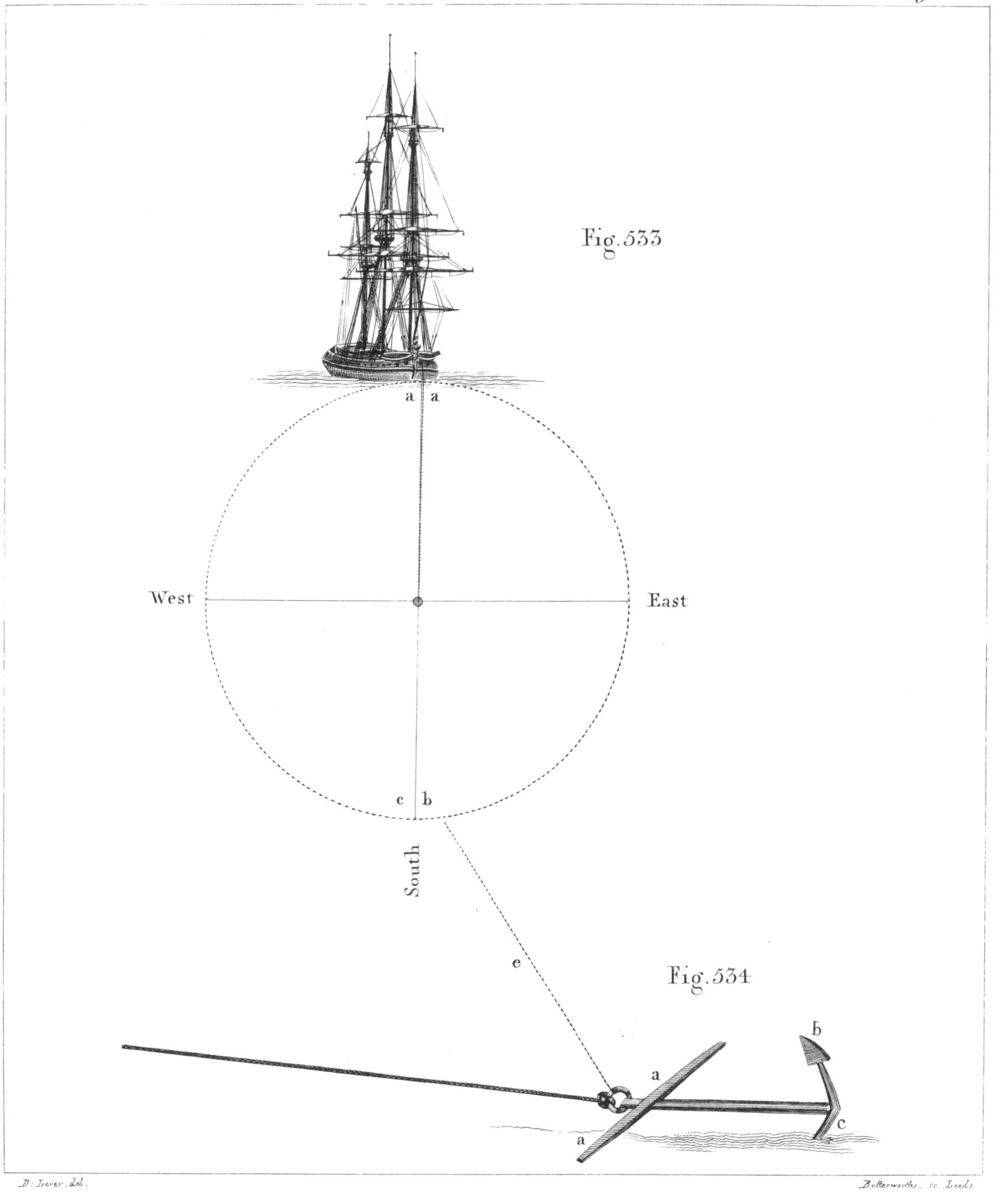

Single Anchor

Fig. 533

West

East

South

e

Fig. 534

a

b

a

c

a a

c b

D. Steel del.

Butterworths. sc. Leeds

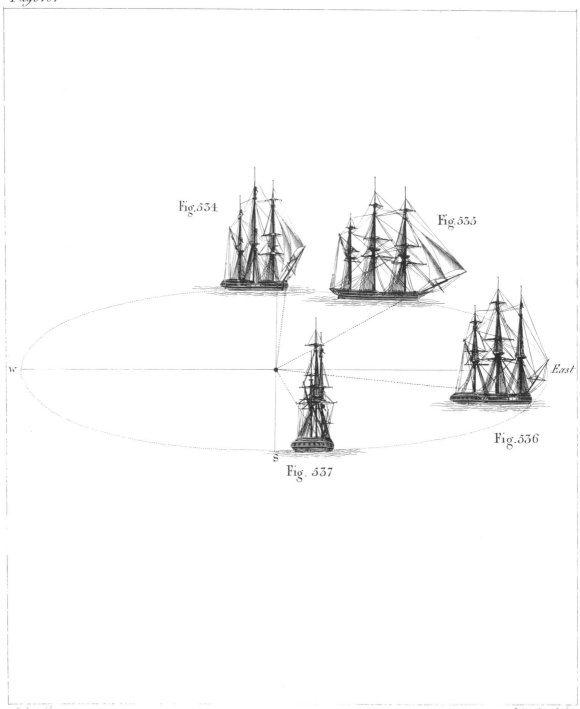

Fig. 534

Fig. 535

Fig. 536

Fig. 537

W

S

East

TENDING to WINDWARD.

The Ship, Fig. 533, in the former page, is riding leeward Tide, the wind at South, and the Ebb setting to the Northward; and she has, on account of their united strength (if it blow fresh), a long Scope of Cable out, the Yards being braced sharp up, to point them to the wind as much as possible. When the Tide begins to slacken, the Cable is hove in to the Windward Service, that there may not be such a length to drag when tending to Windward: and when the weather Tide is set, the wind being then aft, the short Service is sufficient to ride by.

When the Flood begins to set from the Northward, it will naturally cant her Stern so much round, as to bring the wind which is at South, either on the starboard or larboard Bow: in this case, the Jib and Fore Topmast Staysail are set (in general the latter is sufficient), for the purpose of shooting her a-head either to the Eastward or Westward, that the Cable may be kept taught; but as there are particular reasons why a Ship should be shot on one side in preference to the other, it will be necessary to cast her Head so that she may be certain to go the right way: for instance, if the Vessel have a Cutwater, it should be considered that the Cable, when riding to Windward, lies a good deal athwart the Tide by the Sheer (as may be seen by Fig. 537), when it will have a constant tremulous motion up and down; so that to avoid the damage which may be done by the friction, she must be shot over to the Eastward or Westward, that she may lie the whole weather Tide with the Cable out of that Hawse-hole, which is on the same side with the Buoy.

Now if the Ship, Fig. 534, be riding by the larboard Cable, it will be most eligible to cast her on the *starboard* Tack, which will be with her Head to the Eastward, because when she arrives at the situation of Fig. 537, she will have the Cable clear of the Cutwater, and in that position she will lie during the whole *weather* Tide.

To cast the Ship to the Eastward; as soon as the lee Tide slacks, the Helm is put a-starboard, which will give her a Sheer so as to bring the wind on the starboard Bow: the Head Yards are laid a-back with the starboard Braces, the Jib and Fore Topmast Staysail hoisted, like Fig. 534, with the starboard Sheets aft; and the Spritsail Yard may be topped up a-back with the starboard Brace.--- When the Flood begins to set from the Northward, the Helm is put a-port, that the water acting against the larboard or after side of the Rudder may send her Stern to *starboard*, of course assist the Jib and Fore Topmast Staysail to pay her Head off to *Port*. When she is cast with her Head to the Eastward, she must be then set a-head, like Fig. 535, the Head Yards being filled by the larboard Braces, the Helm put a-weather or to *starboard*, and the lee Jib and Fore Topmast Staysail Sheets hauled aft, by which means she will keep the Cable taught, as represented by the dotted Line from the Buoy.

Whilst she is stretching over to the Eastward, she is at the same time driving Broadside to Windward, (or to the *Southward*), and she will continue in that position, till the Tide acting upon her lee side, sends her Stern over the Cable, bringing the Buoy to bear on the larboard Quarter, like Fig. 536, when the Helm is put a-lee (to *Port*), the Head Yards braced to by the starboard Braces, and the Jib and Fore Topmast Staysail hauled down, as in the Figure; because they are of no farther use to keep the Cable taught.* When she was to leeward of it, like Fig. 535, they acted immediately against it; but now that she has gone over it, they would only help to slacken it again, and break her Sheer, which will be mentioned in page 103. Therefore to keep the Cable taught, her Head must be sheered from it, the Helm being a-lee, the after Yards full, and the Head ones pointed to the wind: thus her Head will endeavour to approach the wind by the Helm; but being checked by the Cable, she keeps it taught.

Now the Cable checking her on one side, and the Helm on the other, she is kept in that position till she falls right to Windward of her Anchor, when the Tide being set, she approaches the Stream, and will ride with a Sheer, like Fig. 537, by a check of the lee Helm, the whole weather Tide: the Helm and Yards remaining as last mentioned.

B b

TENDING

---

* *If it blow fresh, the Ship will shoot a-head, and bring the Buoy on the lee or larboard Quarter while to leeward of her Anchor, by the Tide acting on her lee side, as before, and sending her Stern over the Cable---the Helm and Yards are used as above. She will thus fall to Windward, on her proper Sheer.*

TENDING to LEEWARD.

The Helm and Yards are kept in this position the whole Windward Tide, for this reason : if the Helm were put a-midships, and the Ship riding with the Anchor right a-head, she would not lie steadily, but be always sheering first on one side then on the other, the wind in any sudden Squall shooting her a-head so as to slacken the Cable, and the Tide on the lull bringing it taught again with a violent Jerk : but the Helm being put *a-lee*, the *after* Yards filled, and the *Head* ones pointed to the wind, she lies as it were between the wind and the Tide, the Helm biasing one way and the Cable the other. The Helm is only put sufficiently to leeward to keep her on a proper Sheer.

When the Windward Tide slacks, the Cable is kept taught by the same Sheer which she has rode with the whole weather Tide, the Yards being braced as above mentioned. The Tide slackening, the wind will cause her to forge a-head to the Northward, till she comes end on over the Cable, like Fig. 538. In this situation great attention will be required, as Ships riding in this position often break their Sheer against the Helm, as will be mentioned in the next page ; but for the present let it be supposed that she is tending without any accident of this kind occurring : therefore when she is in the station of Fig. 538, end on, the Helm and after Yards not having the Cable to counteract them to *leeward* as before, naturally bring her Head more round to the Eastward, by which her Stern goes over the Cable, and brings the Buoy on the starboard Quarter, like Fig. 539.——(*It is often necessary in light winds, when she brings the Buoy on the weather Quarter, like Fig. 539, to set Sail, the Yards not being sufficient to set her a-head : when this is the case, and the Fore Topmast Staysail is hoisted, the Mizen Staysail must be also run up ; because if the former were set alone, its power lying all forward, and the Cable forming too small an Angle with the Ship to act against it, would pay her Head off, which the latter Sail will prevent. As soon as she brings the wind abaft the Beam, like Fig. 540, the Mizen Staysail must be hauled down, proceeding as before. See next page, Fig. 543).*——When this is the case, the Head Yards must be braced about to fill them, as in the Figure, and the Helm put a-starboard or a-weather, because the Cable must now be brought taught by sheering her Head from it to *leeward* : the Yards being all full send her a-head, and she will keep coming to the Eastward by the Stern flying off. When she brings the wind a little abaft the Beam, like Fig. 540, the Fore Topmast Staysail (and if necessary the Jib) must be hoisted, in which situation she will lie, till according to the power of the wind by the weather Tide ceasing she falls Wind-rode, or the lee Tide have sufficient strength to send her quite to leeward, and forcing her Stern to the Northward, bring her Head to Wind and Tide : the Jib and the Fore Topmast Staysail will then shake, when they must be hauled down, and she will ride leeward Tide as before, like Fig. 533, page 100.

N.B. If the Fore Topmast Staysail were not set when the wind comes abaft the Beam, like Fig. 540, the Cable would draw her Head to wind, and being slackened, she would drag the Bight of it over the Ground till pressed a-stream of her Anchor.

As she is now riding leeward Tide, if it blow fresh, a sufficient Scope of Cable is veered out, and the Yards pointed to the wind : if it increase, the Top Gallant Yards are got down, and the Masts struck or got down on Deck ; and having the Topsails close reefed previously to their being furled, she is prepared for accidents.

BREAKING

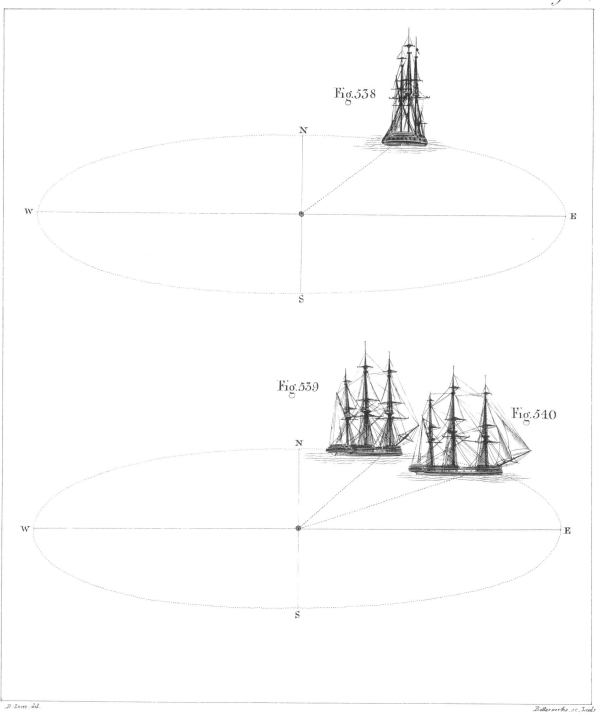

D.Lever del.

Butterworth, sc. Leeds

Breaking the Sheer,

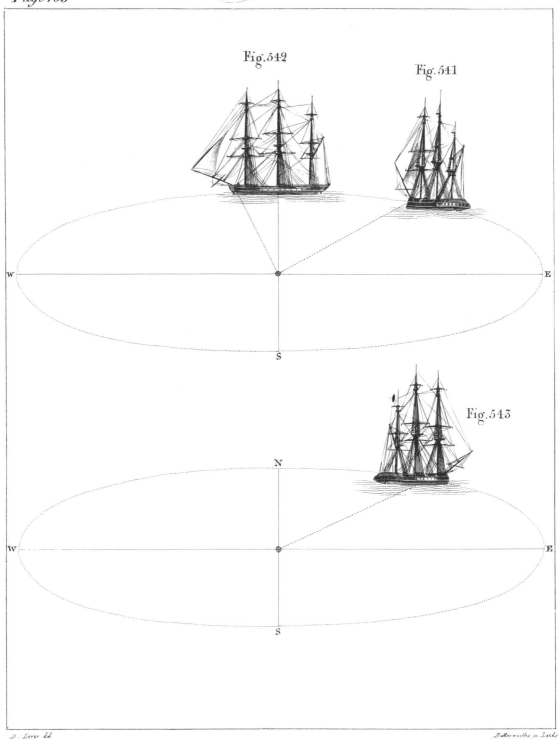

Fig. 542   Fig. 541

Fig. 543

W   E

S

N

W   E

S

BREAKING the SHEER.

Let it be supposed that the Ship has forged *a-head* on the slack of the weather Tide (as shewn in the former page by Fig. 538), having the Helm a-lee, the after Yards full, and the Head ones pointed to the wind, being right end on over the Cable ; and that by the power of the Tide, lulling of the wind, or neglect, she breaks her Sheer against the Helm, bringing the wind on the larboard Quarter, like Fig. 541, and is coming with her Head to the Westward. Then to pay her Head off again, the Fore Topmast Staysail must be hoisted, as in the Figure ; the Helm which was *a-lee* will be now *a-weather* the right way, the after Yards which were full on the other Tack, are now pointed to the wind, and the fore ones which were in the latter position are now full : so that there is every power given to ware her round, and bring the Buoy on the Quarter, when she must be managed as before.

If in shooting a-head she break her Sheer, and get so far over as Fig. 542 ; then if the wind should lull so as to make it doubtful that she would recover, there would be danger of the Tide (which is yet running from the Northward) driving her with a slack Cable over her Anchor : in this case the after Yards must be filled; and the Jib hoisted; (it may be also necessary to hoist the Mizen Staysail) to shoot her over to the *Westward* with a taught Cable, in which position she may remain till the Tide is done, and she falls Wind-rode. If she fall to Windward again, the contrary Helm and Braces must be used to those which were employed when she was to the Eastward. *When a Ship falls to Windward the contrary way to which she has tended the Tide before, there is danger of the Anchor not having turned in the Ground ; it ought therefore to be looked at the first opportunity, as the Cable may have got foul.*

Ships often break their Sheer in tending to *leeward*, after the Buoy is brought on the *weather* Quarter, the Helm a-weather, and all the Yards full, like Fig. 543. This is owing to hoisting the Fore Topmast Staysail before the wind comes on the Beam, when she falls off suddenly, before the Mizen Staysail can be set to catch her : therefore whenever the Sheer is likely to be broken by the Fore Topmast Staysail paying her Head off, the Mizen Staysail is set, and the weather Helm eased ; and when the wind comes near the Beam, it is hauled down again, proceeding as in the former page.

When the Ship is riding *leeward* Tide, if the wind abate considerably, the Cable must be shortened in, that the Bight may not rub on the Ground ; but if it be quite calm at slack water, then she must hove a-peak, because she cannot be tended with a *taught* Cable. When this is the case, particularly if there be any Swell, a piece of old Canvas should be wrapped round the Cable by way of Service ; for, though the time be short that she will remain in that state, yet the Ship being right over her Anchor, will jump so suddenly at times, as to damage it materially, if this precaution be not taken. When the Ship is hove a-peak, the Anchor may as well be looked at, for though it be certain that it has not been fouled, from having always tended with a taught Cable, yet the worming may be damaged close to the Anchor : and if there be no Chain to the Buoy Rope (mentioned page 68), that may also have been materially injured.

The.

The WIND changed THREE POINTS.

Let it now be supposed, that the Wind which was at South, is come round three Points to the Eastward, or S.E. b S : the Ship will then ride more athwart, bringing the Buoy almost on the Beam, and the Cable in that Situation will lift up and down with a tremulous Motion ; therefore if it be out of the Weather Hawse-hole, care must be taken that the Keckling is good.

The Ship, riding in this Situation, must be well watched at slack Water; because this Shift of Wind will cause a S.E. *Swell*, and if she be not carefully attended to, she may be driven over the Buoy: on this Account, it is often necessary to set the Mizen, Mizen Staysail, and Mizen Topsail, like Fig. 544, to send her a-head, and keep her from breaking her Sheer against the Helm. When the Buoy comes on the Weather Quarter, *(as before mentioned in tending to Leeward, page 102, Fig. 539)*, these Sails must be taken in, the Helm put a-weather, and the Head Yards filled, proceeding as there explained She will then ride *leeward* Tide, with the Wind three Points on the larboard Bow; and when the Tide is set, she may have a small Check of the starboard Helm.

At slack Water she will fall *Wind-rode*, with her Head toward the *Weather* Shore, like Fig. 545. And as in tending to Windward before, she was sent to the Eastward, she may be shot that Way again, with the Jib, Fore Topmast Staysail, and if necessary the Mizen Staysail. For the Windward Tide setting to the Southward, by her lying rather athwart like the Figure, will cant her Stern more the same Way, and of course cast her with her Head more to the weather Shore; therefore the Jib and Fore Topmast Staysail being set with the Helm a-weather, or a-starboard, she will shoot over to the Eastward, driving to Windward, till she brings the Buoy on the larboard Quarter, when she must be managed as before shewn in tending to Windward, see page 101, Fig. 536.

The *WIND* right across the *TIDE*.

When the Wind is right across the Tide, she may be either *backed* round, or *sheered to leeward*.— The latter is the Practice in the Royal Navy : and the former in the Coasting Trade.

To BACK THE SHIP.

Suppose the Wind shift round to due East; the Ship, Fig. 546, being sheered to Windward by a Check of the lee Helm, at slack Water braces her Yards a-back, sheets home the Mizen Topsail, hoists it, and lays it a-back also.—She thus keeps the Cable taught, backing round to the *Westward*, and when she arrives at the Situation of the Ship, Fig. 547, *(she will then have the Wind right a-head)*, the Yards are braced about with the contrary Braces, and the Helm changed : thus she will remain till the Tide drives her to the Southward. When the Tide is set from the Northward, the Mizen Topsail may be clewed up, and she will ride sheered to Windward, with a Check of the *lee* Helm, like Fig. 548.

The

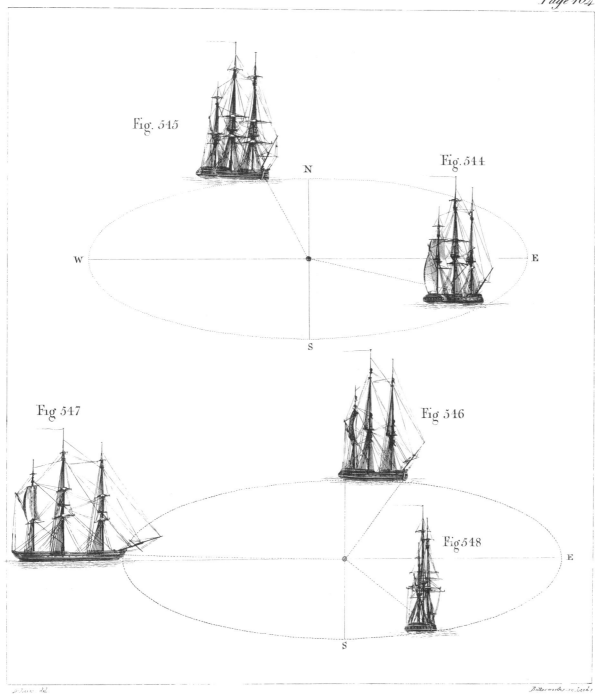

Fig. 545

Fig. 544

N

W   E

S

Fig 547

Fig 546

Fig 548

E

S

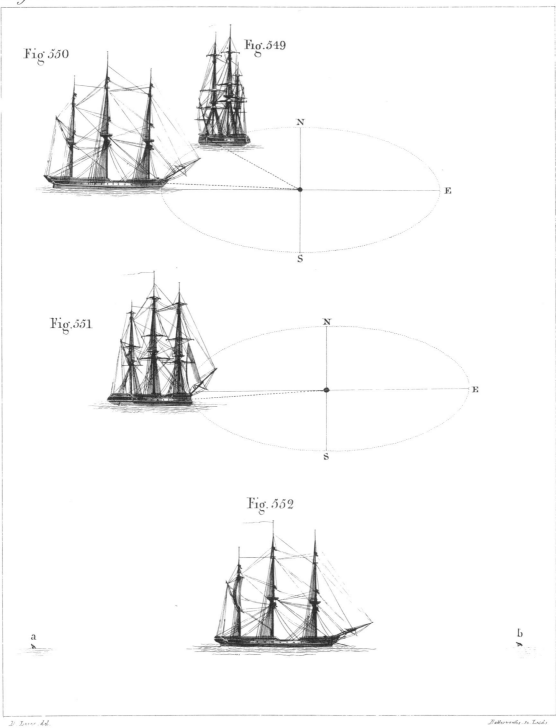

Fig. 550

Fig. 549

Fig. 551

Fig. 552

a

b

D. Lever, del.

Butterworths, sc. Leeds

The Wind right across the Tide------Mooring.

SHEERING TO LEEWARD.

The Ship, Fig. 549, having the Wind at East as before, is sheered to *leeward* with the Helm a-weather : at slack Water she will fall wind-rode, in the Direction of the East and West Line, Fig. 550, and when the Tide from the Northward casts her Stern so much to the Southward as to bring the Wind on the starboard Bow, like Fig. 551, the Fore Topmast Staysail is hoisted with the Sheet to Windward, to keep her steady, and the Cable taught, till the Tide is set ; it is then hauled down.— Thus she swings but over a small part of a Circle each Tide. It would be endless to relate the disputes which have arisen on the different Methods of sheering a Ship with the Wind right across the Tide : Men of great Experience having given their decided Opinions on both Sides.

Mooring.

A Ship is said to be moored when she is secured by more than one Anchor and Cable in different Directions. Suppose the Ship, Fig. 552, to have anchored in good ground, where she can moor, and that she is riding by the starboard Anchor (b), on which she has two or more Cables spliced together : the Tide setting from the Eastward, she veers away two Cables, and being at the Station (a), lets go the larboard Anchor : she then heaves in one Cable of the starboard Anchor (b), with enough of the Mooring Service of the other to freshen the Hawse with, veering away at the same Time upon the larboard Cable, the Anchor of which was dropped at (a). She has then one Anchor to the Ebb and another to the Flood. In veering away upon the starboard Cable to drop the larboard Anchor, if the Tide be not strong, she may be assisted by the Mizen Topsail hoisted a-back, as in the Figure, if the Wind be favourable ; but if the Wind be strong, or the Tide rapid, the Cable must be veered bitted, or it would run out too fast.

C c   Keeping

Blunt includes the following comment, "Ships-of-war, when moored to lay any length of time, have large rings with a swivel, into which all the cables are shackled. By this plan the hawse never fouls.—Am. Ed. (See Fig. 16, plate 112)."
The relevant plate is included as Appendix 24-II.

Keeping a Clear Hawse.

With the Anchors laid as last mentioned, she is said to be moored with a clear or open Hawse to the Northward; because if she swing with her Stern to the South, as described by Fig. 553, each Anchor will lie on that Side where its Cable enters the Hawse Hole; but if she swing with her Stern to the Northward, like Fig. 554, then the Cables will lie across each other, and this is called a *foul Hawse.* If she come several Times the same Way, they will be twisted, so as to render it impossible to veer away either Cable in a Case of Emergency.

If the Ship, Fig. 555, be riding by the *starboard* Cable, with the Wind and Tide of Flood both from the East; then to avoid a *foul Hawse,* she must as before observed, at slack Water swing with her Stern to the Southward, to ride by the *larboard* one with the Ebb from the West. Therefore in order to send her Stern the right Way, the Jib, and Fore Topmast Staysail must be hoisted, with the *starboard* Sheets aft, *(the Jib Sheet may be taken under the Spritsail Yard Arm, the Yard being topped up with the starboard Brace, which will guy it out, and help to cast her),* the Mizen Topsail braced sharp up with the larboard Brace (if it lead aft), like the Figure, and the Helm put a-starboard. The remains of the Flood from the East acting against the *larboard* side of the Rudder, and the Mizen Topsail being a-back, will help to send her Stern to the Southward, and the Jib and Fore Topmast Staysail to cast her Head to the Northward. The wind being at East, she may not begin to cast till the Ebb sets from the West: in which case the Helm must be put a-port, that the Tide against the larboard or after side of the Rudder may help her Stern to the Southward, as before. As soon as she begins to tend, the Mizen Topsail must be taken in, otherwise it will help to throw her Stern back again.

On the slack of the Ebb, which sets from the West, with the wind the same way, the Ship, Fig. 556, to swing with her Stern to the Southward, must put her Helm a-port, and hoist the Mizen Topsail, hauling in a little of the *larboard* Brace: the wind being at East, will act on this Sail to send her Stern to the Southward. If the Driver be at hand, it may be hoisted; or if the Ship carry a Boom Mizen, the *larboard* Guy may be hauled forward, which will greatly assist her.

If the wind be at South, the Ship, Fig. 557, riding by the starboard Cable, at slack water will unavoidably swing with her Stern to the North, consequently cross the Cables, like Fig. 558, the *starboard* Cable being over the *larboard* one, in which situation they will lie during the Ebb; but at the next slack water, when she swings again with her Stern to the Northward, which the Ship, Fig. 559 must do, she will take the Cross out again, like Fig. 560, and ride with the Flood by the starboard Cable, like Fig. 557, with a clear Hawse.

If the wind were at North, the Ships, Figs. 557 and 559, would naturally swing at each slack water with their Sterns to the Southward, and keep the Hawse clear. Care must be taken that the two Cables the Ship is moored by, be not too taught hove in; otherwise she will be girted so as to prevent her swinging well at slack water, and they may be damaged by the strain and friction against the Cutwater.

CLEARING

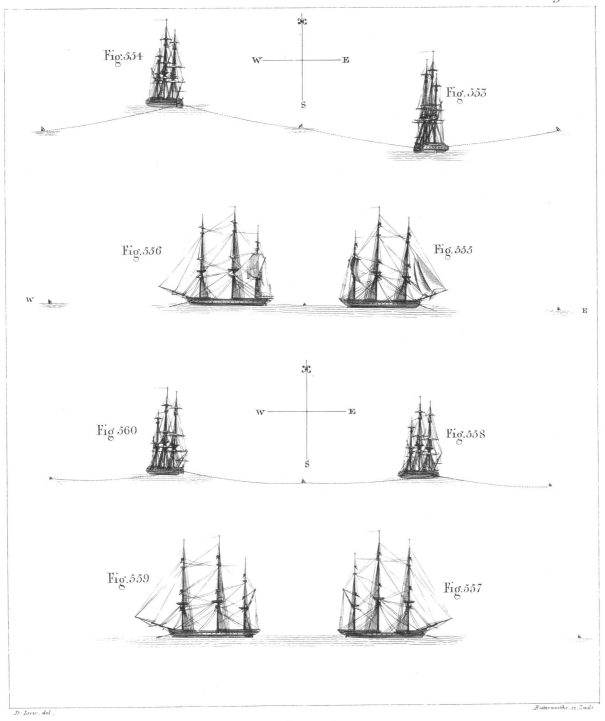

D. Lever. del.

Butterworths. sc. Leeds

Fig. 561 Fig. 562 Fig. 563 Fig. 564

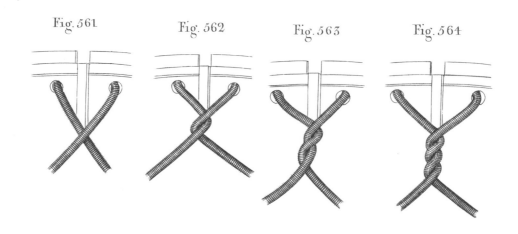

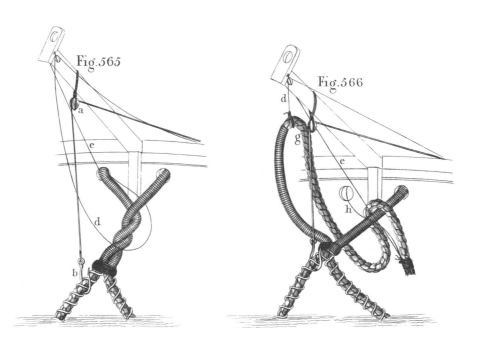

Fig. 565

Fig. 566

D: Lever, del. Butterworth Sc.

CLEARING the HAWSE.

As the wind is liable to shift continually, she must be attended to every slack water, hoisting the Jib and Fore Topmast Staysail with the Sheets to Windward or otherwise, and the Mizen Topsail a-back or full, as occasion may require.

Ships are moored with an open Hawse to that Quarter from whence the most violent wind is to be expected: and it is of the greatest consequence to keep the Hawse clear; for should it blow hard when foul, the Cables cannot be veered away for a greater Scope to ride by. When the Ship cannot be managed by the Helm and Sails, in light winds, a Kedge Anchor and Hawser must be carried out, and she may be hove to it by the Capstern, the Hawser being led in through one of the Quarter Ports; if there be no Capstern, it may be taken through a warping block, and led to the Windlass.

When one Cable lies over another, it is called a CROSS, Fig. 561. When it makes another Cross, Fig. 562, it is called an ELBOW: when a third, Fig. 563, it is called a ROUND TURN: and if it again cross, Fig. 564, a ROUND TURN and an ELBOW.

To clear the Hawse when foul, a Block (a), Fig. 565, is lashed round the Bowsprit, through which a Hawser or Towline is reeved, having a large Hook called a *Fish Hook* (b), bent to its end. A strong lashing is passed round both Cables below the turns. The Fish Hook is placed under the larboard, or riding Cable, before the lashing, which is hove well up by the Hawser. The end of the *larboard* Fore Top Bowline (d), is taken through the starboard Hawse-Hole, being passed *over* and *under* the Cables *(because the starboard Cable, which is the clearing one, is the undermost)*, and bent to the starboard Cable within Board, about two or three Fathoms. The *starboard* Fore Top Bowline (e), must be then over-hauled, led through the Hawse-Hole on its own side, made fast to the end of the Cable, and stopped to it with Spun-yarn in different places: a Rope within Board, called a HAWSE ROPE, is also made fast to the *end* of the Cable.

The *starboard* Fore Top Bowline (e), is then hauled upon (the Stops being cut as they come out of the Hawse-Hole), and as the Bight (g), comes out, Fig. 566, it is triced up by the *larboard* Bowline (d), which is belayed. The Hawse-Rope is then made fast, the *starboard* Bowline cast off, taken over and under the Cables, (as the *larboard* one was), and again made fast near the end. The Hawse-Rope is let go, the starboard Bowline (e), being now bowsed upon, hauls the end of the clearing Cable over the other. The Hawse-Rope (h), being shifted over the Cables, is taken into the Hawse-Hole again, the Cable hauled in by it (the Bowlines being let go and cast off), and bitted. When there is more Cable than can be hauled out in one Bight (g), it must be hung by a slip Rope to the Bowsprit, the Bowline (d), cast off and sent in for another Bight, proceeding as before. If it blow fresh, it will not be safe to trust to the lashing alone; but a Hawser should be made fast to the *starboard* or clearing Cable, with a MIDSHIPMAN's HITCH (see page 9), below the lashing or turns.

This precaution of clearing Hawse is too much neglected; by which, if nothing worse happen, great injury is done to the Cables. It is not uncommon to see large Ships with two round turns in the Hawse: a disgusting sight to an active Seaman.

BACKING

BACKING an ANCHOR, &c.

When a Ship is obliged to anchor in a Road where the water is deep, the Ground bad for holding, and a lee Shore, it has been often recommended to let go one of the Bowers (a), Fig. 567, veering away a good Scope, and stoppering the Cable : then to let go the other Bower, and veer away nearly the whole of the Cable (a), till the other checks her. A stout Hawser (b), must be next bent to the Cable with a Midshipman's Hitch (see page 9), and the end seized down to it : the other end of the Hawser being taken into the Hawse-Hole (c), carried to the Windlass or Bitts, and there made fast. The end of the starboard Cable is then to be hauled out of the Hawse-Hole, and taken with a running Clinch round the larboard Cable (d) : after this, the Stopper (b), must be cut, the Clinch running by the Ship's dragging ; and when she has driven so as to bring it down to the Ring of the larboard Anchor, the larboard Cable is veered away its proper Scope, when she will ride with one Anchor a-head of the other, like Fig. 568.

The difficulty of this method seems nearly insurmountable ; for when it blows so hard as to make something of this nature necessary, there is generally a heavy Sea running, and the Ship may pitch so violently, as to render it almost impracticable (as it must be done without Board) to clinch one Cable round the other. The Stopper (b), from the great strain on it, may not hold. From the time which it would take to accomplish this, the Ship might drive a-shore before it could be effected.

A small Check a-head of the Anchor will prevent its coming home : therefore, when there is a lee Shore, and plenty of Room to veer away a long Scope, the Stream Cable, or even a stout Hawser, should be got upon Deck, and coiled upon a kind of Platform made of Spars on the Forecastle, to keep it clear of Timber Heads, &c. The under end may be taken round the Bows, and bent to one of the Bower Anchors, and the upper one to the Stream or Kedge on the opposite side, letting go the latter when the Ship is hove up in the wind, and the former when the last Fake of the Hawser is clear ; she will thus ride as before, the small Anchor backing the large one.

If the Ship be off a lee Shore, and there is no Room to veer away a length of Cable, then recourse is had to letting go all the Anchors, that she may be secured by their united power : for which purpose the square Sails are handed, like Fig. 569, and she keeps her way under the Staysails : the Anchors are let go, beginning with the weather one (e), then the next to it (f), after it, the foremost one on the *starboard* side, &c. till the whole are gone. The Staysails are hauled down, and she rides like Fig. 570, having all the Anchors a-head, as in the Figure.

BITTS,

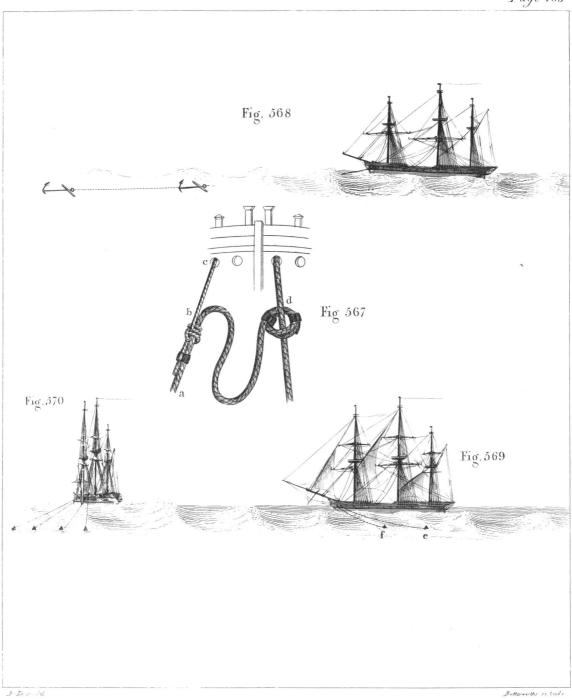

Fig. 568

Fig 567

Fig.570

Fig.569

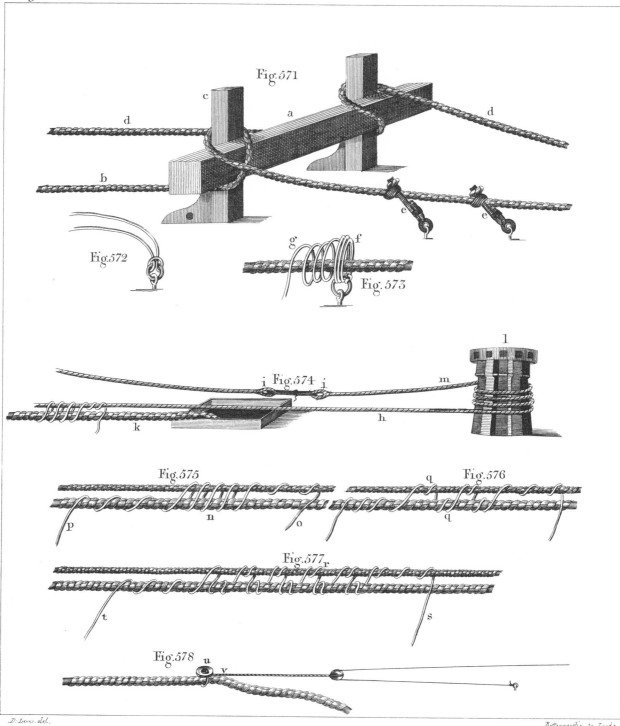

Fig.571

Fig.572

Fig.573

Fig.574

Fig.575

Fig.576

Fig.577

Fig.578

BITTS, NIPPERS, MESSENGER, &c.

The BITTS, Fig. 571, are composed of two strong upright pieces of Timber, firmly secured to the Beams, and have a stout Cross Piece (a), bolted to them. They are used for receiving a Turn of the Cable, and bearing a great portion of the strain upon the Cable which the Ship rides by, together with the Stoppers. The larboard Cable (b), being stoppered before the Bitts, has its Bight put over the Bitt-head (c), *against* the Sun: the starboard Cable (d), has its Bight thrown over the Bitt-head the reverse way, or *with* the Sun.

The STOPPERS (e), are reeved through strong Bolts in the Deck, placed over a large Thimble, and turned in with a Throat and round Seizing (see page 9). A Stopper Knot, see page 6, is clapped on the end of each, and a Laniard being spliced round under the Knot, is passed round the Cable and Stopper, and the end stopped.

RING ROPES are either double or single : the latter are preferred, because the Turns are easily passed. When they are double, Fig. 572, the Bight is put through the Ring, and the ends are reeved through the Bight : when single, an Eye is spliced in one end, put through the Ring, and the end is reeved through the Eye. These are used as Stoppers, and to check the Cable from running out, for which Purpose when veering away, Turns (f), Fig. 573, are taken slack through the Ring and over the Cable : the Worming (g), of the End is also taken slack round the Cable, the Bights of these are held up that they may be no Impediment to the Cable's running out ; but when it is to be checked, the Worming (g), is hauled taught round the Cable, which in running out, draws the Turns (f), also taught, and is jambed to the Ring by them.

The MESSENGER (h), Fig. 574, is a Cablet of sufficient Length to go round the Capstern (l), and to pass slack round the Rollers forward; it has an Eye (i), spliced in each End, which Eyes are secured together by a Lashing. It is passed in the Figure for heaving in the larboard Cable (k) : the upper Part round the Capstern is held on by some Hands at (m). When the starboard Cable is to be hove in, the Lashing is cast off, the Messenger is passed the contrary Way round the Capstern, the heaving Part on the starboard Side being then underneath the Turns, and the Eyes are lashed together as before.

The NIPPERS are passed as follows :——When there is no great Strain on the Cable, as in light Winds and little Tide, a few Turns (n), Fig. 575, are taken round the Cable and Messenger, the End (o), is wormed round the Messenger, and the End (p), round the Cable.—These are clapped on in the Manger, and the Ends of the Nippers are held by Boys, who walk aft with them : when they approach the Main Hatchway, the Nippers are taken off. If the Strain be too powerful for this Method to hold, round turns (q), Fig. 576, are taken alternately round the Messenger and the Cable, and the Ends wormed as before.——When the Strain is very violent, Sand is thrown over the Nipper and Cable, and the former being middled, Fig. 577, the Turns are taken like racking the two Parts of a Laniard, passing a round turn and a racking turn alternately round both the Cable and Messenger. Thus the turns from the Middle (r), aft, are passed *over* and *under ;* from (r) forward, *under* and *over,* the End (s), being wormed round the Messenger, and the End (t), round the Cable forward.

In Merchant Ships, where a Windlass is used, the Cable is held on by a Jigger. The End of the Jigger, Fig. 578, is reeved through a Sheave (u), and knotted. The Sheave being taken over and under the Cable, is placed abaft the standing Part (v), which it jambs when hauled taught to the Cable. One End of the Fall is made fast to an Eye Bolt, &c. aft, and the other is held on, either by Hand, or taken to a Crab on the Quarter Deck.

CASTING

CASTING.

In getting under Way, it should be considered how the Ship is to cast; and whether it be more prudent to shoot a-head, back a-stern, or ware round to avoid other Ships, Shoals, &c. This may be regulated by the Strength of the Tide, bearing of the Wind, the Cable being to Windward or to Leeward, according to the Cast; for all these are of consequence, and require to be well observed.

The Ship, Fig. 579, is riding leeward Tide by the starboard Cable: it will therefore be most eligible to cast her on the starboard Tack, if there be no impediment from Ships lying in the way; because the Cable in weighing will be clear of the Cutwater when she is sheered to bring the Wind on the starboard Bow. Heaving a Stay Peak, the Cable must be stoppered, the three Topsails loosed, sheeted home, hoisted, and a sheer given with the starboard Helm, to bring the Wind on the starboard Bow, (as mentioned in casting for a weather Tide, page 101). The FORE TOPSAIL is braced a-back with the starboard Braces, and the MAIN and MIZEN TOPSAILS sharp up with the larboard ones, (if they lead aft), as in the Figure. If it be intended to shoot her a-head, the Anchor must be hove briskly up. When she has fallen off so as to fill the after Sails (as in Tacking), the Head Yards must be braced about and filled, like Fig. 580: the Helm* must be kept more or less *a-starboard* or *a-weather*, that she may not fly to; for she will not fall off while the Anchor is under the Bows, from the Resistance it causes forward; on which Account the JIB and FORE TOPMAST STAYSAIL are hoisted, as described by the Figure, to render the Steerage easier. When the Ship has shot far enough a-head, the Jib and Fore Topmast Staysail may be hauled down, the Ship brought to by putting the Helm a-lee, the MAIN and MIZEN TOPSAILS hove a-back, and the FORE TOPSAIL kept shivering, like Fig. 581: as she drives, the Anchor may be hove up, and if there be room, catted and fished. When the Anchor is up she will fall off, and the FORE TOPSAIL being filled and the Helm righted, Sail may be set according to Circumstances.

If at weighing, the Vessel must back a-stern when cast, to avoid running foul of another, then the MAIN and MIZEN TOPSAILS must be braced a-back with the *starboard* Braces, as the Fore one was, like Fig. 582, and the MIZEN SHEET hauled aft; the Helm is put a little a-starboard as before, to bring the Wind on the starboard Bow, and the Cable hove briskly in; as soon as the Anchor is out of the Ground, she will get *Sternway*, at which Time the Helm must be put *hard* a-starboard or *a-weather* to keep her to, by the after or starboard Side of the Rudder being pressed against the Water, which forces her Stern to leeward or to port. When she has made her *Stern-board* far enough, the Anchor may be got up with ease: the Opportunity is then taken of her falling off, to fill and make Sail, or ware round on the other Tack, as Occasion may require.

If after making the Stern-board, or at weighing, the Ship must *ware short round*, Fig. 583, the Helm must be put a-lee or to port: *(that the after or larboard Side of the Rudder being pressed against the Water by the Sternway, may send her Stern to starboard)*, the FORE TOPSAIL must be braced *sharp a-back*, the MAIN and MIZEN TOPSAILS *square a-back*, and the JIB and FORE TOPMAST STAYSAIL set with the *starboard* or *weather* Sheets aft; she will then ware sharp round on her Heel, when she must proceed as mentioned in Box-hauling, page 93.

GETTING

---

* *If the Ship (when the Anchor is out of the Ground) get Sternway, the Helm must be still kept a-weather, to prevent her falling off too much.*

Fig 580

Fig. 579

Fig. 581

Fig. 582

Fig. 583

Butterworth sc. Leeds

Getting under Way — Anchoring.

Fig. 584   Fig. 585

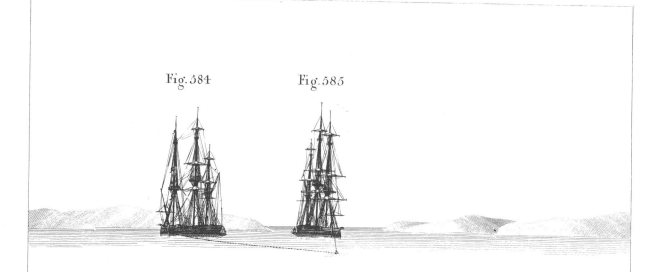

Fig. 586   Fig. 587

P. Lever. del.   Butterworths. sc. Leeds

GETTING UNDER WAY------ANCHORING.

If there be a Necessity for getting under Way on a *lee* Tide, with a Fresh of Wind, it will require great Exertion at the Capstern.

If the Flood be the windward Tide, it is generally the Practice to get under Way at the last Quarter of it, by which means the Ship will not be to cast, the Anchor will be up, catted and fished, and she will save the Tide.

At this Time she will be in the Position of the Ship Fig. 584, which is riding with a Sheer of the Port Helm, as mentioned in riding Windward Tide, page 101, Fig. 537, the after Yards full, and the head ones braced to with the starboard Braces. The Head Yards are filled, the Helm eased, and she falls towards her Anchor, like Fig. 585. If the Tide be strong and the Wind light, the FORE TOP-SAIL may be hoisted to ease the Capstern or Windlass when the Cable is hove in; if the Wind be rather more powerful, the FORE TOPMAST STAYSAIL will be sufficient, or the Topsails hanging loose in the Brails. If it be so strong as to force the Ship a-head, bringing the Cable taught under the Bows, it is seldom attempted to heave the Anchor up with a windward Tide; for in sheering towards her Anchor, to slacken the Cable that it may be hove in, she will bring up suddenly with such violence as to endanger her parting: in which Case it is always judged most prudent to get under Way when the Tide first makes to Windward, heaving in the Slack of the Cable, before she tends so as to bring the Wind aft.

When a Ship comes to an Anchor at the slack of the *windward* Tide, she must be shot a-head with the JIB and FORE TOPMAST STAYSAIL, and if necessary, the MIZEN or MIZEN STAYSAIL. Thus the Ship, Fig. 586, being under the three Topsails, Mizen, Jib and Fore Topmast Staysail, intending to come to an Anchor, takes in the three Topsails, lets go the Anchor at (a), and shoots a-head with the Fore and aft Sails, veering out a sufficient Scope of Cable to tend with, like Fig. 587, bringing the Buoy on the starboard or weather Quarter; when she brings the Wind abaft the Beam by the Mizen sending her Stern to leeward it is taken in, and she then proceeds as described in tending to leeward, page 102, or in breaking the Sheer, page 103.

When the Wind is directly across the Tide, the Ship may be got under Way at any Time, as Sail may be set to stem it. Coming to an Anchor with the Wind in this Direction, there is nothing but to take in Sail, and when the Head-way is done, let go the Anchor, sheering either to windward or to leeward, as mentioned in pages 104 and 105.

A Dictionary of Sea Terms.

A-back. — A Sail is a-back when its *forward* Surface is acted upon by the Wind.

A baft. — The hinder Part of a Ship—Behind—thus *a-baft the Foremast*, means any Thing nearer to the Stern than the Foremast.

A-board. — In the Ship---as the Cargo is *a-board*   A Ship is said to *fall a-board*, when she runs foul of another.   To get *a-board* the Main Tack, is to bring the Clew of the Mainsail down to the Chess-tree.

About. — A Ship is said to be *going about*, when in the Act of Tacking; the Order for which is " *ready about there !* "

A-breast. — Opposite to.

A-drift. — Broken loose from the Moorings.

A-float. — Swimming——not touching the Bottom.

Afore. — That Part of the Ship nearest to the Stem, or Head.

Aft. — Behind——as " *Stand farther aft*" i. e. stand nearer to the Stern.

After. — Hinder—as *the after Ports*—those Ports nearest the Stern.—*After Sails, after Hatchway*, &c.

A-ground. — Not having Water enough to float the Ship, which rests on the Ground.

A-head. — Before the Ship.

A-lee. — The Helm is *a-lee* when the Tiller is put to the lee Side.   *Hard a-lee*, when it is put as far as it will go.

All in the Wind. — i. e. when the Wind blows on the Leeches, or outward Extremities of the Sails, and causes them to shake.

All Hands, hoy ! — The Word given by the Boatswain and his Mates, at the Hatchways, to assemble the Ship's Company.

A-loft. — Up above.   In the Rigging.   On the Yards.   At the Mast Head, &c.

Alongside. — Close to the Ship.

A-midships. — In the Middle of the Ship.   *The Helm is a-midships*, when the Tiller is not put over either to one Side or the other.

To Anchor. — To let the Anchor fall over-board, that it may hold the Ship.

To foul the Anchor. — To let the Cable be twisted round the upper Fluke, &c.

To drag the Anchor. — When the Ship pulls it with her, from the Violence of the Wind.

Anchorage. — Ground fit to anchor in.

The Anchor is a Cock Bill. — i. e. it is hanging by the Stopper at the Cat-Head.

The Anchor is a-Peak. — i. e. near to the Ship : thus at different Distances it is called a *long Peak*, a *stay Peak*, a *short Peak*.

The Anchor is a-weigh, or a-trip. — } i. e. loosened from the Ground by heaving in the Cable.

The Anchor is backed. — i. e. *another* Anchor is placed at a certain distance before it, and attached to it by the Cable of the former being fastened to it, which fixes it firmly in the Ground.

The Anchor is catted. — i. e. drawn up to the Cat-head.

The Anchor is fished. — i. e. its inner Arm is drawn up by the Fish Pendent.

To weigh the Anchor. — To heave it up by the Capstern or Windlass.

The Sheet Anchor — is of the same Size and Weight as the two Bower Anchors and the Spare Anchor; it is a resource, and dependance, should either of the Bowers part, for which purpose the Cable is always kept ready bent with a long Range, that it may be let go on an Emergency.

Best Bower   } Anchors are the two Anchors which are stowed the farthest forward, or near the Bows.
Small Bower }

The Stream Anchor — is used to bring the Ship up with occasionally, or to steady a Ship when she comes to a temporary Mooring.

E e

The

The Kedge Anchor.	The smallest of the Anchors, to which a Hawser or Cablet is generally bent.
An End.	Any Spar or Mast placed perpendicularly. The *Topmasts are an End,* i. e. they are swayed up and fidded, above the lower Masts. *All an End,* i. e. all the Masts are up in their proper Stations.
A-peak.	See Anchor.
Ashore.	On Land. A-ground.
A-stern.	Behind the Ship.
Athwart.	Across. *Athwart-Hawse,* across the Stem. *Athwart-ships,* any thing lying in a direction across the Ship. *Athwart the Fore Foot,* a shot fired by another Ship across the Bows, and a-head.
A-trip.	See Anchor. The Topsails are *a-trip,* i. e. hoisted up.
Avast.	To cease hauling. To stop.
A-weigh.	See Anchor.
A-weather.	The Helm is said to be *a-weather,* when the Tiller is put over to the windward side of the Ship. *Hard a-weather,* when it is put over as far as it will go.
Awning.	A Canvas Canopy placed over the Deck when the Sun is powerful.
To back the Sails.	To expose their forward Surfaces to the Wind, by hauling in the weather Braces.
Back Stays.	Ropes fixed at the Topmast and Top Gallant Mast Head, and extended to the Chains on the Ship's sides.
To Bag-pipe the Mizen.	To bring the Sheet over to the weather Mizen Shrouds, in order to lay it a-back.
To balance the Mizen.	Rolling up a Portion of it at the Peak.
Ballast.	A quantity of Iron, Stone, Gravel, &c. placed in the Hold to give a Ship proper Stability, when she has no Cargo, or but a small quantity of Goods, &c.
Bands.	Pieces of Canvas sewn across the Sail, called *Reef-bands;* also a piece stuck on the middle of a Sail to strengthen it, when half worn.
Bar.	A Shoal running across the Mouth of a Harbour.
Capstern Bars.	Pieces of Timber put into the Holes in the Drum Head of the Capstern, (where they are secured with iron Pins) to heave up the Anchor.
Bare Poles.	Having no Sail up.
Battens.	Slips of Wood nailed on the Slings of the Yards, which are eight square—also over the Tarpaulings of a Hatchway, to keep out the water in stormy weather.
Bays.	In Men of War, the starboard and larboard sides between Decks, before the Bitts.
Beams.	Strong Pieces of Timber across the Ship, under the Decks, bound to the side by Knees. They support and keep the Ship together.
On the Beam.	When the Wind blows at a right Angle with the Keel.
Before the Beam.	When the Wind or Object bears on some Point less than a right Angle, or ninety Degrees, from the Ship's Head.
Abaft the Beam.	When the Wind or Object bears on a Point which is more than a right Angle, or ninety Degrees, from the Ship's Course.
Bearing.	The Point of the Compass on which any Object appears. It is also applied to an Object which lies opposite to any part of the Ship—thus the Buoy, &c. bears on the Beam, the Bow, the Quarter, &c.
Beating to Windward.	Tacking, and endeavouring to get to windward of some Head Land.
Becalmed.	Having no Wind to fill the Sails. The Ship being deprived of the Power of the Wind by the intervention of high Land, a larger Ship, &c.
Beckets.	Short Straps, having an Eye in one end, and a double-walled Knot on the other, for suspending a Yard, &c. till wanted: such are the Beckets for the Royal Yards, for the Bights of the Sheets, &c.
To Belay.	To make fast.
Bend.	A kind of Knot—as a Sheet Bend, &c.—or a Seizing—such as the Bends of the Cable.
To Bend.	To make fast—as to bend the Sails, the Cable, &c.
Bends.	The Streaks of thick Stuff, or strongest Planks in the Ship's sides, on the broadest Part. These are also called *Wales.*
Between Decks.	Any part of the Ship below, between two Decks.

Bight.

Bight.	Any part of a Rope between the ends. Also a Collar or Eye formed by a Rope.
Bilge.	The flat part of a Ship's bottom. *Bilge Water*, that which rests in the Bilge, either from Rain, shipping Water, &c.
Binnacle.	The Frame, or Box which contains the Compass.
Birth.	A place of Anchorage. A Cabin, or Apartment.
Bitts.	Large upright Pins of Timber with a Cross Piece, over which the Bight of the Cable is put; also smaller ones to belay ropes, such as Topsail Sheets, &c.
To Bitt.	To place a Bight of the Cable over the Bitts.
Blocks.	Instruments with Sheaves or Pulleys, used to increase the Power of Ropes.
Block and Block.	When the two Blocks of a Tackle are drawn so close together that there is no more of the fall left to haul upon; also termed *chock a-block*.
To make a Board.	To tack.
To make a Stern Board.	To drive a Ship Stern foremost, by laying the Sails a-back.
Boarding.	Entering an enemy's Ship by force. These men are called *Boarders*.
Boarding Netting.	Network triced round the Ship, to prevent the Boarders from entering.
Boats.	Small Vessels—those belonging to Ships are—the *Long Boat*, the *Launch*, the *Cutter*, the *Yawl*, and the *Jolly Boat*.
Boatswain.	The Officer who has the charge of the Cordage, Boats, Rigging, &c.
Bobstays.	Ropes reeved through the Cutwater, and set up with dead Eyes under the Bowsprit, to act against the power of the Fore Stays—sometimes one of these is taken to the *end* of the Bowsprit, to act against the Fore Topmast Stays.
Bolsters.	Pieces of Wood, or Canvas stuffed, placed on the lower Tressle Trees, to keep the Rigging from chafing.
Bolts.	Iron fastenings, by which the Ship is secured in her Hull.
Bolt Ropes.	Ropes sewn round the edges of the Sails.
Booms.	Large Poles used to extend the Studding Sails, Spanker, &c. Also spare Yards, Masts, &c.
Boom Irons.	Iron Caps fixed on the Yard Arms for the Studdingsail Booms to rest in.
Bows.	The round part of the Ship forward.
To Bowse.	To haul upon.
Bower.	See Anchor.
Bowlines.	Ropes made fast to the Leeches or sides of the Sails, to pull them forwards.
Bowsprit.	A Mast projecting over the Stem.
Box-hauling.	A method of waring or turning a Ship from the Wind.
Boxing off.	Turning the Ship's Head from the Wind, by backing the Head Sails.
Braces.	Ropes fastened to the Yard Arms to brace them about. Also a security to the Rudder, fixed to the Stern Post.
Brails.	Ropes applied to the after Leeches of the Mizen, and some of the Staysails, to draw them up. *
To break Bulk.	To begin to unload.
To break the Sheer.	To swerve from the proper direction in which a Ship should be when at Anchor.
Breaming.	Burning the stuff which is collected on the Ship's bottom during a long voyage.
Breast Hooks.	Pieces of Timber placed across the Bows of the Ship, to keep them together.
Breast Work.	Railing on the fore part of the Quarter Deck, where Ropes are belayed.
Breeching.	A stout Rope fixed to the Cascabel of a Gun, fastened to the Ship's side, to prevent its running in.
Bridles.	The upper part of the Moorings laid in harbours for Men of War. Also Ropes attached from the Leeches of the square Sails to the Bowlines.
To bring up.	To come to an Anchor.
To bring to.	To make a Ship stationary, stopping her way by bracing some of the Sails a-back, and keeping others full, so that they counterpoise each other.
To bring by the Lee.	When a Ship is sailing with the Wind very large, and flies off from it so as to bring it on the other side, the Sails catching a-back; she is said to be brought by the Lee—this is a dangerous position in a high Sea.
To broach to.	Flying up in the Wind so as to bring it on the other side, when blowing fresh.
Bulk-heads.	Partitions in the Ship.
Bull's Eye.	A wooden Thimble.
Bumkin.	A short Boom fitted above the Main Sail, for the purpose of hauling down the fore Tack to. It is supported on each side by a Shroud.

*Blunt includes, "Brail up - The order to haul up a spanker or spencer."

Bunt.	The middle part of a square Sail. Also the fore Leech of a quadrangular Staysail.
Buntlines.	Ropes attached to the foot of a square Sail, to haul it up.
Burton Pendents.	The first piece of Rigging which goes over the Topmast Head, to which is hooked a Tackle, to set up the Topmast Shrouds.
Bush.	Metal let into the Sheaves of Blocks which have iron Pins.
Butt End.	The end of a Plank in the Ship's side.
Buttock.	That part of the Ship's Hull under the Stern, between the Water Line and Wing Transom.
By the Board.	Over the side. A Mast is said to go by the Board when it is carried or shot away just above the Deck.
By the Head.	When a Ship is deeper in the Water forward than aft.
By the Stern.	The Reverse of by the Head.
By the Wind.	When a Ship is as near to the Wind as her Head can lie with the Sails filled.
Cabin.	A Room or Apartment; also a Bed Place.
Cable.	A large Rope by which the Ship is secured to the Anchor. Cables take their names from the Anchors to which they belong, as the *Sheet* Cable, the *best* Bower Cable, &c. they are generally 120 Fathoms in length.
To bitt the Cable.	See Bitts.
To heave in the Cable.	To pull it into the Ship by the Capstern or Windlass.
To pay out the Cable.	To stick it out of the Hawse Hole.
To veer away the Cable.	To slacken it so that it may run out, as in paying out.
To serve the Cable.	To wrap it round with Rope, Plait, or Horse Hide, to keep it from chafing.
To slip the Cable.	To let it run clear out.
Cable Tier.	That part of the orlop Deck where the Cables are coiled.
To coil the Cable.	To lay it on the Deck in a circular form.
Caboose.	The place where the Victuals are dressed in Merchant-men.
Call.	A Silver Pipe or Whistle used by the Boatswain and his Mates, by the sounding of which they call up the hands, direct them to *haul*, to *veer*, to *belay*, &c.
Canted.	Any thing turned from its square position.
Canvas.	Strong Cloth, of which the Sails are made.
Cap.	A Block of Wood which secures the Topmast to the lower Mast.
Capsize.	To turn over.
Capstern.	A Machine for drawing up the Anchor by the Messenger, which is taken round it, and applied to the Cable by the Nippers.
Careening.	Heaving a Vessel down on one side, to clean or repair her Bottom.
Carrick Bend.	A kind of Knot.
To Cast.	To pay a Ship's Head off by backing the Head Sails when heaving up the Anchor, so as to bring the Wind on the side required.
Cat Block.	A large double or three-fold Block used for drawing the Anchor up to the Cat-head.
Cat-head.	A large piece of Timber or Crane projecting over the Bow, for drawing up the Anchor clear from the Ship's side.
Cat-harpins.	Short legs of Rope seized to the upper part of the lower Shrouds, and Futtock Staves, to keep them from bulging out by the strain of the Futtock Shrouds, and to permit the bracing up of the lower Yards.
Cat's Paw.	A light Air perceived by its effect on the Water, but not durable. Also a twist made on the Bight of a Rope.
To Caulk.	To drive Oakham into the seams of the Sides, Decks, &c.
Chains.	Links of Iron bolted to the Ship's side, having dead Eyes in the upper ends, to which the Shrouds are connected by the Laniards.
Channels.	Strong broad Planks bolted to the sides, to keep the dead Eyes in the Chains from the side, to spread the Rigging farther out.
Chappelling.	A Ship is said to build a Chapel, when by neglect in light winds she turns round so as to bring the Wind on the same part which it was before she moved.
Chase.	A Ship pursued by another.
Bow Chase.	A Gun in the fore part of the Ship.

Stern

Stern Chase.	A gun pointing a-stern in the after part of the Ship.
To chase.	To pursue, to follow.
To cheer.	To huzza. *What cheer ho!* A salutation.
Chock a-block.	See Block and Block.
To clap on.	To make fast, as " *clap on the Stoppers*," &c.
To claw off.	To beat to windward from a lee-shore.
Cleats.	Pieces of Wood to fasten Ropes to.
Close-hauled.	As near the Wind as the Ship can lie.
Club-hauling.	Tacking by means of an Anchor.
Clues, or Clews.	The lower Corners of the square Sails.
Coamings.	The Borders of the Hatchways which are raised above the Deck.
Coiling.	Laying a Rope down in a circular form.
Companion.	A wooden Covering over the Cabin Hatchway.
Course.	The Point of the Compass on which the Ship sails. The Mainsail, Foresail, and Mizen, are also called *Courses.*
Crab.	A small Capstern.
To cun the Ship.	To direct the Helm's-man how to steer.
Cut-water.	The Knee of the Head.
Davit.	A Crane of Timber used for fishing the Anchors.
Dead Eye.	A Block with three Holes in, to receive the Laniard of a Shroud or Stay.
Dog-Vane.	A small Vane made of Cork and Feathers, placed on the weather side of the Quarter Deck.
Dolphin.	A wreath of Rope placed round a Mast to support the Pudding.
To douse.	To let fly the Halliards of a Topsail—to lower away briskly.
Down-hauler	A Rope to pull down the Staysails, Topmast Studding Sails, &c.
Drift.	Driving to leeward—driving with the Tide. Drifts are also those parts where the Rails are cut off and end with Scrolls.
Driver.	A large Sail suspended to the Mizen Gaff.
Dunnage.	Wood, &c. laid at the Bottom of a Ship to keep the Cargo dry.
Earings.	Small Ropes to make fast the upper Corners of square Sails, &c.
Ease off.	To slacken.
End for End.	To let a Rope or Cable run quite out.
End on.	When a Ship's Bows and Head Sails are only seen.
Fag End.	The end of a Rope which is untwisted.
Fake.	One Circle of a Coil of Rope.
Falling off.	When a Ship moves from the Wind farther than she ought.
Fid.	A tapered piece of Wood or Iron to splice Ropes with. Also a piece of Wood which supports one Mast upon the Tressle-trees of another.
To fill.	To brace the Yards so that the wind may strike the Sails on their after Surfaces.
Flukes.	The broad Parts or Palms of the Anchors.
Fore.	That part of the Ship nearest to the Head.
Fore and Aft.	The length-way of the Ship, or in the direction of the Keel
Fore Castle.	A short Deck in the fore part of the Ship.
Forging a-head.	Forced a-head by the Wind.
Foul Hawse.	When the Cables are twisted.
To founder.	To sink.
Full and by.	See close-hauled.
Furling.	Making fast the Sails to the Yards by the Gaskets.
Gaff.	A Spar or Yard to which the Mizen of a Ship or the Mainsail of a Brig or Cutter is bent.
Gang-way.	A Platform reaching from the Quarter Deck to the Fore-castle on each side. Also the place where persons enter the Ship.
Gasket.	A piece of Plait to fasten the Sails to the Yard.
Girt.	A Ship is girted when her Cables are too tight, which prevents her swinging.
Goose Neck.	An iron Hook at the end of a Boom.
Goose Wings.	The outer extremities of a Main or Foresail when loose, the rest of it being furled.
Goring.	Cutting a Sail obliquely.

F f   *Gripe.*

*Blunt includes the following, "Clew down the top-sails, top-gallant sails &c. - The order to haul the yards down upon the cap, by manning the clew-lines, &c." and "Clew up the top-sails, top-gallant sails &c. - The order to haul these sails up for furling."

Gripe.	A piece of Timber which joins the Keel and the Cutwater.
Griping.	When a Ship carries her Helm much to windward.
Gunnel.	The upper part of a Ship's side.
Guy.	A Rope to steady a Boom, &c.
Gybing.	When (by the Wind being large) it is necessary to shift the Boom of a fore and aft Sail.
Halliards.	Tackles or Ropes to hoist up the Sails.
To Hand.	The same as to furl.
Hatch-way.	A square Hole in the Deck, which communicates with the Hold or another Deck.
To Haul.	To Pull.
To Hail.	To call out to another Ship.
A clear Hawse.	When the Cables are not twisted.
A Foul Hawse.	When the Cables lie across, or are twisted.
Hawse Holes.	The Holes through which the Cables pass.
Hawser.	A small Cable.
To Heel.	To incline to one side.
The Helm.	A wooden Bar put through the Head of a Rudder—also called the *Tiller.*
To Hitch.	To make fast.
The Hold.	The lower apartment of a Ship where the provisions and goods are stowed.
To Haul Home.	To pull the Clew of a Sail, &c. as far as it will go.
Horse.	A Rope made fast to the Yard, on which the Men stand.
Hull.	The Body of a Ship.
Jewel Blocks.	Blocks at the Topsail Yard Arms, for the Topmast Studding Sail Halliards.
Jigger.	A Purchase used in Merchant Ships to hold on the Cable.
Junk.	Pieces of old Cable, out of which Mats, Gaskets, &c. are made.
Jury Masts.	Temporary Masts, stepped when the others are carried or shot away.
Keckling.	Old Rope passed round the Cable at short distances.
Kink.	A twist or turn in a Rope.
To Labour.	To pitch and roll heavily.
Land-fall.	Discovering the Land.
Larboard.	The left Side.
Launch ho !	To let go the top Rope when the Topmast is fidded.
Leeward.	That Point towards which the Wind blows.
Lee-lurch.	When the Ship rolls to leeward.
Lee-way.	The lateral Movement of a Ship to leeward.
Lee Tide.	When the Wind and Tide are the same Way.
Lizard.	A small piece of Rope with a Thimble, spliced into a larger one.
Looming.	The appearance of a distant Object, such as a Ship, the Land, &c.
Lubber.	A Sailor who does not know his Duty.
Luff.	A direction to the Steer's-man to put the Helm to leeward.
Luff Tackle.	A large Tackle, consisting of a double and a single Block.
Lying to.	See to bring to.
To Man the Yards.	To send Men upon them.
Messenger.	A Rope attached to the Cable, to heave up the Anchor by.
Mizen.	The aftermost Sail in a Ship.
To Moor.	To secure a Ship by more than one Cable.
Moorings.	The place where a Vessel is moored. Also Anchors with Chains and Bridles laid in Rivers for Men of War to ride by.
Neap Tides.	Those Tides which happen when the Moon is in her Quarters, and are not so high as the Spring Tides.
Neaped.	A Ship is said to be neaped when she is left on Shore by these Tides, and must wait for the next Spring Tides.
To near the Land.	To approach the Shore.
No Near.	A direction to the Helm's-man to put the Helm a little a-weather, to keep the Sails full.
Nippers.	Plaiting or Selvagees to bind the Cable to the Messenger.
Off and on.	Coming near the Land on one Tack, and leaving it on the other.
Offing.	Out to Sea—from the Land.
Orlop Deck.	The lowest Deck in the Ship, lying on the Beams of the Hold. The place where the Cables are coiled, and where other Stores are kept.

*Blunt includes, "Haul up the courses - The order for clewing up the fore-sail, main-sail and mizen (if a square sail)."

Overboard.	Out of the Ship.
Overhauling.	To haul a fall of Rope through a Block till it is slack. Also examining a Ship, &c.
Painter.	A Rope by which a Boat is made fast.
Palm.	See Fluke.
To Pass.	To hand any thing from one to another; or place a Rope or Lashing round a Yard, &c.
To Pay.	To rub Tar, Pitch, &c. on any thing with a Brush.
To Pay off.	To make a Ship's Head recede from the Wind by backing the Head Sails, &c.
To Peak up.	To raise the after end of a Gaff.
Plying.	Turning to windward.
Pooping.	A Ship is said to be pooped when she is struck by a heavy Sea, on the Stern or Quarter.
Port.	To the left side. This term is used to the Helm's-man to put the Helm to the left, instead of the word *"larboard"*—to make a distinction from the affinity of sound in the word *starboard.*
Preventer.	Any thing for temporary security; as, a Preventer Brace, &c.
Quarter.	That part of a Ship's side between the Main Chains and the Stern.
Racking a Fall.	Seizing the parts of a Tackle-fall together by cross turns.
Rake.	The projection of a Ship at the Stem and Stern, beyond the extent of the Keel—also the inclination of a Ship's Masts either forward or aft from a perpendicular Line.
Range of Cable.	A sufficient length hauled up, to permit the Anchor to drop to the bottom.
To rattle down the Shrouds.	To fix the Ratlings on them.
To reef.	To reduce a Sail, by tying it round the Yard with Points.
To reeve.	To put a Rope through a Block, &c.
To ride.	To be held by the Cable. To " ride easy" is when a Ship does not labour much. To " ride hard" is when the Ship pitches with violence.
To rig.	To fit the Rigging to the Masts.
To right.	A Ship is said to right when she rises to her upright position, after being laid down by a violent squall.
To right the Helm.	To put it a-midships, or in its fore and aft position, parallel to the Keel.
To round in.	To haul in a Brace, &c. which is not very tight.
To rouse in.	To haul in the slack part of the Cable.
To run down.	When one Ship sinks another by running over her.
To scud.	To sail before the Wind in a Storm.
To scuttle a Ship.	To make holes in her bottom to sink her.
To serve.	To wind any thing round a Cable or Rope, to prevent its being chafed.
To seize.	To make fast, or bind.
To sheer.	To go in and out, and not in a direct course.
To ship.	To put any thing on board.—To " *ship a Sea,*" when the Sea breaks into the Ship.
To shiver.	To make the Sails shake.
The Slack of a Rope, &c.	That part which hangs loose.
To slip a Cable.	To let it run out to the end.
To slue.	To turn any thing about.
To sound.	To find the bottom by a leaden Plummet.
To take a Spell.	To be in turn on duty at the Lead, the Pump, &c.
To spill.	To take the Wind out of the Sails by the Braces, &c. in order to reef or hand them.
To splice.	To join two Ropes together, by uniting the Strands.
Spoondrift.	A continued flying of the Spray and Waves over the Surface of the Sea.
To spring a Mast.	To crack or split it.
A Spring.	A Rope made fast to the Cable at the Bow, and taken in abaft, in order to expose the Ship's side to any direction.
Spring Tides.	The highest Tides at the Full and Change of the Moon.
To stand on.	To keep in the Course.
To stand by.	To be ready.
Starboard.	The right side.
To steer.	To manage a Ship by the movement of the Helm.
To stopper the Cable.	To keep it from running out, by fastening short Ropes to it, called *Stoppers.*

Strand.	One of the Divisions of a Rope.
Stranded.	When one of the Divisions is broken. Also when a Ship is run on Shore so that she cannot be got off, she is said to be stranded.
To stretch.	To stand on different Tacks under a press of Sail.
To strike.	To beat against the bottom. Also to lower the Flag in token of submission. Lowering the Topmasts is commonly termed, *striking* them.
To surge the Messenger.	To slacken it suddenly.
To sway.	To hoist up the Yards and Topmasts.
To swing.	To turn a Ship from one side of her Anchor to the other, at the change of the Tide.
To tack.	To turn a Ship by the Sails and Rudder against the Wind.
Taught.	A corruption of Tight,
Taunt.	Long, lofty.
Tending.	The movement of a Vessel in swinging at Anchor.
Tier.	The place where the Cables are coiled.
Traverse.	To sail on different Courses.
Trying.	Laying to in a Gale of Wind, under a small Sail.
Turning to windward.	Tacking.
Twice-laid Stuff.	Rope made from the Yarns of a Cable, &c. which has been half worn.
To veer and haul.	To pull a Rope and then slacken it.
To unbend.	To cast loose.
To unmoor.	To reduce a Ship to a single Anchor, after riding by two.
To unreeve.	To pull a Rope out of a Block.
To unrig.	To deprive a Ship of her Rigging.
To unship	To take any thing from the place in which it was fixed.
Waist of a Ship.	The part between the Main and Fore Drifts—also a term sometimes used for the spare or waste Anchor, from its being stowed near the Fore Drift, or Fore Part of the Waist.
Wake.	The Track left by the Ship on the Water which she has passed over.
Wales.	See Bends.
To Ware.	To turn a Ship round from the Wind.
To warp.	To move a Ship by Hawsers, &c.
Watch.	A division of the Ship's company who keep the Deck for a certain time. One is called the *starboard,* and the other the *larboard Watch.*
Water-logged.	The state of a leaky Ship when she is so full of Water as to be heavy and unmanageable.
Way of a Ship.	Her progress through the Water.
To weather a Ship.	To get to windward of her.
A weather Tide.	A Tide or Stream which runs to windward.
Weather-beaten.	Any thing worn or damaged by bad weather.
To weigh.	To heave the Anchor out of the Ground.
To whip.	To bind the end of a Rope with Yarn, to prevent its untwisting—also to hoist any thing by a Rope which is reeved through a single Block.
Wind's Eye.	That point from which the Wind blows in a direct Line.
Between Wind & Water.	That part of the Ship's bottom which is just at the surface of the Water, or what is called the *Water Line.*
To wind a Boat, &c.	To turn it round from its original Position.
Wind-rode.	When the Ship is kept a-stern, &c. of her Anchor solely by the Wind.
To windward.	Towards that point from whence the Wind blows.
To work to windward.	To make a progress against the Wind by *Tacking.*

F I N I S.

T. Gill, Printer, Leeds.

PREFACE OF THE AMERICAN EDITOR.

—◦∞◦—

In preparing this book for the press, the American Editor has availed himself of every facility which this great sea-port could afford.

It is some thirty-four years since, his vocation then being upon the deep, that he purchased one of these books in England ; and, although then behind the day in the improvements in the rigging of American ships, it was found to be a work of great utility.

Since that time the changes in the mode of rigging, and in diminishing the unnecessary weight aloft, combining lightness with strength, have been greater than for the preceding hundred years, if a fair judgment can be formed from a comparison of the different works upon the subject.

These improvements have been effected mainly, it is believed, by American ingenuity. Our shipmasters have been free to act, untrammelled by any control save that of their own good sense and experience ; and the result is, that we now can challenge the world to produce so many symmetrically rigged and serviceable ships as exist in our mercantile marine.

Let us give one instance :—on a voyage to India, in 1818, the ship which we were on board of, was rigged in the common way ; the yards encumbered with straps, &c. In the course of the voyage every yard was stripped, gromets were worked to fit the yard arms ; into them cringles were put, to which the brace blocks, lifts, &c., were spliced. This was the beginning of the present neat mode of fitting yards, as the same shipmaster, in building a new ship shortly afterwards, fitted her with the iron straps now in use.

In the present work, several of the plates containing the old cumbrous mode of rigging have been retained, as there are ships now rigged in that way ; and it was thought best to leave them, that the learner, for whom this book is intended, might make a comparison

Much new matter has been introduced ; such as the Tables on Rope, Canvas, Guns, Spars, Clippers, and Forbes' New Rig.

The Editor neither seeks nor shuns criticism : if there is any of his part of the work to approve it will gratify him ; if to condemn, he will mend it. Any suggestion from a seaman, will be duly appreciated.

NEW-YORK, January, 1854.

Within the cap, four stout pieces of oak or locust (locust is the best) are bolted, two on each side, called *Bees* (e) and (e 1); through these, in modern rigged vessels, the fore-top-mast and fore-stays are rove. (f) is the outer bowsprit shroud dead-eye, and (g) the outer bob-stay dead-eye; they are fastened to the bowsprit with an iron strap.   About one half out, is a piece of wood called a Saddle (h); and when ships carry a sprit-sail yard, (which is very seldom done in the Merchant Service), cleats are put on for the parral.   The gammoning (i) is now an iron strap, which sets up with a nut and screw.   (See (a) 158).

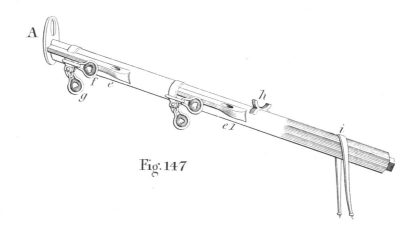

Fig. 147

APPENDIX 3

Getting in a new Mast by the old one without Sheers_Gammoning

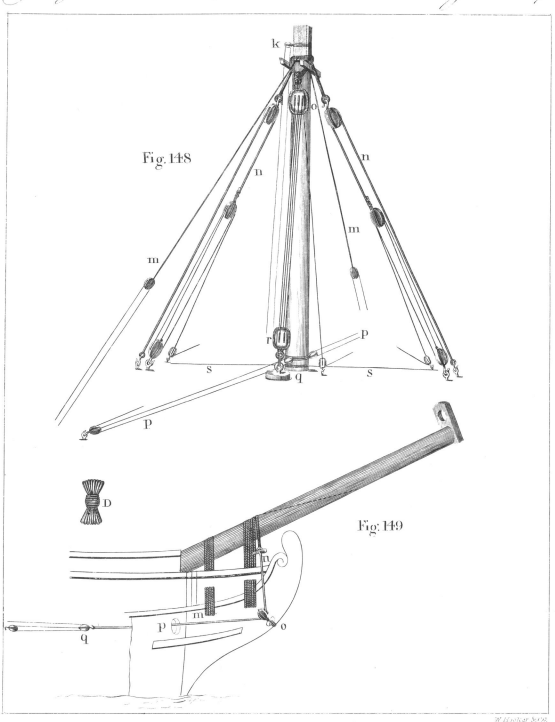

Fig. 148

Fig: 149

BOB-STAYS.

The BOB-STAY COLLAR, or STRAP, Fig. 156,

When not made of iron as in the plate, is wormed, parcelled, and served, having an eye spliced in each end. A dead-eye is placed in the bight, and a round seizing (see page 9) is clapped on. This lies underneath the bowsprit, and the lashing is passed through the eyes over the upper part of it. In large vessels, there are two of these, one placed before the other.

BOWSPRIT SHROUD COLLARS,

Of which there are two, are lashed over the bowsprit in the same manner, with a heart or dead-eye, one lying on each side ; but more frequently in merchant ships the hearts are both seized into one collar, Fig. 157, and the lashing is passed through the eyes over the bowsprit. The ends of all the lashings are whipped, and seized down to the standing part. In the plate, Fig. 158 the collars are iron straps, which is the mode of all modern ships.

The BOB-STAYS, Fig. 158,

In vessels, are of chain or rope: when of rope, they are wormed, parcelled and served, led through a dead-eye, which is fitted through iron plates, (r) let into the stem and cutwater, and have the two ends spliced together. A dead-eye (m) is seized in with a round seizing (see page 9), the splice laying on the upper side of it. They are set up thus: a rope called a *Laniard* (n) is spliced to the heart or dead-eye, under the bowsprit, passing alternately through the heart or dead-eye (m), in the bob-stay, and the one it is spliced to : the double block of a luff-tackle (o) is hooked to a cat's-paw or Black-wall hitch (see Figs. 57 and 59, page 8) on the laniard : the single block (p) hooks to a selvagee round the night-head. This is bowsed taught, and another luff-tackle (q) being hooked in the same manner to the fall of this, it is set up. The laniard is then nippered with rope-yarn (see page 9), and the tackles taken off. This purchase of the tackles is called *Luff-upon-Luff*. The end is taken through between the seizing and dead-eye (m) : one turn is taken round the single part of the bob-stay, the remaining turns round both parts, and the end stopped ; or if it be long, it may be frapped round the parts of the laniard (n). When of chain, a dead-eye is fitted to the upper part, and it is set up as above.

Vessels which have no figure head, such as coasters, whose cat-heads are in general very forward, have their bob-stays led through a hole in the stem, like Fig. 159. They have a double block turned into the collar (a), and a single one (b) is seized in the bob-stay. The reason why they have not dead-eyes, is because, when the anchor is hove up, the bob-stay lying so near the bows, the stock is apt to get foul of them. They are therefore let go occasionally, and the bights of the bob-stay are triced up to the bowsprit, as in the figure. This is the case with the English colliers.

The BOWSPRIT SHROUD, Fig. 160, or 160 (d),

Has a hook and thimble (r) spliced into one end and a heart or dead-eye (s) into the other. It is served over. The lower end (r) is hooked to an eye-bolt in the bends forward, and the upper one (s) is set up with a laniard, to the heart or dead-eye in the collar, with luff-upon-luff, like the bob-stay.

Bobstays.

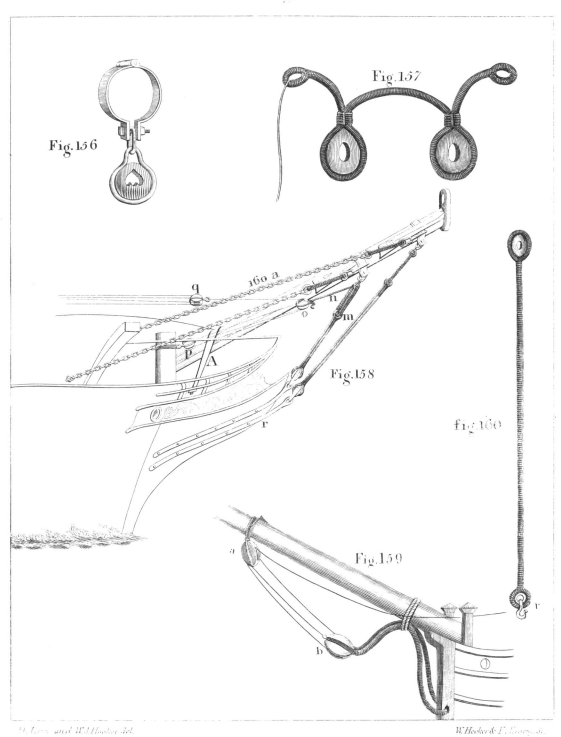

Fig. 156

Fig. 157

Fig. 158

Fig. 159

fig. 160

SHROUDS sometimes are cable-laid; but they are now generally shroud or hawser-laid. (See page 2). They are taken round two fids, or short posts (a, c, Fig. 164).

In fixing the FORE RIGGING, warp only two pairs the proper length: (i. e.) from the tressle-tree on the opposite side to the partners: then stretch them hand-taught. At one end, lay them one *without* the other: at the other end, one *upon* the other. Drive in another fid (b) at one foot distance, to lengthen the next two pairs: warp them as before, and so proceed, according to the number of pairs wanted; driving in a fid at the same distance. Cut them asunder at (a), where the bights are laid one *upon* the other. Thus the bights at c, d, &c. will be the middle of a pair of shrouds.

Sometimes the fids, for increasing the length between each pair, are driven in at the end (a) where the bights lie one *upon* the other.

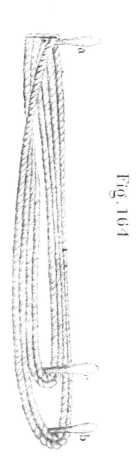

Fig. 164

In staying the mast, the stay is rove through the dead-eye or collar (f), on the bowsprit, Fig. 174. A selvagee is clapped on the stay at (d), and the double block of a luff-tackle (e) is hooked to it. The stay being leathered and well smeared with grease, to make it pass freely, the single block of the luff-tackle is attached to the end of the stay by a strap : the single block of another luff-tackle (g) is hooked to the fall of that; and the double block (h) to a selvagee or pair of slings, round the bowsprit (i); the fall leading in on the forecastle. The stay is then set up by the purchase, and when sufficiently so, the parts are nippered with racking turns (see page 9) as before. The end is then secured to its own part, by two or three round seizings. In men of war, the lower masts are generally bowsed forwards by the runners and tackles, before they are stayed.

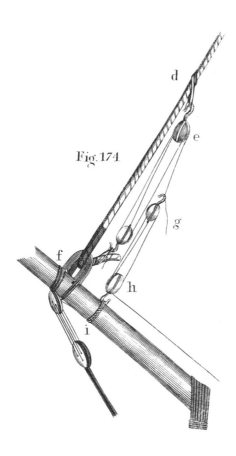

Fig. 174.

The MAIN STAY, Fig. 201,

Is fitted with an eye similar to the fore stay, Fig. 168. The end is rove through a heart, bolted to the upper breast-hook or the bowsprit bitts: it is then set up on its own part, and secured the same as the fore stay; (see Fig. 203). In merchant ships, the main stay is in two parts, leading down on each side of the fore-mast; in the wake of which it is leathered, or served and cleated, (Fig. 203), to prevent its working up and down on the mast.

Sometimes there is a collar, (Fig. 202), having a heart seized in at (a), with a round seizing (see page 9). This collar is wormed, parcelled, and served: in the end of the short leg, there is an eye spliced (b); and the long leg being taken over the breast-hook, or through a large ring-bolt forwards, its end (c) is reeved through the eye (b), and seized to the standing part with one throat, and two or three round seizings, (d). (See page 9.)

Sometimes a heart is iron-bound, or strapped, to a large bolt (w) in the bows, Fig. 203, and set up as above. A pendent, called a JUMPER, has an eye spliced in one end, and a thimble in the other: the eye is seized to the stay (y), abreast of the fore-mast; and the thimble at the lower end has a laniard spliced into it, which is reeved alternately through an eye-bolt in the deck (z) and the thimble. This eye-bolt, which is a little distant from the mast on the starboard side, guys the stay off, and keeps it from working too much.

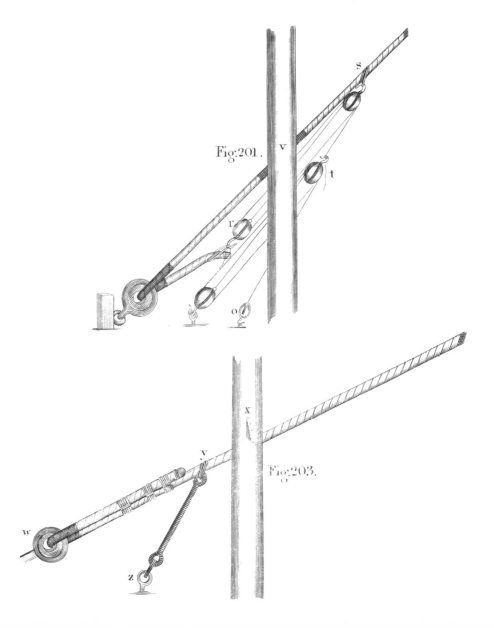

Fig. 201.

Fig. 203.

Is fitted the same as the main-stay, and led down to the deck forward of the fore-mast, where the ends are rove through hearts secured and placed a little above the main stay : then set up and secured on its own part (see Fig. 205.) The advantage of this plan over the old way of leading to the fore-mast head, is too obvious to need comment : as in the case of the loss of the fore-mast under the old plan, the main top-mast was pretty sure to go with it.

[We well remember a night in which the Rufus King lost her bowsprit and foremast, and the difficulty there was in preventing the main top-mast from following suit, from the main top-mast stays being secured to the head of the fore-mast.—*Amer. Ed.*]

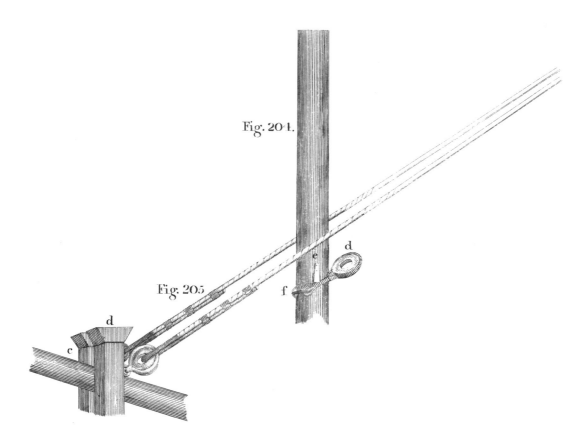

Fig. 204.

Fig. 205.

THE MIZEN STAY, Fig. 211,

Is often doubled; in which case an eye is spliced in both ends: it is passed round the main-mast, Fig. 211, and a cleat placed over it; then carried over the head of the mizen rigging. A short distance below the top a round seizing is put on to make the collar: it is then set up by lashings through the eyes and by a Spanish windlass.

If it is single, the stay is fitted with the ordinary collar, Fig. 169, and led through an iron strap on the main-mast, Fig. 211, (d), and secured to its own part after being set up, as the main stay, Fig. 203. But another method is to have a heart, iron-bound, and an iron strap round the main-mast, Fig. 212. On one side of the hole may be cut a sheave-hole (b) for the mizen stay-sail down-hauler.

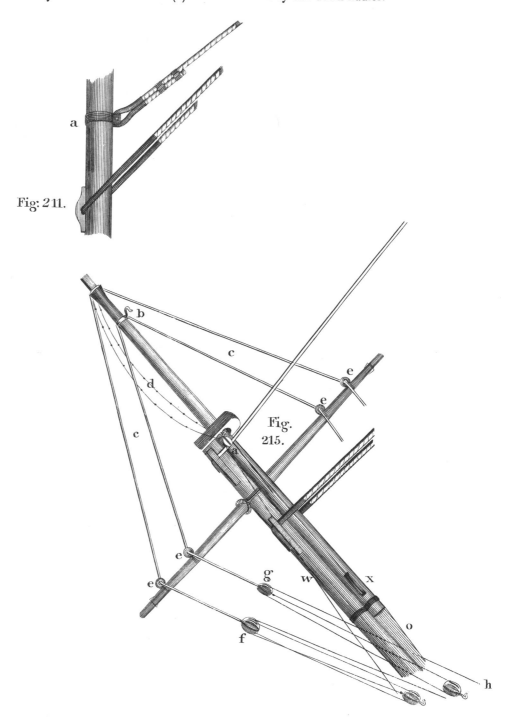

Fig: 211.

Fig. 215.

JIB-BOOM—SPRIT-SAIL YARD—JIB-GUYS—MARTINGALE, &c.

—ↁↁↁ—

The head of the jib-boom is fitted with an iron strap, to which there are eye-bolts attached, and the different pieces of rigging after mentioned are spliced or hooked in.

Ships which carry SPRIT-SAIL YARDS, have them sometimes slung like Fig. 1. An iron strap (c) goes round the BOWSPRIT, having a kind of hinge (d) to lie underneath it. Another iron strap (e) goes round the SPRIT-SAIL YARD at the slings, having a swivel eye-bolt (f) on the upper side. This eye is placed in the hinge (d): a bolt (g) having an eye in the end, is put through the hinge and eye, and a forelock (h) secures it.

The SPRIT-SAIL YARD, by this mode, is topped with great facility: and by the lifts, it is got fore and aft instantly, hanging by the swivel, and being secured by lashings.—When it is required to be got in, the *top or yard rope* is hove upon, and the bolt taken out of the hinge.

Another mode is adopted for a SPRIT-SAIL YARD, Fig. 2. An iron strap, with a double eye-bolt on both sides of the bowsprit (m), Fig. 2, is fitted round the mast: in this another eye-bolt, Fig. 2, (i), is put, bolted and forelocked. This allows the yard to be triced in, and laid parallel to the bowsprit when in dock. In such cases the yard is in two pieces.

A DOUBLE DOLPHIN STRIKER, or MARTINGALE, Fig. 3, may go with a hinge (o) fastened on the bowsprit cap, close under the hole for the jib-boom, and secured with an iron strap (p) at the lower part of the cap. This is fitted with a hinge and pin, to open when the dolphin striker is either triced up, in coming into dock, or when it is unshipped. (They are now generally single.)

Between the two legs of the dolphin striker is an iron bar, having a roller (q), and two iron braces (r). There are three sheave-holes, 1, 2, 3, in each leg, and a small hole underneath them (s).

The MARTINGALE STAY (t) reeves through the roller (q), leads through a thimble (u) in a strap round the bowsprit: and it sets up with a luff-tackle purchase to an eye-bolt in the bows.

The MARTINGALE GUY (v) leads through a thimble in the strap on the bowsprit, through the upper sheave-hole (1), reeves through a block (w) strapped round the jib-boom end, back again through the second sheave-hole (2), and through another thimble in the strap round the bowsprit. The other end is hitched or seized to a timber-head, or an eye-bolt in the bows.

The FLYING JIB MARTINGALE GUY, leads through a thimble in the strap on the bowsprit, and through the lower-sheave-hole (3), reeves through a block (y) at the end of the flying jib-boom, and through the hole (s). A double wall-knot (see page 5), is then cast on the end. The same operation takes place in the other leg of the dolphin striker.

The AFTER GUY (x) goes with a running eye round the end of the dolphin striker (z), leads through a thimble in a strap round the bowsprit, and sets up with a luff-tackle purchase as before.*

When no sprit-sail yard is carried, the JIB-BOOM may be equally secured by guys to an *outrigger* or *boomkin*, Fig. 5, or to the cat-heads. This method is followed by most ships, on account of the great weight of a yard, equal in size to the fore top-sail yard, lying so far out when a ship is pitching, which adds considerably to the strain on the bowsprit. These OUTRIGGERS, or HORNS, are sometimes of iron, and in the above mentioned ships are rigged out just abaft the CAT-HEADS. Blocks are strapped to them for the falls, in one of the methods represented in the Figure.

---

* The martingale (t) might be bent to the traveller, and a martingale stay taken from the jib-boom end, reeved through a block (a) in a span at the end of the dolphin striker, and through a block on the bowsprit as before.

Spritsail Yard, Jib Guys, Martingale &c.

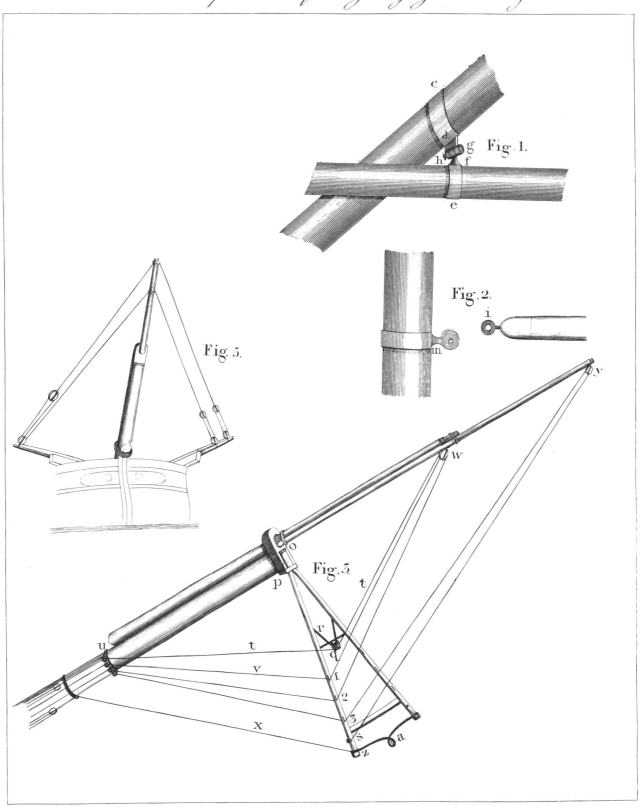

Fig. 1.

Fig. 2.

Fig. 5.

Fig. 3.

RIGGING THE LOWER YARDS, Fig. 218.

—◦◦◦—

Iron straps are fitted to the yard-arm with three eye-bolts, into which are hooked or spliced the horses, lifts, braces and reef-tackle blocks.

The iron straps for the slings, quarter and clue garnet blocks, are fitted on. The jack-stays (h), which are sometimes of rope or iron, but most commonly of oak, are fastened to the yard. These are to bend the head of the sail to. This work is usually done before the yard is taken on deck.

The horses (c) for the men to stand on are hooked or spliced to the strap; they are rove through thimbles spliced into short ropes called stirrups (d). A thimble is spliced into the other end of the horse (c), and it is lashed to the yard by the quarter block (g).

The stirrup (d) has an eye spliced in one end for the horse to reeve through; the other end is secured on top of the yard by a staple drove into the yard.

The brace blocks (k) are hooked into the yard-arm strap, and the reef-tackle blocks (1) also: they are either double or single, as may be required.

The YARD-TACKLE PENDENTS (e) are next put over. They have an eye spliced in one end to fit the yard-arm: and in the other end there is a thimble to hook the double block of a luff or a long tackle to. When these tackles go without pendents, a strap with a thimble in (g) is put over the yard-arm for the hook of the tackle. These tackles are used for hoisting in the boat, provisions, &c., and when not wanted, are triced up to the yard by a line called a *Tricing Line*. This is reeved through a block strapped round the yard, and hanging underneath it at (h) about the distance of the pendent's length within the arm-cleats. When a pendent (e) is used, there are *two* tricing lines: and the last mentioned is called the *outer* one. The *inner* one is reeved through a block seized to the futtock stave; and a thimble being spliced in the end, the single block of the yard-tackle is hooked to it. When no pendent is used, but merely the strap (g), there is but one tricing line, which generally reeves through an iron staple under the yard, and through a small block strapped to the truss pendent, at the seizing, close to the yard, belaying to a cleat on the mast below.

The TOPSAIL-SHEET BLOCKS,

When they are used, are strapped, and placed over the yard-arms. Top-sail sheets are now rove through a sheave-hole fitted in a sheave at the yard-arm.

Sometimes the *top-sail sheet block* is spliced into the lift (N), leaving beneath the seizing an eye for the yard-arm, which is served over. When the lifts go *double*, the lift block (O), and the top-sail sheet block (P), are generally strapped together, the former above the latter (o p).

The QUARTER BLOCKS, (Q),

Are strapped with iron. These are large blocks hanging below the yard, under the slings, within the cleats (q), and for the top-sail sheets.

The CLUE-GARNET BLOCKS, (r),

Strapped in the same manner, hang underneath the yard, just without the cleats, on each side: they are hooked into an iron strap. There are two *bunt-line blocks* on each side (s), placed as in the Figure: these stand on the upper part of the yard. The *leech-line blocks* (t), stand also above the yard. These are secured to the yard by staples, or seized to the jack-stay.

Rigging the lower Yards.

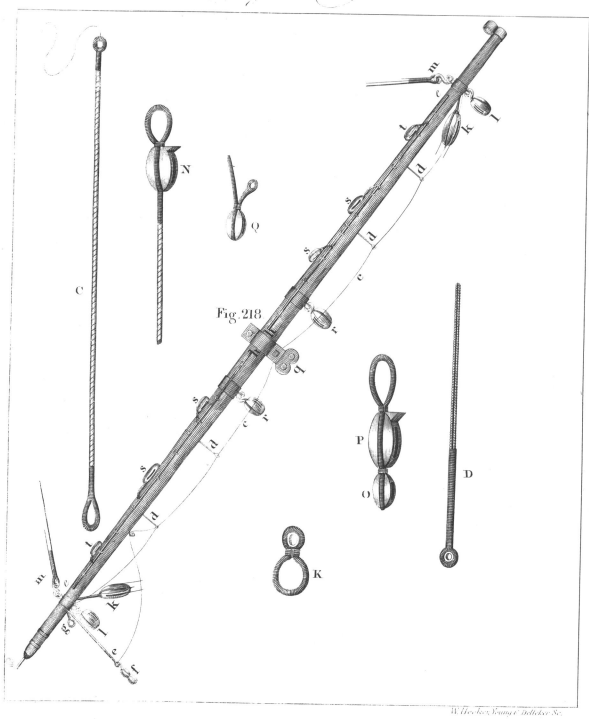

Fig. 218

APPENDIX 12

Lower yards are now slung with chains, Fig. **233**.   A stout piece of oak is scarfed on the forward foot of the tressle-trees, and the chain (c) is secured to it, shackled and bolted to the yard.

Trusses (b), Fig. **233**, are now, in most merchantmen, fitted in the way in the plate : an iron band is secured around the mast, and the truss, after being secured to the yard, plays in a goose-neck.   The advantages of this plan are, that the yard keeps clear of the rigging, and there is no labor in over-hauling trusses, and the yard works with one-fourth less labor ; but on the other hand there is more danger of the trusses being carried away, than when made of rope.

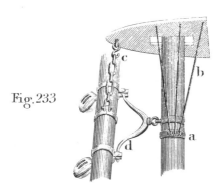

Fig. 233

APPENDIX 13

The LOWER CROSS-JACK YARD,

Is slung to the mizen-mast like the other lower yards to their respective masts.   It is rigged the same as the fore-yard when there is a sail to be bent to it, (which is not very common), with this exception, that the brace blocks (d and g), Fig. **242**, are on the forward part of the yard ; as mizen braces lead forward to the after main shroud.

When there is no sail to be bent to it, the geer necessary is omitted.   Fig. **242** represents a mizen-yard with top-sail sheet blocks ; sheave-holes are generally used, and are better.

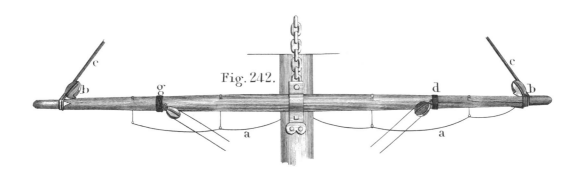

Fig. 242.

The TOP-SAIL YARDS are retained to the masts by PARRALS, which answer the same purpose that the trusses do to the lower yards. There are several kinds of parrals; the Fig. 253 is of iron, secured into an iron brace on the yard by a screw. Fig. 253 (1), is a cylinder of iron, which is leathered and placed over the mast: the parral is then secured around it, and it runs up and down with the yard. Fig. 253 (a), is a chock of wood bolted to the yard, scored out to the diameter of the mast, and leathered. It is then secured to the mast by an iron strap, bolted and keyed, or a lashing through eye-bolts on the after part of the chock, as shown in the plate. The advantages of these parrals are, that they keep the yards steady, and render the use of rolling tackles unnecessary. For another kind of parral, see next page.

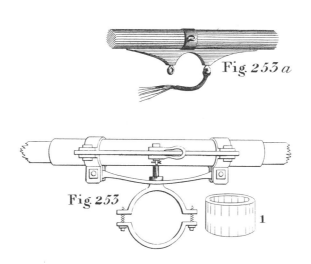

Fig. 253 a

Fig. 253

1

APPENDIX 15-I

MIZEN GAFF.

At the inner end, or throat of the gaff, Fig. 263, jaws (m) are made to receive the after part of the try-sail mast, with a bevel proportionable to the stiving of the gaff. To these jaws is fixed a parral with trucks (k). An eye-bolt (n) is driven in the upper part of them, and a small one underneath. It is there scarfed and hooped. There is an eye-bolt (b) also fitted to the peak end, like the mizen-yard. A jack-stay is fitted on the lower part of the gaff to bend the sail to. The gaff is sometimes slung, and sometimes hoisted. It is slung thus, Fig. 264:

An eye-bolt (d) is fitted into the iron strap which holds the futtock-shrouds on the after part of the mast; on the forward end of the gaff there is a goose-neck, which, after being put into the eye-bolt, is keyed. The after part of the gaff has an iron strap, to which is hooked the slings and the guys or vangs (d): the slings (b) are hooked on to the after part of the tressle-trees, or to the mizen-cap. In the standing gaff, as shown in Fig. 266, hanks are put over for the head of the sail, and it hauls out with an out-hauler (c), through a sheave-hole at the end of the gaff, led through a block (e) hooked into the lower part of the tressle-trees. In other cases the sail is bent to a jack-stay, and is hauled up by brails.

To get this gaff up for rigging, Fig. 265, the lower block of the mizen top-sail halliards is hooked to a selvagee (w) in the middle of it: a tail-tackle is made fast with a double block to the mizen tressle-tree (x), and the tail of the single one is hitched round the throat. In some vessels, the mizen top-sail yard is lashed down to the cap; but where the fore part of the cap projects out sufficiently, the bight of the tye (y) is taken with a hitch round it; or the bight of the tye may be taken under the cap between the masts, and put over the fore part of it, like Fig. G. The gaff is hoisted up by the tail-tackle and top-sail halliards, and slung as before described.

When the gaff traverses up and down the mast, Fig. 266, a double or single block, according to the size of it, is strapped with a hook and thimble, and hooked to the eye-bolt in the throat (a): another double block (b) is hooked into an eye-bolt in one of the tressle-trees. The fall (c) is reeved alternately through these blocks, and called the THROAT HALLIARDS. In some ships the upper block (b) is hooked to an iron strap round the mizen-mast head.

The peak halliards are rove like Fig. 266, through a double block (c) at the top-mast cross-trees, then through a single block at the end of the gaff, then through the block (c), and back through (e), from whence it is led and hooked to the mizen cap. This gaff has on it a jack-stay (f) to bend the sail to. The blocks (g) answer either for down-haul or vang blocks.

Mizen Gaff

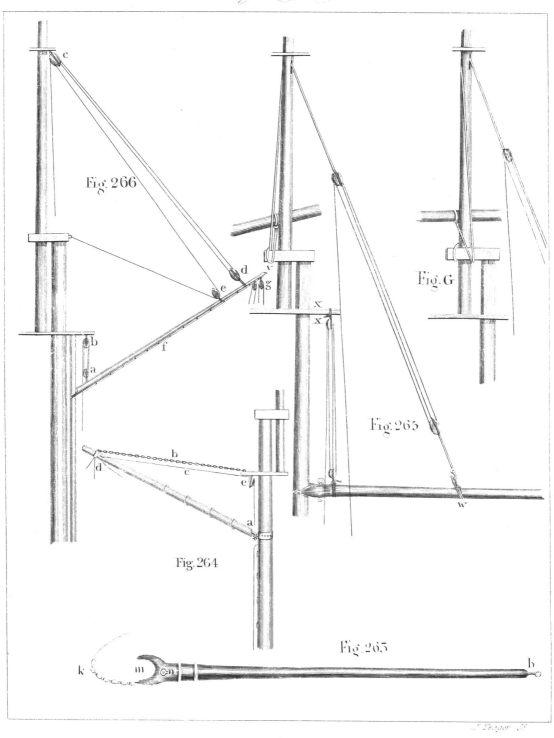

Fig. 266

Fig. 264

Fig. 265

Fig. G

Fig. 263

TOP-GALLANT MAST RIGGED.

A pair of shrouds (n), Fig. 274, are put over on the *starboard* side, then a pair on the larboard: and as there is an odd shroud on each side, the leg of the last pair (o) is led down as a back-stay, and set up in the channel, or in the stool for the top-mast back-stay, with dead-eyes; or, in small vessels, with thimbles. Men of war have two top-gallant back-stays on each side.

The shrouds are seized with eyes like the top-mast ones: and they are served round the eyes, and in the wake of the holes in the cross-trees   In the foremost pair, just below the eye-seizing, a thimble is seized, for the top-gallant lifts to reeve through.

The STAY (m), instead of a mouse being raised, has the end spliced in the standing part, forming a collar: and it is served over, as before mentioned, for the top-mast stay.   Sometimes the stay has no collar; but the end is spliced round a thimble on an iron traveller, Fig. M, which is placed over the pole-head after the rigging is put over; but in this case the pole should be made very strong, particularly that of the main top-gallant mast, for the stay going up with the royal-yard, the strain of it, and the top-gallant stay-sail (the halliards of which must reeve through a block on the traveller) will be entirely on it.

The ROYAL BACK-STAYS (q) and stay (s) are next put over the head of the pole, and are stopped from coming down by cleats nailed on for that purpose: after which, the truck (P p), which has a sheave-hole on each side for the pennant halliards, is placed on the tenon of the pole-head, having a mortise cut in for that purpose.

The mast is then swayed up by the top or mast rope, the fid thrust through the square hole in the heel, the top-rope eased, and then unreeved: and the top-gallant top-block is unhooked, and lowered down below.

Round the head of the top-mast, at (a), there is an iron strap for the futtock-shrouds: they are of iron, similar to the lower ones.   The top-gallant rigging is rove through them, and set up on its own part after the mast is stayed.

The fore top-gallant stay, (Fig. 275), is rove through a sheave-hole at the end of the jib-boom, outside of the rigging; it is then led in-board to a small heart alongside the fore top-mast stay, and set up on its own part.

The top-gallant rigging sometimes has a laniard spliced round the thimble in the end of the top-gallant shroud (r), Fig. T, which connects it to another thimble (t), seized in a strap round the futtock plate.   The top-burton tackle being over-hauled, the laniard of each shroud is cat's-pawed to the hook of its single block, and they are set up by the people in the top.   Or a SPANISH WINDLASS, Fig. 276, being made, by laying one end of a handspike (b) over the iron rail of the top, and the other in a becket on the shroud, the laniard (c) is taken round it, and set up by a heaver (d):

Or the TOP-GALLANT SHROUDS are led across like Fig. 277, (which shews the aft side of the top-mast): they are set up to thimbles in the opposite futtock plates: this is a great ease to the futtock stave and top-mast rigging; and the lee rigging, by these means, is kept taught, as they act like bentick shrouds below.

The FORE TOP-GALLANT BACK-STAY (o), Fig. 274, in some ships, has a thimble turned into the lower end; and it is set up to another dead-eye in a chain-plate for that purpose, a jigger-tackle, being clapped on the back-stay, with a midshipman's hitch (see page 9), and the hook of the lower block cat's-pawed to the laniard.

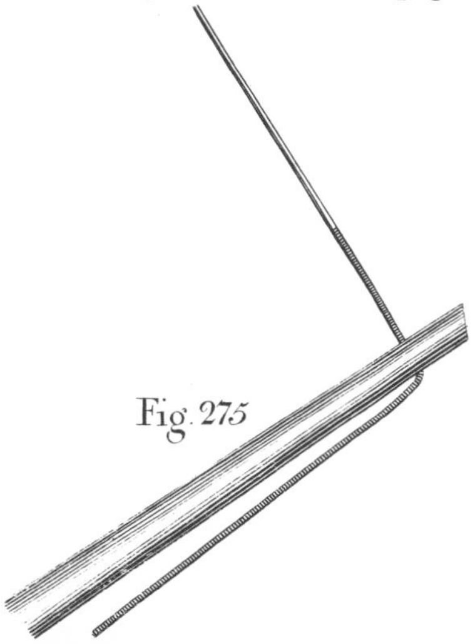

Fig. 275

The **CLEWS** (h) are now made of iron, as in the plate, (h), Fig. 294. (K) is bent into the horse-shoe form, with an eye at each end, in which there are two thimbles, to which the leech and foot ropes are spliced; across this clew there is an iron bar, round which the clew-garnet or clew-line blocks are strapped: this is the most approved plan. The tacks and sheet blocks, if double, are hooked into this clew; if single, the tack and sheet itself are hooked and moused.

Fig. 294.

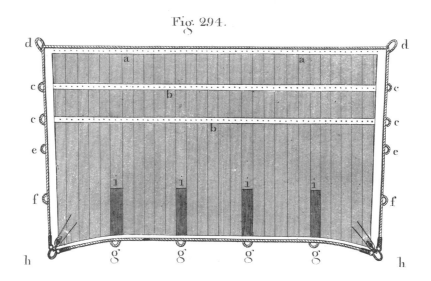

Fig. 295.

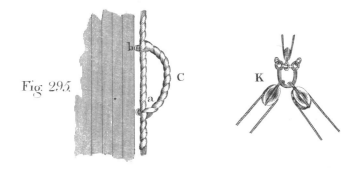

The CLEW-LINE BLOCKS are fitted the same as the clew-garnet blocks of the fore-sail. (See page 52.

The clew-lines, Fig. 311, on each side, are reeved through the blocks on the top-sail yards, then through the blocks at the clew (r), and the ends are hitched round the yard, without the blocks : the leading parts (t) go through the lubber's hole.

The TOP-SAIL SHEETS, which generally are chains long enough to lead below the quarter blocks, from which they are of rope, to the deck, are hooked into the clews with sister hooks ; or, if all the rope, the top-sail sheet having a double walled knot, double crowned (see page 5) on the end, is thrust through the clew, the knot (u) lying aft. The sheet is served to prevent its chafing in the blocks, and against the lower yard : it is reeved through the sheave-hole at the lower yard-arm (w), then through the quarter block (x), lying under the yard at the sling cleats, and through a sheave-hole in the top-sail sheet bitts.

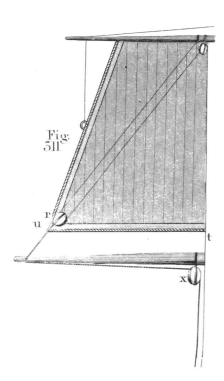

Fig. 311

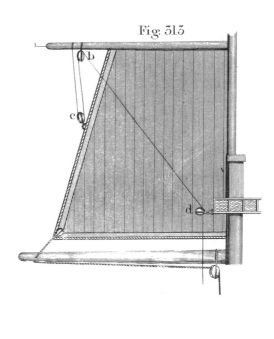

Fig. 313

Spritsail topsail — Staysails.

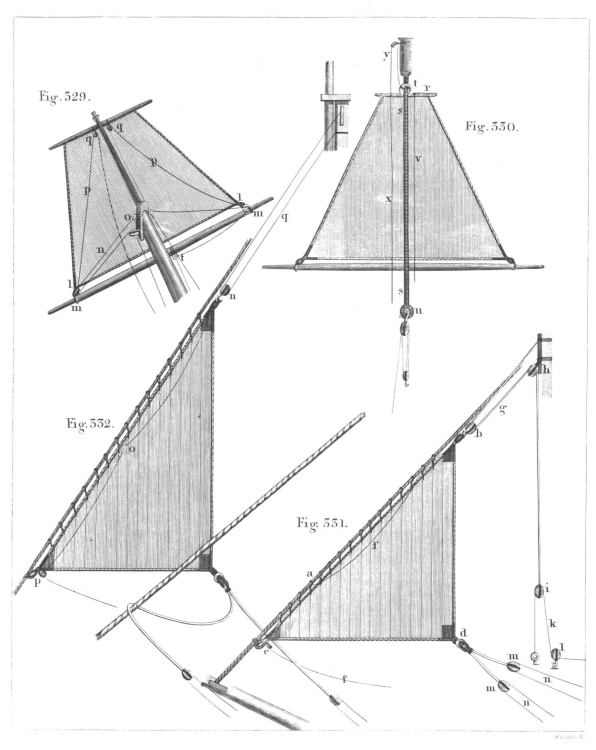

Fig. 329.

Fig. 330.

Fig. 332.

Fig. 331.

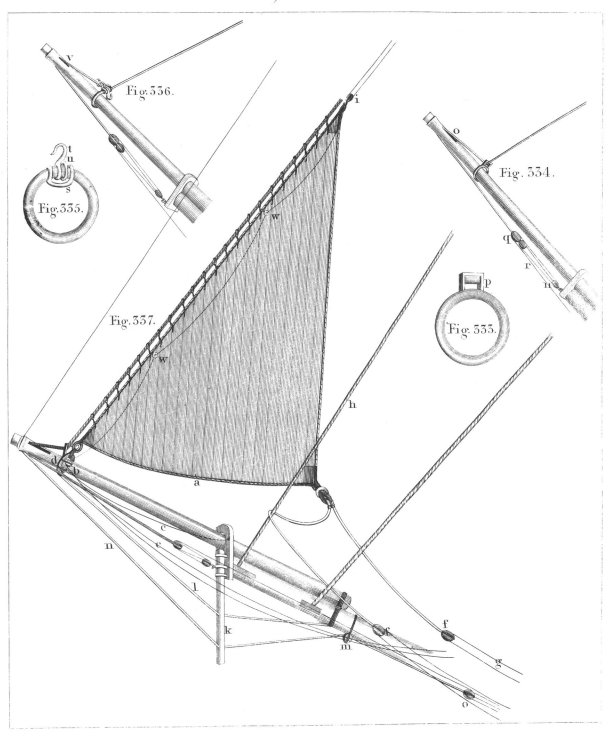

Fig. 336.

Fig. 335.

Fig. 334.

Fig. 337.

Fig. 333.

The FORE AND MAIN SPENCERS, Fig. 346.

The sail is made with a mast leech, which is bent to a batten or a jack-stay (a) on the mast; hoops are put on the gaff, and the head of the sail is bent to them, and the sail is hauled out upon the gaff by an out-hauler (b).

The sheet (c), which is either single or double, is hooked to an eye-bolt in the water-way.

The sail is furled by brails (d), of which there are generally three; the head brail is bent to the head cringle, and led through a block at the throat of the gaff to the deck : the middle brail is bent to a cringle in the after leech, as far distant from the gaff as the block on the mast is distant from the throat of the gaff: the lower or foot brail is bent according to the same rule.

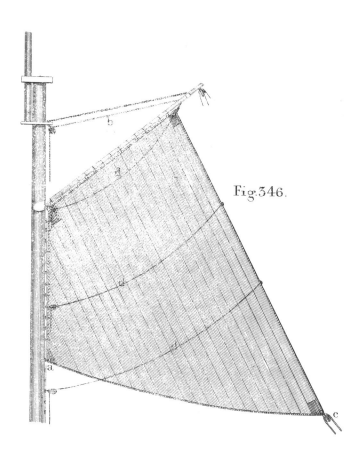

Fig. 346.

MIZEN, OR SPANKER.

The fore and aft sail, Fig. 355, is called by either of those names, excepting when a square sail is bent to the cross-jack yard, which is the case in some of our modern packet ships, such as the Liverpool and Victoria.

The mizen in such ships is bent like the fore-sail, page 52, and the other sail is called the spanker.

Around the mizen-mast at (d), there is an iron strap with an arm, on which the try-sail mast, (if there is one), rests, and in which there is an eye-bolt, through which the goose-neck of the spanker boom plays.

The boom is fitted with a block at (f) for a sheet, which is connected by a fall with another at the taffrail amidships. Guys (h) are hooked to the outer end of the boom: on the inner end of the guys, blocks are spliced and connected with other blocks by falls, which are hooked into the boomkins, or on the quarter. When going free the lee guy is hooked forward to steady the boom.

There are three different modes of bending and using a spanker. The first mode, Fig. 355, is that the head is bent to a jack-stay on the gaff; the luff is bent to hoops on the try-sail mast; the tack (m) is lashed to the heel of the mast, and the clew (n) lashed to the boom: the gaff is hoisted by peak and throat halliards: down-haulers are fixed to the throat and peak of the gaff.

The second is by a gaff slung, Fig. 355. The head of the sail is bent to the gaff on a jack-stay; the luff is bent to a jack-stay on the mast; the clew is hauled out by an out-hauler (g) to the end of the boom.

Brails (d) are lashed to cringles on the after leech and foot, to furl the sail.

The third is also a slung gaff. The luff is bent as Fig. 355, but the head and foot are both hauled out by out-haulers. (See Fore and Main Spencers, Fig. 346).

Mizen & Spanker.

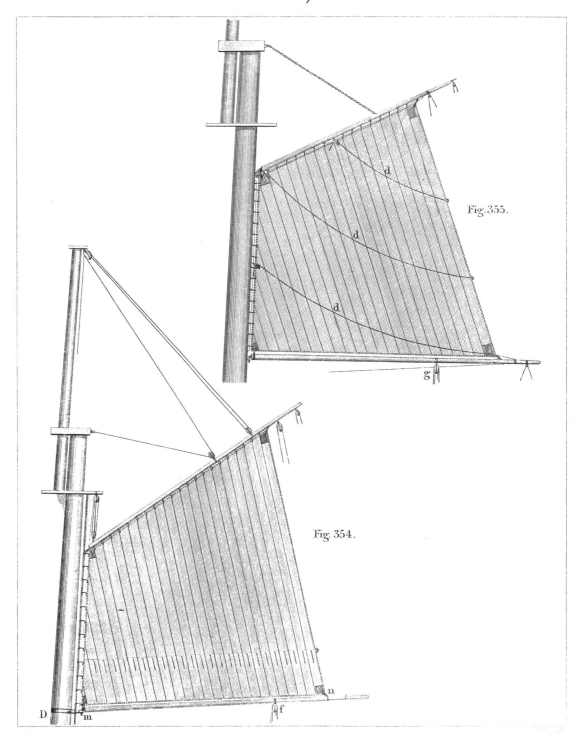

Fig. 355.

Fig. 354.

ANCHORS, &c.

Vessels called Barques, Fig. 357, rigged in this manner, can sail with a hand or two less, and answer very well for working through narrows, there being no square-sail on the mizen-mast to brace round.

In some few vessels, the main brace, Fig. 357, leads through a block at the aftermost fore shroud, and the main top-sail brace, through a block strapped to an eye-bolt in the after part of the fore cap, the standing part being hitched round the fore-mast head; the top-gallant brace leads to the after part of the fore top-mast cross-tree.

The aftermost shroud of any mast rigged with a boom, and gaff which traverses, the sail having reefs in, should be served the whole length: and the aftermost top-mast back-stay should go with a block and runner, as mentioned for the breast back-stay: the former, that it may not be chafed when going large, and the latter, to make room for the boom to be guyed forwards.

AN ANCHOR is a large instrument of iron, shaped like Figures 358 and 359: (a), the flukes or palms; (b), the bills; (c), the shanks; (d), the arms; (e), the stock, made of oak, bolted together, hooped, and furled, secured by the nut, (g); (f), the iron hoops; (h), the eye for the ring; (k), the ring, and (m) the crown of the anchor. In the Navy, the bower and sheet anchors are of the same size, as are their cables.

There are many kinds of anchors; that of Porter's seems to be of the most approved of the modern kind, Fig. 364, (a).

The advantages of a Porter's anchor are,

1. It is impossible to foul it, as when the lower fluke has taken hold, the upper lays flat upon the shank.

2. It cants and bites much quicker than any other anchor.

3. It is more convenient for stowage, as it can be taken to pieces.

[Fig. 364 (a), represents one of Porter's anchors in the ground: the flukes, it will be seen, play upon an axis in the crown; the ring is different from the old kind, in being of the horse-shoe form, which is the case with most anchors to which chains are to be bent.—*Am. Ed.*]

English men-of-war carry six anchors, viz: two bowers, one sheet, one spare, one stream, one kedge. In a first rate, the weight would be about twenty-one tons; in a frigate, twelve and a half tons; and in a corvette, about nine tons. Merchant ships, four anchors, viz.: two bowers, one stream, and one kedge.

A first rate has ten cables, viz.: five bowers and one stream, (hemp); three bowers and one stream, (iron). A frigate nine cables, viz.: four bowers and one stream, (hemp); three bowers and one stream, (iron). A corvette, eight cables, three bowers and one stream, (hemp); three bowers and one stream, (iron). Merchant ships have three chains, viz.: two bowers and one stream. (For Anchors, Chain Cables, and comparison of strength, see page 112).

There is an advantage in having an extra bower or sheet anchor, as no ship can stand A 1 at Lloyd's with less than three bower anchors.

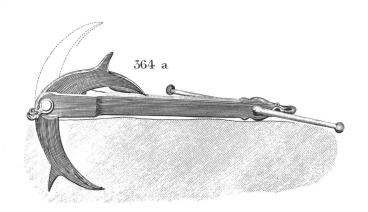

364 a

CHAIN CABLES—WINDLASS—STOPPERS.

Fig. 10 represents part of a chain cable bent to the anchor.   These cables are now in general use.

A stout shackle, (c) is passed over the ring (e) : and this ring is attached to the end of the shank (f) by the bolt (g), which is secured by the forelock (h).

To every link of the chain a bar is placed across, to prevent them from being drawn together : and at every seventh fathom a shackle and swivel is placed.   Thus it may used as a mooring chain.

This cable is used with either a windlass or a capstern.—When the former is carried, the part (i), Fig. 11, is entirely cased with iron : it rises gradually on each side : and on the starboard side it has projections (k) raised something in the manner of thumb cleats.   These prevent the chain from riding, and always keep it in its place.

An IRON ROLLER, like Fig. 12, is sometimes fixed before the hawse-hole where the chain-cable enters : and another of the same kind is fixed within board.—The cable abaft the windlass passes through an IRON STOPPER, Fig. 13 : the *horns* (o) keep it from slipping out.   It is held on by *iron hooks* like (L) : these are from two to three feet in length.   When necessary, the upper part, or lid of the stopper (p) is let down ; when it will appear like Fig. 14.   An iron bar or crow, being put into the hollow of a raised strap (m), it is pressed down : and this completely jams the chain.

In merchant ships these stoppers are not now used ; the ordinary deck stoppers (e), Fig. 571, are preferred, or the kind called devil's claw, Fig. 573 (a).   A round turn and a half is taken round the windlass, for the purpose of holding on better.

Fig. 15 represents the ring-stopper now in use : it is of chain.   The advantage of it over the old kind is, that the short end is let go, and there is no long part to fly or jam.

The Table on the next page is compiled from various sources : the chains are heavier in proportion to the tonnage, and the weight of the anchor, than is generally used in American vessels.   Those marked with a dagger (†) are the proportions used in the U. S. Navy.

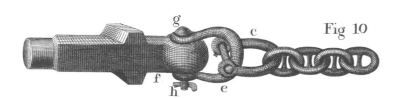

Fig 10

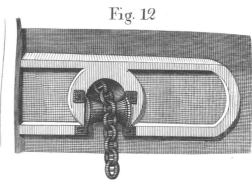

Fig. 12

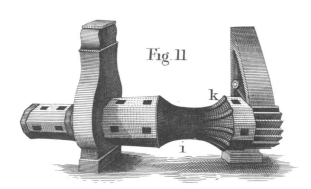

Fig. 11

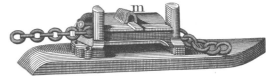

L

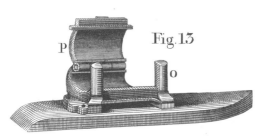

Fig.13

Fig 14

Fig.15

Fig.16

HEMP AND CHAIN CABLES.

A TABLE,*
Showing the comparative strength and weight of Hemp and Chain Cables.

** Size.	Threads.	*** Weight.	Equal to Chain.	lbs. per Fathom.	Proof.	Weight of Anchor.	Register Tonnage.	Size.	Threads.	Weight.	Equal to Chain.	lbs. per Fathom.	Proof.	Weight of Anchor.	Register Tonnage.
inches.		cwt. qrs. lbs.			tons.	cwt.		inches.		cwt. qrs. lbs.			tons.	cwt.	
2	27	0 3 26						14½	1098	40 1 12	1⅜	116	25	28†	
2½	36	1 1 8	5/16	5½	¾			15	1170	43 0 1		106	33	17	360
3	54	1 3 25						15½	1251	45 3 26	1½	115	36	18½	400
3½	72	2 2 16		8	1½			16	1332	48 3 24		125	40	20	450
4	99	3 1 6		11	2½			16½	1413	51 3 21					
4½	108	3 3 24		14	3½	2	20	17	1503	55 1 0	1⅝	162	37	38†	
5	135	4 3 23						17½	1593	58 2 6		145	48	25	550
5½	162	5 3 22		18	4½	2½	30	18	1683	61 3 13	1¾				
6	189	6 3 21						18½	1782	65 2 1		170	56	30	700
6½	216	7 3 21		24	6	3	40	19	1881	69 0 17	1⅞	210	45	50†	
7	252	9 1 1		28	7½	3½	50	19½	1980	72 3 4					
7½	288	10 2 9						20	2088	76 3 1		195	64	37	850
8	333	12 0 26	¾	32	9	4	60	20½	2187	80 1 16	1 15/16	226	49	70†	
8½	378	13 3 15		38	11	4½	75	21	2295	84 1 14	2				
9	423	15 2 25						21½	2403	88 1 10					
9½	468	17 0 22	⅞	44	13	5½	95	22	2520	92 2 16	2	230	72	45	1000
10	522	19 0 21	1	50	15	6½	120	22½	2646	97 1 3					
10½	576	21 0 19	1					23	2763	101 2 8	2⅛	270	60	95†	
11	630	23 0 18		56	19	8		23½	2880	105 3 14					
11½	684	25 0 15	1⅛	63	19	9½	180	24	3006	110 2 1	2⅛				
12	747	27 1 23	1⅛	71	21½	11	210	24½	3132	115 0 16					
12½	810	29 3 3						25	3258	119 3 2	2⅛				
13	882	32 1 19		79	24	12½	240	25½	3393	124 2 26					
13½	954	35 0 7	1¼	88	27	14	280	26	3528	129 2 22	2⅛				
14	1026	37 2 24		96	30	15½	320				2¼	314	66	105†	

Number and Size of Cables, Hawsers, and Messengers allowed to the different class Vessels in the U. S. Navy.

CABLES. No. & Size.	SHEET. No.	SHEET. Inch.	BOWERS. No.	BOWERS. Inch.	STRE'M. No.	STRE'M. Inch.	HAWSERS. No.	HAWSERS. Inch.	MESSENGERS. No.	MESSENGERS. Inch.	CHAIN CABLES. No.	CHAIN CABLES. Size of Iron in Inches.
74 of 3 decks	1	25	5	24	1	15½	6	11,10,9,8,7,6	3	14½	2	2 3-16
" 2 d'ks, 1st class	1	24	5	23	1	14½	6	11,10,9,8,7.6	1	13½	2	2 1-8
" " 2d "	1	23	5	22½	1	14	6	10,9,8,7,6,5	1	13	2	2
Razee												
Frigates												
1st class	1	22½	5	22	1	13	5	10.9,8,7,6	1	13	2	1 7-8
2d class	1	22	4	21	1	12	3	7,6,5	1	11½	2	1 3-4
Sloops												
1st class			3	16	1	9	3	6,5,4	1	10	2	1 1-2
2d class			3	15	1	8	2	6,5	1	8	2	1 3-8
3d class												
Brigs & Schooners			3	12					1	7	2	1 1-4

Weight of Anchors, exclusive of Stocks, for the different classes of Vessels in the U. S. Navy.

Class of Vessel	BOWERS AND SHEET. No.	BOWERS AND SHEET. Weight.	STREAM. No.	STREAM. W't.	KEDGES. No.	KEDGES. W't.	W't.	W't.	W't.	W't.	W't.
74 of 3 decks	4	10,500	1	3,200	6	1,400	1,200	1,000	800	700	600
" 1st class, 2 d'ks	4	9,500	1	3,000	5	1,200	900	750	600	500	
" 2d " "	4	8,500	1	2.800	5	1,000	900	750	600	450	
Razee	4	8.500	1	2,600	5	1,000	900	750	600	450	
Frigate, 1st class	4	7,000	1	2,600	4	900	700	600	400		
" 2d "	4	5,000	1	1,400	4	850	700	600	400		
Sloop, 1st class	4	3,800	1	1,000	3	600	450	300			
" 2d "	4	{ 1 of 3,200 / 2 " 3.000 / 1 " 2,800 }									
" 3d "											

All the Rope used in the U. States Navy is tested before it is used, and the following strength is required, viz :

For a cable yarn........................140 lbs. | For standing rigging yarn.............112 lbs.
„ running rigging yarn.............125 „ | „ ball-rope yarn........................100 „

In the Whaling service there is a superior kind of rope, called *whale-lines :* these are light and strong—size 1¾ inch, of 30 thread, 120 fathoms length, weight 110 lbs.; and it is required to bear a strain of 100 lbs. to the yarn.

---

* In this Table the weight of the rope is that of 100 fathoms in length ; of the chain, the weight of a fathom ; the weight of the anchor generally used with such sized hemp or chain, and the size of the vessel. This, of course varies according to the judgment—but the table shows the general usage. 29

Ed. Notes:

**The cable's size in this Table is its circumference, not its diameter.*

***In the terminology of the day, "cwt" (hundredweight) was 112 pounds and "qr" (quarter) was 28 pounds, making the tabulated weight of 100 fathoms of 2-1/2" hemp cable 148 pounds.*

CANVAS.

American Canvas is of two kinds—*Phenix Mill and Cotton Duck.*

1st. The PHENIX MILL CANVAS is made from flax into bolts, 40 yards long, 20 inches wide; and the different qualities weigh as follows, viz:

No. 1,............47 1-2 lbs. Avoirdupois.	No. 5,...........30 lbs. Avoirdupois.
" 2,............42 1-2 " "	" 6,............25 " "
" 3,............35 " "	" 7,...........22 1-2" "
" 4,............32 1-2 " "	" 8,............20 " "

The experiments of the Navy go to establish that 20 inches wide makes the strongest seam and the best sail, every way.

Vessels-of-war, according to their class, take as follows for a single suit of sails, viz:

A Three-decker,..........18,805 running y'ds.	Frigate, 2d class,.........12,080 running y'ds.
Ship of the line, 1st class,...18,479 " "	Sloop, 1st " .... 9,637 " "
" " " 2d " ...17,171 " "	" 2d " .... 8,275 " "
Frigate, 1st " ...14,603 " "	Schooner, 1st" .... 3,102 " "

2d. COTTON DUCK, which is 22 inches wide, and numbers from one to eight; number one being the heaviest. There are several manufactories of this article. This is used mostly for fore-and-aft vessels. Occasionally, square rigged vessels have sails made of it; and lately, some East-Indiamen out of this port, have had whole suits of sails made of it.

HOLLAND DUCK.—Of this canvas there are two widths, 24 inch and 31 inch. This duck is now mostly used for square rigged vessels, for top-sails and courses. It was formerly much used on coasting vessels; (that is, sloops and schooners); but Cotton Duck being a closer canvas, holds the wind better, and coming something cheaper, now takes the precedence.

ENGLISH CANVAS.—Of which there are many kinds. The first in order is the

LEITH DUCK.—It is 24 inches wide, and generally considered the best duck in use for square sails. Second to that is the NAVY DUCK.—This is also 24 inches wide, and for weight, (number one being the heaviest), numbers from that to eight. The number *one* is suitable for fore and main top-sails, fore courses, fore and main stay-sails, spencers, and brigs' try-sails. No. *two*, for square main-sails, and mizen top-sails, for the largest size ships. No. *three*, for smaller class of vessels' square main-sails and mizen top-sails, and fore and main top-gallant sails, jibs and spankers of the largest size ships. No. *four*, for smaller class vessels' top-gallant sails and jibs. No's. *five* and *six*, for flying jibs, top-mast and lower studding-sails, and mizen top-gallant sails. No's. *seven* and *eight*, for top-gallant studding-sails, royals, and top-mast and top-gallant stay-sails.

RUSSIA DUCKS.—These are numerous. The three best which are put in the order of quality, and are suitable for the heavy sails of ships, brigs, &c., are D. Brusgins, I. Brusgins, and M. Zotoff. Next comes the HALF DUCK, for top-gallant sails and jibs. Then, the HEAVY RAVENS DUCK, which is used for mizen top-gallant sails, top-mast, and lower studding-sails; and, sometimes, for fore and main top-gallant sails and flying jibs of small brigs and schooners. The last is RAVENS DUCK; which is used for royals and top-gallant studding-sails. Most of the Russia Canvas is used for small vessels. It is not as much used as formerly.

GUNS.

It was the intention of the American Editor, on the commencement of this work, to have added some pages on Gunnery; but finding it would add materially to the size of the book, he has confined himself to a statement as shown in the Tables of the weight of the guns in use by the principal European powers, as taken from Belcher, and that of our own service; for which, with the remarks, he is indebted to the kindness of Commodore A. S. Wadsworth, U. S. Navy.

Those wishing to see into the practice of guns are referred to Sir Howard Douglas, on Naval Gunnery, and Totten's Naval Text Book.

A TABLE,

Showing the Calibre and Length of Iron Guns, with the Standard weight and diameter of Shot adopted by several European powers.

	ENGLISH.		IRON.		FRENCH.		SPANISH.		DUTCH.		PORTUGUESE.		RUSSIAN.	
Prs.	Calibre.	Dia. Shot.	Length.	Weight	Dia. Shot.	Weight Shot.	Dia.	Weight	Dia.	Weight	Dia.	Weight	Dia.	Weight
*10 inch	. . . .	. . . .	9.4	84.0.0										
†68 inch	8.0080	7.8480												
42	6.8208	6.6844	9.6	67.0.0	. . . . . .	. . . . . .	. . . . . .	. . . . . .	. . . . . .	. . . . . .	7.49	59.09	6.860	45.40
32	6.2297	6.1051	9.6	55.0.0	6.3496	36.00	6.840	45 0	6.400	36.87	6.800	35.12	6.470	38.08
24	5.6601	5.5469	9.0	47.2.0	5.808	27.55	6.030	30.84	5.920	29.18	5.930	29.32	6.000	30.38
18	5.1425	5.0397	9.0	40.0.0	5.074	18.37	5.520	23'65	5.450	22.77	5.400	22.14	5.450	22.77
12	4.4924	4.4026	9.0	32.0.0	4.610	13.78	4.800	15.55	4.760	15.16	4.700	14.60	4.760	15.16

* Inch shot, new gun.   † 8 inch, new gun.

Length, Weight, Calibre, Charge, &c. of Ordnance generally used in the Naval Service of the United States.

NATURE OF GUN.	LENGTH.		WEIGHT		Proportionate Weight of Shot to the Gun.	CALIBRE.	Diameter of the high Shot Gauge.	Diameter of the low Shot Gauge.	SERVICE CHARGE	PROOF CHARGE fired twice.		
	ft.	in.	cwt.	qrs.		in.	in.	in.	lbs. oz.	Powder. lbs.	Shot.	
10 inch	9	4	87	2	1 to 77† 1 .. 98‡	10	9 90	9 80	10	20	1 solid, 127 lbs.	42 pr. chamber.
8 inch	8	10	63		1 ..110† 1 ..150‡	8	7 90	7 80	8	18	1 solid, 64 lbs.	32 pr. chamber.
42 pounder	9	4	71		1 ..190	7	6 90	6 80	12	21	2	
32 pounder	9	4	62		1 ..217	6 40	6 30	6 20	10	16	2	
32 pounder	8	6	51		1 ..180	6 40	6 30	6 20	8	12	2	
32 pounder	8	0	42		1 ..150	6 40	6 30	6 20	6	10	2	24 pr. chamber.
24 pounder	9	0	49		1 ..229	5 82	5 72	5 62	8	12	2	
24 pounder	6	7	32		1 ..150	5 82	5 72	5 62	5	9	2	
42 lb. carronade .	4	7	26		. . . .	7	6 90	6 80	4 8	8	1	
32 lb. carronade .	4	2	21		. . . .	6 40	6 30	6 20	3 4	6	1	

† Solid shot.   ‡ Hollow shot.

GUNS AND GUN CARRIAGES.

Service charges are reduced as may be necessary—for heavy guns to a 4th and 5th, and for carronades to a 12th and 14th the weight of the shot.

A gun should never be charged with two shot without a wad between them, as without it one of the shot will almost invariably break in the gun, and the fragments becoming wedged, will either burst the gun or injure the bore.

Guns are proved, after examining them as to their several dimensions, by placing a skid under the trunnions; and they are fired at a small elevation and suffered to recoil on the ground. The trunnions are examined with a hammer, and the bores and vents are carefully inspected with a searcher.

The length of a gun is measured from the after part of the base ring to the face of the muzzle.

The following variations only are allowed from the given dimensions of Guns.

		Inch.
In diameter of the bore,	{ more	0.04
	{ less	0.00
In the exterior when turned	more or less	0.05
Diameters when not turned,	{ more	0.20
	{ less	0.05
Length — of the bore,	more or less	0.20
of breech and cascable,	" "	0.20
of the runforce,	" "	0.20
of the chace, including muzzle,	" "	0.15
from base ring to trunnions,	" "	0.20
Depth of cavities — in the bore or vent		0.00
on the exterior surface,		0.25
on the trunnions, within 1 inch of the rim base,		0.10
on the trunnions, elsewhere		0.25

Weight of Gun Carriages used in the U. S. Navy.

Weight of a 10 inch gun carriage,	6,093 lbs.
" 8 " " "	1,788 "
" 42 lb. " "	1,615 "
" heavy 32 " " "	1,320 "
" light 32 " " "	1,272 "
" 24 " medium "	987 "
Weight of a 42 lb. carronade carriage,	1,236 "
" 32 " " "	788 "
" 24 " " "	620 "

Note.—The elevating screws, beds, and quoins, are included in the above weights. Beds and quoins average 70 lbs.

Shot are inspected by passing them through a cylinder of the diameter of the largest size of the shot, and afterwards examined with a gauge of the smallest diameter, to determine their size. A portion of them are dropped 25 or 30 feet, on a bed of iron; and they are each examined with a hammer and steel point. All shot are rejected which are not perfectly spherical in their form—which are of rough and uneven surface—which have cavities of the depth of 2-10ths of an inch from the surface—which are not of full weight and of proper size, and made of good iron.

The strength of powder is ascertained by the distance which an ounce (Avoirdupois) of the powder will throw a 24 pound ball, without windage from the established eprouvette, fired at an elevation of 45°. But this proof is by no means satisfactory. The standard range for powder used in the Navy is 250 yards. Cannon powder is packed in well seasoned white oak barrels, which hold 100 lbs., leaving a space of two inches between the powder and the head. Priming powder is packed in kegs and half barrels, containing 25 and 50 lbs., respectively. In the magazines of ships the cartridges are all filled and stowed in copper boxes, which are water tight.

Percussion locks are now generally used in the Navy. Those made by Mr. Hidden, with a sliding hammer, are deemed the best.

RANGES OF SEA ORDNANCE.

—◦◦◦—

In no department of the Naval service is there so little certainty known as in this. The conditions which determine the path and force of a ball are in themselves so various, and so difficult of attainment, that a mere recapitulation of them would satisfy any mind that no ordinary obstacles interpose to prevent a full solution of the question. Still, there may be obtained, from long and careful practice, such tabular results as may enable a young officer, with moderate experience, to form some idea of the capacity of sea ordnance. There is nothing which our service stands more in need of, and the Secretary who feels disposed to confer a lasting benefit on the Navy, cannot fail to do so, by directing a full and accurate inquiry into this matter.

In support of these remarks, the following ranges, attributed to the 24 pounder, are taken from the tables of some of the best authorities.

AUTHORITY.	LONG IRON 24.					
	CALIBRE.	LENGTH.	CHARGE.		RANGE.	
		feet.			yards.	
Pocket Gunner.........200	24	$9\frac{1}{2}$	$\frac{1}{3}$	Point Blank.....	297	English...No. 1.
Pocket Gunner.......197 ⎰ Beauchant.......... 20 ⎱	24	$6\frac{1}{2}$	$\frac{1}{4}$	" "	258	" .. " 2.
Aide Memoire.............	26	$9\frac{1}{2}$	$\frac{1}{3}$	Nat. P. Blank...	639	French... " 7.
Man. de l'Artilleur.........	26	$9\frac{1}{2}$	$\frac{1}{3}$	" " ...	682	" ... " 8.
Exercises of 1811..........	26		$\frac{1}{3}$	" " ...	640	" ... " 9.
Pocket Gunner.........201	24	$9\frac{1}{2}$	$\frac{1}{8}$	Point Blank.....	360	English... " 3.
" " 200	24	$9\frac{1}{2}$	$\frac{1}{6}$	" "	265	" ... " 4.
" "	24	$6\frac{1}{2}$	$\frac{1}{4}$	" "	288	" ... " 5.
Beauchant.............	24	$6\frac{1}{2}$	$\frac{1}{8}$	" "	247	" ... " 6.

The difference of Point Blank range between the French and English guns, of nearly similar calibre, is attributable to the different signification conveyed by the term " Point Blank" in the two services. In the French, the upper surface is levelled, and the point where the path of the shot intersects the line of sight, is the Point Blank range. This is expressly stated in the Text-book, and cannot escape the notice of the reader. Hence the cylinder of the gun has a certain elevation, varying with the pattern of the gun, from 1° 11' to 1° 29'. In the English tables, the cylinder of the gun is supposed to be levelled, and the point where the shot strikes the horizontal plane produced from the platform on which the gun-carriage stands, is taken as the Point Blank. Captain Simmons asserts that the English Point Blank is known to every body to be " the distance which the shot flies before it is brought down by gravity to the plane which is parallel to the axis of the bore of the gun, and tangential to the gun wheels, or fore trucks." But there is some reason to doubt if this be so well known, for those who write on Naval Gunnery say nothing about it, and the very definition of Simmons lacks precision ; for we can as well infer from it that the English Point Blank is derived from a horizantal bore as a horizontal line of metal.

But what can be depended on from the various ranges of a 24 pound shot, as given above by English authorities ! No doubt the most palpable discrepancies are mere typographical errors—but such should never be suffered to remain in tables of range. On the whole, there is much reason to doubt whether the Point Blank range of a 24, with $\frac{1}{3}$ charge, ever reached so far as 300 yards.

The English tables being generally current in the U. S. Navy, are not given here ; but as many may be desirous of having some of the authorities to which French naval officers are referred by their government, the following succinct statement is taken from Montgery : it is French Point Blank, equivalent to our line-of-metal range ; and, except the ranges of the carronades, the distances are quoted by Montgery from Churruca :

POINT BLANK IN YARDS.

NATURE OF GUN.	ELEVATION OF BORE.	ROUND SHOT.	GRAPE.
	° ′		
Long 39	1 32	639	320
" 24	1 29	639	320
" 19	1 30	639	320
" 12	1 25	586	320
Carronade. . . .39	3 43	905	480
" 24	3 19	800	430

More extensive tables are given in the Manœuvrier, also taken from Churruca, captain in the Spanish Navy, by Captain Willaumez, of the French service. In these is given the number of feet to be aimed at, above or below the mark to be struck.

———

SHOT—SHELLS.

This species of projectile has recently been introduced into the several principal navies, and now forms a part of the armament of all heavy ships. Shells have been used ashore and afloat for a long time ; but in the Navy they were only projected from heavy mortars ; and in the land service, though thrown horizontally, yet, from light pieces, called howitzers, of so little efficiency as to make slight impression, except on masses of men in the open field. In 1822, Col. Paixhans, an officer of French artillery, published a work proposing the use of shells fired horizontally from heavy ordnance on board of shipping ; at the same time, he insisted strenuously on the necessity of having the armament of a vessel of one calibre, and proposed the pattern of a gun, which he thought preferable to any other for shell service. The principle on which this gun is modelled is by no means original, being almost identical with that of the Congreve gun, which, when tried, failed, in the estimation of many good judges, to throw a round shot with equal force and precision to the old pattern.

The idea of firing shells from heavy ordnance being presented to notice simultaneously with the pattern of his own gun, by Paixhans, has caused both to be so closely associated, that in common opinion they are considered one and the same thing ; which is so far from being the case, that while shells within their proper limits must be very effective, it may be well considered an open question, whether one kind of gun or another is best adapted to give the shell range and precision.

Two sets of experiments were made by order of the French Government—one, to test the effect of shells on a line-of-battle ship, which proved fully equal to that anticipated ; and another, to determine and compare the range of the Paixhans 86 with the long 39 and other calibres.

APPENDIX 29-III

The following results are extracted from the publication of Col. Paixhans:

Experiments made at Brest in October, 1834, *on the range of Bomb Cannon of* 86¼, *compared with that of the sea gun, and on the ranges of solid shot compared with that of hollow shot.*

In recommending peculiar pieces for the horizontal projection of bombs, I sought to prove that they would possess *a range equal to that of the present sea artillery, and even greater;* the first trials at Brest in December, 1823, and January, 1824, have proved this to be the case. The result, which is inconsistent with received opinion, was attributed to the reduced *windage* of my gun; and it is true, that to this, in connection with the increase of calibre, it was principally due.

It then became desirable to know to what extent the ordinary gun could be improved by reducing the windage; new trials were therefore instituted, ashore, for greater accurracy, and the ranges of the bomb cannon 86¼ were compared with those of guns and carronades of 39 and 26, using in the latter balls sufficiently large to produce a windage equal to that of the new piece.

As it was wished at the same time to compare the range of hollow shot with that of solid shot, trials were made with both in the calibres 86¼, 39 and 26.

The results are given in the table, in which I shall only refer to the ranges of the 86¼ and long 39, omitting those of the 26 and carronades; for the long 39 being the heaviest in service, will suffice, *a fortiori*, for the comparison in view.

For the 26 and the carronades a summary will answer.

The solid shot of 86¼ calibre weighed from 86¼ to 89½ pounds; the hollow, from 60½ to 62½. The solid shot of 39 having been chosen from the heaviest, weighed from 41 to 42 pounds; and the hollow, from 28 to 29 pounds.	RANGE IN YARDS.			
	BOMB CANNON 86¼.		ORDIN. LONG 39.	
	Solid.	*Hollow.*	*Solid.*	*Hollow.*
	At an elevation of 3 degrees.			
Charge of Powder.	2089	1918½		
	1502¾	1918½		
For the 39, 7,757 pounds,	2089	1886¼	2110¼	1875¾
" 86¼, 10,793 "	1502¾	1534¾	1577¼	1715¾
	1460	1598½	1598½	1522
	2216¾	1939¾		
Mean Range,	1810	1799½	1762	1704½
	At an elevation of 5 degrees.			
	2110¼	1886¼		
	2110¼	1952½	2282¾	1818¼
	2067½	2025	2430	2072
Same charge.	2451¼	1918½	2540½	1875¾
	1897	1907¾		
	2131½	1897		
Mean Range,	2128	1931¼	2417½	1922
	At an elevation of 8 degrees.			
Charge.	2221	2280¾		
	2210¼	2434	2280¾	2099½
For the 39, 9,714 pounds,	2218¾	2421¼	2349	2423½
" 86¼, 13,355 "	2483¼	2402	2419¼	2513
	2238	2227½		
	2242¼	2397¾		
Mean Range,	2269	2360½	2349¾	2345¼
	At an elevation of 10 degrees.			
	2376½	2621¾		
	2472½	2604¾	2579	2711¼
	2366	2589¾	2749¾	2493¾
Same charge.	2423½	2483	2930¾	2312¾
	2615¼	2610		
	2660	2419		
Mean range,	2485¾	2554¾	2753¼	2506
	At an elevation of 16 degrees.			
Charge.	3223	3442¼		
	3836¾	3719½	3655½	3389
For the 39, 12,951 pounds,	3525½	3932¾	3943½	3378½
" 86¼, 17,809 "	3529¾	3794	3747¼	3229¼
	3922	3329½		
	3612¾	3421		
Mean range,	3608	3606½	3782	3332½

From these trials, Paixhans infers,—that there is little foundation for the belief that shells have such an inferior range; and also, that his 86 pounder ranges nearly equal to the long 39.

With the enormous discrepancies that exist among the several rounds, it is to be doubted whether such important conclusions are at all admissible; or, indeed, that any conclusion can be fairly deduced, except that the ranges of these, and all calibres from 18 up, should be submitted to a rigid scrutiny, and some hundred rounds fired from each piece upon the water; noting the recoil of the gun on a level platform; distance of first graze and extreme range; number of ricochets; deflection of shot from vertical line; difference of range between two shot fired together from the same gun; and using shot from the greatest windage to that fitted close with a patch, with and without sabots: the ordnance to have vent pieces, which are to be replaced whenever the vent is perceptibly enlarged.

It would have been more satisfactory if Paixhans had stated distinctly whether the elevation given in his tabular results, referred to the bore of the gun or the line of metal; because the angle of the latter, being 2° greater in his gun than that of the long 39, in consequence of the greater thickness at the breech, must therefore give a greater inclination to the bore, if the gun be elevated by the line of metal.

That there is some such relation between the ranges of a solid shot of 86 and one of 39 lbs., cannot be denied; but this is not to be attributed to the particular form of the Paixhans gun—it arises from the well known fact that the surface of the ball does not increase in the same ratio as its weight, and hence that the momentum of the larger projectile is increased greatly, while the resistance it meets with has but a trifling addition. Here, then, is the advantage which Paixhans has availed himself of, and which might have given a fairer character to the Congreve pattern, and to that of Bloomfield, if, instead of a calibre of 24, they had thrown a ball of 80 or 100 pounds. There are good reasons for thinking that a light calibre, after the Paixhans model, would hardly be more successful with the corresponding long gun than those of the same character that preceded it.

————

The following data from Simmons are brought together, with the view of showing the English opinion on this subject.

Comparative penetrations of solid shot from 42 and 84 pounders, charge of each ⅓—medium windage of 42 and 84 = 125 in.—and of shells from the French 86, charge ⅕ the weight of shell, and windage ¾ of one tenth; also, solid shot from the French 39, charge ⅓ and windage 18 in.

RANGE IN YD'S	RELATIVE PENETRATING FORCE.			
	42 POUNDER.	84 POUNDER.	FRENCH 39 POUNDER.	FRENCH 86 PR. SHELL.
500	85,921	114,597	80,209	60,224
800	66,846	91,288	55,434	40,909
1000	46,583	75,065	43,852	32,242
1200	37,076	62,060	34,968	25,173
1500	26,699	44,978	25,329	17,832
2000	16,305	30,729	15,616	10,827
2500	10,714	20,909	10,378	7.254
3000	7,570	14,827	7,400	5,367

The following selection is made from the old tables by way of comparing the ranges of shot and shells, and to give some idea of the conclusion that would be made by following these results. The shells were 5½ inch, fired from a long 24 of 9½ feet and 49 cwt., charge 3 lbs. Having no ranges of 24 pound shot with a like charge, those from an 18 pounder are given, of 9 feet and 40 cwt.; also, the range of shells from a heavy 5½ inch Howitzer of 10 cwt., charge 3 lbs., and shot from an 18 of 9½ feet and 42 cwt.

RANGES IN YARDS.

ELEVATION.	SHELLS.				SHOT.		
	LONG 24.		HOWITZER OF 24.		LONG 18—9 FEET.		18 POUNDER 9½ FEET.
	1st Graze.	Extreme Range.	1st Graze.	Extreme Range.	1st Graze.	Extreme Range.	1st Graze.
Point blank					325	1,620	308
1°	277	1,424	479	....	577	1,857	503
2	526	1,464	722	....	695	1,793	757
3	740	1,600	921	....	965	1,723	1,058
5	1,182	1,733	1,325	....	1,517	2,100	1,365
8	1,520	1,744	1,721	....	....	....	1,980

Such are the different ranges attained with one charge, those of shot from the two kinds of long 18 pounders are discordant enough. The ranges of shells from the long 24 weighing 16¼ lbs. are by no means very inferior to those obtained by Paixhans. The ranges of one 18 pounder are from those obtained in 1813, the other on Sutton Heath in 1810, and both given by respectable authority. Considerable as the differences are, it is not improbable they are both right—for they are far less than the differences existing between many of the rounds recorded in the experiments made to test the Paixhans gun. Something of the kind may always be expected where the ranges are tried on land; for, in addition to the variety of soil which may be found at intervals of 200 or 300 yards, there is scarcely ever a perfect level obtainable of any great extent. Hence if the ball meet with a wet spot it may lodge, or lose much of its force—if it strike on hard ground it may glance off and go farther—an inclination of the soil upwards or downwards will produce nearly like effects. These obstacles do not intervene when the range is tried on water, though it may be much more difficult to note the distance. That it can be done, is evidenced by the fact that the tables of Captain Churruca, of the Spanish navy, were formed from trials of this kind. The Point Blank ranges already given, are abridged from his tables by Montgery.

NOTE.—The American Editor is indebted to his friend, Lieut. John A. Dahlgren, U. S. Navy, for the article on the " Ranges of Sea Ordnance."

SPARS.

—✺—

The tables annexed give the length of the spars in some of our most approved ships. It will be seen that there is no rule; but the judgment of the builder decides.

American ships, however, are much lighter sparred than English ships, as will be seen by reference to the Table on next page, taken from the Art of Mast-making.

—◆—

TABLE.

	Ship *Liverpool.* feet. inches.		Ship *Ashburton.* feet. inches.		Ship *Pat'k Henry.* feet. inches.		Ship *Victoria.* feet. inches		Ship *St. James.* feet. inches.		Ship *Courier.* feet. inches.	
	Length..175 10 Breadth.. 36 9 Depth.. 22 2 Am. tons..1077 2/95		Length..166 2 Breadth..36 6 Depth..21 9 Am. tons .1015 3/95 Eng. " 926		Length..160 0 Breadth...34 10 Depth...21 10 Am. tons 881 38/95 Eng. " 1014 including poop.		Length..133 9 Breadth..35 3 Depth..21 9 Am. tons.868		Length..133 9 Breadth...32 8 Depth....20 6 Am. tons.641 10/95 Eng. " 619		Length..116 0 Breadth...27 0 Depth....16 10 Am. tons.380	
NAMES OF THE MASTS AND SPARS.	LENGTH OF SPARS.		LENGTH OF SPARS.		LENGTH OF SPARS.		LENGTH OF SPARS.		LENGTH OF SPARS.		LENGTH OF SPARS.	
	Masts.	*Yards.*	*Masts.*	*Yards.*	*Masts.*	*Yards.*	*Masts.*	*Yards.*	*Masts.*	*Yards.*	*Masts.*	*Yards.*
FORE......	78 feet.	65 feet.	79 feet.	66 feet.	78 feet.	65 feet.	72½ feet.	61 feet.	69 feet.	60 feet.	58 feet.	49 feet.
Top........	44 ,,	51 ,,	45½ ,,	52½ ,,	44 ,,	51 ,,	43½ ,,	50 ,,	41 ,,	50 ,,	34 ,,	39 ,,
Top-gallant.	24 ,,	37 ,,	24½ ,,	38 ,,	24 ,,	37 ,,	25 ,,	35½ ,,	22 ,,	34 ,,	18 ,,	30 ,,
Royal......	17 ,,	28 ,,	17 ,,	29 ,,	17 ,,	28 ,,	15½ ,,	27 ,,	15 ,,	25 ,,	12 ,,	24 ,,
Sky-sail....	11 ,,	......	......	......	11 ,,	......	......	......	......	......	9 ,,	20 ,,
MAIN......	80 ,,	69½ ,,	81½ ,,	68 ,,	80 ,,	69½ ,,	75½ ,,	67 ,,	73 ,,	61 ,,	60 ,,	52 ,,
Top.......	46 ,,	55 ,,	47 ,,	53½ ,,	46 ,,	55 ,,	44 ,,	54 ,,	43 ,,	51 ,,	36 ,,	42 ,,
Top-gallant.	26½ ,,	41 ,,	26 ,,	40 ,,	26½ ,,	41 ,,	25 ,,	38½ ,,	23 ,,	36½ ,,	19 ,,	33 ,,
Royal......	20 ,,	32 ,,	19 ,,	31 ,,	20 ,,	32 ,,	15½ ,,	29 ,,	16 ,,	26 ,,	13 ,,	26 ,,
Sky-sail....	13 ,,	......	......	......	13 ,,		......	......	......	......	10 ,,	22 ,,
MIZEN or Cross Jack ⎰	73 ,,	55 ,,	76 ,,	55 ,,	73 ,,	55 ,,	69½ ,,	49 ,,	65 ,,	39 ,,	54 ,,	42 ,,
Top.......	37½ ,,	42 ,,	38 ,,	42 ,,	37½ ,,	42 ,,	37 ,,	39¾ ,,	35 ,,	49 ,,	27 ,,	33 ,,
Top-gallant.	20 ,,	30 ,,	20 ,,	31 ,,	20 ,,	30 ,,	20½ ,,	28½ ,,	17 ,,	26½ ,,	15½ ,,	26 ,,
Royal......	14½ ,,	22 ,,	13 ,,	22 ,,	14½ ,,	22 ,,	12½ ,,	22 ,,	12 ,,	19 ,,	11 ,,	22 ,,
Sky-sail....	10 ,,	......	......	......	10 ,,	......	......	......	......	......	8 ,,	......
*Bowsprit..	28 ,,	......	29½ ,,	......	30 ,,	......	25 ,,	......	28 ,,	......	20 ,,	......
†Jib-boom...	24 ,,	......	21½ ,,	......	25 ,,	......	21½ ,,	......	25½ ,,	......	17 ,,	......
†Flying ditto	16 ,,	......	16 ,,	......	16 ,,	......	14 ,,	......	20½ ,,	......	11 ,,	......
Span'r boom.	42 ,,	......	43 ,,	......	......	......	......	......	38 ,,	......	33 ,,	......
Gaff.......	39 ,,	......	41 ,,	......	......	......	......	......	......	......	24 ,,	......

* Out board.   † Outside cap.

The above, with the exception of the Courier, are New York built ships. The Courier was built in Newburyport, Massachusetts.

TABLE,

Showing the Dimensions of Masts and Yards used in the English Merchant Service.

NAMES OF THE MASTS AND YARDS.	1100 TONS.				1000 TONS.				900 TONS.				600 TONS.				400 TONS.			
	MASTS or BOOMS.		YARDS.		MASTS or BOOMS.		YARDS.		MASTS or BOOMS.		YARDS.		MASTS or BOOMS.		YARDS.		MASTS or BOOMS.		YARDS.	
	Length Ft. In.	Dia. In.	Length Ft. In.	Dia. In.	Length Ft. In.	Dia. In.	Length Ft. In.	Dia. In.	Length Ft. In.	Dia. In.	Length Ft. In.	Dia. In.	Length Ft. In.	Dia. In.	Length Ft. In.	Dia. In.	Length Ft. In.	Dia. In.	Length Ft. In.	Dia. In.
MAIN	90 0	30	80 0	20	87 0	29	78 0	19	86 0	28	76 0	18½	78 0	24	62 0	15½	70 0	21½	50 0	13
Top	56 0	17¼	57 6	13½	52 0	16½	54 0	13	50 0	16	52 0	12½	48 0	15	48 0	12	41 0	13	39 0	10
Top-gallant	27 0	9	37 0	8	26 0	9	36 0	8	26 0	9	34 0	8	23 0	8	32 0	7½	23 0	7½	29 0	6½
Royal	20 0	6½	23 0	5	19 0	6½	22 0	5	19 0	5½	21 0	4½	......	......	......	......	15 0	5	20 0	5
FORE	84 0	29½	76 0	18½	81 0	29	72 0	18	79 0	28	70 0	17	73 0	23½	58 0	14½	65 0	21	49 0	12½
Top	52 0	17¼	52 0	13	50 0	16½	52 0	12½	48 0	16	50 0	12	46 0	15	46 0	11½	40 0	13	39 0	10
Top-gallant	26 0	9	36 0	7¾	24 0	9	34 0	7½	23 0	9	32 0	7½	22 0	8	30 0	7½	21 0	7½	27 0	6
Royal	18 0	6	21 0	5	17 0	6	20 0	4½	17 0	5½	19 0	4½	......	......	......	......	14 0	6	19 0	4¾
MIZEN	78 0	21	68 0	13	76 0	20	66 0	12½	76 0	20	64 0	12	68 0	16	60 0	10½	62 0	15	30 0	7½
Top	39 0	12	38 0	9	38 0	12	38 0	9	37 0	12	35 0	8½	30 0	10½	32 0	8	30 0	9½	30 0	7½
Top-gallant	20 0	6½	26 0	5	19 0	6½	26 0	5½	19 0	6	23 0	5	18 0	5½	22 0	4½	16 0	5	20 0	5
Royal	12 0	5	16 0	4½	10 0	4½	11 0	4												
Bowsprit	58 0	30	54 0	11¼	54 0	29	54 0	11¼	54 0	28	50 0	10½	50 0	24½	48 0	9½	47 0	21	36 0	7½
Jib-boom	40 0	12	38 0	8	40 0	12	36 0	8	40 0	12	36 0	8	36 0	10½	32 0	7	34 0	10		

TABLE

Of Masts and Spars of Vessels of the United States Navy. Prepared by FRANCIS GRICE, *Naval Constructor, U. S. Navy Yard, Brooklyn.*

	120 GUNS. PENNSYLVANIA.		80 GUNS. DELAWARE.		74 GUNS. FRANKLIN.		44 GUNS. POTOMAC.		22 GUNS. ALBANY.		22 GUNS. LEVANT.		16 GUNS. YORKTOWN.		10 GUNS. BRIG TRUXTON.	
Length between perpendiculars,	212 feet 11 in.		199 feet 2 in.		190 feet 10 in.		177 feet 10 in.		150 feet 7 in.		134 feet 7 in.		119 feet 7 in.		102 feet 6 in.	
Breadth, extreme,	57 " 6 "		54 " 6 "		51 " 7½ "		46 " 2 "		39 " 6 "		36 "		32 " 11 "		28 " 2 "	
Depth,	24 " 3 "		21 " 7 "		19 " 9 "		21 " 2 "		18 "		15 "		15 "		13 "	
Custom H. Tonnage,	3104.65 95		2602.34		2243.34		1684.14		1041.90		770.3		569.30		329.89	
MASTS AND SPARS.	MASTS.	YARDS.	MASTS.	YARDS.	MASTS.	YARDS.	MASTS.	YARDS.	MASTS.	YARDS.	MASTS.	YARDS.	MASTS.	YARDS.	MASTS.	YARDS.
	ft. in.	ft. in.	ft. in.	ft. in.	ft. in.	ft. in.	ft. in.	ft. in.	ft. in.	ft. in.	ft. in.	ft. in.	ft. in.	ft. in.	ft. in.	ft. in.
FORE	121	100	115	96	105	90	95	84	84 1	77	72	65	65 6	60 9	65 6	55
Top	63	75	63	71	63	67	56	62	50	57	43	49	42	45 6	37 6	42
Top-gallant	37 6	48	32	46	37	45	29	41	25 3	39	23	32	21	30 6	19	28
Royal	22	23	22	33	22	30	20	27	16	28	15	22	13	20 6	13	20
Pole	17		11		6		10		8		5		6		5	
MAIN	132	110	124 6	107 6	117	105	105	95	89 7	77	80	75	72	67 6	68 3	55
Top	70	82	70	78	70	77	63	71	50	57	47	56	45	50 6	37 6	42
Top-gallant	41	52	41	52	41	51	32	30	25	39	24	37	22	34	19	28
Royal	24	36	24	36	24	35	22	20	16	28	16	25	14	22 9	13	20
Pole	18		12		6		11		8		5		7		5	
MIZEN	†99	80	97	80	98	80	84	66	‡70 3	47	66	53	§54 6	52		
Top	55	52	55	52	53	49	46	45	38	39	37	36 6	32	34		
Top-gallant	33	33	29	33	33	32	24	30	19	25	20	29 6	16	21		
Royal	20	23	20	23	20	21 9	16	19	13	17	13	15	12	14		
Pole	14		10		5		8		6		4		5			
Bowsprit, outboard	54		56		48		45 9		32 8		33		30		22	
Jib-boom, from cap	43		40		36		32 9		29		25 6		22 9		21	
Flying Jib-boom	24		21		20		21 3		19		14 6		13 3		15	
Spanker Boom	61 6		60		60		50		41		35		34		50	
Gaff	38 10		38		38		30		35		28		28		32	

† Steps on the Orlop Deck.   ‡ Steps on the Berth Deck.   § Mast Head in a line with Main Tressletrees.

Note.—It has been decided by the Bureau of Construction and Equipment, U. S. N., that the yards, top-mast, top gallant mast, on the fore and main mast, should be alike hereafter. The rule is to take the mean of the present spars as the standard, for instance:

The fore yard of the Potomac is...84 feet.

The Main " " " ....95 "

179

The mean is the size of the fore and main yards,...................... 89 6   [*Am. Ed.*]

APPENDIX 30-III

The dimensions given in this page are those of the *Queen of the West*, the largest and most complete merchant-ship ever built in the United States.

She was built by the firm of Brown & Bell, of New-York, of whom it may be said, that their monuments are upon the waters ; and to whom the Editor is indebted for the details below.

	MASTS.						YARDS.					
	LENGTH.		MAST HE'D		DIAMETER		LENGTH.		DIAMETER		YARD ARM.	
	ft.	in.	ft.	in.	ft.	in.	ft.	in.	ft.	in.	ft.	in.
FORE	80		14	6	2	4	68		1	6⅛	4	
Top	48		9		1	4	53	6	1	2¼	3	9
Top-gallant	25	6	2	6	0	10½	39	6	0	9⅜	2	6
Royal	17	6	....		....		29		0	6½	1	9
Skysail	14	7										
Pole	9	11										
MAIN	82		14	6	2	4	73	6	1	7⅝	4	3
Top	48		9		1	4	59		1	3¾	4	
Top-gallant	26	6	2	6	0	10¾	45		0	10⅝	2	9
Royal	19	6	....		....		34	6	0	7¾	2	
Skysail	15	7										
Pole	10	6										
MIZEN	75		11	3	1	10½	57	6	1	3⅜	3	9
Top	39	6	7	6	1	½	44	6	0	11⅞	3	6
Top-gallant	20	6	2		0	8	32		0	7½	2	3
Royal	14	6	....		....		23		0	5⅛	1	5
Skysail	12											
Pole	8											
Bowsprit, outboard	29	6	Bed.....		2	5						
Jib-boom, outside the cap	26	6	End.....		2	3	Cap.....		1	4		
Flying Jib-boom	17		End.....		7		Cap.....		0	10		
Spanker boom	46		Slings...		0	10						
Gaff	43		Pole.....		7		Slings....		0	8		

DIAMETER OF YARDS.

	ft.	in.	in.
Lower Yards	3	9 to	1
Topsail "	3	9 "	1
Top-gallant Yards	4	3 to	1
Royal "	4	6 "	1

STATION OF MASTS.

	ft.	in.
From forward of the stem to centre of fore-mast	34	8
From forward to centre of the main-mast	61	10
From centre of main to centre of mizen-mast	49	8
From centre of mizen-mast to after side of post	34	0
Whole length on deck	180	2

DIMENSIONS.

	ft.	in.
Length of keel to half scarf	162	0
Whole length	164	6
Breadth of beam	37	8
Depth of lower hold	14	6
Depth between decks	7	4½

Measuring 1,168$\frac{20}{95}$ tons.

FASTENINGS.

Copper and iron fastenings used in constructing and completing the ship, 98,000. lbs.

DESCRIPTION OF PLATE.

"QUEEN OF THE WEST."

1. Bowsprit.
2. Jib-boom.
3. Flying Jib-boom.
4. Flying Jib.
5. Jib.
6. Fore Top-mast Stays.
7. Fore Stays.
8. Jib Martingales.
9. Flying Jib do.
10. Martingale.
11. Fore-mast.
12. Fore-yard and Sail.
13. Fore Top-mast.
14. do. Top-sail Yard and Sail.
15. do. Top-gallant Mast.
16. do. do. Yard and Sail.
17. do. Royal-mast.
18. do. Royal Yard Sail.
19. do. Lift.
20. do. Braces.
21. do. Top-sail Braces.
22. do. Top-gallant Braces.
23. do. Royal Braces.
24. do. Top-gallant Stay.
25. Main Sky-sail Stay.
26. do. Royal Stay.
27. do. Top-gallant Stay.
28. do. Top-mast Stays.
29. do. Stays.
30. Fore Spencer Gaff.
31. do. Top-mast Back-stays.
32. do. Top-gallant do.
33. do. Royal-mast do.
34. do. Rigging.
35. do. Top-mast Rigging
36. do. Top-gallant Rigging.
37. Bob-stays.
38. Bowsprit Shrouds.
39. Slings Fore-yard.
40. Fore Sky-sail Stay.
41. Main Yard and Sail.
42. do. Top-sail Yard and Sail.
43. do. Top-gallant Yard and Sail.
44. do. Royal Yard and Sail.
45. do. Sky-sail Mast.
46. Burgee, or Private Signal.
47. Main Royal-mast.
48. do. Royal Brace.
49. do. Top-gallant Mast.
50. do do. Brace.
51. do. Top-mast.
52. do. Top-sail Brace.
53. do. Lifts.
54. do. Brace.
55. do. Rigging.
56. do. Top-mast Back-stays.
57. do. Top-gallant do.
58. do. Royal do
59. do. Spencer Gaff.
60. Mizen Stay.
61. do. Top-mast Stay.
62. do. Top-gallant Braces.
63. do. Royal Stay.
64. do. Yard and Sail.
65. do. Top-sail Yard and Sail.
66. do. Top-gallant Yard and Sail.
67. do. Royal and Sail.
68. do. Sky-sail Mast.
69. do. Royal Mast.
70. do. Top-gallant Mast.
71. do. Top-sail.
72. do. Lifts.
73. do. Top-sail Braces.
74. do. Top-gallant Stay.
75. Spanker Gaff.
76. Spanker Boom.
77. do. Sheets.
78. American Ensign.

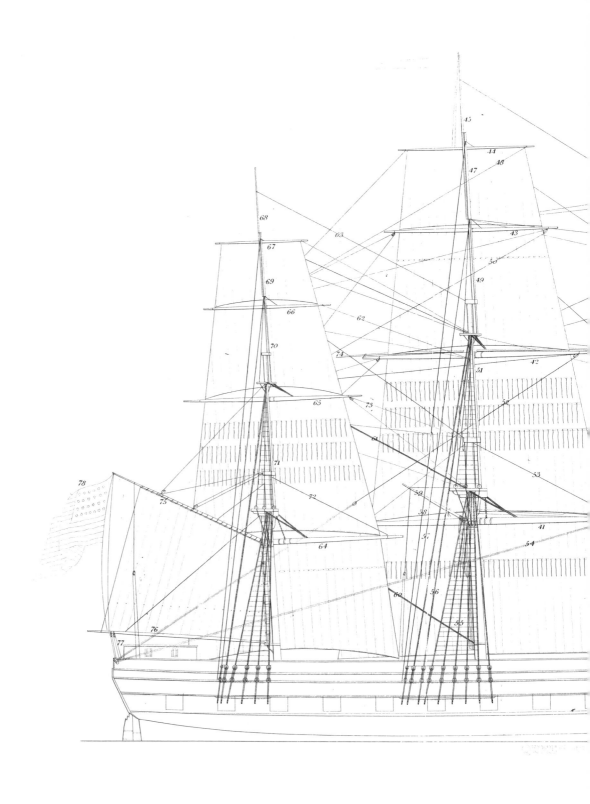

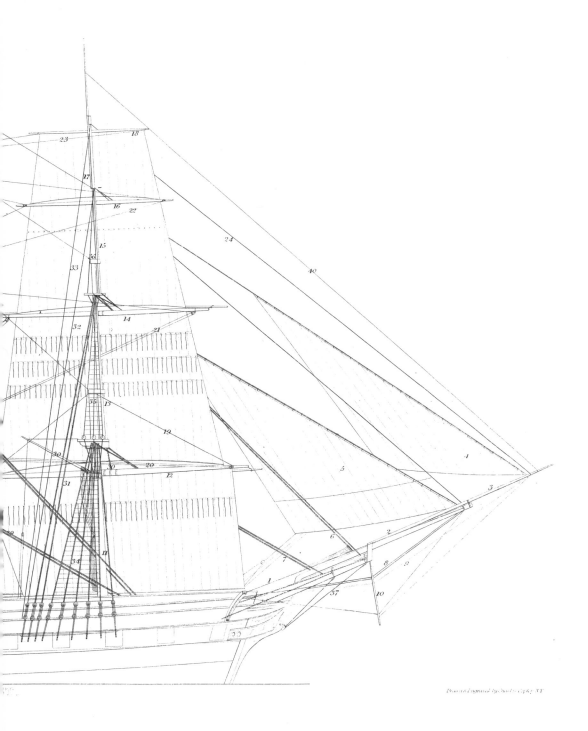

APPENDIX 32-I: **Clippers**

Within ten years an entire new class of vessels have been built, entitled Clippers, which combine great beauty with great speed.

The first approaching that class of vessels, we believe, were the Ships Helena and Montauk, followed by the Rainbow and Sea-Witch, which were Clippers in earnest. The California trade gave a great impulse to this class of vessels; and, from ships of 600 tons we have advanced until we now have many over 2,000 tons, larger, we believe, than any ship at the battle of Trafalgar; and we now have one, the Great Republic, larger than any sailing vessel in the world, built by Donald McKay, of Boston.

We give the dimensions and spars of three Clippers built by W. H. Webb, of New-York, and also of the Great Republic.

SWORD-FISH.

Length of keel to half scarf,	162	feet.
Whole length on deck,	170	"
Breadth of beam,	36	"
Depth of hold,	20	"
Depth between decks,	7½	"
Measurement in tons, (Carpenter's,)	1250	
Do do (Custom-House,)	1000	

NAMES OF THE MASTS AND SPARS.	LENGTH. ft.	LENGTH. in.	MAST HEAD. ft.	MAST HEAD. in.	YARD ARM. ft.	YARD ARM. in.	DIAMETER. in.
FORE-Mast,	76		13	6			30
" Top-mast,	44	6	7	8			16
" Top-gallant,	23						11
" Royal,	15						7
" Sky-sail,	10						
" Pole,	6	6					
MAIN-Mast,	79		14				30
" Top-mast,	46		8				16
" Top-gallant,	24						11
" Royal,	16						7
" Sky-sail,	10	8					
" Pole,	7						
MIZEN-Mast,	69		11				23½
" Top-mast,	36		6	3			12
" Top-gallant,	18	9					8¼
" Royal,	12	6					5½
" Sky-sail,	8	4					
" Pole,	5	6					
FORE Yard,	66				4	9	17½
" Top-sail,	54	6			5	3	14½
" Top-gallant,	37				2	4	9½
" Royal,	28				1	8	6½
" Sky-sail,	19	6			1		4¾
MAIN Yard,	74				5		19½
" Top-sail,	61				5	6	15½
" Top-gallant,	41	6			2	8	10
" Royal,	31	6			1	10	7
" Sky-sail,	21	6			1	2	5
MIZEN Yard,	52				4	3	13½
" Top-sail,	42				4	6	10½
" Top-gallant,	27	9			1	9	6½
" Royal,	20	6			1	4	5
" Sky-sail,	13					9	4
Bowsprit outboard,	25	top				28by	38
Inner Jib-boom,	18						16
Outer do	12						
Pole,	8						
Spanker-boom,	42						10
" Gaff,	35		5	6			8
Swinging Boom,	42						9
Width Fore-top,							14
" Main "							14½
" Mizen-top,							11¼

FLYING DUTCHMAN.

Length of keel to half scarf,	182	feet.
Whole length on deck,	190	"
Breadth of beam,	38	"
Depth of hold,	21½	"
Depth between decks,	7½	"
Measurement in tons, (Carpenter's,)	1600	
Do do (Custom-House,)	1200	

NAMES OF THE MASTS AND SPARS.	LENGTH. ft.	LENGTH. in.	MAST HEAD. ft.	MAST HEAD. in.	YARD ARM. ft.	YARD ARM. in.	DIAMETER. in.
FORE-Mast,	81		14				30
" Top-mast,	47	3	8				16¾
" Top-gallant,	27						11½
" Royal,	18						7¾
" Sky-sail,	11	9					
" Pole,	8						
MAIN-Mast,	85		14	6			31
" Top-mast,	48		8	3			16¾
" Top-gallant,	27	6					11½
" Royal,	19						7¾
" Sky-sail,	12						
" Pole,	8						
MIZEN-Mast,	73		10	6			23½
" Top-mast,	38		6	6			12¾
" Top-gallant,	21	3					8¾
" Royal,	14						5½
" Sky-sail,	9						
" Pole,	6						
FORE Yard,	74				5		19½
" Top-sail,	60				5	6	15
" Top-gallant,	42				3		10½
" Royal,	32				2	6	6½
" Sky-sail,	24				1	6	5½
MAIN Yard,	81				5 to 6		21
" Top-sail,	66				6		15½
" Top-gallant,	46				3	6	10¾
" Royal,	34				2	6	6¾
" Sky-sail,	25	6			1	6	5½
MIZEN Yard,	56				4		14
" Top-sail,	47				4	6	11
" Top-gallant,	32				2	6	7¼
" Royal,	23				1	6	
" Sky-sail,	16				1		3½
Bowsprit, outboard,	28	6					28 by 30
Flying Jib-boom, (16 feet outside,)	10						
Jib-boom,	14						
Spanker-boom,	52		4	6			
" Gaff,	35		6				
Ringtail Spar, outside	16						
Width of Fore-top,	14	6					
" Main-top,	15	0					
" Mizen-top,	11	6					

YOUNG AMERICA.

Length of keel to half scarf,.............225 feet.
Whole length on deck, ...235 "
Breadth of beam, ...41 "
Depth of hold,.....................26 "
Depth between decks, ...7⅔ "
Measurement in tons, (Carpenters',.......2500
Do   do   (Custom-House,) ... 2000

GREAT REPUBLIC.

Whole length on deck, ...325 feet.
Breadth of beam,......................53 „
Depth of hold, ...39 "
Measurement in tons, (Carpenter's,).....
Do   do   (Custom-House,)... 4,552
Measurement for stowage, ...5,560 tons.
Carries, with dead weight and proper mixed cargo, 6,500 tons.

YOUNG AMERICA

NAMES OF THE MASTS AND SPARS.	LENGTH. ft.	in.	MAST HEAD. ft.	in.	YARD ARM. ft.	in.	DIAMETER. in.
Fore-Mast,	92	....	16	6	....	....	36
" Top-mast,	53	6	9	....	....	....	18
" Top-gallant,	36	....	6	....	....	....	13
" Royal,	24	....	4	....	....	....	8½
" Sky-sail,	16	....	2	8	....	....	5½
" Pole,	10	8	....	....	....	....	3¾
Main-Mast,	96	....	17	....	....	....	36
" Top-mast,	56	....	9	6	....	....	19
" Top-gallant,	37	9	6	4	....	....	13½
" Royal,	25	....	4	2	....	....	9
" Sky-sail,	17	....	2	9	....	....	6
" Moon-sail,	11	6	2	....	....	....	4
" Pole,	8	....	....	....	....	....	....
Mizen-Mast,	84	6	13	6	....	....	29
" Top-mast,	44	....	7	4	....	....	15
" Top-gallant,	29	6	5	4	....	....	10¼
" Royal,	19	6	3	4	....	....	6¾
" Sky-sail,	13	....	2	2	....	....	4½
" Pole,	8	6	....	....	....	....	3
Fore Yard,	82	....	....	....	4	6	22
" Top-sail,	69	8	....	....	6	2	16¾
" Top-gallant,	51	....	....	....	2	9	11¾
" Royal,	40	....	....	....	1	7	8¾
" Sky-sail,	30	6	....	....	....	9	6¼
Main Yard,	86	....	....	....	5	....	23
" Top-sail,	73	....	....	....	7	2	17¾
" Top-gallant,	52	8	....	....	3	4	12½
" Royal,	41	4	....	....	1	8	9
" Sky-sail,	31	....	....	....	1	....	6½
" Moon-sail,	24	6	....	....	....	6	4½
Mizen Yard,	68	....	....	....	3	6	17¾
" Top sail,	57	....	....	....	5	....	14
" Top-gallant,	41	8	....	....	2	....	9½
" Royal,	32	4	....	....	1	6	6¾
" Sky-sail,	25	....	....	....	....	6	5
Bowsprit, outboard,	28*						
Inner Jib-boom,	18	....	....	....	....	....	17½
Outer Jib-boom,	14	....	5	....	....	....	
Spanker-boom,	62	....	3	....	....	....	14
" Gaff,	40	....	6	6	....	....	9
Swinging Boom,	64	....	....	....	....	....	14½
Width of Main-top,	18	6					
" Fore-top,	17	9					
" Mizen-top,	14	6					

GREAT REPUBLIC

NAMES OF THE MASTS AND SPARS.	LENGTH. ft.	in.	MAST HEAD. ft.	in.	YARD ARM. ft.	in.	DIAMETER. in.
Fore-Mast,	130	....	36	....	....	....	44
" Top-mast,	76	....	12	....	....	....	24
" Top-gallant,	28	....	....	....	....	....	18
" Royal,	22	....	....	....	....	....	15
" Sky-sail,	19	....	....	....	....	....	11
" Pole,	12						
Main-Mast,	131	....	36	....	....	....	44
" Top-mast,	76	....	12	....	....	....	24
" Top-gallant,	28	....	....	....	....	....	18
" Royal,	22	....	....	....	....	....	15
" Sky-sail,	19	....	....	....	....	....	11
" Pole,	12						
Mizen-Mast,	122	....	33	....	....	....	40
" Top-mast,	69	....	10	....	....	....	22
" Top-gallant,	22	....	....	....	....	....	16
" Royal,	19	....	....	....	....	....	10
" Sky-sail,	15	....	....	....	....	....	8
" Pole,	8						
Spanker-Mast,	110	....	14	....	....	....	26
" Top-mast,	40						
Fore-Yard,	110	....	....	....	6	....	26
" Lower top-sail	90	....	....	....	5	....	24
" Upper "	76	....	....	....	4	6	19
" Top-gallant,	62	....	....	....	4	....	15
" Royal,	51	....	....	....	3	6	12
" Sky-sail,	40	....	....	....	3	....	9
Main Yard,	115	....	....	....	6	....	28
" Lower top-sail	90	....	....	....	5	....	24
" Upper "	76	....	....	....	4	6	19
" Top-gallant,	62	....	....	....	4	....	15
" Royal,	51	....	....	....	3	6	12
" Sky-sail,	40	....	....	....	3	....	9
Mizen Yard,	90	....	....	....	5	....	24
" Lower top-s'l	76	....	....	....	4	6	19
" Upper "	62	....	....	....	4	....	15
" Top-gallant,	51	....	....	....	3	....	12
" Royal,	40	....	....	....	3	....	9
" Sky-sail,	29	....	....	....	2	....	6
Bowsprit, outboard,	30	....	....	....	....	....	44
Inner Jib-boom,	22	....	....	....	....	....	22
Outer Jib-boom,	14						
Spanker-boom,	40						

* From K't H'd centre of bowsprit 36 in.

FORBES RIG.

FORBES RIG

The plate shows the new rig of R. B. FORBES, Esq., of Boston. Mr. FORBES's description says :— " The lower yards and the top-gallant yard are in the same position as in the ordinary rig ; but the top-sail and top-gallant sail are so divided as to make three sails instead of two. The top-sail being exactly of the size of an ordinary double reefed top-sail, the yard being parrelled to the heel of the top-mast, where the top-masts are fidded forward of the lower mast-head ; and to the head of the lower mast where the top-masts are (as they ought to be) fidded abaft the mast-head ; this renders it necessary to have the lower mast-heads longer, by several feet, than in the old rig. The next sail above the top-sail, representing the upper half of the top-sail of the old rig and a fraction of the old top-gallant sail, is called the top-gallant sail, and the old rig top-gallant sail is, in the new rig, called the royal, while the royal of the old rig becomes the skysail of the new rig. As I consider it important to have the sail as much in the body of the ship as possible, and, at the same time, so dispose of the canvas and spars that the sails can be used in different places, I make the foreyard of the same length (excepting a slight difference in the yard-arms) as the main top-sail yard ; the fore top-sail yard the same as the main top-gallant yard, the fore top-gallant yard the same as the main royal yard, and so on with the mizen, so that the yards and sails on the fore fit on the main one stage higher up, those on the mizen fit on the fore one stage higher, and on the main two higher.

" There must, of course, be a difference in the diameter between lower yards and top-sail or top-gallant yards, although they may be of the same length. The principal advantages of this rig over the old are, that, by clewing down top-gallant sails in a squall, the ship is practically reduced to double reefed top-sails by the watch in a moment, the sails are more easily managed, set better on a wind, can be furled snugger in a gale, and are much less subject to wear out ; in short, the ship can be taken care of in bad weather by the watch as well or better than the ship, rigged after the ordinary fashion, by all hands.

" I advocate fidding the masts abaft for the following reasons, both in steamers and sailing vessels :— The top-gallant masts and royal masts can be housed without interfering with the sails next below ; so that top-gallant sails can be carried with the royal masts housed, and top-sails can be carried when the top-gallant masts are housed. The strain on the trussle trees is also divided between the top-mast (say top-gallant of new rig) and the lower yard, which, in merchant ships, generally hangs to the chock formed of the lower mast-head.

" Each top-sail and top-gallant sail has only one reef in it, and the points are fitted so that the sail reefs to a jack-stay on the yard above the bending jack-stay or batten, both legs of the points being before the sail, as in a man-of-war's courses. There is another advantage in the new rig, which is, that, in case of carrying away a top-gallant mast, (top-mast of old rig) you can still set double reefed topsails, and you can get up another top-mast in any weather, and often when it would not be safe to attempt it in the old rig.

" Besides the advantages named the rig has many others, among which may be mentioned that the ship is kept more steadily on her course, as it is very seldom necessary to luff and to bear away to take in reefs, as in the old rig. When running for land in thick blowy weather the ship, with the new rig, can carry nearly full sail and still be ready to haul her wind suddenly and " claw off," and may often make her port by day-light, when the ship with the old rig would not be able safely to accomplish this. The ship, with the new rig, when running before a fresh gale, may round to safely to sound, by simply clewing down top-gallant sails, when the ship with the old rig would lose much time by clewing down top-sails, or run more risk to save this trouble. The sails are much more easily managed, and are more durable, being in smaller sheets, and on a wind they set better.

" Against all these advantages there are some disadvantages ; namely—the new rig does not look so neat ; it is *in the first cost* more expensive, but in the long run more economical. There is a slight loss of power by having the sails smaller ; but, as they are much more manageable, this is soon made up. Some people, who have not tried the rig, object to the increased number of ropes, but as these facilitate operations I do not deem the objections valid.

" There is one very strong recommendation, and this is, that no Master who has tried the rig at sea, that I am aware of, makes any objection to it.

" Some say, who have only seen it on paper, or alongside the wharf, 'it may answer very well for the Atlantic trade, but it is not necessary for the Pacific and China trade.'   To this I would only refer to the weather off Cape Horn and Cape of Good Hope, and to that in the Bay of Bengal and China Seas during the contrary monsoons, and ask any seaman whether he would not often like to put his ship under double reefs and keep her going, and make all sail again *with the watch*.   It almost always happens that when the ship is leaving Bengal, or China, or Manilla, during the S. W. monsoon, for home, the crew is enfeebled by disease and hard work loading the ship ; then the rig is found to be a great relief to all hands.

" Its advantages, when working through narrow straits in squally weather, cannot but be apparent to the most cursory observer.   When obliged to anchor in such places is it not a great advantage to have the top-sails set, with top-gallant sails clewed down, or furled, ready to start on the first favorable chance, and yet ready to make snug in case of a sudden squall without calling all hands ?

" Take the case of a ship leaving Liverpool only half manned, and of these some are out of working condition—the ship gets sail on her after a fashion to make an old tar weep—it comes on to blow— the ship often has to put back or to anchor in an exposed place, simply because she cannot be decently handled.

" In short the *new rig*, or the old ' North Sea Schooner Rig,' applied to a ship, makes her more safe and vastly relieves the responsibility of master and officers, the risk to underwriters, and last, not least, the labors of the sailors, and must come into general use sooner or later.

" R. B. FORBES."

To this it may be added, Mr. Forbes's plan has this great advantage, that the vessel is always making headway and under control, which is not the case with vessels under the old plan ; when reefing top-sails on a wind, they are sure to make much leeway whilst so doing.

REMARKS

UPON THE DRAUGHT OF WATER AND DIMENSIONS

OF

PROPELLER VESSELS FOR WAR PURPOSES.

BY S. M. POOK, U. S. Naval Constructor.

The first thing to be taken into consideration is the object for which the vessel is designed. A war ship, then, may be considered a gun carriage, and that vessel that can carry the gun with the least expense into shoal places, for the protection of harbors or coasts, may be considered the best adapted for defence; but a larger class of vessels, drawing a greater depth of water, are considered better for sea purposes and for offence.

The draught of water of any steam vessel of war is limited by the dimensions of the ship, and if a light draught of water be desirable, the vessel must be small in proportion to the lightness of the draught that may be required.

A vessel able to carry an effective armament with ten days' fuel, water and provisions for a six month's cruise, will probably draw the following draught of water in proportion to their size,

400 tons from 9 to 10 feet when loaded.

600   „   10 to 11 „   „   „

800   „   11 to 12 „   „   „

1,000 „   12 to 13 „   „   „

1,200 „   13 to 14 „   „   „

1,400 „   14 to 15 „   „   „

1,600 „   15 to 16 „   „   „

1,800 „   16 to 17 „   „   „

2,000 „   17 to 18 „   „   „

2,200 „   18 to 19 „   „   „

2,400 „   19 to 20 „   „   „

It will be found in practice that vessels fitted out in the usual manner for war purposes, and built strong as is required for war steamers, taking those heretofore built as the basis, that the draught of water will be about equal to two-fifths of the breadth of the beam, and that the total displacement at that depth will not be more than once and one half the tonnage, (carpenter measure,) allowing the vessel to be five and a half times the breadth for the length, and the depth to be half the breadth; for example, say a vessel be 1,000 tons, being 34 feet beam, 187 feet long and 17 feet deep, her draught of water equal two-fifths breadth is 13.6 feet, and at this depth she will displace 1,500 tons of water when fully equipped for sea.

The weight of the hull will be ....700 tons.

„   „   cables and anchors .... 33 „

„   „   rigging, spars, sails, boats, &c. .... 45 „

„   „   sea stores................................. 22 „

„   „   men, tanks, cask, water, provisions, &c...........170 „

„   „   guns, shell, powder &c. .... 80 „

„   „   engines, boilers, filled coals, &c. ....450 „

Total displacement................1500 tons.

The above supposes the frame to be of live oak, and built strong for war purposes; but if the frame be made of white oak, and the ceiling and plank be of yellow pine, the hull might be reduced in weight about one-seventh, which would lighten the vessel about 9 inches, making the load draught 12 feet 9 inches; and if the fuel be only for five days instead of ten days, as calculated, her draught will be reduced about 9 inches more, making the draught about 12 feet, below which it will be found difficult to reduce the draught of a ship of 1,000 tons, equipped for sea and properly armed for war purposes.

By comparing the estimated weights which go to make up the total displacement, it will be found that four-fifths of the whole is due to the weight of the hull, spars, rigging, cables, anchors, engines, boilers and coals, leaving only one-fifth available for cargo, such as guns, powder, shot, men, provisions, water, &c.; this will give us 300 tons for a ship of 1,500 displacement. Now it is curious to compare the difference and see what is gained by increasing the dimensions of this vessel to double this tonnage. If the vessel be 2,000 tons and 3,000 tons displacement, we have 600 tons available for cargo by the same rule, the weight of the ship, engines, coals, &c. increasing in proportion as the ship is enlarged, this vessel being increased to 43 feet beam, her draught of water is increased to 17 feet 2 inches water, being 42 inches more draught than the vessel of 1,000 tons. Now if the small vessel were brought down to the same draught, 17 feet 2 inches, instead of 13 feet 6 inches, it would add, (at 11 tons per inch,) 462 tons, which added to 300 tons available at 13 feet 6 inches, it would make 762 tons available for cargo in a vessel of 1,000 tons against only 600 available for a vessel of 2,000 tons at the same draught of water. The question is only whether there be room for stowage or working the guns in the small vessel if armed in the same manner; if there should be found sufficient room for this purpose, the small vessel could carry the same weight of armament on 15 inches less draught of water than the larger vessel, or say small vessel 16 feet against the larger 17 feet 2 inches, both vessels being armed with the same weight of armament, men, provisions, &c.

By increasing the size, then, we add to the cost double the sum and increase the draught of water 15 inches, as well as the continual expense of coals and wear and tear. Before we build a propeller vessel of war, it would be well to limit the quantity of coal, water, provisions, and stores, and consider well the object for which the ship is designed, that the ship have not one foot more space allowed than is absolutely necessary for the purpose for which she is designed.

The above calculation supposes the power of steam sufficient to drive the ship at the rate of 10 miles per hour, when loaded down to two-fifths of the breadth of beam.

But the velocity is dependent upon the power applied to the weight, and the velocity would be increased or diminished as the vessel and cargo is increased in weight, or her draught of water is reduced. Vessels built for commercial purposes may be built one-fourth lighter than war vessels, and the difference of the weight of hull may be added to the cargo: but commercial steamers should be built with reference to the distance of the trip they are intended to make without coaling, while it might be economical to steam with great velocity for short voyages. I should think that it would be the reverse to attempt a higher speed than 10 miles for long voyages, as the quantity of coals required to keep up high velocities not only adds much to the expense, but displaces the cargo. It is easy to calculate, that a vessel's speed may be so great that to go a distance of 1,000 miles she must be loaded with coals.

ISBN 0-921335-71-7

9 780921 335719